The Origins of Modernism

The Origins of Modernism

Eliot, Pound, Yeats and the Rhetorics of Renewal

Stan Smith

HARVESTER WHEATSHEAF

New York   London   Singapore

First published 1994 by
Harvester Wheatsheaf
Campus 400, Maylands Avenue
Hemel Hempstead
Hertfordshire, HP2 7EZ
A division of
Simon & Schuster International Group

Typeset in 10/12 pt Sabon
by Photoprint, Torquay, Devon

Printed and bound in Great Britain by
Redwood Books Limited, Trowbridge, Wiltshire

British Library Cataloging in Publication Data

A catalogue record for this book is available from
the British Library

ISBN 0–7108–0632–9 (hbk)
ISBN 0–7108–1164–0 (pbk)

2 3 4 5 98 97 96

For Vaughan Parker Smith

born 10 August 1992

and for the eyes of dogs to come

waiting for Doggy

It is so difficult to begin with something – or to return to the beginning. We would like most of all to place ourselves outside the world and to see where and how it begins. To begin before the beginning, to go behind the beginning. Not even the attempt to articulate this can happen. It can only be represented in an inarticulate cry and with that eliminate itself . . . . It is just not possible to begin before the beginning.

(Wittgenstein)

Contents

Acknowledgements

This book began as a paper on Class, Gender and Polyphony in Modernist Poetry at the Higher Education Teachers of English Conference at the University of Newcastle in 1983, some of which survives in Chapters 4 and 7. Earlier versions of the former and of Chapter 8 respectively first appeared in *English* and *The Irish University Review*. A slightly different version of Chapter 9 first appeared in *Yeats Annual* in 1988. Elements of Chapter 2 were aired at a conference on T.S. Eliot and his Legacy at the University of Glasgow in 1988, and parts of Chapter 10 in a keynote lecture at the Royal Irish Academy symposium on Literary Theory and Irish Literature in 1991. The conclusion extends an argument first made in a lecture at the Triennial Conference of the International Association for the Study of Anglo-Irish Literature at Maynooth College in 1979. I am grateful to editors and conference organisers for the opportunity they provided first to develop these ideas.

Much of the penultimate reading, thinking and writing was accomplished while I was a Visiting Professor at the Università degli Studi di Firenze in 1987, and I am extremely grateful to that university for the opportunity to think about Modernism in one of its originary sites, as well as the area where for one Modernist at least it was finally 'wrecked for an error' (*Pisan Cantos*). I should also like to record my gratitude and affection to many friends in Florence for their hospitality and stimulus, in particular that Virgilian guide and provocateur Valerie Wainwright-Dari.

The University of Dundee was kind enough to grant study leave to complete this work in 1992; my particular thanks go to Principal Michael Hamlin, for his generous and consistent support for the development of English Studies there over the last few years. Sue Roe and then Jackie Jones at Harvester Wheatsheaf deserve much gratitude for persistent encouragement, some little faith and much patience, in ensuring this book reached completion.

The staff of the British Library and of Cambridge, Birmingham, Florence and Dundee University Libraries are to be thanked for their invaluable assistance. The library of the British Institute in Florence, though small, contains deposits from the 1920s and 1930s which made possible some of the precise dating contained herein. Particular thanks should go to Rupert Hodson and his staff there, as to John Bagnall and the staff at Dundee University Library.

Rob Watt offered, as usual, shrewd observations on several versions of the text, as well as the moral support any book needs when it hovers before completion. As ever, Jennifer Birkett was a perpetual encouragement and an ideal reader, as well as the source of much information and insight. To her go my love and gratitude.

Chapter One

'A new start': Promises after the event

'My feet are at Moorgate, and my heart
Under my feet. After the event,
He wept. He promised "a new start."
I made no comment. What should I resent?'
(*The Waste Land*, ll. 296–9)

Dated statements

T.S. Eliot (wrote Ezra Pound in the *Criterion* in July 1932) 'displayed great tact, or enjoyed good fortune, in arriving in London at a particular date with a formed style of his own. He also participated in a movement to which no name has ever been given'.[1] It is a peculiarity of the origins of Modernism that, in an era when writers everywhere inscribed themselves under a deliberate banner, this most momentous of movements should emerge anonymously, and wait more than a decade to be named. The name of 'Modernism' arrived after the event, its origins wrapped in obscurity. Laura Riding and Robert Graves in *A Survey of Modernist Poetry* in 1927 offered the formal christening. Their discussion, however, makes it clear that the epithet had been in circulation for some time, to the extent that they believed it 'now possible to reach a position where the modernist movement itself can be looked at with historical (as opposed to contemporary) sympathy as a stage in poetry that is to pass in turn, or may have already passed, leaving behind only such work as did not belong too much to history'.[2]

The uncertainty about a name is compounded by uncertainty about the date of birth. For if Pound writes of Eliot 'arriving in London at a particular date', it is, we note, 'with a formed style of his own', so that

Eliot's Modernism at least predates that arrival. Eliot first visited London in February 1911, after spending some months in Paris and before going on to Germany and Northern Italy. He had indeed begun 'The Love Song of J. Alfred Prufrock' and 'Portrait of a Lady' before he left the United States in October 1910, and was to complete the former in Munich and the latter after his return to Harvard in October 1911. He next visited Britain *en route* for a summer school at Marburg University in 1914, where the outbreak of war compelled him to flee back to London, arriving on 21 August 1914.[3] To compound these complications, when Pound goes on in the same memoir to elucidate the 'particular date' which witnessed the origin of Modernism, his time-scale has shifted:

> That is to say, at a particular date in a particular room, two authors, neither engaged in picking the other's pocket, decided that the dilutation of *vers libre*, Amygism, Lee Masterism, general floppiness had gone too far, and that some counter-current must be set going. Parallel situation centuries ago in China. Remedy prescribed 'Emaux et Camées' (or the Bay State Hymn Book). Rhyme and regular strophes.
>
> Results: Poems in Mr Eliot's *second* volume, not contained in his 'Prufrock' (*Egoist* (1917), also 'H.S. Mauberley.'
>
> Divergence later.

In the shift between paragraphs, a divergence has already occurred, for the foundation date of an incognito Modernism has itself shifted from 1911 or possibly 1914 to 1919–20, the occasion of *Hugh Selwyn Mauberley* and 'Mr Eliot's *second* volume'. Nor is this all. In another of his journalistic essays from the early 1930s, 'We Have Had No Battles But We Have All Joined In And Made Roads', Pound backdates and collectivises those origins, calling in 'the LONE whimper of Ford Madox Hueffer' (later Ford), and his 'more pliant disciples . . . [F.S.] Flint, [Douglas] Goldring, and D.H. Lawrence' as progenitors, as 'In the dim mainly forgotten backward of 1908 and 1910 a few men in London groped toward the "revolution of the word".'[4]

Pound himself first arrived in London in 1908, and presumably includes himself among the godfathers. In 1929, a special number of Eugene Jolas's journal *transition* had proclaimed a 'Revolution of the Word' originating largely in the work of James Joyce.[5] Pound is at pains here to set the record straight by establishing a proper paternal lineage. Joyce, after all, had been the discovery of himself and Eliot, who had published and propagated his work in the pages of *The Egoist* and *The Little Review* throughout the second decade of the century. Pound is therefore polemically insistent about departure dates: 'the literary historian will err if he tries to start "the revolution of the word" a decade or so later with the emergence of Mr Joyce's epigons and jejune admirers.'

Retrospection, it seems, has been the hallmark of Modernism from the start, whether it is a question of its conception, birth or christening. Yet the name was always in waiting. Twenty years before his *Criterion* piece, writing to Harriet Monroe, editor of the Chicago journal *Poetry* in September 1914 of his recent 'discovery', T.S. Eliot, Pound came tantalisingly close: 'He is the only American I know of who has made what I can call adequate preparation for writing. He has actually trained himself *and* modernized himself *on his own*.'[6] None of the other 'promising young', he says, have managed to combine these two achievements. From its inception, then, Modernism is a double-edged promise. Modernising, a total up-to-dateness, has to be combined with a training in the classics. Originality must be matched by a sense of origins. It is, Pound goes on to say, 'such a comfort' to meet someone you don't have to tell to 'remember the date (1914) on the calendar'. That date on the calendar, for Modernism, is the most up-to-date in the world: today – the very moment of writing, at the cutting-edge of the new. But the other side of the coin is that today rapidly becomes yesterday, and there is nothing more out-of-date than yesterday's news.

Foregrounding the date of writing is a common feature of Pound's criticism and not absent from his poetry: the significance of the internal datings of 'Envoi' and 'Mauberley' in *Hugh Selwyn Mauberley*, for example, has generated much debate. Pound's criticism, to remain up-to-date, has repeatedly to be post-dated. For example, an essay already called 'A Retrospect' in *Pavannes and Divisions* in 1918 incorporates an earlier piece put in its place by a footnote '(Dec. 1911)'; a subsequent footnote distances the author from his past opinions: 'Let me date this statement 20 Aug. 1917.'[7]

One of the most significant instances of such backdating occurs at the beginning of the 1929 revision of *The Spirit of Romance*, first published in 1910.[8] Here a '*Praefatio ad Lectorem Electum*' outlines the various time zones that coexist in a merely geographical present:

> It is dawn at Jerusalem while midnight hovers over the Pillars of Hercules. All ages are contemporaneous. It is B.C., let us say, in Morocco. The Middle Ages are in Russia.

At this point a footnote in the 1929 edition adds, tersely, '1910'. For in 1929 'Russia' is no longer the Middle Ages but, under a new name and management, appears to be the most up-to-date state in the world, exempt from that capitalist crisis for which 1929, the year of the Wall Street Crash, is the shorthand. Pound's 1929 Postscript to this Preface brackets the book as no more than a 'partial confession of where I was in the year 1910.'[9] Modernism, much concerned with the simultaneity of all art, a case argued in *The Spirit of Romance* as much as in

'Tradition and the Individual Talent', is also mightily preoccupied with its own continuous self-updating.

Pound's review of *Prufrock and Other Observations* in *Poetry* provided the opportunity for a similar dissociative postscript when reprinted in his *Literary Essays*. Beginning by citing de Gourmont on contemporaneity, it observes that 'Mr Eliot's work interests me more than any other poet now writing in English.' The reprinted essay, edited by Eliot himself, acquires the cautionary footnote: 'A.D. 1917', a date, as we shall see later, which has its own special significance in the calendar of modern letters.[10]

Comfort, curiously, is what concerns Pound in this review of *Prufrock* as in his comments to Harriet Monroe above. Envisaging a new start, a new art, even as European civilisation staggers to its doom on Western and Eastern Fronts, the review finds it 'a comfort to come upon complete art, naive despite its intellectual subtlety, lacking all pretence'. The opposition of 'naive' and 'complete' corresponds to that between 'modernised' and 'trained' in the letter to Monroe – another version, in fact, of that between the contemporary and the traditional: 'I should like the reader to note how complete is Mr Eliot's depiction of our contemporary condition.' There is in these poems, he says, 'no rhetoric, although there is Elizabethan reading in the background'. 'He has placed his people in contemporary settings', used 'contemporary detail'. Along with Joyce's *Ulysses*, 'Eliot has a like ubiquity of application. Art does not avoid universals, it strikes at them all the harder in that it strikes through particulars.' 'His men in shirt sleeves, and his society ladies, are not a local manifestation; they are the stuff of our modern world, and true of more countries than one.'

At the end of another essay of the 1930s, '*Prefatio Aut Cimicum Tumulus*', Pound again proffers 1917 as the seminal year for Modernism, taking up the 'Elizabethan' connection but distinguishing Eliot's revivification of dead writers and discourses from the antiquarian revivalism of a previous generation, and linking his own work to Eliot's achievement:

> I might also assert that Eliot going back to the original has derived a vastly more vivid power than was possible to the century and more of Elizafiers who were content to lap the cream off Lamb and Hazlitt or to assume a smattering of Elizabethan bumbast from Elizabethan derivers. *Quod erat demonstrandum. Quod erat indicatum*, even by the present disturber of repose anno 1917 and thereabouts.[11]

Eliot's originality lies in going back to the original, but this is quite distinct from a secondary copying of sources. On the contrary, Eliot and his originals become *contemporaries*. The intervenient 'Elizafiers' of whatever century are by contrast not simply *past* but irredeemably *passé*.

In the preface to *The Spirit of Romance* Pound had been at pains to establish this distinction:

> All ages are contemporaneous. . . . The future stirs already in the minds of the few. This is especially true of literature, where the real time is independent of the apparent, and where many dead men are our grand-children's contemporaries, while many of our contemporaries have been already gathered into Abraham's bosom, or some more fitting receptacle.[12]

'Real time' is an eternal present where all that is truly living coexists. Literature provides privileged access to it, for literature offers us the subjective interior of dead lives as if *we* were living them for the first time. It is, in this sense, a kind of spiritual *possession*, and indeed the vocabulary of mediumship recurs in the theorising of the Modernists. But such re-invented immediacy does not mean that history has no time-depth. The past may exist only in our retrospective construction of it, but precisely because of this it is incumbent on us to distinguish living continuities from mere inert survival. What Eliot in Modernism's final retrospect in 'Little Gidding' was to redefine in 1942 as 'a pattern / Of timeless moments' cannot be dissociated from a History which is 'now and England'.

Originals

The paradoxes are dense in Pound's idea of 'tradition'. He argues in 'The Tradition' in *Poetry* in 1913 that

> A return to origins invigorates because it is a return to nature and reason. The man who returns to origins does so because he wishes to behave in the eternally sensible manner. that is to say, naturally, reasonably, intuitively. . . . He wishes not pedagogy but harmony, the fitting thing.[13]

Every original literary movement starts by inventing its origins, as the 'harmony' from which it draws and to which it aspires, seeking to fit, seeking 'the fitting thing'. Yet these 'origins' are not really in the past. Rather they are found in a present behaviour which realises an 'eternally sensible manner'.

The tension between 'origin' and 'originality' catches a central contra-diction of Modernism. To be *original* is to reproduce, or re-produce, that which is there already. Paul Valéry makes the point in his 'Letter About Mallarmé', talking of the nature of 'influence':

> Whether in science or the arts, if we look for the source of an achievement we can observe that *what a man does* either repeats or refutes *what*

someone else has done – repeats it in other tones, refines or amplifies or simplifies it, loads or overloads it with meaning; or else rebuts, overturns, destroys and denies it, but thereby assumes it and has visibly used it. Opposites are born from opposites.

We say that an author is *original* when we cannot trace the hidden transformations that others underwent in his mind.[14]

By this reckoning, none of the great Modernists could be called 'original', since a great part of their originality lies precisely in flaunting those traces and transformations, demonstrating self-consciously the operations they have performed on their sources. Their 'originality', in Valéry's terms, lies not in suppressing the texts they rework, but in concealing the way such operations transform the traditional concept of 'influence', by making *influence* itself, the inflowing of sources, their central thematic. Modernism's originality, that is, lies in making the transformative act of translation, adaptation, repetition its real content.

'Translation', Pound wrote in 'A Few Don'ts' in *Poetry* in March 1913, is 'good training, if you find that your original matter "wobbles" when you try to rewrite it.'[15] But translation, in this sense, is more than just 'training', and not just one of several activities for Modernist writers. It is, rather, a key to their whole artistic process. For what translation foregrounds is the fact of cultural relativity, at the very moment that it invents a timeless 'tradition' where all art coexists. The Modernists relativise their own productions by relativising the productions they quote, echo, distort, respond to – in a word, 'translate'. In the Provence poems of Pound's *Personae* it can be difficult to decide at any one point whether the date is 1309 or 1909, and whether the speaker is Cino or Bertrans de Born or Pound himself. 'The Bowmen of Shu' opens *Cathay*[16] with the most up-to-date of buttonholings, starting with a 'Here we are' (compare Gerontion's 'Here I am') which fuses not then and now but two present tenses millennia apart. The Bowmen of Shu may be located on the Chinese frontier with the Mongols in 'Reputedly 1100 B.C.' (Pound's note); but when they ask 'Will we be let to go back in October?' they speak in the frustrated accents of the Western Front in 1915. The two moments fuse in a real time which creates 'that sense of sudden liberation; that sense of freedom from time limits and space limits; that sense of sudden growth' which 'A Few Don'ts' identifies as the achievement of 'the greatest works of art'.

'An "Image"', Pound says here, 'is that which presents an intellectual and emotional complex in an instant of time.' This 'complex' is created by what his 1914 essay on 'Vorticism' in *The Fortnightly Review* describes as a geometrical 'equation' between two moments, in which time itself seems neutralised.[17] The moment of the reader is brought fully alive by this instantaneous co-presence of the moment of the actual writer (Pound) with that of his imagined persona. When, however, the title-page of *Cathay* declares that these poems are 'For the most part from the Chinese of Rihaku, from the notes of the late Ernest Fenollosa, and the decipherings of the Professors Mori and Ariga', Modernism's confidence trick is at its most blatant. The immediacy of these 'translations' recedes down an endless avenue of scholarship, where two Japanese professors 'decipher' the notebooks of an American scholar who is decidely 'late'. Not so belated as Pound himself, however, since the 'Rihaku' whose experience is so vivaciously brought to life here is an artefact of imperfect transmission in that very process. For 'Rihaku' is no more than the Japanese transliteration of the name of the Chinese poet Li Po, translated into English here not from Chinese but from Fenollosa's translation of an intermediate Japanese translation. The 'instant of time' is instantaneous because it is a fabrication, in the present. In the many mediations between Li Po and Pound, a wholly imaginary 'intellectual and emotional complex' has been created, transcending cultures and histories, which is entirely contemporary: the *illusion* of unmediated rapport with the dead.

Such instantiations are frequent in Pound. His brilliantly evocative version of 'The Seafarer' in *Ripostes* in 1912[18] converts the 'burghers' (towndwellers) of the original into an anachronistic, non-existent Anglo-Saxon bourgeoisie. The equation forged between ancient and modern universalises the individual talent's sense of exile in a world ruled by the cash-nexus. But the forging is also a forgery, creating a configuration of the present with an 'original' which never existed. A self-effacing modern voice speaks ventriloquially through the masks of all those *personae* assumed in the first wave of Modernist texts, constituting itself in its contemporaneity at the moment that it defers totally to the voice it revives. What we are aware of finally in reading such poems is not the felt immediacy of the past but our modern remove from such originary authenticity. This is not Walter Benjamin's messianic 'time of the now', but a plangently late Romantic view of history as dispossession, in which, as for the poor in W.H. Auden's *Spain*, ' "Our day is our loss." '

In 1934 Pound wrote in the introduction to *Make It New* that 'an epic is a poem including history'.[19] When *The Cantos* compound times, juxtaposing John Quincy Adams and Kung, Justinian's Byzantium and the Medici's Florence, they offer an image of history not as a causal process of constant transformation and differentiation, a narrative which develops and progresses, but as mere repetition, a repertoire of homologies which are overlaid in a spurious 'real time', what the last fully drafted Canto, CXVI, sums up as 'the record / the palimpsest'.[20]

The very first Canto[21] prefigures the central dilemma of the whole work, offering, in Pound's English reworking of the Renaissance Latinist Andreas Divus' 1538 reworking of Homer's *Odyssey*, a palimpsest of narratives in which the story is always about to begin again. In its present published form, the opening of 'A Draft of XXX Cantos' as first published in 1930, it offers a version of material already repeatedly reworked since its first publication as three Cantos in *Poetry* in 1917. This forever unfinished 'Draft' itself begins in the middle of things, on a co-ordinating conjunction ('And then went down to the ship'). It ends in the middle, too, with a conjunction that points onward, through a colon which promises more, to the next Canto, where this particular story is decisively not resumed ('Bearing the golden bough of Argicida. So that:').

The various 'versions' of the story of Odysseus allude to an originary event they cannot, by definition, define. We never have the events themselves, only some new telling of them, and, as Jane Harrison had written in 1882,

> Homeric scholars and comparative mythologists tell us that the stories with which the Odyssey is thick-strewn were not invented by Homer; that he took the folk-lore that lay ready to hand, and wove its diverse legends into an epic whole; that many of his myths are the common property of both Aryan and non-Aryan peoples.

Prefiguring subsequent scholarship, including that which influenced Joyce and may account for Phlebas the Phoenician in *The Waste Land*, she wrote of their origins in a narrative tradition ultimately not Greek at all but Phoenician.[22]

The ancient and accumulated tellings drawn on in these Cantos promise ' "a new start" ', with all the irony of the quotation marks intact, warning that we have heard it all before. They constitute a rite of passage as empty of significance as that blank colon through which reader and narrative alike pass, not to any goal, but simply to the next 'draft' of a vast poem that remained by its very nature unfinished on Pound's death. With affectionate irony, Joyce makes the same point at the beginning of *A Portrait of the Artist as a Young Man*, deploying the immemorial familiar formula 'Once upon a time and a very good time it was too' as both the content of his fiction – the start of a nursery tale told by Dedalus senior – and as its form, the originating words of Modernism's founding *Bildungsroman*.

Much of the pathos of Modernism's relation to its origins can be discerned in what Pound and Eliot say about their major authenticating patriarch, Dante. One observation of Eliot's will suffice here: not the Dante essay which concludes his 1920 collection *The Sacred Wood*, and starts from a remark of Valéry's on the place of philosophy in 'modern poetry', but the essay on Blake which precedes it.[23] Eliot here contrasts Blake's 'eccentricity' and 'formlessness' with the consummate form of Dante, which he attributes to 'a more continuous religious history', that of 'the Latin traditions'. 'Blake did not have that more Mediterranean gift of form which knows how to borrow as Dante borrowed his theory of the soul; he must needs create a philosophy as well as a poetry.' Eliot relates this inability to 'borrow' to 'a similar formlessness' in what he calls Blake's 'draughtsmanship', most evident in the longer poems: 'You cannot create a very large poem without introducing a more impersonal point of view, or splitting it up into various personalities.' What Blake lacks and Dante reveals is an impersonality that derives from a dramatic or dialogic method inseparable from 'a framework of accepted and traditional ideas'. The dialogism of poetry for Eliot, then, lies in its capacity to 'borrow', to submit one's mere originality to the true originals, impersonalising the individual voice by dispersing it among the voices of tradition. Pound makes a similar point in *The Spirit of Romance*, stressing that Dante writes a *Commedia*, a *drama*.

A central conflict, between two different kinds of polyphony, is re-enacted again and again throughout the Modernist corpus. For in calling up that 'communication / Of the dead ... tongued with fire beyond the language of the living' of which 'Little Gidding' speaks,[24] the Modernist texts seek to repress those living and imperative voices that constantly break in from that 'immense panorama of futility and anarchy which is contemporary history' which Eliot dismissed so derisively in his famous review of *Ulysses*.[25] When, in 'Little Gidding', Eliot turns to Dante and Virgil as well as Pound, Mallarmé and many others to construct the 'familiar compound ghost' of his Modernist tradition, their voices are fused, indissociably, in the presiding monotone of his ghostly interlocutor. By contrast, that moment in Canto XXVI of the *Purgatorio*, the source of many of Eliot's allusions, which invokes Dante's 'influences', those predecessors who underwrite 'modern use' ('*l'uso moderno*'), enacts a displacement of origins down the chain of poetic signifiers which problematises the whole question of 'influence'.[26]

Dante here defers to the ghost of Guido Guinicelli as his poetic source, only to hear Guido speak in turn of Arnault Daniel as 'father of me, and of others my betters'. It is not Dante himself but Guido who describes Arnault Daniel as '*il miglior fabbro*', the phrase Eliot applied to Pound in the dedication to *The Waste Land*. And indeed it is Pound, in a chapter of *The Spirit of Romance* called 'Il Miglior Fabbro', who first called attention to this passage, where, he says, 'This device of praising Daniel by the mouth of Guinicelli is comparable to that which Dante uses in the "Paradiso", honoring St Dominic and St Francis in the speech of a Franciscan and a Dominican respectively'.[27] Dante, that is, is singled out by Pound for his relativising of discourse, rendering all utterance dramatic by making it the speech of some one, interested party, and in the process undermining the whole pretention to impersonality and objectivity which is so much a part of Eliot's idea of Tradition. This displacement of an authenticating origin, complicating the whole idea of patriarchal succession, is implicit at the very start of the *Divine Comedy*, which, while it defers to remotest origins, setting up Virgil for guide, starts not at the ancient source but in the contemporary middle of things, 'Nel mezzo del cammin di nostra vita'. Beginning *in medias res*, the *Divine Comedy* adheres to the prescriptions of Aristotle's *Poetics*, and it goes forward by returning, finding itself ('*io mi ritrovai*') at the moment that it admits to being lost.

Eliot refigures this moment on several occasions, not only in 'Little Gidding' but also in 'Ash Wednesday' and in 'East Coker', which speaks of being 'in the middle way', '*entre deux guerres*'. But if 'The Dry Salvages' asks 'Where is there an end of it?', the actual, unanswerable question *Four Quartets* asks and sidesteps at once is 'Where is there a beginning of it?' For all its evocation of the authorising discourses, *Four Quartets* (like the broken Coriolanus revived for a moment at the end of *The Waste Land*, who seeks to become in Shakespeare's words 'author of himself, and kn[o]w no other kin') speaks out as an individual talent which has substituted its own mind for the mind of Europe. In the process, it has set the seal on one tendency of Modernism, which is to subdue its warring voices to the dominant monologue of the text, creating a pattern of timeless moments unanswerable to history. Yet everywhere the great texts of Modernism struggle against their own domineering tendencies, inscribing in their texture the very resistances and counter-voices they seek to occlude. In this, they have learned more thoroughly than they realised from Dante, ironically reproducing in their structures not the unitary conviction they attribute to the *Divine Comedy*, but its actual decentred, polyphonic and self-unravelling plurality and the fractious and fractured 'contemporary history' they seek to ignore. It is in this urgent modern conflict that we can discern the true origins of Modernism.

Riding and Graves in 1927 offered a shrewd diagnosis of the duplicity at the heart of Modernism's sense of cultural time.[28] On the one hand, Modernism had rejected 'the underlying conception of a crude, un-differentiated, infinite, all-contemporaneous time, and of a humanity co-existent with this time, a humanity consolidated as a mass and not composed of individuals', in the name of 'relative time – the sense of many times going on at once'. Having established itself,

> modernist criticism . . . found it convenient . . . to insist on the traditional character of Poetry as an *art*, to reintroduce . . . 'classical' time by emphasizing the element of contemporaneousness. . . . poetry now attempted to stabilize itself by reverting to an absolute time-sense.

But they are wrong to see this as two successive phases, in which 'the modernist generation is already over before its time, having counted itself out and swallowed itself up by its very efficiency – a true "lost generation"' so that 'Already, its most "correct" writers, such as T.S. Eliot, have become classics'. Rather these two moments, of revolt and of restoration, always coexisted in dynamic instability in the fabric of Modernism. Its end (intention, terminus) was always implicit in its beginning, as 'East Coker' acknowledged: 'In my beginning is my end.' To be Modern is to be constantly self-superseded. If, finding itself in the middle way exactly 'Twenty years largely wasted' after the writing of *The Waste Land*, this poem can echo without the irony of quotation marks the promise of that earlier poem's faithless seducer, observing that 'every attempt / is a wholly new start, and a different kind of failure', this is because, as Mikhail Bakhtin observes, 'Genre lives in the present, but it always remembers the past, its beginnings'.[29]

Late news

'Modernist' may be an epithet applied in hindsight to a disparate collection of writers, but it is also a real element in their discourse of themselves. Already in 1918 Pound's *Pavannes and Divisions* had collected several fugitive but already canonical pieces about 'Twentieth century poetry, and the poetry which I expect to see written during the next decade or so' under the heading 'A Retrospect'.[30] A further retrospect, 'Date Line', opens the volume *Make It New* in 1934.[31] Directed towards 'the careful historian of the 1910's', 'Date Line' offers a calendar of dates in the intellectual and publishing history of Modernism. Criticism's dual function is to look simultaneously forward and backward: 'to forerun composition, to serve as gunsight', combined with 'the general ordering and weeding out of what has actually been performed. . . . so that the next man (or generation) can most readily find the live part of it, and waste the least possible time among obsolete issues'. Criticism must then 'efface itself when it has established its dissociations'. The essay concludes by undermining its own careful date-filing in a manner which recalls the Preface of *The Spirit of Romance*:

'There is a TIME in these things. It is quite obvious that we do not all of us inhabit the same time.'

'Make It New' is Pound's perennial Modernist command. But in his 1918 'Retrospect', 'new' had carried with it the odium of 'so much scribbling about a new fashion in poetry'. Newness was certainly in fashion in the 1910s, as we can see from the very names of the journals in which Eliot and Pound wrote. There is *The New Age*, of course, but there is also the original title of *The Egoist*, ambiguously calling up another preoccupation of the decade, *The New Freewoman*. The rhetoric of newness infiltrates the most unlikely places in Pound's writings. Thus, he commends Mussolini in *Jefferson and/or Mussolini* (1935) for what sounds like a specifically Modernist achievement: 'restorations, new buildings, and, I am ready to add off my own bat, AN AWAKENED INTELLIGENCE in the nation and a new LANGUAGE in the debates in the Chamber.'[32] But 'newness' is clearly a contrary matter. The pithy aphorism in *ABC of Reading* that 'Literature is news that STAYS news'[33] does not really dispose of *Mauberley*'s link between newness and the 'accelerated grimace' of an age that demands constant novelty where 'We have the Press for wafer' and 'the modern stage' dispenses with 'Attic grace'.

At times, the rhetoric of the New in Pound overrides that of the Modern. In the early essay 'The New Sculpture' he inveighs against 'Modern civilisation' which has 'bred a race with brains like those of rabbits'. Now 'we artists', he says, 'the heirs of the witch doctor and the voodoo . . . so long the despised, are about to take over control. And the public will do well to resent these "new" kinds of art'.[34] In *Guide to Kulchur* (1938) a cryptic memo contrasts Dante's continuing newness with a degenerate modernity which links journalism and the educational apparatus in a common stink: 'Dante's Inferno, XXI, line 139. It's the last line = voice of the modern press and the bulk of the professoriate and of pedagocracy.' The line Pound refers to is translated with a significant blank in the Temple Classics text he used: 'and he of his — had made a trumpet'. Press and pedagocracy have replaced 'Tradition' with an arsy-versy modern 'curriculum' which, in being posited on the fashionable, is always-already out-of-date: 'The modern and typical prof holds his job because of his slickness . . . because he crawls under the buggy rug of a moth-eaten curriculum.' By contrast, a truly modernising and trained completeness would 'make [its] *Gestalt* of Kung, Homer, the middle ages, renaissance, the present, with the greek decline in its due proportion . . . and the peripheries':

> Plenty of chance for a NEW Quattrocento. Plenty of chance for a gang of scholars with gumption enough to overhaul the whole congeries, measure off Greece against China, plus technical progress,

> but, in no case go to sleep
> on lies, on subsidies, on foundations of our truly contemptible universities,
> of pot-bellied toadying presidents of fat beaneries. In no case swallow fat
> greasy words which conceal three or four indefinite middles.[35]

In the age of mechanical reproduction, as *Hugh Selwyn Mauberley* observed in 1919, even music has succumbed to fashionable repetition:

> The tea-rose tea-gown, etc.
> Supplants the mouseline of Cos,
> The pianola 'replaces'
> Sappho's barbitos.

The hand-cranked pianola here becomes the expressive icon of a mass-produced modernity, its tune struck mechanically from the holes in a rotating cylinder, tirelessly producing the same notation without the need for an individual talent. In Eliot's 'Portrait of a Lady' similarly 'a street-piano, mechanical and tired / Reiterates some worn-out common song' in a world where the exceptional is swamped by the common, and even personal desire is a second-hand replaying of 'things that other people have desired'. In *The Waste Land* the pre-recorded music of the gramophone and 'the automatic hand' of the secretary, like her purely mechanical copulation, epitomise the condition of the new. The quotation marks which bracket ' "replaces" ' in Pound's poem actually enact the replacement of which the word speaks, substituting its own 'up-to-date' (i.e. clichéd) secondariness for whatever it replaces. Modernity is not an original discourse but, from the start, a repetition, erasing that which it overrides. There can be no real replacement, only self-conscious and secondary 'replacements', the act of substitution itself foregrounded as the latest thing.

The pianola thus becomes part of the tradition of itself, its main achievement the act of *replacement* which has become an end in itself. Each person and thing signals its own replaceability. Yet the endlessly replayable tune that exists independently of the time of its origin and the time of its performance is in one sense the very epitome of the Modern. It is precisely what constitutes that 'pattern of timeless moments' which for Eliot and Pound lies at the heart of Tradition. 'Making it new', 'modernising', have regularly to be dissociated by Pound's rhetoric from the degenerate realm of 'news' and 'modern civilisation' because Modernism is itself compromisingly intertwined with the latter, in some senses a symptom of the very process it revolts against.

What Pound identifies as the antithesis of his Modernism in *Hugh Selwyn Mauberley* is precisely what a subsequent discourse nominates as 'postmodernism', the cult of permanent replacement which is Modernism's intimate other. Postmodernism is in a sense coeval with

Modernism, its originary twin, the perpetual but repressed other which reminds, when Modernism puts on the airs and graces of universality and timelessness, of its own named and dated contemporaneity, and therefore of its transience. More so than one would think, in fact. A letter to the *Times Literary Supplement* in 1993 reports that the National Art Library of the Victoria and Albert Museum has recently acquired a volume called *Postmodernism and Other Essays*, by Bernard Iddings Bell, published by Morehouse Publishing Company, Milwaukee, in 1926. Thus, amusingly, the term 'postmodernism' in a book title predates by a year what is generally thought to be the first comparable usage of 'Modernist', in the title of Graves's and Riding's *Survey of Modernist Poetry*. Truly, Modernism has always been simultaneously behind and ahead of itself.[36]

Modernism began by promising 'a new start' after the event, but not really believing its promises. *Hugh Selwyn Mauberley* starts with an obituary for its author, E.P., 'late' before he has even begun, and it ends with a series of 'epilogues' for 'Human redundancies'. E.P. is 'out of key with his time', 'Wrong from the start', struggling to make it new by reviving a dead art. He is 'born / In a half-savage country, out of date', the last phrase ambiguously applicable both to him and his origins, his end preceding his beginning. In its course the sequence bestows various 'tin wreaths' on a way of life which seems already posthumous, as a retrospective disenchantment sweeps through the whole generation that survived the Great War, 'learning later'. At the centre of all the poem's bustle lies a void, 'Mouths biting empty air', where the 'mandate / Of Eros' is merely a 'retrospect', 'noted a year late', unredeemable by desperate attempts at 'Emendation, conservation of "the better tradition"'. 'The Love Song of J. Alfred Prufrock' likewise hinges upon an event that does not occur, first in empty prospect and then in empty retrospect. Promises evaporate almost before they are uttered. Each of these 'new', 'original' poems is inscribed everywhere with the melancholy of that desperate impossible command 'Make it new'. At the site of the origin there is only an emptiness, the absence of significance, 'the heart of light, the silence' where, like the characters of *The Waste Land*, we 'know nothing', a void scrawled over with the traces of our vain reiterations. As James Joyce knew, remembering is also invention, for if 'Imagination is memory', it is also something 'erigenating from next to nothing'.[37]

Coming second

Seeking originality – the New – in a return to origins, Modernism was a deeply contradictory phenomenon, at once revolutionary and reactionary. Beyond Dante lies Virgil, and beyond Virgil, Homer, mediated by many retellings but still presiding over the opening of *The Cantos* and the ultimate source of those burning cities at the end of *The Waste Land*. Reviewing *Ulysses* in *The Dial* in 1923, Eliot wrote famously of its use of 'the mythical method' to make manageable 'the immense panorama of futility and anarchy which is contemporary history'.[38] In dealing with contemporary history, however, *Ulysses* enters into ironically belated relation with the world it depicts. Retrospect is built into its very structure. This is in part because its narrative reworks the lineaments of an ancient story, Homer's account of Odysseus' ten-year return home to Ithaca after the Trojan War, and of his son Telemachus' searches for him. But, even more importantly, the novel establishes a retrospective relation to the everyday modern events it inscribes. It may be set in the peaceable world of Dublin in June 1904, but the time and place of its writing are indicated in the last words of the text as 'Trieste-Zurich-Paris, 1914–1921', at the heart of a continent at war. *Ulysses* is thus already the postscript on a lost innocence, a fictive *nostos* or descent into the realm of the dead like that Odysseus remakes at the start of Pound's *Cantos*.

Joyce spoke to Frank Budgen of wanting 'to give a picture of Dublin so complete that if the city one day suddenly disappeared from the earth it could be reconstructed out of my book'.[39] This anecdote deserves more consideration than it usually receives. *Ulysses* contains allusions to many sacked cities, 'fabled by the daughters of memory' like those in Dedalus's schoolroom vision of 'the ruin of all space, shattered glass and toppling masonry, and time one livid final flame'.[40] Although the *Odyssey* is the structural model for *Ulysses* the book is equally haunted by the *Iliad*'s vision of the doom of Troy. For nearly three millennia the city of Troy, which had 'disappeared from the earth', had been regularly and variously 'reconstructed' from Homer's epic, until Heinrich Schliemann's excavations at Hissarlik in 1870 uncovered its authentic ruins.[41] This was very late news indeed. More recently, between 1900 and 1906 – that is, in the very 'present' of the novel's narrative – Sir Arthur Evans's excavations at Knossos had exposed the original of that 'Labyrinth' Stephen Dedalus's mythical namesake had reputedly built for King Minos of Crete.[42] (Pound recalls this archaeologically rewritten Minos in the last poem of *Mauberley*.) Knossos too showed signs of violent destruction around the putative date of the Trojan War. In the first two decades of the twentieth century, these ancient events were once again topical news and, from 1914 onwards, they spoke to a specifically modern condition.

The world of Bloomsday, so carefully dated to 16 June 1904, is an idyllic antebellum one. But, while Joyce was writing, Dublin itself in 1916 went up in flames, torn by a nationalist insurrection against British rule which, by the time *Ulysses* was published in 1922, had turned into full-scale civil war. In their timeless but dated particularity, in all the vivid immediacy of their daily routines and irregularities, Leopold and Molly Bloom and Stephen Dedalus come second to the Odysseus, Penelope and Telemachus they unwittingly post-figure. But they also stand in problematic relation to that ten years' war from which, in the *Odyssey*, Odysseus spent ten years returning. For them, war is still ten years in the future. Their destinies written in advance by the fables which, unbeknown to them, their narrative reproduces, at once belated and previous, these characters move in circuits as predetermined as the Labyrinth of Minos or the circles of Dante's inferno. (Joyce, Pound wrote in his *Dial* review in June 1922, 'has set out to do an inferno, and he has done an inferno'.[43]) Dedalus's premonitions of apocalypse prefigure a fate of which the text has prior knowledge but which for him is mere fantasy. In its reworking of the *Odyssey*, *Ulysses* promises ' "a new start" '. What it retells, however, is the oldest story in the world. If contemporary history is a nightmare from which Modernism was trying to awake in such 'timeless' texts as *Ulysses*, it is also the authenticating context of its claims to authority.

Ulysses, Pound wrote in that same review, was 'as unrepeatable as Tristram Shandy', thus, in the very act of proclaiming it unique, naming its precedent. This is a prevailing paradox of Modernism, which regularly creates novelty out of what W.B. Yeats was to identify, in one of his last poems, as the enumeration of old themes. Eliot described Yeats in 1953 as 'a late developer' who only 'emerged as a great modern poet about 1917, [when] we had already reached such a point that he appeared not as a precursor but as an elder and venerated contemporary'.[44] It is a point with which Yeats would agree. 'We were the last Romantics', he acknowledged in 'Coole Park and Ballylee, 1931', in retrospect acknowledging his generation as the last belated adherents of 'Traditional sanctity and loveliness'. Now, he goes on, in a note familiar from *Mauberley*,

> Where fashion or mere fantasy decrees
> We shift about – all that great glory spent –
> Like some poor Arab tribesman and his tent.[45]

Neither 'the book of the people' nor Homer can fill this void. The high horse is riderless, 'Though mounted in that saddle Homer rode'. Homer, indeed, is the figure of a determining absence, a mere trace, not the site of an originating plenitude. Twelve years earlier, reacting in 1919 in 'Meditations in Time of Civil War' to the anarchy and futility of contemporary history, Yeats had already identified Homer with an 'abounding glittering jet' transformed in the space of a line from a figure of fulness to one of emptiness, turned inside out like Yeats's gyres into 'some marvellous empty sea-shell flung / Out of the obscure dark of the rich streams'.[46]

'The Second Coming', written in January 1919, and collected in *Michael Robartes and the Dancer* in 1921,[47] represents one of Yeats's deepest impulses, to fit the passing moment into a great movement of supernatural forces that make a mockery of local times and places. Critics instructed by Modernism usually argue that Yeats universalises each little local catastrophe into a vision of apocalypse which transcends history. Certainly the movement from particular to general is a regular procedure in Yeats's finished work, even when his poems bear in their title the date of the events which occasion them. It is a way of disembarrassing Modernism of its political and historical complicity, exculpating it from responsibility for the various unpleasant extremisms it espoused in its long life (including in his and Pound's case at least an unambiguous support for Fascism).

In reality, such poems become much more polemic and time-bound *because* they don't name their actual target. Yeats's revulsion at the murder of the Tsar's family, which the drafts reveal to be the occasion of the poem,[48] is suppressed in its successive rewriting, until the finished poem makes sweeping statements about the nature of historical change in general as a process which is *always* for the worse, always a matter of 'blood-dimmed tides', in which *everywhere* the 'ceremony of innocence' is drowned. The 'blood-dimmed tide' of 'The Second Coming' is the 'filthy modern tide' with its 'formless spawning fury' which, in 1938, 'The Statues' casts as antithetical to all that 'We Irish, born into that ancient sect' stand for.

Such ancientness is not antique but timeless, an order of mythic contemporaneity where the casual, incomplete narratives of history are invaded and subsumed by myth, and Pearse can transfigure the ragged fighting in a mundane Dublin Post Office by summoning Cuchulain to his side. By presenting their ferociously partisan sentiments in the guise of disinterested cosmic vision, poems such as 'The Second Coming' and 'The Statues' seek endorsement for their reactionary sentiments, and encourage readers to find confirmation for their local prejudices in the commanding universals of art. This is complicated when, as here, the moral posture of the poems is deeply ambivalent. For it is clear that, while Yeats laments the destruction the poems envisage, he also exults in that destruction as a necessary prelude to renewal, part of that 'widening gyre' of history which in *A Vision* in 1925 he presented as the inevitable movement of the modern era.

The note Yeats wrote for 'The Second Coming' tries to extract it from contemporary events by insisting upon its millennial vision. The moment of the poem becomes caught up in a pattern of abstraction which purges it of all historical contingency. History, according to Yeats, is composed of two vast interlocking gyres, one inside the other, rotating in opposite directions, one expanding as the other contracts, around a common centre. Historical events are shaped by the turbulence created by their conflicting pulls:

> The end of an age, which always receives the revelation of the character of the next age, is represented by the coming of one gyre to its place of greatest expansion and of the other to that of its greatest contraction. At the present the life gyre is sweeping outward, unlike that before the birth of Christ when it was narrowing, and has almost reached its greatest expansion. The revelation which approaches will however take its character from the contrary movement of the interior gyre. All our scientific, democratic, fact-accumulating, heterogeneous civilisation belongs to the outward gyre and prepares not the continuance of itself but the revelation as in a lightning flash, though in a flash that will not strike only in one place, and will for a time be constantly repeated, of the civilisation that must slowly take its place.[49]

The two thousand years of the Christian era are now to be replaced by their antitype, a monstrous antithetical replay of its themes embodied in that Antichrist foretold in the book of *Revelation*. The new knowledge ('but now I know') is at once a disenchanting and the augury of a new covenant. What salvages the poem from desperation is a peculiarly comforting consolation: the idea of repetition and recurrence. Across the greatest historical transformations, nothing ever really changes. The gyres merely swirl back and repeat themselves in antithetical mode. Inscribed in the very texture of this cataclysmic process is its secondariness. 'The Second Coming' is, after all, precisely that: a second, parodic inversion of an earlier event. On a cosmic scale, it resembles the pianola which in the same year ' "replaces" ' Sappho's barbitos in Pound's poem. In what, in the event, turned out to be the last of many retrospects on his work, Yeats repeated in 'The Circus Animals' Desertion' a few weeks before his death his recognition that all his originality derived from repetition, the rhetorical question answering and confirming itself performatively as it was put: 'What can I but enumerate old themes?'

Alas!

The Thames-daughter's flat numbed account of her seduction at the head of this chapter is one of those little cameos of lament with which *The Waste Land* abounds. Recalling the automatic indifference of the secretary in an earlier moment, the quotation marks of that ' "new start" ' echo Pound's ' "replaces" ', secondary verbal formulae which performatively refer only to themselves. In miniature, the passage could be taken as a statement about Modernism itself, its promises of a fresh beginning in hindsight revealed to be, as Ezra Pound put it in his elegy for E.P., 'Wrong from the start ... out of date'. Like Tiresias, the Thames-daughter has 'foresuffered' it all, for even suffering is not original. The euphemistic fetishisation of 'the event' is both blunt and evasive. The echoing '-ent' sound hints at a 'repent' which is ubiquitous and unspoken throughout the poem, figured in the rebukes of Ezekiel at the start and picked up just after this true-life confession by the recollection of Augustine's confessions and repentance. 'The Event' – what might it be that is acknowledged here as it is repressed? What violation of the flow of history has to be annealed, healed over, by the consoling postcoital insincerities of the violator?

All 'new starts' involve not just recovery but repression. What is forgotten as much as what is remembered constitutes the event. Modernism as an ideological operation refuses its origins in the national, class and gender politics of its day, promising through the 'mythical method' egress from the nightmare of history, plucking from the air a live tradition as a substitute for the 'immense panorama of futility and anarchy', situating itself both before and after but never *in* the realm of historical Event. At the same time, it draws its energies from the very forces it seeks to evade through displacement, transference, and deferral. Tiresias is the trope of Modernism itself, which returns to the origin only to flee real beginnings, which goes back to the source only to deny the event. In opening up that complex of blindness and insight figured by the blind seer ('What Tiresias *sees*, in fact, is the substance of the poem'), we can begin to restore Modernism to its true, contemporary origins.

As if in defiance of their contingent historicity, Modernist texts repeatedly date themselves, whether the transitional 1919/1920 at the heart of *Mauberley*, Eliot's *Poems – 1920*, Joyce's 'Trieste-Zurich-Paris, 1914–1921', Yeats's 'September 1913', 'Easter 1916', 'Nineteen Hundred and Nineteen', 'Coole Park, 1929' and 'Coole Park and Ballylee, 1931', or Auden's 'September 1, 1939' and, most famously, 'Spain 1937'. Each of these datings both stresses the immediate moment of composition and endows the text with its own luminous envelope of instant retrospection. The pattern by which myth appropriates history is revealed most clearly in the conjunction, in the title of 'Easter 1916', of dated historical moment and the timeless ritual of resurrection. The most overtly political poem to come out of the Modernist tradition, Auden's *Spain*, focuses these contradictions. Published as a separate

pamphlet in 1937, the poem attempted to restore authenticity and depth
to the real by moving the Modernist project back into history. The
grand narratives are all superseded, the opening section tells us, by the
urgency of the here and now. But the freestanding text *Spain* (1937) was
to find itself renamed a mere three years later as 'Spain 1937', one of a
series of 'Occasional Poems' in the volume *Another Time*.[50]

This careful post-dating, like Pound's critical afterthoughts distancing
him from the 'partial confession of where I was in the year 1910',
reminds us how ephemeral the Modern is. It inscribes postmodernity in
a title which ever thereafter is put in its place, fixed in a perpetual
yesterday which disowns its original historical urgency, even though its
key and repeated 'message' is 'to-day the struggle'. Publishing a revised
poem under a revised, temporising title, in a sequence which emphasises
both the occasional and the second-hand (French, '*d'occasion*') nature
of the text, in a volume called *Another Time*, Auden 'places' the poetic
text in 'another time', in a kind of aesthetic aorist, absolved of historical
complicity. For, as he says in a companion elegy for his Modernist
mentor W.B.Yeats, 'poetry makes nothing happen', it is simply 'a way of
happening, a mouth'. It does not direct a future; rather, it *is* a perpetual,
speaking presence.

It might seem odd for a poem so supposedly wedded to the 'Marxist'
concept of 'History' to be identified as a 'postmodernist' text. But if we
look at what Auden actually does to the concept of History we can see
that it is far from Marxist but far, too, from the concept of 'Tradition'
which animates the Modernist corpus. If Modernism appropriated its
cultural antecedents, it did not supersede them. Rather it entered into
symbiosis with them, drawing its life-blood from what it came to
'replace', incorporating them in its own 'pattern of timeless moments'.
Though it appropriated and made new its many pasts, it retained what
'Tradition and the Individual Talent' called 'a perception not only of the
pastness of the past, but of its presence'. But Modernism is the *only* past
postmodernism has, a 'past' without time-depth. Postmodernism
reduces its host to a mere surface, the mute body upon which it inscribes
its own secondary discourses, sustaining itself like a bacteriophage in the
denial of its original, incorporating by replacing and erasing as it
incorporates. And this is precisely what Auden's poem does to the
concept of historical time in 'Spain'.

The poem proclaims an absolute rupture with all that has preceded it,
flattened now to a single abstraction: 'Yesterday all the past'. Its
perspectives take in the same sweeps of prehistory and history as Eliot's
'Tradition', from the Magdalenian cave-paintings and Homer to the
present, from the cromlech and 'the belief in the absolute value of
Greek' to the retrospects of 'the classic lecture / On the origin of

Mankind'. It does this only to renounce it absolutely. It is a remarkable transaction, in which millennia of human evolution, summed up in that bare phrase 'all the past', are condensed to a single flat 'Yesterday'. By the time the poem is reprinted in its revised form as 'Spain 1937', it has itself become part of that 'Yesterday', part of its own prehistory, a superseded text to which 'History' has already said 'Alas'. For Auden, in his already postmodern perspective, all this has been superseded by a state of emergency where the diachronic has turned into pure synchrony, past and future suspended in the moment: 'But to-day the struggle'. But this today is not the site of fullness. On the contrary, it is totally empty: ' "Our day is our loss" ', a day as 'flat' and 'ephemeral' as the political pamphlet and the boring meeting, a day as 'makeshift' as the consolations which sustain it. In the condition of the postmodern, 'We are left alone with our day, and the time is short'. In this foreshortening of time, 'History' itself is projected into an unimaginable future detached from 'the struggle', where its function, turning into story, will be simply to record a retrospective epitaph for the defeated: 'Alas'. This flattened, foreshortened present is as bleak and comfortless as any envisaged in some Lyotardian radical-chic version of the 'end of history'. And this terminal state, at the end of Modernism, after the event, is precisely where it began.

Chapter Two

Returning to the origin: Mr Eliot's literary revolution

Or whatever the date was

The first edition of T.S. Eliot's *Selected Essays*, published in 1932, carries the subtitle *1917–1932*. Admirably precise, the dates demarcate the successful critical career to which the volume witnesses. They are, however, omitted from all subsequent editions – ostensibly because, as Eliot's Preface to the 1951 edition informs us, the volume was subsequently enlarged to include material from *Essays Ancient and Modern* otherwise unavailable.[1]

There is a simpler, if more puzzling explanation for the omission. In the Contents list of the 1932 volume only one essay is dated 1917. That is the essay placed first in the collection as its keynote text. This essay is 'Tradition and the Individual Talent'. In the 1951 edition of the *Selected Essays*, however, the essay is dated 1919.

1919 is indeed when the essay was first published, appearing in two parts in *The Egoist* in September and December 1919.[2] A letter from Eliot dated 18 December 1919 informs his mother that he has just finished writing the second part of the essay.[3] The essay was reprinted within a year, without any special foregrounding, as the third essay of *The Sacred Wood*.[4] Now any author, particularly one as prolific as Eliot, can misremember the date of an essay. Few, however, would go so far as to enshrine that mistake in the title of a major, definitive collection. Dating the 1932 collection suggests the wish to establish an authoritative canon. It proposes a 'correct' intellectual profile of Eliot's critical output. To this end the essays are arranged not chronologically, but according to theme, so that a section of general essays on drama precedes one of variously written essays on Elizabethan and Jacobean dramatists, and so on. Essays from three decades are mixed together, as if to reinforce that claim for the synchronicity of all 'Tradition' described in the opening essay. Works of criticism, like works of art, compose a simultaneous order, unity and presence.

In the circumstances, Eliot's mis-dating in April 1932 could not be more peculiar. But he persisted in the error thirty years later in the Preface he added, in 1963, to a new edition of *The Use of Poetry and the Use of Criticism* published in 1964.[5] This book, originally published in 1933, collected the Charles Eliot Norton Lectures which Eliot gave at Harvard University during the winter of 1932–3, just after *Selected Essays* first appeared in print. In those lectures, Eliot set out to examine the poetic and critical traditions leading up to his own work. The 1963 Preface speaks of 'Tradition and the Individual Talent' as 'perhaps the most juvenile and certainly the first to appear in print' of all his essays. He reprints this volume, he says, 'in the faint hope that one of these lectures may be taken instead of *Tradition and the Individual Talent* by some anthologist of the future', and goes on: 'That, the best known of my essays, appeared in 1917, when I had taken over the assistant editorship of *The Egoist* on Richard Aldington's being called up for military service, and before I had been asked to contribute to any other periodical.'

At the beginning of the 1961 lecture which gives the title to *To Criticize the Critic* (1965), Eliot asserts that

> I know more about the genesis of my essays and reviews than about those of any other critic; I know the chronology, the circumstances under which each essay was written and the motive for writing it, and about all those changes of attitude, taste, interest and belief which the years bring to pass.[6]

And, he goes on,

> When I publish a collection of essays, or whenever I allow an essay to be republished elsewhere, I make a point of indicating the original date of publication, as a reminder to the reader of the distance of time that separates the author when he wrote it from the author as he is today. But rare is the writer who, quoting me, says 'this is what Mr Eliot thought (or felt) in 1933' (or whatever the date was).[7]

Ironic then that, in spelling out the three periods of his criticism, Eliot should proceed to place 'Tradition and the Individual Talent' in the period of writing which he says ended in 1918, 'when *The Egoist* had come to an end', and to reiterate the anecdote about replacing Aldington. This, certainly, is what Mr Eliot thought (or felt) in 1933, and again in 1961 and 1963. But, though he is clearly in his own estimation 'the subject supposed to know', it is not correct. We need to enquire what it was in the genesis, or the 'original date of publication', or 'the chronology, the circumstances under which each essay was written and the motive for writing it', which accounts for such a persistent misremembering.

It is probable, from the evidence, that for most of his life Eliot ascribed the beginning of his critical activity to an imaginary writing-act in 1917. The correction to '1919' in 1951 may well be the work of a copy-editor more concerned with factual than symbolic history. There is a certain relish to this. A Modernism much concerned with simultaneity, with the past as co-presence, and with hindsight masquerading as foresight, misplaces its own founding moment, the point at which it first theorised itself. In its very inception, Modernism is not present to itself, is, indeed, ahead of itself by two whole years. In my beginning is, perhaps, not my end, but my absence.

But why should 1917 have such a significance for Eliot? What could it have been in 1932–3 that led him so to misdate his by then classic essay? Attempting to read out an answer to this question from Eliot's criticism we come close, I would suggest, to the hidden agenda of his criticism and poetry alike, and, in the process, uncover some of the more secret places of Modernism.

Clues to the symbolic history contained in this mistake are offered in the course of *The Use of Poetry and the Use of Criticism* itself. The 1963 Preface ends by explaining that 'As for the opening paragraph of the first lecture . . . the United States were at that moment on the eve of the presidential election which brought Franklin D. Roosevelt his first term of office.' That paragraph is, however, a quotation from a letter by Charles Eliot Norton himself written in 1876, which predicted, of an earlier presidential election, that ' "a reorganisation of the parties seems not unlikely. . . . But any radical change is not to be hoped for." '[8] To Eliot's original audience, until he identified his source, the passage would have sounded like Eliot's own direct comment on the mood of America on the day of the lecture, 4 November 1932, four days before Roosevelt's landslide victory.

Eliot invokes contemporary politics only to disclose that what sounds like his own immediate reaction to current events is really a quotation half a century old from the man who gave his name to the lecture programme itself. We are expected to infer from this that such observations are timeless, not because they are perennially relevant, but because their perenniality reveals only their abiding irrelevance. And this, ostensibly, is the premise on which the lectures are founded: 'The present lectures will have no concern with politics; I have begun with a political quotation only as a reminder of the varied interests of the scholar and humanist whom this foundation commemorates'.

To speak of politics in 1932–3 as merely one of many 'varied interests', reducing it to the status of a superior amusement, a hobby, is a symptomatic Eliotic demotion. This is only the first of many repressions of the political in the course of these lectures. Almost teasingly, in another symptomatic move, the opening quotation calls up a preoccupation which is repeatedly repressed in their course, but which resurfaces with a persistence that testifies to the power of the repressed material. If politics, in 1932 as in 1876, simply recycles the same perennial trivia, then the urgent social responsibility Norton brought to politics is largely valueless: nothing really changes, no matter how much we care. Eliot's subsequent quotations, however, indicate that he is far from convinced of that of which he wishes to persuade his audience. His own subterranean concerns recur like a leitmotiv in the text.

Thus Eliot selects a letter of Norton's of December 1869 whose appositeness to the present subverts the pontifical composure with which he disposes of it:

> 'The future is very dark in Europe, and to me it looks as if we were entering upon a period quite new in history – one in which the questions on which parties will divide, and from which outbreak after outbreak of passion and violence will arise, will not longer be political but immediately social.'[9]

Norton's letter alludes to the impending Franco-Prussian War. French defeat the following year confirmed his prognosis, when a class-based politics erupted violently in 1871 in the short-lived Paris Commune, hailed by the Soviet Union throughout the 1920s as the predecessor of its own workers' state. As a young man Eliot had witnessed the collapse of the old imperial order and the groundswell of proletarian revolution throughout Europe which followed the Great War. He had worked for Lloyds Bank on the financial implications of the reparations agreements and the post-war redrawing of European boundaries in the Treaty of Versailles. He knew that internal revolution followed close on the heels of inter-imperialist war and imperial collapse. The letter to his mother in December 1919 mentioned above added that his New Year resolution was 'to write a long poem I have had on my mind for a long time' – *The Waste Land* – and went on to speak of the current collapse of Central Europe: 'the destitution, especially the starvation in Vienna, appears to be unspeakable. I suppose Americans realise now what a fiasco the reorganisation of nationalities has been: the "Balkanisation" of Europe'.[10]

Less than three weeks later (6 January) he returned to the theme:

> I wonder if America realises how terrible the condition of central Europe is. I can never ~~forget~~ quite put Vienna out of my mind. And I have seen people who have been in Germany and they are most pessimistic about the future, not only of Germany, but of the world.[11]

The inability to forget/quite put Vienna out of his mind gives precise historical urgency to the vision, from Lausanne, of 'that city over the mountains / Cracks and reforms and bursts in the violet air' in *The Waste Land*. His pervasive pessimism, in 1919, about the future not only of Germany but of the whole of Europe would have been more than borne out in November 1932. Norton's worries, then, can hardly be far from Eliot's own:

> 'Whether our period of economic enterprise, unlimited competition, and unrestrained individualism, is the highest stage of human progress is to me very doubtful; and sometimes, when I see the existing conditions of European (to say nothing of American) social order, bad as they are for the mass alike of upper and lower classes, I wonder whether our civilisation can maintain itself against the forces which are banding together for the destruction of many of the institutions in which it is embodied, or whether we are not to have another period of decline, fall, and ruin and revival, like that of the first thirteen hundred years of our era.'[12]

Eliot seems to concur in Norton's quoted belief that ' "No man who knows what society at the present day really is but must agree that it is not worth preserving on its present basis" '. And, lest the point be missed, he indicates in which particular bosoms this jeremiad will find the loudest echo: 'These are words to which many who approach contemporary problems with more dogmatic assumptions than Norton's can give assent.' For 'dogmatic', read 'communist'.

Nevertheless, Eliot sets against this apparent political urgency a countervailing concern of Norton's, that, in Eliot's words,

> The people which ceases to care for its literary inheritance becomes barbaric; the people which ceases to produce literature ceases to move in thought and sensibility. The poetry of a people takes its life from the people's speech and in turn gives life to it.

Despite the populist inflexion here, reminiscent of Yeats, the antithesis invokes the patrician tone and authoritarian tenor of Matthew Arnold's *Culture and Anarchy*, exactly contemporary with Norton's letter, and pointing the same lessons about the dangers of proletarian insurrection. Arnold was to be the subject of Eliot's sixth lecture. For Arnold, as, it would appear, for Eliot, a supposedly disinterested 'culture' is the best antidote to political and social barbarism.

In 1932–3, fears of a new dark age in Europe were far from academic. The most pressing context of Eliot's lecture schedule is not the election of Roosevelt, but something closer to that prophesied by Norton and Arnold in 1869. Two days after Eliot's first lecture on 4 November 1932, elections to the German Reichstag, in which Hitler controlled the largest single bloc, showed gains for the Communists. By the time of the final lecture on 31 March 1933, Hitler had been appointed Chancellor (30 January), and, in the wake of the Reichstag burning, blamed on the Communists, had suspended civil liberties and freedom of the press (27 February); his National Socialist German Workers' Party had won (5 March) the largest number of seats in further elections, and with the help of the right-wing Nationalists, had an overall majority in the Reichstag; and (23 March) enabling laws had granted Hitler dictatorial powers until April 1937. As Eliot composed his lectures, Europe was on the brink of a darkness more profound than that of 1869.[13]

It would be surprising if in the winter of 1932–3 Eliot's lectures did *not* respond to the momentous events unfolding in Europe. But, at first sight, there is no mention of them. Perhaps those events appear more omen-laden in retrospect than they did at the time to a middle-aged, Mussolini-sympathising Maurrasian, who later in 1933 was to speak, in lectures at Virginia University, in terms reminiscent of Hitler of a western civilisation 'worm-eaten by Liberalism', of the United States as 'invaded by foreign races', of the need for a population to be 'homogeneous', linked by 'blood-kinship' and not 'adulterated' by other races, and to observe, of New York, 'reasons of race and religion combine to make any large number of free-thinking Jews undesirable'. This second set of lectures was published in 1934 as *After Strange Gods*.[14] After Munich, Eliot suppressed the volume. But in the polarisation of Europe between the two barbarisms of Fascism and Communism, Eliot had little doubt that 'civilisation' was safer in the hands of Fascism. He was to write in his January 1937 'Commentary' in *The Criterion* of Franco's Spanish insurrection that 'one might be persuaded to believe that the rebels . . . had finally and reluctantly taken to arms as the only way left in which to save Christianity and civilisation.'[15] What is most striking in *The Use of Poetry* is the peculiarly oblique, even devious way in which current events are *deflected*, not *reflected*. It takes a prefatory note thirty years later to spell out the nature of the contemporary allusion. An innocent reader, not supposed to know whatever the date was, would have no sense of the configuration these lectures make with the immense panorama of futility and anarchy which is contemporary history.

The modern mind and the revolution of the word

The subtext of Eliot's preoccupations is revealed in the lecture called 'The Modern Mind' delivered on 17 March 1933, only a week after Hitler had achieved an absolute majority in the Reichstag. Here Eliot almost capriciously acknowledges the existence of that most contemporary phenomenon of the 'modern mind', Communism, not in political but in literary-critical terms. Attempting to explain the origins of literary innovation, he finds precedent for his own views in an unexpected source: Leon Trotsky, now, like Eliot, an expatriate. Trotsky's *Literature and Revolution* is, he says, 'the most sensible statement of a Communist attitude that I have seen.' He is particularly impressed by Trotsky's remarks on 'the relation of the poet to his environment':

> 'Artistic creation is always a complicated turning inside out of old forms, under the influence of new stimuli which originate outside of art. In this large sense of the word, art is a handmaiden. It is not a disembodied element feeding on itself, but a function of social man indissolubly tied to his life and environment.'[16]

There are larger implications to this observation, which so strikingly links the leading practical theoreticians of Modernism and of Marxism in a common definition of the origins of a literary moment. But it is its immediate, polemic function I want to pin down here.

Throughout the lectures, Eliot conducts a running battle with the Shelleyan model of poet as prophet and unacknowledged legislator. He is surprised, then, to find Trotsky's 'conception of art as a handmaiden' in 'striking contrast' to Shelley's idea of 'art as a saviour', drawing 'the commonsense distinction between art and propaganda'. Eliot develops his theoretical affinities with Trotsky by noting that the latter is 'dimly aware that the material of the artist is not his beliefs as *held*, but his beliefs as *felt* (so far as his beliefs are part of his material at all)'. The idea of 'felt' belief as the raw material of poetry can be found throughout Eliot's early essays, in 'Tradition', 'The Metaphysical Poets', and so on. But an earlier remark indicates what really lies behind his unexpected summoning of Trotsky in witness. Acknowledging I.A. Richards's shrewd identification of Canto XXVI of Dante's *Purgatorio* as a source for *The Waste Land*, Eliot rejects Richards's claim that religion has been replaced by sex as the pre-eminently modern theme, in *The Waste Land* and elsewhere. On the contrary, he says, 'My contemporaries seem to me still to be occupied with it, whether they call themselves churchmen, or agnostics, or rationalists, or social revolutionists.'[17]

It is hardly necessary for Eliot in March 1933 to distance himself from his younger contemporaries, that generation of leftists he had recently begun to publish at Faber and Faber. Stephen Spender's *Poems* (1933), Auden's *The Orators* (1932), and his *Paid on Both Sides* (1930), the latter first printed in the columns of Eliot's own *Criterion*, are certainly among 'the work of some of the more interesting younger poets to-day' he had earlier spoken of as influenced by Pound's 'Seafarer'.[18] But there is little chance that his audience will identify Eliot's Modernism with theirs. The gratuitousness with which he calls up without naming these writers establishes his own sense of the link between his work and theirs, even as he dissociates himself. Like him, his younger contemporaries are still preoccupied with religion, though this may now have a 'social revolutionist' inflection.

Throughout the lectures there are signs of Eliot's amused if anxious recognition of his role as the father-figure of a Modernist literary revolution now identified in its second generation with the political revolution of Marxism. In this he and Pound fulfil for the 'social revolutionists' a role similar to that the second generation of Romantics attributed to Coleridge and Wordsworth. Both the latter, he says, were 'not merely demolishing a debased tradition, but revolting against a whole social order'. This is a question not just of reform but of revolution: 'If Wordsworth thought he was simply occupied with reform of language, he was deceived; he was occupied with revolution of language.' But the 'revolution of the word' is precisely what Eugene Jolas had proclaimed as Modernism's legacy in the journal *transition* between 1927 and 1929.[19] Eliot assures his audience that he does not wish to associate himself with any particular tendency of modern criticism, 'least of all the sociological'[20] – where 'sociological', as subsequently, stands in for 'socialist'. Elsewhere in the lectures, however, he echoes drily the hard-boiled tones of 1930s leftism with remarks such as 'Tell that, we might add, to the Unemployed.'[21]

The lecture on Wordsworth and Coleridge acknowledges the analogy with himself and Pound, only to repudiate it. 'I myself can remember a time', he says, 'when he and I and our colleagues were mentioned by a writer in *The Morning Post* as "literary bolsheviks" and by Mr Arthur Waugh . . . as "drunken helots".' But he and Pound believed, he says, that they were 'affirming forgotten standards, rather than setting up new idols'. Wordsworth's revolution of the word is thus reappropriated to a tradition of literary restoration, for he 'was only saying in other words what Dryden had said, and fighting the battle which Dryden had fought'. Eliot rejects the *class* basis of Wordsworth's linguistic practice: he speaks, really, like himself, 'rather better, we hope, than any actual class'.[22] Nevertheless, class is an important key to his work. The 'remarkable letter' Wordsworth wrote to Charles James Fox (which Eliot quotes at length) espouses a 'doctrine which nowadays is called distributism' (as Eliot knows but does not say, this was a significant element in the Social Credit policy Pound espoused and propagandised on behalf of). 'You will understand a great poem like *Resolution and Independence* better', he tells his audience, 'if you understand the purposes and social passions of its author; and unless you understand

these you will misread Wordsworth's literary criticism entirely.' And
then he adds, in an aside resonant with personal feeling:

> Incidentally, those who speak of Wordsworth as the original Lost Leader
> (a reference which Browning, as I remember, denied) should make pause
> and consider that when a man takes politics and social affairs seriously the
> difference between revolution and reaction may be by the breadth of a
> hair, and that Wordsworth may possibly have been no renegade but a
> man who thought, so far as he thought at all, for himself. But it is
> Wordsworth's social interest that inspires his own novelty of form in
> verse, and backs up his explicit remarks upon poetic diction; and it is
> really this social interest which (consciously or not) the fuss was all
> about. . . . Except on this point of diction, and that of 'choosing incidents
> from common life', Wordsworth is a most orthodox critic.[23]

The formula 'the *original* Lost Leader' presupposes a modern replacement. The language of the passage registers Eliot's own acknowledgement
that he is the candidate, his Modernist revolution transformed into that
reactionary concept of 'orthodoxy' shortly to be adumbrated in *After
Strange Gods*. Against a new generation of 'literary bolsheviks' who
have taken their cue from his early work, in tones which both disown
and acknowledge a lineage, Eliot insinuates the continuity of 'revolution
and reaction'. It is not that rebellious youth is followed by reactionary
middle age. What Trotsky calls 'the influence of new stimuli which
originate outside of art' inflects an ambivalent Modernism one way or
the other.

Eliot's co-option of Trotsky leads him into indiscretions which further
expose this ambivalence. Modernism emerged from a social and
political crisis, self-consciously aware of the social conditions of its
production. A decade later, it has sought to repress that knowledge. But
a new generation of Modernists has returned to the source, to that
scandalous insurrection which, like the corpse buried in the garden in
The Waste Land, has once again begun to sprout.

In developing the model of literary change he found in Trotsky, Eliot
identifies himself with the 'ruined man' Coleridge, while Pound
resembles the ideologically driven Wordsworth. Given Eliot's self-styled
Anglican Classical Royalism, the identification is remarkable. Only the
cautious solemnity of his prose allows him to home in on a final
stability:

> Wordsworth's revolutionary faith was more vital to him than it was to
> Coleridge. You cannot say that it inspired his revolution in poetry, but it
> cannot be disentangled from the motives of his poetry. Any radical change
> in poetic form is likely to be the symptom of some very much deeper
> change in society and in the individual. I doubt whether the impulse in
> Coleridge would have been strong enough to have worked its way out, but

for the example and encouragement of Wordsworth. I would not be understood as affirming that revolutionary enthusiasm is the best parent for poetry, or as justifying revolution on the ground that it will lead to an outburst of poetry. . . . I only affirm that all human affairs are involved with each other, and that consequently all history involves abstraction, and that in attempting to win a full understanding of the poetry of a period you are led to the consideration of subjects which at first sight appear to have little bearing upon poetry.[24]

In the original summing-up of his Wordsworth lecture, Eliot called up a scenario of permanent revolution, in which all periods of stasis are unstable (though some are more unstable than others). If Wordsworth's and Coleridge's 'age of change' corresponds, in Eliot's implicit model, to the originating moment of Modernism, then the age of Matthew Arnold represents the illusory stability in which Eliot now finds himself:

Even if it be true that change is always making ready, underneath, during a stable period, and that a period of change contains within itself the elements of limitation which will bring it to a halt, yet some stabilisations are more deeply founded than others. It is with Arnold that we come to a period of apparent stabilisation which was shallow and premature.[25]

Effecting a restoration amidst social disintegration, Eliot's lecture series lurches through the same crises, seeking refuge in the ponderous surface assurance of Matthew Arnold after the 'distasteful' and 'repellent' excesses of Shelley, only to find that there is no sanctuary there. A sense of conflicts too deep to be resolved frets raggedly at the foundations of the lectures. The note appended at the end of the Wordsworth/Coleridge lecture runs a reprise of many of Eliot's early positions, but this time from the opposite side:

What I see, in the history of English poetry, is not so much daemonic possession as the splitting up of personality. If we say that one of these partial personalities which may develop in a national mind is that which manifested itself in the period between Dryden and Johnson, then what we have to do is to re-integrate it; otherwise we are likely to get only successive alternations of personality. Surely the great poet is, among other things, one who not merely restores a tradition which has been in abeyance, but one who in his poetry re-twines as many straying strands of tradition as possible. Nor can you isolate poetry from everything else in the history of a people.[26]

When he goes on to say that it is 'rather strong' for Herbert Read 'to suggest that the English mind has been deranged ever since the time of Shakespeare', concluding, 'If the malady is as chronic as that, it is pretty well beyond cure', what Eliot seeks to exorcise is the resurrected corpse of his own famous assertion, in 'The Metaphysical Poets' in 1921, that 'In the seventeenth century a dissociation of sensibility set in, from

which we have never recovered'. But if the ghost of his own youthful
insurgency rises to haunt him now, the image of the re-twining of
straying strands resuscitates that earliest attempt to reconcile revolution
and restoration, 'Tradition and the Individual Talent' itself.

The violent stimulus of novelty

'Tradition and the Individual Talent' is posited on the refusal of
difference. Yet it speaks of a poetic and critical revolution which
overthrows the whole existing order of things. The breaking down of
strong habitual barriers, in the account in *The Use of Poetry*,
corresponds exactly to the overthrow of the whole prior order of
tradition, in the supervention of novelty; the quick re-forming of these
barriers corresponds to the return of a new simultaneous order. In
'Tradition', this happens so discreetly, and Eliot argues for it so
discreetly, that nothing seems to have altered in the process, though a
whole new interpretation has seized power. It is this revolution by
stealth that exposes the dilemma of Modernism.

In classic Freudian terms, Oedipus has overthrown the father and
installed himself as patriarch in turn. But in order to legitimise his new
regime, he has to insist not only on its continuity with the old but on
their identity. Everything has changed, and so it appears that nothing
has changed. In the words of Peter Brooks, explaining Freud's account
of the dynamics of transference in the process of analysis:

> [T]he transference succeeds in making the past and its scenarios of desire
> relive through signs with such vivid reality that the reconstructions it
> proposes achieve the *effect* of the real. They do not change past history –
> they are powerless to do that – but they rewrite its present discourse.
> Disciplined and mastered, the transference ushers us forth into a changed
> reality.[27]

The language of patriarchal succession pervades 'Tradition'. British
critics fetichise originality, it argues, preferring in an author 'those
aspects or parts of his work in which he least resembles anyone else',
'the poet's difference from his predecessors':

> Whereas if we approach a poet without this prejudice we shall often find
> that not only the best, but the most individual parts of his work may be
> those in which the dead poets, his ancestors, assert their immortality most
> vigorously.

If the patriarchal ghosts walk abroad again in the armour of the new
'individual talent', this does not involve 'following the ways of the

immediate generation before us in a blind or timid adherence'. On the contrary, such adherence 'should be positively discouraged', for 'novelty is better than repetition'. Rather, restoration becomes original in a return to remotest origins, to the most ancient fathers (Homer and the Magdalenian cave painters, for instance). Tradition requires 'the historical sense', which is 'a perception, not only of the pastness of the past, but of its presence', a sense of the 'contemporaneity' of all past works, which compose 'a simultaneous order' in the present. 'No poet ... has his complete meaning alone. His significance, his appreciation, is the appreciation of his relation to the dead poets and artists. You cannot value him alone; you must set him, for contrast and comparison, among the dead.' A work finds its 'significant emotion' only when it enters the chain of signification, the 'simultaneous order' of a synchronic Tradition. The new work alters 'the *whole* existing order', yet 'supervention' immediately gives way to 'conformity between the old and the new'. One minute, there is the old 'existing order ... complete before the new work arrives'. Then, as if by magic, the new has arrived, the existing order is altered in a way which readjusts 'the relations, proportions, values of each work of art toward the whole', and nobody has seen it happen. Eliot's 'historical sense', paradoxically, suppresses the history of its own most significant operations. History is expunged from Eliot's account of Tradition, because history itself is the site of the primal crime.

In the 1932 *Selected Essays* 'Tradition' is twinned with 'The Function of Criticism'[28] as the theoretical framework within which the whole book is to be read. In this 1923 essay Eliot has already stepped back from the dangerous revolutionism of *The Waste Land* and 'Tradition'. The essay repeats the latter's claim that 'The existing monuments form an ideal order among themselves', and reiterates that what is at issue is 'essentially a problem of order', of providing those ' "organic wholes", as systems in relation to which, and only in relation to which, individual works ... have their significance'. 'Tradition' speaks of the poet creating his work through the extinction of personality, a continual 'surrender' of personality to something greater. 'The Function of Criticism' makes this a much more overtly political act, speaking of that 'something outside of the artist to which he owes allegiance, a devotion to which he must surrender and sacrifice himself in order to earn and to obtain his unique position'. But the sacrifice is not really that difficult, since it is only to something in which he is already at home: 'A common inheritance and a common cause [which] unite artists consciously or unconsciously', creating between 'true artists of any time ... an unconscious community'. In 1923, the impact of the Treaty of Versailles in destroying those 'organic wholes' from which meaning derived was only too apparent to Eliot. The 'common inheritance' was only too obviously fragile.

The essay clings to the idea of order because of a deep anxiety about political upheaval. Even his attack on Matthew Arnold in 'The Function of Criticism' reinstates the key terms of Arnold's call to order, and it is Arnold's horror at the Hyde Park mob in *Culture and Anarchy* that surfaces in his imagery:

> But on giving the matter a little attention, we perceive that criticism, far from being a simple and orderly field of beneficent activity, from which impostors can be readily ejected, is no better than a Sunday park of contending and contentious orators, who have not even arrived at the articulation of their differences.[29]

Instead, then, of 'quiet co-operative labour' and the composing of differences, 'in the common pursuit of true judgment', there is a scramble of opinions, instead of 'the endeavour to discipline' there is the growth of 'personal prejudices and cranks'. Eliot's own rhetoric grows increasingly intemperate in reflection of this deterioration, for by the next sentence we 'begin to suspect that the critic owes his livelihood to the violence and extremity of his opposition to other critics'.

The insistent political subtext of the metaphors in these essays of 1919–23 cannot be ignored. What is being repressed in all their tergiversations is the moment of rupture itself. For novelty to supervene, order has to be breached. There has to be contention and disorder. There has to be the tearing down, if ever so slightly, of the Hyde Park railings. Eliot himself effected such a violent revolution on the site of tradition. His demolition of the Victorians and Romantics, the dethroning of Milton, the *coup d'état* which enthroned the Metaphysicals and the Jacobean dramatists at the centres of power, and replaced Shakespeare with Dante, effected an enormous and far-reaching revolution, unsettling the whole concept of an 'English Tradition'. The subsequent sections of *Selected Essays* testify to the Jacobin thoroughness of Eliot's literary revolution. What cannot be admitted, as its publication in 1932 commemorates the first decade of the new critical and poetic regime, is precisely the partisan street-fighting, the guerrilla warfare of (Eliot's own word) 'obnubilation', the search-and-destroy missions, the critical Terror, that made this revolution such a total success.

We can see the same process at work in the evolution of the poetry. *The Waste Land*'s revolutionary poetic breakthrough had overthrown the unitary voice of Tradition, scattering the authority of a central and centralising speaker into the myriad fragments of utterance only tenuously held together by the device of Tiresias, that 'mere spectator'

Eliot's notes somewhat desperately claim 'is yet the most important personage in the poem, uniting all the rest'. The original title Eliot gave the poem indicates just how subversive of centralised textual authority he believed it to be: 'He Do the Police in Different Voices', a marginal voice reproducing the voices of power as entertainment, with all the ironies that involves. But the drive of Eliot's critical superego is to restore unity to this barbarous polyphony, reinstate the police powers of Tradition over this explosion of difference, until the multiple individual talents are once again beating obedient to controlling hands.

Four Quartets achieves this restoration much more effectively, using the centripetal harmonising drives of music and religion to reintegrate a history unravelled into partial personalities, reduced to a Sunday park of contending orators. At a time of total war, with London in flames, the poet in 'Little Gidding' walks the streets of what is no longer an unreal city, to confront the 'familiar compound ghost' of tradition. The assurance he finds there enables him, by the end of the poem, to impose cultural unity upon the most divisive period of English history, the Great Rebellion and Civil War, driving the contending voices of 'Englishness', Milton and Marvell's Protestant Parliamentary Republicanism, Herbert's Anglican Royalism, the quietism of Nicholas Farrar and the Little Gidding community, into 'a single party', united in 'the constitution of silence', folded back into itself like the multifoliate (English) rose. 'Constitution' here, like 'party', is a word riddled with plurality, its political meaning suggesting that the only constitution that could reconcile warring parties would be one that subjected all to the same discreet agreement not to speak their differences. The only good constitution, the poem suggests, is a dead one.

In both *Four Quartets* and *The Use of Poetry* Eliot is concerned to restore a unitary voice to a disintegrated tradition. If the 'national mind' is split up into 'partial personalities', it is the use of poetry, and of criticism, to labour for their reintegration, 're-twining' the straying strands. But Eliot's remarkable literary achievement, his 'radical change in poetic form', came when he allowed that difference to run riot, in a polyphonic text transformed by 'the example and encouragement' of Pound's 'revolutionary enthusiasm'. In an essay which was really written in 1917, 'Reflections on *Vers Libre*', Eliot had found a bloodless revolution an improbable scenario, in words which recall Wordsworth's 'Preface to Lyrical Ballads':

> In an ideal state of society, one might imagine the good New growing naturally out of the good Old, without the need for polemic and theory; this would be a society with a living tradition. In a sluggish society, as actual societies are, tradition is ever lapsing into superstition, and the violent stimulus of novelty is required.[30]

In 1933, such an awareness, long buried, rises to haunt all the talk of stability and order. In his Arnold lecture Eliot identifies with the 'relative and precarious stability' of the age in which Arnold was 'neither a reactionary [nor] a revolutionary'. But Arnold himself, far from offering security, becomes the signifier of an unsuccessful drive to restoration. The attempted reprise of 'Tradition and the Individual Talent' in the Arnold lecture seeks to mute its revolutionary implications by stressing one of its key evasions, the concept of *readjustment*:

> From time to time, every hundred years or so, it is desirable that some critic shall appear to review the past of our literature, and set the poets and the poems in a new order. This task is not one of revolution but of readjustment. What we observe is partly the same scene, but in a different and more distant perspective; there are new and strange objects in the foreground, to be drawn accurately in proportion to the more familiar ones which now approach the horizon, where all but the most eminent become invisible to the naked eye.[31]

The topographical analogy does not however restore order. The text swirls dizzily without coming to rest in any secure position. The next, optical metaphor cranks up the instability. The critic,

> armed with a powerful glass, will be able to sweep the distance and gain an acquaintance with minute objects in the landscape with which to compare minute objects close at hand; he will be able to gauge nicely the position and proportion of the objects surrounding us, in the whole of the vast panorama.

The last image recalls, unsettlingly, Eliot's reference to the 'immense panorama of futility and anarchy which is contemporary history' in his review of Joyce's *Ulysses*. It also points forward to that mortifying image of the theatre of history swept into the wings in *Four Quartets*: 'And we know that the hills and the trees, the distant panorama / And the bold imposing facade are all being rolled away'. Far from reinstating a solid terrain for Tradition, Eliot seems almost to have given the whole game away: this canonical space is nothing more than a *trompe l'oeil*.

What is to be done?

The lecture's immediately subsequent metaphor for critical change is overtly political: 'among more independent minds a period of destruction, of preposterous over-estimation, and of successive fashions takes place, until a new authority comes to introduce some order.'[32] The *rappel à l'ordre* is not a new note in Eliot's writing, echoing as it does the question of a bemused Fisher King at the end of *The Waste Land*:

'Shall I at least set my lands in order?' That 'New Order' had not taken long to arrive. On 3 March 1933, two days before elections widely expected to give Hitler, already Chancellor, the mandate he needed, there is a chilling edge to the phrasing. The language of order and authority throughout these lectures is not innocent, though it is held in check by what can seem a tolerant liberal scepticism which observes that 'each new master of criticism performs a useful service merely by the fact that his errors are of a different kind from the last'. But this new error is useful because it is corrective of old error. The argument differs little from Eliot's justification for Fascism in his *Criterion* editorials as 'the only way left of saving Christianity and civilisation', whose excesses can be ironed out later.

Order, however, walks on the abyss. Eliot's lecture concludes that 'I feel, rather than observe, an inner uncertainty and lack of confidence and conviction in Matthew Arnold: the conservatism which springs from lack of faith, and the zeal for reform which springs from dislike of change.' Arnold was 'somewhat disturbed. He had no real serenity, only an impeccable demeanour.' The note has recurred throughout the lecture. Arnold creates a 'disturbance of our literary values'. He occupied 'the painful position . . . between faith and disbelief', so that 'the vanishing of . . . religious faith has left behind only habits',[33] just as Eliot sees himself in *Four Quartets*, in words that explicitly echo Arnold's position 'between two worlds, the one dead, the other powerless to be born'. Arnold may believe that 'Poetry is at bottom a criticism of life', but Eliot knows that 'At the bottom of the abyss is what few ever see, and what those cannot bear to look at for long.'[34]

To rephrase this in the blunter terms of *Four Quartets*, 'human kind / Cannot bear very much reality', is to see that Eliot's position here is far from liberal scepticism. Eliot simultaneously identifies and contrasts himself with Arnold. His own desire for transformation, in 1917 or 1919 or 1922, sprang from lack of faith, and his desire for order from dislike of change. The two find resolution in a reactionary radicalism that wants to overthrow everything and 'restore' something that is completely new. The latent nihilism that infused the young Eliot's impulse to pull down the bold imposing façade of a dead Tradition still underlies that interest in a new order and authority that will 'master' an anarchic, futile history.

The radical nature of Eliot's revolutionism is succinctly characterised in the penultimate paragraph of the Arnold lecture, disguised as an observation on *style*. Against Arnold's compulsive moralising Eliot sets what he calls 'the "auditory imagination"'. But what might seem a merely technical concern, the 'feeling for syllable and rhythm', becomes at once and surprisingly an atavistic impulse uprooting the whole organised psyche, 'penetrating far below the conscious levels of thought and feeling, invigorating every word; sinking to the most primitive and forgotten, returning to the origin and bringing something back, seeking the beginning and the end.'[35]

This is what *Four Quartets*, also preoccupied with the convergence of the beginning and the end, is to call 'The backward look behind the assurance / Of recorded history, the backward half-look / Over the shoulder, towards the primitive terror'. If the terror here is domesticated by further reflections on art's fusion of 'the old and obliterated and the trite, the current, and the new and surprising, the most ancient and the most civilised mentality', the radical disturbance of 'returning to the origin' cannot be ignored, in 1933. That sudden surprising excursus into the underworld has brought up too much repressed material, and no amount of 'impeccable demeanour' can restore the illusion of serenity.

For Eliot, the genuine poetic revolution effected by Modernism lay in 'returning to the origin and bringing something back'. Innovation is more than the 'supervention of novelty'. It is the recovery of that which has been forgotten. It brings the 'primitive' back from 'the origins'. This is not the 'tiresome' critic whose 'stiffness' and 'pontifical solemnity' are regretted in the 1928 Preface to *The Sacred Wood*, but a more desperate and a more interesting Eliot, the true voice of Modernism, who wrote in the review 'War Paint and Feathers' in *The Athenaeum* in the same month as the first part of 'Tradition' (October 1919):

> The maxim, Return to the Sources, is a good one. More intelligibly put, it is that the poet should know everything that has been accomplished in poetry (accomplished, not merely produced), since its beginnings – in order to know what he is doing himself. He should be aware of all the metamorphoses of poetry that illustrate the stratifications of history that cover savagery.[36]

In the Conclusion to the Norton lectures, on 31 March 1933, the repressed material returns again, in one of those carefully veiled personal confessions Eliot scatters around his criticism. Here, he fuses the return to the origin with 'stimuli which originate outside of art'. In uncharacteristically un-classical terms which he himself compares to Housman's idea of poetry as a 'morbid secretion', he observes 'that some forms of ill-health, debility or anaemia, may . . . produce an efflux of poetry in a way approaching the condition of automatic writing':

> To me it seems that at these moments, which are characterised by the sudden lifting of the burden of anxiety and fear which presses upon our daily life so steadily that we are unaware of it, what happens is something *negative*: that is to say, not 'inspiration' as we commonly think of it, but the breaking down of strong habitual barriers – which tend to re-form very quickly . . . – [offering] sudden relief from an intolerable burden.[37]

In speaking of his own 'automatic writing' Eliot taunts us that 'no critic has ever identified the passages I have in mind', though he acknowledged elsewhere that it is the opening sequence of 'What the Thunder Said' in *The Waste Land*, a section which the poem's notes link emphatically to 'the present decay of Eastern Europe'. In the Eliotic unconscious, then, there is a recurrent and anxiety-laden link between poetic creation, 'breaking down strong habitual barriers', and political revolution.

The fourth lecture had spoken of Coleridge as, once 'visited by the Muse', 'a haunted man', 'a ruined man'.[38] It is a metaphor which can easily be applied to the lectures themselves. They are haunted by contemporary history, and their very struggle to keep out politics, announced at the beginning, and to ignore what Norton called the 'decline, fall, and ruin and revival' associated with politics, is recorded in every other turn of the text. It is in this struggle to repress that their ruin originates, and it is in preserving the traces of this conflict between poetry and history that they have a more abiding value than that Eliot allowed when he spoke of them in his 1933 Preface as 'another unnecessary book'. Poetry, 'this disturbance of our quotidian character which results in an incantation, an outburst of words which we hardly recognise as our own (because of the effortlessness)'[39] corresponds to a continental upheaval in which unreal cities like Vienna and London crack and reform and burst in the violet air.

Everywhere in these lectures, the spectre that walks abroad, haunting Europe, disturbing the universe, is that of revolution. Returning to the origin requires, in Trotsky's words cited in 'The Modern Mind', a 'turning inside out of old forms', which only arises when there is pressure from forces which 'originate outside of art'. Eliot the elder statesman may wish to fend off such terrors, but the poet is also drawn to their sinister seductions. Castigated in his youth as a 'literary bolshevik' with revolutionary designs on the apparatus of tradition, the Eliot of the early 1930s feels a pang of recognition in the new forces, of left and right, that challenge a cultural order 'worm-eaten with Liberalism'.[40]

The concluding peroration of *The Use of Poetry* generalises this analogy into a wider theory of poetry's social function, that 'use' which has provided the title of the whole lecture series:

> It [poetry] may effect revolutions in sensibility such as are periodically needed; may help to break up conventional modes of perception and valuation which are perpetually forming, and make people see the world afresh, or some new part of it. It may make us from time to time a little more aware of the deeper, the unnamed feelings which form the substratum of our being, to which we rarely penetrate; for our lives are

mostly a constant evasion of ourselves, and an evasion of the visible and sensible world.[41]

But this is going too far. A self-exemplifying evasion cuts short the confession, and ends the lecture series, by acknowledging the 'fear that I have already, throughout these lectures, trespassed beyond the bounds which a little self-knowledge tells me are my proper frontier'. Eliot has indeed constantly trodden this frontier, as if he knew that here alone, in the margins, lies the real significance of his argument. The 'breaking down of strong habitual barriers' is not to be tolerated. The 'unspeakable' consequences of the Treaty of Versailles, he had written to his mother in 1919, in that letter which speaks of completing 'Tradition and the Individual Talent' and wanting to start *The Waste Land*, should make 'Americans realise now what a fiasco the reorganisation of nationalities has been: the "Balkanisation" of Europe' – and, by implication, of 'the Mind of Europe', that mysterious entity which, for the author of 'Tradition and the Individual Talent', comprised the whole of culture from Homer until now, but which *The Waste Land* had seen as a heap of broken images, fragments shored against a ruin. No wonder, then, that the lecture ends not in crossing a frontier, but in a summons back into the constitution of silence, as 'The sad ghost of Coleridge beckons to me from the shadows'.[42]

In 1919 'Tradition and the Individual Talent' had also discreetly 'propose[d] to halt at the frontier of metaphysics or mysticism', but not before its last sentence had made one last curious gesture towards contemporary history. 'Surrendering himself wholly to the work to be done', it says, the literary revolutionary

> is not likely to know what is to be done unless he lives in what is not merely the present, but the present moment of the past, unless he is conscious, not of what is dead, but of what is already living.

'What is to be done?' had been adopted by Lenin in 1902 from the title of a nineteenth-century Russian novel as the title of what was to become his most widely-cited pamphlet on revolutionary strategy. The pamphlet's reputation preceded its English translation, which came later than German and other translations. Eliot's Oxford mentor (and probable lover of Vivienne Eliot), Bertrand Russell, the 'Mr Apollinax' of *Prufrock and Other Observations*, was sufficiently interested in the new Soviet state to visit it in spring 1920. Later that year he reported on his visit in *The Practice and Theory of Bolshevism*,[43] a book which shows a thorough acquaintance with the theory as much as with the practices. By 1919, the question 'What is to be done?' was something of a catchphrase in revolutionary circles. It is likely to have been known to someone working for Lloyds Bank on the implications of 'the present decay of eastern Europe' for the European monetary system. There is a striking parallel between Eliot's individual talent, 'surrendering himself wholly to the work to be done' in effecting a literary revolution, and the self-sacrificing Bolshevik cadre described by Russell, who 'spares himself as little as he spares others ... lives an austere life ... not pursuing individual ends, but aiming at the creation of a new social order'.[44]

The hidden agenda of such texts as 'Tradition and the Individual Talent' is exposed by Eliot's persistent mis-dating. If a tardy history delayed its actual writing for another two years, 1917 was in retrospect the necessary symbolic moment for such an essay to be published. Throughout Eliot's life then a deep unconscious association links his slyly subversive text with the momentous events of a Europe in revolutionary ferment. In 1919 the Red Army under Trotsky's command was sweeping unresisted across the frontiers of eastern Europe, as Modernism was advancing on all fronts against an enfeebled cultural orthodoxy. For Eliot, the moment of Modernism coincided with the moment of Bolshevism in which traditions and frontiers were also overthrown in the creation of a new order. If, in retrospect, 1917 and not 1919 was the memorable date, Eliot's misremembering can be understood. For if this year did not give birth to 'Tradition and the Individual Talent', what it did witness were two even more momentous events, the first shots in the revolution of the word brought about by two 'literary Bolsheviks', the Lenin and the Trotsky of Modernism: publication of Eliot's *Prufrock and Other Observations* and of Ezra Pound's *Homage to Sextus Propertius*.

Chapter Three

Disturbing the universe: *Prufrock and Other Observations*

Cheering oneself up

J. Alfred Prufrock has known them all already, known them all, the eyes that fix you in a formulated phrase, the voices dying with a dying fall. Perhaps his retarded delivery, thrust into the world in June 1915 in the pages of *Poetry* (Chicago), and not published in a collection until 1917, though completed by 1911, has sophisticated but also jaundiced his outlook. The room he contemplates entering is a room he also knows in advance, a room where the women come and go talking of Michelangelo, as they have done it seems forever. As they talk of Michelangelo, so they will talk of him, for *they* also know *him* already. The phrases in which these midwives to his fully-grown persona will fix him are not the spontaneous expression of an authentic, original response any more than his prediction of what 'They will say'. This is one reason why he can anticipate their words. Discourse goes round and round in a perpetual circuit, without ever touching anything new.

'Let us go, then, you and I. . . .' The poem opens with an invitation which is in fact a *fait accompli*, precluding any alternative, as that quietly interpolated 'then' suggests. Neither party to the dialogue has a choice in the matter. The real debate and the real decisions have taken place even before the poem starts, for the streets are pre-scripted texts, which 'follow like a tedious argument / Of insidious intent' (we are not told what they follow, so that the verb hangs intransitively unfulfilled) and lead to a predetermined end, a conclusion which lacks an object, which is simply another beginning in another 'overwhelming question'. Language returns upon itself. The narratives are all pre-empted. They neither originate from nor belong to the subject who utters them. We

42

must not ask 'What is it?' We must simply enter the discourse, after which it is too late for questions.

The opening passage of the opening poem of Eliot's first volume, 'The Love Song of J. Alfred Prufrock', has already written the scenario for all that is to come. It was of this poem that Pound wrote to Harriet Monroe, editor of *Poetry* (Chicago), in 1914:

> Eliot ... has sent in the best poem I have yet had or seen from an American. PRAY GOD IT BE NOT A SINGLE AND UNIQUE SUCCESS. ... He is the only American I know of who has made what I can call adequate preparation for writing. He has actually trained himself *and* modernised himself *on his own*.[1]

The 'supervention of novelty' of which Eliot was to write in 'Tradition and the Individual Talent' has already occurred, but nothing has changed. The new thing talks only about the old things, their irreplaceability, and the 'ideal order' they make among themselves, as the women chatter of Michelangelo. There is a central paradox here. This poem, which has strong claims to be the primal, founding text of Modernism, certainly represents what 'Tradition and the Individual Talent' calls 'the introduction of the new (the really new) work of art' among the 'existing monuments'. Eliot has fulfilled Pound's requirement for a modern poetry: he has *made it new*. But in that new making he speaks throughout of an always-already finished business, of stale reiteration. Prufrock's anticipations, his anxious self-reassurance that 'indeed there will be time', pass without noticing into a disenchanted retrospect, a postmortem on a non-event. An original act, something which might have disturbed the universe, has not happened. And if it had, 'would it have been worth it, after all?' The poem turns over the same questions endlessly, lifting and dropping them on its plate.

Yet something new *has* occurred. The new, the really new work of art, 'modifies' the existing order by *bracketing* all that has gone before. Eliot at times uses actual brackets as a stylistic device in his poems (there are four sets in 'Prufrock', three in 'Portrait of a Lady'), thereby achieving the same ironic distance Pound affected by scattering around quotation marks. But the framing and distancing is achieved primarily by the sudden shifts of point of view, perspective and argument. 'Prufrock' does to the conventional narratives of which the poem is constituted what Edmund Husserl (whom Eliot read in Marburg in 1914 while trying to write a sequel to 'Prufrock', 'The Love Song of St Sebastian'),[2] wrote of as the primary philosophical act: the bracketing, the parenthetical distantiation of experience.

Prufrock endeavours to see life steady and see it whole by framing it within a perspective that detaches the speaking subject from that of which he speaks. Thus 'the whole order' is 'modified', which is to say, *put into another mode*, by the recognition that it is not nature but artifice – that it is, precisely, an ensemble of ways of seeing and interpreting constructed through language. Prufrock has the last word because it is, after all, his 'love song' which constitutes the world from which he recoils. The narrative of 'Prufrock' becomes itself a new meta-narrative which puts all the jostling, discontinuous, contradictory internal narratives into a new and ironic relation: the totally new because self-conscious experience of stale recurrence itself.

Prufrock inhabits a closed discursive universe. There can be no innovation in this world. Though he knows exactly what is to come next he is not, like John the Baptist, a prophet, because *everybody* knows in advance what is likely to happen. Discourse itself permits only certain options, and within that range there is a formula for coping with everything – for, that is, absorbing the new initiative, fixing it in a formulated phrase, so that it does not disturb the closed universe of predictable occasions, so that it leads only to the same overwhelming and conclusive and already concluded question. Prufrock's deepest distress is that 'It is impossible to say just what I mean!' – which may suggest that the truly original thing lacks a language in which to manifest itself. It is more likely, however, that this protestation is itself a formulaic empty disclaimer. After all, the phrase is simply a variation on what he has speculated the woman will say, one of the formulae appropriate on such occasions to head off the embarrassingly pre-dictable move: ' "That is not what I meant at all. / That is not it, at all" '. Prufrock's prolepsis becomes a kind of epitaph for an event which will not occur. Perhaps this speculative, finally imaginary disturbance of the universe – a proposal or proposition of a sexual kind, we can assume from the poem's title – is not a departure from the script, but itself a predictable and pre-scribed thing. The 'overwhelming question' then becomes no more than an insignificant exchange in a familiar scenario, the pre-text of humiliation and retraction.

It is predictable, then, that Prufrock should turn to that currently fashionable stereotype of misunderstood and dilatory egregiousness to save his dignity, even as he disclaims any pretensions to greatness. He is not, nor was 'meant to be', Prince Hamlet – that is out of the question. He will not unpack his heart with words, fall a-cursing like a drab, nor consider that overwhelming question, 'To be, or not to be', though its answer is implicit in his (predictably *fin de siècle*) identification with John the Baptist. Nevertheless, his implicit assumption is that he *is*, like Hamlet, primarily a man of words, not deeds, 'full of high sentence' (his identity sliding into the wordy Polonius and the even wordier Osric here) but like them finally empty of meaning. The various roles he tries on from the play all turn on language as secondary commentary, inferior to deeds, from Horatio the prince's philosopher-confidant to the jesting, word-playing Fool.

The Boston Evening Transcript in 1909 carried a report on an interview with Sigmund Freud, then giving a series of visiting lectures at Harvard, in which Freud quoted at length Hamlet's remarks to Rosencrantz and Guildenstern about being played on like a pipe, being predictable, fathomable, the heart of his mystery plucked. Eliot, then a student at Harvard, was attending the seminars of Josiah Royce, the academic who had invited Freud to lecture.[3] Equally second-hand, the escapist sexual fantasy of the mermaids, drawn from Matthew Arnold and similar romantic sources, also hinges on non-communication ('I do not think that they will sing for me'). What Prufrock is doing here is very similar to what Eliot attributes to Othello in 1927, in an essay which also refers to Husserl's phenomenology, 'Shakespeare and the Stoicism of Seneca'. He is

> *cheering himself up*. He is endeavouring to escape reality . . . turning himself into a pathetic figure, by adopting an *aesthetic* rather than a moral attitude, dramatizing himself against his environment. He takes in the spectator, but the human motive is primarily to take in himself.[4]

Linking himself negatively with Hamlet, Prufrock offers another version of such '*bovarysme*, the human will to see things as they are not'. If he seems an improbable candidate for the Senecan mode, one might recall Eliot's definition of Stoicism as 'a philosophy suited to slaves. . . . the refuge for the individual in an indifferent or hostile world too big for him', a definition which drolly turns the tables on the author of the canard against Christianity by suggesting that Nietzsche himself 'is the most conspicuous modern instance of cheering oneself up'. And, Eliot goes on, 'even Hamlet, who has made a pretty considerable mess of things . . . dies fairly well pleased with himself'. If Prufrock feels, like Hamlet trapped in the Revenge Tragedy he despises, that all he can do is replay already written roles, he is merely repeating an unoriginal discovery, for in that earlier 'period of dissolution and chaos', Eliot tells us, 'Antony says, "I am Antony still", and the Duchess, "I am Duchess of Malfy still"; would either of them have said that unless Medea had said "*Medea superest?*"'

Nor does the recession stop here, for Seneca himself was 'following the Greek tradition . . . he developed familiar themes and imitated great models'. Right back to the origins, there is no originality. Except, that is, Prufrock's originality of repetition, which says, not 'I am Hamlet still' but rather 'I am not Prince Hamlet, nor was meant to be'.

Appetites in arrears

'Bovaryisme' is very much the mood of 'Portrait of a Lady', another poem which rewrites its sources, in this case that Matthew Arnold whose 'Forsaken Merman' is recalled and inverted in Prufrock's final self-pitying soliloquy, and who himself keeps watch over the shelves of 'Cousin Nancy'. As B.C. Southam has pointed out:

> Throughout the 'Portrait' Eliot seems to suppose the reader's acquaintance with 'The Buried Life', on which he provides a kind of modern commentary, a rewriting of Arnold's serious dramatic monologue as a *conversation galante*, a complex statement, with shifting tones of irony, quite different from the relative simplicity of Arnold's singleness of tone and feeling.[5]

Not only is the lady herself a bundle of exhausted words, re-used clichés, but so is the poem, its very title derivative of Henry James, its themes and motifs second-hand, its overall narrative a reworking of a third-rate poem from a previous generation, mediated by a derivative Laforguian irony that turns its romantic postures into absurd pastiche. Even the lady's affected *'cauchemar'* is archly cited, as if in quotation marks, from the French poet. The ' "dying fall" ' with which the poem contemplates its own end derives not only from *Twelfth Night*, but more immediately from the poem which precedes it in *Prufrock and Other Observations* (the 'Love Song' itself, line 52). Both poems in their turn defer to James's story 'The Aspern Papers' (a text also to be deployed in 'Burbank with a Baedecker') where quotation marks also register the phrase's formulaic quality. In a final complex involution, in James's story it also applies to one writer's retreading of a previous, now dead writer's haunts, in which 'some note of his voice seemed to abide ... by a roundabout implication and in a "dying fall" '.[6] Eliot's 'roundabout implication' here involves his text in a remarkable act of auto-referentiality.

The only *real* deed in such a world would be that which is entirely, brilliantly original. Since this is impossible, all action is utopian. The speaker of 'Portrait' wishes, like Prufrock or Hamlet, to act decisively. But when desire strikes its commonness appals, linking him shamefully to all those other vulgar doers and desirers. Touched like them by a 'mechanical and tired' pianola repeating 'some worn out common song' in the street, he finds human solidarity only in banal repetition. Subjectivity here is not the Romantic ego's spontaneous, self-authenticating self-articulation, but the replaying of an exhausted text. Song is no longer the always original lyric *voice*, but a pre-inscribed *writing*, fixed in sterile repetition, on a paper roll which is an up-to-date version of the self as *tabula rasa*.

Eliot wrote Section II of 'Portrait of a Lady' first, in February 1910, though it was not published until it appeared in the New York little magazine *Others* in 1915. Its opening line, 'Now that lilacs are in bloom', corresponds almost exactly to the opening line of Rupert Brooke's 'The Old Vicarage, Grantchester', dated May 1912, and published in Edward Marsh's *Georgian Poetry 1911–1912* in December 1912: 'Just now the lilac is in bloom'.[7] Since it is highly unlikely that either poem influenced the other, the coincidence suggests that they share a common source in the hackneyed phrases of some current popular song, of exactly the type that might be played on a street piano. The tired exasperation at one's own derivativeness, 'Recalling things that other people have desired', is inadvertently confirmed by the coincidence of Eliot's and Brooke's phrasings. Personal memory, like public history, is constructed by an order of discourse that exists beyond and before the self. These 'things' are as unnamed and unspecific as those 'other people', constituted simply in their otherness. The lady's clichés return with the same predictability; her voice also plays a familiar tune on a tired instrument, as obvious and insistent as the rhyme:

> The voice returns like the insistent out-of-tune
> Of a broken violin on an August afternoon.

The poem had opened with a similar irony at the expense of an overblown Romantic fashion in histrionic performers, 'let us say' likewise diminishing the significance of any particular event, musician or composer:

> We have been, let us say, to hear the latest Pole
> Transmit the Preludes through his hair and finger-tips.

Elsewhere in *Prufrock and Other Observations* the title 'Preludes' ironises the idea of a transcendent martyred soul by reminding us of the thousand sordid images of which that soul is really constituted. Romanticism itself dwindles to the interplay of a few clichéd signifiers: Chopin, Polishness, wild hair, sensitive fingers. Originality resides only in the self-regarding theatricality which simulates spontaneity: 'You will have the scene arrange itself, as it will seem to do.' Like the generic Pole, the young man invited to tea is only 'the latest' in a line, without personal distinction, expendable, replaceable, like the tunes of the pianola. If this particular subject resists his type-casting, he can be dismissed in a formulated phrase which reduces heroism to cliché: ' "You are invulnerable, you have no Achilles' heel." ' Like Prufrock, the young man is also 'Prepared for all the things to be said, or left unsaid.' In an ethos of 'velleities and carefully caught regrets', even the 'definite "false note"' of lust, absurdly hammering out a different kind of 'prelude of its own' in capricious (goatlike) monotone, can be orchestrated by a quick change of air. Relationships are no more than a complicated negotiation of preconceived positions ('This is as I had reckoned'), in which even the death of one party has to be calculated for in advance with a rehearsed response, no longer an original or final event but simply another manoeuvre in a minuet of advantages.

'Rare and strange' life is, says this woman whose life is 'composed', but 'composed so much of odds and ends' which are as 'common' and 'worn out' as the street-piano's reiterated tune. She might be describing Eliot's poems themselves, at once wholly original and yet composed entirely of the odds and ends of contemporary conversation. Indeed, in the years to come Eliot was frequently to cite Ariel's song from *The Tempest*, vaguely echoed here, as a metaphor for an art such as this, which converts the mundane into 'something rich and strange', just as he was to rework in several rather finer contexts her clichéd consolatory phrase, 'Our beginnings never know our ends'. When they 'Discuss the late events, / Correct [their] watches by the public clocks', they are not bringing themselves up-to-date in some Poundian programme of modernisation. Rather, caught in a world where events are always belated, poems and personae alike seek refuge in an evasive textuality: to fix the Lady in writing, pen in hand, is the only way to avoid being transfixed in one's turn. Re-inscription is the only original act.

In 'Preludes' there is the same predictability as evening and winter settle into their routines. Morning 'comes to consciousness' bleakly aware of its own banally repeated rituals, coming to an impersonal awareness of itself in the consciousness of an unspecified observer, much as, in the criticism, Eliot speaks of the mind primarily as a vehicle or catalyst in which emotions, images and feelings come into existence. As rooms are furnished with mass-produced items, so is consciousness, as the repetition of 'thousand' underlines:

> One thinks of all the hands
> That are raising dingy shades
> In a thousand furnished rooms. . . .
> You dozed, and watched the night revealing
> The thousand sordid images
> Of which your soul was constituted.

These images flicker on the ceiling like the collective fantasies of a prose kinema. But they are not constituted by the soul, and they do not issue from it. The night reveals them; and it is the soul which is constituted by them. The soul's escape lies in 'such a vision of the street as the street hardly understands'; yet, ironically, such vision is created only by back-formation: the soul is merely the 'conscience of a blackened street', with a play on the French usage of *'conscience'* as consciousness returning us to the beginning of Section II. It is deliberately unclear whether soul or street is 'impatient to assume the world' because, as Eliot observes in his thesis on Bradley, consciousness is not abstractable from the objects of consciousness. What that conscience reflects is a world manufactured by the discourse of 'evening newspapers' and 'certain certainties', where fancies curl and cling around images like the newspaper curled in the hair overnight or wrapped around the feet by the wind in grimy scraps.

In 'Portrait', the lives and indiscretions the unnamed speaker reads of are as hackneyed and disposable as the newspaper in which he reads of them. Throughout Eliot's verse the newspaper represents a textuality endlessly changing and endlessly the same, like the expendable because repeatable lives it reports. 'The Boston Evening Transcript' gives away the secret of all these transactions. Its very title contains a sly double narrative: it is the singular and apparently original text of a poem called 'The Boston Evening Transcript'. But it is also the title of another text, a text we cannot read here but which we see being delivered to Cousin Harriet, announced like a divine visitation in the last words of the poem, a text that, renewed daily, is always different yet always in each new edition *the* real and unique *Boston Evening Transcript*. For a newspaper is an odd kind of text, when one considers it in relation to its origins. It has as many *antecedents* as there are previous editions, yet at the same time each most recent edition is the one and only, original and authoritative text. It is, therefore, self-originating, having no *origins* beyond itself. Yet at the same time each new edition merely repeats that transcription of the Boston evening which is its *raison d'être*.

Transcription is rendered problematic in the poem's own transcribing of the production, distribution and consumption of a newspaper. After the title, the newspaper is named three times, at formally key moments at the beginning, middle and end of the poem. The newspaper, like the poem, authorises and homogenises its readers, divorcing them from 'the appetites of life', constituting them by back-formation as, simply, 'The readers of the *Boston Evening Transcript*' (the newspaper, the poem?). The newspaper overwhelms life as its title dominates the Aristotelian turning-points of the poem's narrative. 'The Boston Evening Transcript' makes explicit the motif of the newspaper in Eliot's verse, as the sign of a textuality that inscribes, collectivises, diminishes, demeans, erases – the very condition of the modern, where the worlds revolve, not like Ptolemy's or Dante's in a lucid, rational space, but worn-out, exhaustively recycled, in a void without centre. The 'real' exists here as debris, usable only as fuel, the secondary burning of the permanently secondhand.

The moon of 'Rhapsody on a Windy Night', like any whore, has heard it all many times. So has the undertaker in 'Aunt Helen', 'aware that this sort of thing had happened before'.

Cousin Nancy in the poem of that name 'smoked / And danced all the modern dances. / Her aunts were not quite sure how they felt about it / But they knew that it was modern', in contrast with 'The army of unalterable law' represented by the books of Arnold and Emerson on the shelves, apostles of a dead tradition. Like Prufrock, however, we are not fooled by this spurious modernity, so like that 'challengingly original Modern Girl' to be mocked by Percy Wyndham Lewis in *Tarr*.[8] We know the type. Indeed, we have 'known them all before, known them all'. We know that the formulated phrases which confer modernity are what two decades later Eliot was to identify as 'conventional modes of perception and valuation which are perpetually forming' to ensure that 'our lives are mostly a constant evasion of ourselves, and an evasion of the visible and sensible world'.[9] The very epigraph of the volume's closing poem, 'La Figlia Che Piange' ('*O quam te memorem virgo . . .*'), receding via Italian 'figlia' to Latin 'virgo', reminds us that this is no original romantic interlude and no 'challengingly original Modern Girl', but an oft-repeated event, stage-managed by a speaker who runs and re-runs the episode in memory, trying out different variants, reducing any original to the mere aesthetic trace of 'a gesture and a pose'. 'Preludes' sums up the mood of the whole volume, defining all supposedly new experience as in reality nothing more than repetition, 'masquerades / That time resumes'. In the mode of *Hamlet*, between the 'late events' and such preludes to action falls the shadow, where the present disappears in a fumbled exchange of words, words, words.

Yet Prufrock, in registering the stale, flat and unprofitable nature of an existence lived at second-hand, is a genuine original: his modernity lies precisely in knowing that he is not original, in a sense more complex than that of *Ecclesiastes*, one of his precedents. Wyndham Lewis again, in *Tarr*, gives us the theorised version, speaking of 'the secrets and repressions that it is the pride of the modern to disclose with a conventional obscene heroism', the foremost of which is that 'a man is always his *last* appetite, or his appetite before last. And that is no longer an appetite'.[10] Modernity resides in the recognition that the self lives in arrears, in a self-conscious relation to the clichés it endures. Prufrock's response to his ageing finds its novel modernity in a ludicrous and trivial revolt into youthful fashion: 'I shall wear the bottoms of my trousers rolled.' No other protest against age in the whole of world literature had ever sounded this note of pathos and absurdity. Prufrock's historical uniqueness lies in the ironic weary flatness and deflation with which he recognises his own stale predictability.

Never anything anywhere

The past, Eliot tells us in 'Tradition and the Individual Talent', is 'that which we know', and it 'directs' the present. But it is also 'altered by the present as much as the present is directed by the past'. So the present is in fact directed by a past it has created in its own image – is altered, in a way, by itself. This is the closed universe Prufrock inhabits, which precludes any real innovation, since any new event is merely the re-working of some already worn-out narrative. But it is also the paradox of Modernism itself, of its attempt to make it new by going over the old ground. For the ground cannot be the same. In the ensemble the present forms with innumerable possible pasts and futures – all those speculative subjunctive possibilities which link the comic futility of 'Prufrock' with the beautiful pathos of 'La Figlia' – is constituted a discourse which is always a dialogue, the dialogue of the historically constituted subject with the discursive contexts which constitute it. Eliot's personae are historical, not timeless. They are the past that they know, but in knowing it they are different from their past. And the world of Prufrock, on this reckoning, is also the critical universe of essays such as 'Tradition', which speak of a major literary revolution in terms that minimise the enormity of the change taking place.

Eliot's metaphor for literary creation in 'Tradition and the Individual Talent' has unexpected correspondences with the *personae* of these early poems. The poet's mind is like the catalyst of 'finely filiated platinum . . . introduced into a chamber containing oxygen and sulphur dioxide'.[11] The analogy stresses the before and the after, but leaves magical the instant of combustion that actually transforms the whole, producing the new work of art but leaving the catalyst unaffected. In the same way, in the essay's larger account of the 'supervention of novelty' which occurs when a new work of art joins the existing monuments, the actual moment of transformation in which everything is rearranged gets left out of the transaction. A single paradigm links these two propositions. In both cases, two elements are brought together by a third, the catalyst, to produce the fourth, the new synthesis. In the smaller analogy, 'the mind of the poet is the shred of platinum'. In the larger, it is the intervention of the individual talent. But in both instances, this third is a mere empty effectivity, enduring, like Prufrock, 'a continual surrender of himself as he is at the moment to something which is more valuable. The progress of an artist is a continual self-sacrifice, a continual extinction of personality'.

The essay's air of confident scientificity conceals a deep epistemological confusion. The 'extinction of personality' seems to involve something more than simply remaining like a catalyst, 'itself . . .

apparently unaffected . . . inert, neutral and unchanged'. This is a very peculiar kind of catalyst, since it also supplies the materials to be catalysed: it 'may partly or exclusively operate upon the experience of the man himself', and 'the experience . . . the elements which enter the presence of the transforming catalyst, are of two kinds: emotions and feelings'. The simile is complicated by a third role assigned to the mind of the artist, which besides being the inert agent and the raw material is also the receptacle or flask in which the experiment takes place, 'a more finely perfected medium in which special, or very varied, feelings are at liberty to enter into new combinations'.

The schizoid dissociation threatens to swamp the analogy. But, as a metaphor, it corresponds very closely to the position of Prufrock, who is both observer and observed, the site of action and inaction and the inert witness to them, at once the object and subject of events and the empty space in which they transpire. Attempting to rescue his analogy, Eliot inflicts a major fission on 'the mind of the poet' by shifting discursive context from a chaotic chemistry lab to the realm of social psychology and then the dinner table: 'the more perfect the artist, the more completely separate in him will be the man who suffers and the mind which creates; the more perfectly will the mind digest and transmute the passions which are its material.' The new concept of 'passions' is clearly distinct from both 'emotions' and 'feelings', though the distinction of each from the others is never specified. The idea of the chemical catalyst still flickers feebly in an illustration from Canto XV of the *Inferno* which purports to demonstrate but really only distracts attention from the crumbling 'explanation':

> The last quatrain gives an image, a feeling attached to an image, which 'came', which did not develop simply out of what precedes, but which was probably in suspension in the poet's mind until the proper combination arrived for it to add itself to. The poet's mind is in fact a receptacle for seizing and storing up numberless feelings, phrases, images, which remain there until all the particles which can unite to form a new compound are present together.

The 'new compound' of the poem reproduces on a smaller scale the 'new order' of tradition. There is no explanation of how this new thing '"came"'. (The quotation marks recall a similar gratuitous act of '"replacement"' figured by the same device in Pound's contemporaneous *Mauberley*.) It was merely 'in suspension' until 'the proper combination arrived'. Eliot cannot theorise that arrival any more than Prufrock can explain how he arrived at his overwhelming question. We know, however, that it is not a simple *development* out of what precedes it. It is, rather, a genuine *supervention* of novelty which breaks with causal determinism – a qualitative revolutionary change. The 'new compound' arrives only when all the various 'particles' are brought together in the 'receptacle' of the poet's mind.

This receptacle is no more inert than the earlier catalyst turned out to be. It is not only a place for 'storing up' chemicals, it is also actively involved in 'seizing' them. The conflict here, between the passive 'storing' and the active 'seizing', registers the strain of trying to impose a conservative model of changelessness on the dynamic literary transformations of Modernism. What the clinical metaphor refuses is that historical dimension which is the element and agency of literary as of social revolution. That repressed dimension returns to haunt what at first sight seems the last gasp of the chemical analogy in the next paragraph, where the 'process' of creation is no longer a passive 'combination' of elements effected by an inert third party, but an active 'fusion' under intense 'pressure':

> For it is not the 'greatness', the intensity, of the emotions, the components, but the intensity of the artistic process, the pressure, so to speak, under which the fusion takes place, that counts.

In his account of tradition, as of the composition of the poem, Eliot has no device for explaining the insertion of the diachronic into the synchronic. We are left instead with a succession of synchronies, complete in themselves, and an uncrossable epistemological space between them. Where does the supervention come *from*? Does it arrive fully formed? Are there no warnings of its coming? Are there no ripples after it has arrived, but just an instantaneous readjustment of all the parts, leaving a new and complete stasis? How do we reconcile the idea of an inert catalyst, unchanged by what it effects, standing outside its achievement, indifferent, no doubt paring its finger nails, with the idea of the artist's mind undergoing a perpetual sacrifice and extinction of personality? How can the artist at once be detached from the new combination and absorbed in it, his 'emotions and feelings' fused in the new compound in the way that the individual talent is subsumed into the perpetually renewed synchrony of tradition?

Well, 'There will be time to murder and create. . . . for a hundred visions and revisions, / Before the taking of a toast and tea'. Prufrock also moves surreptitiously from contemplating his daring to disturb the universe as a future event ('Should I . . . Have the strength to force the moment to its crisis?') to seeing it as a past non-event ('And would it have been worth it, after all?'), from, that is, vision to revision, without ever passing through the realm of action. No new start here, no 'event' to come after, but only a gap where, in the words of 'The Hollow Men',

> Between the idea
> And the reality
> Between the motion
> And the act
> Falls the Shadow.

Eliot supplied an account of the actual agency of change a decade and more later, in that passage of *The Use of Poetry and the Use of Criticism* I have discussed in the previous chapter: supervention occurs 'under the influence of new stimuli which originate outside of art'. Here lie the true origins of Modernism, in an external history which, far from being a panorama of futility and anarchy upon which art imposes order, transforms the order of art as, in the words Eliot quotes from Trotsky, a 'function of social man indissolubly tied to his life and environment'. The individual talent is an 'impersonal' catalyst because its main function is to act as the carrier of *social* meanings, that is why it is a vehicle of 'significant emotion' – that is, of emotion which carries signification.

The poetry tells us more about this social meaning. The relation of individual talent to tradition and of the catalytic mind of the poet to its contents is reproduced in the cognitive processes of Tiresias and Prufrock. The catalytic mind of the poet remains 'apparently unaffected . . . inert, neutral, and unchanged' and yet is identical with the gases it synthesises and the medium in which they meet. In the same way, Tiresias 'although a mere spectator and not indeed a "character", is yet the most important personage in the poem, uniting all the rest'. Similarly, just as 'Tradition' is a unity composed of the multiplicity of diverse talents, constantly reformed as each new voice intrudes into the discourse, so 'all the women are one woman, and the two sexes meet in Tiresias. What Tiresias *sees*, in fact, is the substance of the poem.' The individual talent is possessed by all the living dead of tradition: 'Someone said: "The dead writers are remote from us because we *know* so much more they did." Precisely, and they are that which we know.' Knowledge of the dead is Tiresias' special insight, as a necromancer: 'I had not thought death had undone so many'; Prufrock too likens himself to Lazarus, 'back from the dead, come back to tell you all'.

Prufrock is the 'catalyst', the inert agent of change, but he is also external to the action of the poem, standing at a distance from it, the 'receptacle' which transcends and contains it all. He is, paradoxically, also the object of the action, his emotions and feelings the raw material on which it works. He wonders, self-ironisingly, whether he 'dare / Disturb the universe'. But even the most universe-disturbing super-vention of novelty seems to leave no trace. In this room where there is time to murder and create, time for a hundred visions and revisions, reversable minute by minute, the taking of a toast and tea will continue as if nothing has happened.

Like the individual talent, Prufrock experiences a perpetual extinction of personality, a sacrifice of the self, figured repeatedly in every metaphor and metamorphosis of the text, from the etherised patient, the cat-fog that falls asleep, the self reduced to something 'formulated . . . pinned and wriggling on a pin', the vision of the pair of ragged claws, the somnolent afternoon, the beheaded John the Baptist, the refusal of John's prophetic as of Hamlet's princely status, the deferring of identity and deferring to others, the extinguished and returned Lazarus, the withdrawal of meanings, the inability to say just what he means, and the final vision of mermaids, which ends with an awakening which is also a drowning. Like Tiresias, he is simultaneously the most important personage, uniting all the rest, and the most marginal and insignificant, a mere inert catalyst and receptacle. Like the new work of art, he wants to transform everybody there, arrange them all around him, and he wants not to be noticed at all.

What is figured here is the condition Eliot himself wrote of, with remarkable if evasive insight, as his own predicament, that of the returning émigré, come to claim his inheritance, but acknowledging his multiple expropriations, in a letter to Herbert Read in 1928:

> Some day I want to write an essay about the point of view of an American who wasn't an American, because he was born in the South and went to school in New England as a small boy with a nigger drawl, but who wasn't a southerner in the South because his people were northerners in a border state and looked down on all southerners and Virginians, and who so was never anything anywhere and who therefore felt himself to be more a Frenchman than an American and more an Englishman than a Frenchman and yet felt that the USA up to a hundred years ago was a family extension.[12]

'Never anything anywhere', whether on the shores of Asia or in the Edgware Road, Eliot's aesthetics, like his *personae*, are the projection of a complex of national, class and gender positions – or, more accurately, depositions. Just as Eliot's metaphors for the production of poetry dissolve into a contradictory plurality when expounded, so polyphony inserts itself into the heart of his unitary tradition, dissolving the unity of the self into a multitude of dispossessions, leaving the rightful inheritor in possession of precisely *nothing*. ('On Margate Sands', we recall, 'I can connect / Nothing with nothing'.) Indeed, in an apparently gratuitous aside in 'Tradition and the Individual Talent', Eliot observes that 'The point of view which I am struggling to attack is perhaps related to the metaphysical theory of the substantial unity of the soul.'

The poet, he argues, does not have a unitary ' "personality" ' to express, but a particular medium, which is only a medium and not a personality, in which impressions and experiences combine in peculiar and unexpected ways'. The poet is, in fact, not an individual talent at all, but 'different voices', a bundle of discourses without a corporeal body. But though the voices come and go, talking of Virgil, Dante and Michelangelo, the patriarchal authority of tradition remains unchanged and unchallenged. In every literary revolution, the ultimate signifier of power abides our presence. Thus the poet aims, not to express his passing and local personality, which is a mere enabling medium, but that 'significant emotion', i.e. that signifying emotion, which is the sign of power itself.

Eliot's metaphor of the inert catalyst in 'Tradition' owes its origin to an observation of Keats's which he was to cite, many years later, in his fifth Norton lecture at Harvard: 'Men of genius are great as certain ethereal chemicals operating on the mass of neutral intellect — but they have not any individuality, any determined character — I would call the top and head of those who have a proper self Men of Power.'[13] it is the implicitly political context of Keats's remark which illuminates the subtext of 'Tradition and the Individual Talent'. (That Keats is in his mind in this essay is confirmed by a reference to the Nightingale Ode.) Keats is talking about the way men of genius exert influence rather than offering direct leadership, like the men of power. The antithesis of genius and power highlights why it is so important for Eliot to stress the passivity and inertness of the catalyst. The metaphor allows the mind to be an agent of change without being its victim. It allows for stability and autonomy in the midst of combustion, disturbing the universe by provoking it to disturb itself.

Disturbance is the subtle subtext of Eliot's ostensibly neo-classical criticism, a concept which, we have seen in the last chapter, lies behind some of his key critical formulations. The concept is disturbingly frequent in Eliot's criticism. But its *locus classicus* is perhaps an essay in *The Egoist* in 1918 signed under the Prufrockian pseudonym 'T.S. Apteryx'. Expositing Ford Madox Hueffer's *Observations* on the shape of the prospective postbellum world, and remarking, *a propos* 'the imminent ascendancy of Japan', that 'the degeneracy of one civilisation does not seem to be inevitably accompanied by the rise of another', he goes on:

> Mr Hueffer's warning is certainly just, and could perhaps be stated in more general terms. What we want is to disturb and alarm the public; to upset its reliance upon Shakespeare, Nelson, Washington, and Sir Isaac Newton. . . . To point out that every generation, every turn of time when the work of four or five men who count has reached middle age, is a *crisis*. Also that the intelligence of a nation must go on developing, or it will deteriorate. . . . That the forces of deterioration are a large crawling mass, and the forces of development half a dozen men.[14]

Nearly twenty years after *Prufrock and Other Observations*, in 1935, 'Burnt Norton' resumes Prufrock's dilemma, depicting a subject preempted before he starts out, knowing that whichever turning he takes he will end in the same place, a place of unfulfilment, for 'What might have been and what has been / Point to one end, which is always present'.[15] The speaker of 'Burnt Norton' is more modest than Prufrock, not wondering whether to dare disturb the universe, but only to what purpose his words disturb the dust on a bowl of rose-leaves.

'Burnt Norton' theorises the linguistic nature of the closure within which Eliot's *personae* find themselves trapped, the closure which also seals off his perpetually renewed Tradition from the currents of any actual history. Language in its perpetual restlessness always eludes the subject which tries to fix it sprawling on a pin, dislocating and disturbing time itself so that 'the end precedes the beginning, / And the end and the beginning were always there / Before the beginning and after the end'. No wonder, then, that

> Words strain,
> Crack and sometimes break, under the burden,
> Under the tension, slip, slide, perish,
> Decay with imprecision, will not stay in place,
> Will not stay still.

The signifier slips, slides, as the syntagmatic chain returns on and repeats itself in new ways, returning to the origin in straining towards a conclusion. Words not only passively suffer strain and tension, they actively strain after the unformulable. In 'Prufrock' our question is rebuffed before it can be asked by a similar negativity, just as Prufrock bites his tongue before the predictable response. It is impossible to ask, as to say, just what it means, because we cannot question a signifier which is itself ultimately 'an overwhelming question', not any specific enquiry, but the simple point of inquisition itself, an empty sign: '?'. 'Words, after speech, reach / Into the silence', as that question mark presumes an unspoken response, the 'unheard, unspoken / Word ... unspoken, unheard' of 'Ash Wednesday'.[16] Voices die with a dying fall, to be succeeded by 'the still unspeaking and unspoken Word'. The authority of the spoken and of the speaker is subverted in the very utterance, which is an authoritative admission of the failure, the predetermined *end* of speech. Words 'will not stay in place, / Will not stay still', because they have no place, no secure subject and no secure history, in which to come to rest. Eliot's literary revolution may have disturbed no more than the dust on a bowl of blown roses, but, in its very celebration of ineffectuality, it also disturbed the universe. And after such knowledge, 'Where shall the word be found, where will the word / Resound?'

Chapter Four

The poetry of a democratic aristocracy: *Homage to Sextus Propertius*

Imperial posts

Ezra Pound's definition of the image in his 1914 essay 'Vorticism' is well known: 'The image is not an idea. It is a radiant node or cluster . . . a VORTEX, from which, and through which, and into which, ideas are constantly rushing.'[1]

What is less remarked is that this is also a pattern of historical perception. Pound may, in the same year, have written in *The Egoist* of British culture as a 'malebolge of obtuseness'.[2] Nevertheless, in the cage at Pisa in 1945, it is to the London of the 1910s that he obsessively returns to explain how it all went wrong. When *Canto LXXX* ends with the plaintive cry 'God knows what else is left of our London / my London, your London', this is not just a lament for lost youth or a bombed city. Rather it's a dirge for squandered opportunities, for a lost set of cultural and political possibilities. During those years, 'Chesterton's England of has-been and why-not' had also been a vortex from which and through which and into which ideas had been constantly rushing – ideas which might have blown open that 'malebolge of obtuseness'. That they did not is, in a sense, why we fail to grasp the Englishness of Modernism, preferring to see it instead as the brainchild of two Americans and two Irishmen.

Pound wrote in *The New Age* in 1919 that 'The capital, the vortex, is that which draws intelligence into it, not that which builds up a wall for its own protection.'[3] From 1908 to 1922, off and on, London was this vortex, resisting that provincialism of time and space Pound indicted in so many of his essays. 'The Roman poets', he wrote to Iris Barry, 'are the only ones we know of who had approximately the same problems as we have. The metropolis, the imperial posts to all corners of the known world.'[4] If the progenitors of Modernism were semi-colonials, American and Irish, it was their complex and contradictory relation to the English metropolis that brought Modernism together; and it was this that finally took it apart.

A 'radiant node or cluster', unstable, ready to fall apart, 'Modernism' was the brief convergence of native and exotic elements within the vortex of a metropolitan culture in decline, yet still with global hegemony. Its fractured, subversive discourses, ironic, satiric, parodic, correspond to profound structural disturbances in British society at the beginning of this century, disturbances brought to a head, but not caused, by the Great War and the European collapse that ensued. The texts of Modernism register this disturbance in terms of a shifting interplay of *polyphony* and *intertextuality* – the one a democratic, open-ended responsiveness to the many voices of the present, the other a closed, autocratic celebration of the unitary text of tradition. This was a social and political crisis of legitimation, in which the hegemonic discourse of an imperial and patriarchal culture was challenged and subverted by the voices excluded from it: voices of another class, another nation, another sex. What these various 'others' inserted into the univocal discourse of the dominant culture was a real heterogeneity and difference, in Derrida's strong sense of the word. The polyphony of Modernist texts is a sign of this disruption. But, from the beginning, the pull of intertextual allusion back to a normative literary tradition threatened to re-incorporate disruption, render it safe and acceptable.

Intertextuality, introduced to literary criticism by Julia Kristeva in her study *Desire in Language*, was seen there simply as an extension of the Russian Formalist Mikhail Bakhtin's *polyphony*, the key term in his *Rabelais and his World*.[5] There Bakhtin set up an opposition between two modes of literary discourse: the monologistic and the dialogical. The first he associates with the epic tradition, which seeks to impose a single voice and monolinear narrative upon events, to proclaim a unitary and irrefutably single truth which cannot be diverged from without error and apostasy. This is the discourse of science, of 'history' (historiography); it speaks with the voice of authority. The second he associates with the Socratic dialogues, with Menippean satire, with the carnivalesque tradition. This culminates in the modern novel, which substitutes the polyphony of a collective subject for the solitary voice and omnipresent authority of the epic author. The dialogical mode speaks with the many voices of the oppressed; it belongs to the popular and democratic tradition.

For Bakhtin, the dialogical necessarily excludes poetry, whether it is the single self-important voice of the epic or the lonely plaint of the lyricist. Yet one of the major achievements of Modernism was to bring the dialogical mode into the ambit of poetry – not by transforming the epic, or by writing novels in verse, but by creating a new form, a semi-narrative sequence composed of disjunctive episodes, working by the accretion of fragmented lyric moments which gesture towards a narrative cohesion never realised, perpetually deferred to some moment beyond the poem. *The Waste Land*, with its absent centre in the heart of light, the silence, is the epitome of this; but sequences like 'Meditations in Time of Civil War', *Hugh Selwyn Mauberley, Homage to Sextus Propertius*, poems where the cohering perspective is always elsewhere, felt, intuited, but not grasped, in the gaps between each moment, all belong to the same mode. In such poems, the central 'subject' of the epic tradition – both as the articulating voice of the poet and as the protagonist of the poem – is displaced, marginalised, loses itself in the labyrinth of an external world it finds it increasingly difficult to comprehend, where it can connect nothing with nothing, or where, as in the *Cantos*, its way out of the Inferno is perpetually delayed by each new accumulation of cultural and historical debris, so that, in the final words of an unfinished poem:

> i.e. it coheres all right
>   even if my notes do not cohere. . . .
> But to affirm the gold thread in the pattern. . . .
> To confess wrong without losing rightness:
> Charity I have had sometimes,
>   I cannot make it flow thru.
> A little light, like a rushlight
>   to lead back to splendour.[6]

The desire for coherence is the epic delusion of Modernism. The acknowledgement that it doesn't cohere, that diversity cannot be reduced to uniformity, is its saving grace. Part of that cultural debris is precisely that intertextuality which for Kristeva is simply another aspect of polyphony. For it is what she calls 'the foreign discourse constantly present in the speech that it distorts' which causes that block and obstruction with which the *Cantos* end.[7] The 'imperial posts to all corners of the known world' bring home, in the end, an unassimilable plurality, the white man's burden of an alterity that cannot be shrunken and contained to the contours of a parochial 'Tradition'.

A company of actor-authors

Pound's *Homage to Sextus Propertius* (1917) is a *locus classicus* of Modernism's debate between epic and dialogical modes.[8] The precise terms in which Pound conceptualised it can be found in his quick run-through of the literature of early western Europe from the troubadours to Camoes, published in 1910 as *The Spirit of Romance*. Pound's terms in many ways prefigure those of Bakhtin, and provide an essential prelude to a reading of the poem.

In his '*Praefatio Ad Lectorem Electum*', as we have seen in the first chapter, Pound makes it clear that he is engaged in a double sifting – a sifting of both past and present:

> It is dawn at Jerusalem while midnight hovers above the Pillars of Hercules. All ages are contemporaneous. It is B.C., let us say, in Morocco. The Middle Ages are in Russia. The future stirs already in the minds of the few. This is especially true of literature, where the real time is independent of the apparent, and where many dead men are our grandchildren's contemporaries, while many of our contemporaries have been already gathered into Abraham's bosom, or some more fitting receptacle.[9]

And, he continues, 'What we need is a literary scholarship, which will weigh Theocritus and Yeats with one balance, and will judge dull dead men as inexorably as dull writers of today.' If the present is to provide occasions for a new poetic impulse, there has to be a new seeing of the inheritance, a clearing of the rubble.

All this is familiar enough, and characteristically Poundian. But it is important to note how different Pound's formulation is from the ostensibly similar one Eliot makes in 'Tradition and the Individual Talent' nine years later. Pound is here talking about a *discontinuous* history, of 'differentiated histories' in Derrida's term. Contemporaneity is not the co-existence of *all* the past in the mind of the present. Rather it is a matter of a fractured, disjunctive series of time-zones held together within a collective present which cannot be totalised, seen steady and whole, by any one individual (dawn in Jerusalem, midnight in Morocco). Otherness, the existence of other points of view which cannot be brought within any easily forged consensus by the individual talent, is already inscribed in his metaphors. And, proceeding from that, it is obvious that for any one individual some synchronies are available and others are not – are excluded, or have to be repelled. The Elect, whether as writers or readers, have to struggle to forge a 'real time', a genuine synchrony, from these discrepant moments. In the process they will become a creative elite. Pound's geographical analogy decentres in advance that unitary 'tradition' Eliot was in process of constructing, emphasising not only the contemporaneity of all ages, but also their dispersal. The success of Pound's project will be the forging of 'the poetry of a democratic aristocracy' like that he admired in medieval Provence, 'which swept into itself, or drew about it, every man with a wit or a voice'.[10] The oxymoron indicates the political ambiguity of Modernism, as the dynamic metaphor prefigures the image of the vortex.

The Spirit of Romance keeps up a perpetual jostling of Bakhtin's two modes. It is there, principally, discussing allegory in the *Romaunt de la Rose*, in the statement that 'Objective narrative art precedes the subjective narrative'; and in the observation that 'The mediaeval author is not yet able to shed himself in completely self-conscious characters; to make a mood; slough it off as a snake does his skin and then endow it with an individual life of its own.' And Pound contrasts this emphatically with what 'Dante did triumphantly in the *Commedia*'.[11]

Since Dante is the proclaimed model for the *Cantos*, what Pound has to say of him here is of considerable moment. And it is the dramatic, the dialogical element that he foregrounds, in opposition to the epic, or monological, mode. Thus, having rejected the egotistical sublime of Wordsworth and Whitman, it is to Milton that he turns for the major contrast with the Italian poet:

> Milton resembles Dante in nothing; judging superficially, one might say that they both wrote long poems which mention God and the angels, but their Gods and angels are as different as their styles and abilities. Dante's God is ineffable divinity. Milton's God is a fussy old man with a hobby. Dante is metaphysical, where Milton is merely sectarian. *Paradise Lost* is conventional melodrama, and later critics have decided the Devil is intended for the hero, which interpretation leaves the whole without significance. Dante's Satan is undeniably and indelibly evil. He is not 'Free Will' but stupid malignity. Milton has no grasp of the superhuman. Milton's angels are men of enlarged power, plus wings. Dante's angels surpass human nature, and differ from it. They move in their high courses inexplicable.[12]

'Difference' is the significant concept here. 'Melodrama' is monological: it makes its moral norm, its 'point of view', heavily apparent. There is only one allowed way of interpreting it, and to try to deconstruct it by, for example, reversing hero and villain is to render it nugatory. Milton's God speaks with Milton's voice. But so do Milton's men and Milton's angels. This is the definition of 'sectarian': it substitutes its own univocal definitions of reality – there is only one way of being human – for the catholicity which includes difference, heterogeneity, of Dante's vision. Dante, Pound concedes, may run the risk theologically of being accounted a Manichaean, but it is this which make his work essentially dialogical, dramatic.

For Pound, the true comparison for Dante is not with the epic Milton but with the dramatic Shakespeare: 'Shakespear alone of the English poets endures sustained comparison with the Florentine', though, of course, 'It is idle to ask what Dante would have made of writing stage plays, or what Shakespear would have done with a "Paradise".'[13] In a later comparison, Pound is even more emphatic: 'Dante is many men, and suffers as many. Villon cries out as one.'[14] And it is precisely to the dialogical tradition, initiated according to Bakhtin by the Socratic dialogues, that Pound assigns Dante, again with an insistence on heterogeneity:

> Shakespear would seem to have greater power in depicting various humanity . . . but recalling Dante's comparisons to the gamester leaving the play, to the peasant at the time of hoar-frost, to the folk passing in the shadow of evening, one wonders if he would have been less apt at fitting them with speeches. His dialogue is comparatively symbolic, it serves a purpose similar to that of the speeches in Plato, yet both he and Plato convey the impression of individuals speaking.[15]

Dante's writing of a Divine *Comedy* is not, then, an accidental thing. The word 'comedy', with all its levelling, egalitarian and dramatic associations, its polyphonic opportunities, is what essentially distinguishes such a 'long poem' from the Miltonic epic. Lacking an appropriate critical vocabulary, Pound is nevertheless emphatic as to what the *Divine Comedy* is *not*:

> The *Divina Commedia* must not be considered as an epic; to compare it with epic poems is usually unprofitable. It is in a sense lyric, the tremendous lyric of the subjective Dante; but the soundest classification is Dante's own, 'as a comedy which differs from tragedy in its content,' for 'tragedy begins admirably and tranquilly,' and the end is terrible, 'whereas comedy introduces some harsh complication, but brings the matter to a prosperous end'. The *Commedia* is, in fact, a great mystery play, or better, a cycle of mystery plays.[16]

In the *Cantos* Pound attempted a similar 'long poem' which is not an epic but a polyphonic comedy, evoking Dante as his mentor and revelling in the same interplay of serious and comic, refined and scatological. But Pound does not set up a simple antithesis of narrative and drama in *Spirit*: the divide runs right down the middle of narrative itself, separating the monological epic from other forms. Thus *El Cid*, a narrative poem, reveals 'constant drama not only in the action, but in the contending passions of the actors'; while the dialogue forms of the troubadour poetry are linked by him to the improvisatory polyphony of the 'Comedia del Arte', in which:

> The comedians choose their subject; and each man for himself given some rough plan, worked out his own salvation – to wit, the speeches of the character he represented. That is to say, you had a company of actor-authors, making plays as they spoke them.[17]

This is more than a literary idea. It is also a model for social organisation. Through spontaneous self-dramatisation a 'democratic aristocracy' can find its salvation in corporate action, and thus break out of Prufrock's impasse, daring, as Mussolini's *fascisti* were soon to do, to disturb the universe.

Writing against the grain

Pound is significantly discriminating in his exploration of what we now call intertextuality. His distinctions all emphasise the two-way trans-action that obtains between the new poet and his predecessors, in which success is defined in terms of the ability to make it new, rather than slavishly imitate an authoritative tradition. Thus, of Shelley's debt to Dante he remarks: 'I doubt if Shelley ever thought of concealing the source of much of his beauty, which he made his own by appreciation', adding 'the best of Shelley is filled with memories of Dante'.[18] He speaks disapprovingly, however, of 'the Miltonic maximum of the twenty-four allusions to the classics and Hebrew Scriptures, in a passage of twenty lines'.[19] Again, Milton is the butt of his criticisms, and Shakespeare closest to Dante. Discussing Spanish and Elizabethan imitations of early Tuscan sonnets, for example, he observes: 'Great poets seldom make bricks without straw; they pile up all the excellences they can beg, borrow or steal from their predecessors and contemporaries, and then set their own inimitable light atop of the mountain'; and goes on to add: 'As Shakespeare wrote the finest poetry in English, it matters not one jot whether or not he plundered the Italian lyrists in his general sack of available literature'.[20]

These are clearly three different ways of relating to that 'foreign discourse' of which Kristeva speaks – that otherness represented by tradition that inserts itself right into the heart of the new poem: reverential recollection, showy namedropping, and the ransacking of a condottiere. Pound's relation to his predecessors may be any of these, despite his strictures on Milton, but his characteristic stance, in the early verse, is a different one: that of dissonant recall.

In the last chapter of *The Spirit of Romance* he suggests that the exact nature of the influence exerted by the classics on the Renaissance can be determined best in 'those works where it appears least affected by other influences – that is, the works of the men who were the most persistent in their effort to bring the dead to life, and who most conscientiously studied and followed their models'. These, the neo-Latin poets of the Renaissance, eschew, one might say, the polyphonies of the present, the better to re-awaken the intertextual possibilities of a defunct poetic: 'they alone do no violence to their medium; their diction is not against the grain of the language which they use'.[21] Just before this, discussing

Camoens, he had made a distinction which corresponds to Bakhtin's between monological and dialogical:

> An epic cannot be written against the grain of its time: the prophet or the satirist may hold himself aloof from his time, or run counter to it, but the writer of epos must voice the general heart.[22]

Being 'against the grain' of one's age and one's language are thus for Pound intimately linked with the rejection of epic, on the one hand, and of the predominance of the intertextual over the polyphonic on the other. It is precisely the subversion of established tradition by a diction which speaks of otherness, of those excluded, 'vulgar' voices from beyond the 'literary' sphere which makes for the vigour and renewal (and the poet for Pound must always 'make it new') of a modern, and Modernist, poetic. Earlier, discussing Lope de Vegas' ironic, sometimes playful, sometimes savage counterpoint of artifice and the demotic, he had observed: 'Works of art attract us by a resembling unlikeness'.[23]

In *Four Quartets* T.S. Eliot speaks of tradition as an absolute authority and presence, the familiar compound ghost which usurps the present, for the voices of the dead are 'tongued with fire beyond the language of the living'. In these poems, Eliot uses all the resources of literary allusion to underwrite a unitary vision of a history which is now and England – a unity so monological that it is capable of resolving even the divisions of a civil war that took one man to the block and another, in a supposedly opposite camp, to die blind and alone. This is one impulse of Modernism. But when Pound, in *Homage to Sextus Propertius*, calls the dead to his aid, evoking not only the elegist to whom his poem pays 'homage' but a whole host of names back to Homer invoked by Propertius in his turn, this is not to stifle the present with the burden of tradition. Rather it is to brush that tradition 'against the grain', to use it for purposes contrary to its supposed intent, to turn, for example, the myth of Imperial Rome required by Imperial Britain against the uses to which it had been put in the nineteenth century, and to use it instead to subvert those imperial pretensions – pretensions which, in the year of publication, 1917, were justifying the deaths of a multitude, and of the best among them. 'The electric current gives light where it meets resistance', Pound says in *The Spirit*. Far from succumbing to the baying of the 'general heart' for German blood and jingoistic unanimity, Pound in *Homage* seeks that illumination which comes from resistance, writing against the grain of his time.

In *Spirit* he had written that 'the living conditions of Provence gave the necessary restraint, produced the tensions sufficient for the results, a tension unattainable under, let us say, the living conditions of imperial

Rome.'[24] In 1917 in Propertius he found an alternative tradition to that of the epic, a tradition descending from Callimachus and passing beyond to Provence, that could be set athwart the 'Martian generalities' of an imperial Rome and an imperial Britain, to shed new light on a darkening era, and bring new life to 'the language of the living'. Significantly, Pound launches his assault on the 'distentions of Empire' by opening up a new front, detecting a new and unfamiliar 'resembling unlikeness' between the two patriarchal, imperial orders, one which calls into question the very values privileged by the customary comparisons between nineteenth-century Britain and first-century Rome. It is this 'dissonant recall' of the full range of Latin poetic possibilities that allows Pound to deconstruct the epic tradition, with its 'distentions of Empire' and the distentions of language which under-write it. In this poem Pound turns intertextuality against itself, for instead of affirming a single link with the homogeneous past, he offers instead a melange of conflicting, competing modes, which restore that past to its true heterogeneity and in the process allow the pressing voices of the present to make their claims on the general ear.

Neither Calliope nor Apollo

Calliope, the Muse of Epic, and Apollo, the god of poetry as order, rationality, public service, are centrally refused in the poem:

> Neither Calliope nor Apollo sing these things into my ear,
>   My genius is no more than girl.

But throughout, gathering to her the epithets and appurtenances of Venus, such a 'girl' is not to be underestimated. For, if Cypris (Venus) is spoken of as his 'cicerone', Propertius also clearly recognises the terrifying power of the love goddess. At the end of Section II of the poem, Calliope distances herself from the other Muses as one who will consort neither with Venus nor Propertius, looking 'with face offended' on the poet who spurns the delights of war, content (like Yeats, perhaps, whose 'Wild Swans at Coole' was published in *The Little Review* in June 1917), to spend his time with the white swans sacred to Venus:

> 'Night dogs, the marks of a drunken scurry,
> 'These are your images, and from you the sorcerizing of shut-in
>   young ladies . . .'
>   Thus Mistress Calliope,
>   Dabbling her hands in the fount, thus she
> Stiffened our face with the backwash of Philetas the Coan.

Pound knows what he is up to here. There is, in the original, no sense of Calliope's contempt for the poet. Her face is not 'offended', nor does she so conspicuously dismiss him as not her type (there may be a pun about printer's ink in 'fount'). Instead, in the 1912 Loeb translation Pound used as a crib, she simply 'sprinkled my lips with the draught Philetas loved', in benediction rather than reproach.[25] By translating 'viragit' as 'stiffened', Pound has stiffened the tone of Calliope here. There is also no trace in the original of the seediness Pound's version associates with the erotic Muse, 'Night dogs' being a deliberate mistranslation of 'nocturnaeque canes', 'For thou shalt sing . . . through the dark'. The same deflection of the original had already excised Calliope from the first section of *Homage*, where her benign presence ('But the Muses are my comrades, and my songs are dear to them that read, nor ever is Calliope aweary with my dancing') is replaced by an extraneous reference to Numa Pompilius, an anachronistic aside about a frigidaire patent, and a generalising remark to the effect that the Muses' companions, 'weary with historical data', will prefer his dance tune.

In Pound's version, Calliope's reproaches are couched in cadences that recall that pseudo-historical, epic tradition (the repeated 'Nor . . . Nor' construction here and elsewhere being a prime device of the genre). Propertius, on the contrary, has announced from the beginning an alternative ancestry, where 'Grecian orgies' and 'the dance' rather than combat are the principal mode of encounter between mortals – that tradition represented by the 'shades' of Callimachus and 'Coan ghosts' of Philetas. There is complex irony here, of course, for both these poets were Alexandrian lyrists, grammarians, pedagogues, cataloguers, haunting the famous library of a declining empire, sprinkling their pastorals with much laboriously acquired learning. Propertius' protestations have to be taken *cum grano salis*. He may claim to speak for 'A young Muse with young loves clustered about her', and to ride in a 'new-fangled chariot'. But in his contempt for the out-weariers of Apollo and their 'Martian generalities' his erasers have not really rubbed out all precedents in the name of a new and original discourse. The vaunted return to origins is itself a literary trope with an ancient lineage. Propertius is too much an accomplice in his immediate world not to feel its pull.

Propertius' contempt for the patriotic clichés of Livy and subsequent annalists of Roman reputations, for Transcaucasian celebrities who 'belaud Roman celebrities' and (punning on Pound's own name) 'expound the distentions of Empire', is pronounced in the name of 'something to read in normal circumstances. . . . a few pages brought down from the forked hill unsullied. . . . a wreath which will not crush my head'. But in Propertius' Rome, as in Pound's London in 1916–17, the imperial theme had become 'normal circumstances'. Pound wrote to

Iris Barry in August 1916, discussing Propertius among other Greek and Latin models, of 'the gulph between' Sapphic lightness and 'Pindar's big rhetorical drum TINA THEON, TIN' EROA, TINA D'ANDREA KELADESOMEN'.[26] Within three years he was to make a bitter pun on this very line in *Mauberley*, in an indictment of wartime Britain which casts a light, too, on Propertius' desire for 'a wreath which will not crush my head': 'O bright Apollo, / . . . What god, man, or hero / Shall I place a tin wreath upon!' This wreath, of course, is both the tawdry, mass-produced substitute of a fraudulent tradition, and the tin helmet of the trenches, challenging all 'loud-mouthed products'. But jingoism has spread its snares widely. Propertius sees its corrupting effect, for example, in his friend Lynceus, who has betrayed him by seducing his girl, and whose betrayal seems intimately linked to his literary and political failings: the venereal infection ('a swig of poison' jabbing a knife in his vitals) he seems to have passed on to Propertius implicitly parallels the martial infections of a rhetoric which, though it makes a hash of Antimachus, persists in imitating Aeschylus, and now, like any mid-western tourist in Europe, intends to 'do Homer'.

Propertius evinces general contempt for the sycophants of the epic tradition, currently represented by Virgil, whose *Aeneid* establishes him as the official heir to Homer, listing Caesar's ships as the *Iliad* did those of the Greeks, 'proving' Augustus' lineal descent from the Trojan Aeneas. Elevated to the dubious status of 'Phoebus' chief of police', Virgil rapidly deteriorates into a self-important traffic cop, commanding Roman and Greek authors to 'make way' and 'clear the street' for 'a much larger Iliad . . . on the course of construction / (and to Imperial order)'.

Pound wrote to A.R. Orage at some length in 1919, of *Homage*, that

> If possible I shd. even have wished to render a composite character, including something of Ovid, and making the portrayed figure not only Propertius but inclusive of the spirit of the young man of the Augustan Age, hating rhetoric and undeceived by imperial hogwash'.[27]

Nevertheless, it is clear that Virgil is doing quite nicely out of his commission as poetic 'chief of police', and there is more than a tinge of jealousy to Propertius' resentment. One way to prove that it is not lack of talent but predilection which keeps him from the epic 'high-road to the Muses' is to show how easy it is to turn out this militaristic trash. If it is up-to-date, in this last age, to sing of tumult, leaving Venus to the 'primitive ages', then of course he will not baulk at being up-to-date. He too will sing of war 'when this matter of a girl is exhausted'. He is even prepared to offer a sample of this 'more stately manner', though it is rapidly redefined as a 'large-mouthed product':

'The Euphrates denies its protection to the Parthian and apologizes
  for Crassus,'
And 'It is, I think, India which now gives necks to your triumph,'
And so forth, Augustus . . .

Such rhetoric, however, is subverted by *double entendre*: his ironically
portentous 'lowly cantilation' pulls to 'cantilever', underpinning the
phallic opportunities of rising to a 'timely [i.e. time-serving] vigour';
'Virgin Arabia' shakes in her inmost dwelling and foreign lands 'shrink'
in 'postponement' of Roman 'domination'; the poet speaks slyly of his
own readiness to 'follow the camp' in 'singing the affairs' of the imperial
cavalry. That these innuendoes are deliberate is confirmed by the
reference to the Pierides themselves. For although this is sometimes the
surname of the Muses, it also alludes to the nine daughters of Pierus,
king of Emathia, who daringly named them after the nine Muses.
Challenged to compete with the real Muses, they were defeated and
changed into birds. The opening of this section, which speaks of it being
time to cleanse Helicon, 'to lead Emathian horses afield' with a census of
Roman chiefs, is to be read ironically. Propertius is saying that any
attempt to replace the true Muses by imperial fiat is not only misguided
but hubristic on the model of Pierus. The 'august Pierides' are to be
understood as Augustus' fake Muses. It is not that 'I have not the
faculty' to ape the rhetoric of imperial apologists; it is that this would be
betray the true Muses.

In order to declare his independence from the political allegiances of
Empire, the poet has also to break with the literary traditions which
underwrite it. Pound has Propertius do this by a deliberate subversion of
the epic mode itself, an irreverently playful turning inside-out of the
genre which invents a new narrative mode – within the poem as
'content', but also in the embodied form of the poem itself. Propertius'
poem, that is, hints at a whole cycle of erotic *Iliad*s, of which this is the
first, to replace the epic proper, his punning colloquialisms finding 'a
volume in the matter' when she dresses to kill, 'new jobs for the author'
in her sinking to sleep, fusing Penelope's distaff concerns with Odysseus'
sailor's tales, by spinning 'long yarns out of nothing':

> And if she plays with me with her shirt off,
> We shall construct many Iliads.

Plebeian processions

If the erotic 'epic' becomes a satiric inversion of and assault on the
martial epic proper, gathering to itself a host of antitheses – of Apollo
and Bacchus, Mars and Venus, Rome and Greece – the largest and most

complex antithesis is that of tradition and newness, seen repeatedly as one between wearisome 'historical data' and the quite different 'time-bar' of the 'dance tune'. What underlies and unifies both elements of the antithesis, however, is the inescapable reality of death. It is the deaths of heroes that the epic records; but it is the death of lovers that adds a plangency to every love poem. From the beginning of *Homage*, the poet is aware of this dimension within which all human acts are assessed and evaluated:

> I shall have, doubtless, a boom after my funeral,
> Seeing that long standing increases all things regardless of quality.

Like those heroes whose case Homer stated, the poet-lover will also have his dog's day. Yet this is little consolation. His songs may offer a fine tombstone over his lovers' beauty, but, no more than the 'expensive pyramids' of Egypt or Mausolus' monumental effigies, do they offer 'complete elucidation of death'. If, amidst universal mortality, 'Stands genius a deathless adornment', this last stand is a merely cosmetic imitation of potency. The most powerful and finely cadenced moment in *Homage* is the vision of an underworld in which victor and vanquished, Roman and Carthaginian alike, make that last crossing of a frontier, 'Moving naked over Acheron / Upon the one raft, victor and conquered together, / Marius and Jugurtha together, one tangle of shadows'. Caesar may continue to plot against India, 'Tibet shall be full of Roman policemen' (the anachronism draws obvious parallels with British imperial dreams), but death ignores all imperial pretensions. Without bathos Propertius can thus turn to consider his own funeral with its 'small plebeian procession', the three books he takes as a not unworthy gift to Persephone, the obsequies of one ' "once the slave of one passion" ', now truly and finally enslaved. Whether Adonis lamented by the Cytharean herself, or Propertius mourned by Cynthia, differences of rank and status no longer apply: 'Vain call to unanswering shadow, / Small talk comes from small bones'.

Propertius can move from the erotic to the elegiac without difficulty, as he can invoke the bawdy and the risqué (thinking, for example, of the 'devirginated young ladies' who will enjoy his poems 'when they have got over the strangeness') because his verse moves in a discourse which turns 'small talk' into a kind of heroism, in which ' "Soft fields must be worn by small wheels" ' (quoting Apollo himself) and the kind of 'nasty things' said at a funeral carry as much weight as the gravest obituary. Beyond the patriarchal imperial platitudes lies a world of difference, where many discourses jostle in the marketplace, the sailor speaking of winds, the ploughman of oxen, the soldier of wounds, and 'We, in our narrow bed, turning aside from battles', espouse a different rhythm,

And my ventricles do not palpitate to Caesarial *ore rotundos*,
Nor to the tune of the Phrygian fathers.

Language shares its mystery with the forces of sexuality and death
alike, the great levellers which collapse all antinomies, all distinctions of
master and slave, class and nation, respectable and profane. Even the
gods can be moved to pettiness by sexual rivalry or lust; Jove is an 'old
lecher' and Venus may be 'exacerbated by the existence of a comparable
equal', while death too is an insatiable rake collecting beautiful women
in hell, 'his tooth in the lot'.

Death presides as sovereign over an era of 'democratic aristocracy' in
which beauty and fortune alike last only for a season. Propertius' own
verses share in the same levelling tendency, reducing all simple
oppositions to a larger heterogeneity in which antitheses dissolve in a
swirl of possibilities. Wanting to write of love in a world dominated by
bellicose epic bullfrogs, he has himself to write of war, if only as
'background'. The desire to write in the tradition of the Greek love idyll
brings him face to face with death. The pursuit of the new and the wish
to return to an old naive mode collide, to create a form which is neither
one nor the other, but a novel amalgam of established, even obsolete
modes: this elegiac–satiric sequence, its moods varying, polychromatic.
This third form, mixed, impure, is not a love poem but a poetry of erotic
encounters offered as an ironic commentary on the encounters of
warfare, as the elegiac in turn undermines the values of the erotic,
leaving us only with the certitudes of a language that outlives them all.

Certain emotions vital to me in 1917

Propertius would, he says, write 'war poetry' if his love commanded it –
obey 'Like a trained and performing tortoise'. But this is to make war
merely an adjunct of his passion. Taking up the image of 'Jove protected
by geese' (with its origins in Livy) from earlier in the poem, he takes one
last swipe at a public opinion clamouring for martial rhythms.
Propertius, as the Loeb translation points out, makes here 'a punning
reference to the poetaster Anser (= goose) suggested by Vergil, *Ecl.* IX.36'.
Pound consummately translates this sly dig by an updating play on the
name of Rupert Brooke, the public's latest model of poetic rectitude:

> For the nobleness of the population brooks nothing below its own
>   altitude.
> One must have resonance, resonance and sonority . . . like a goose.

Nevertheless, Pound and Propertius alike find themselves, at the end of
this sequence, gathered into a tradition. The dialogical mode in which

both poets have been working has constantly undermined any stance in which they might be fixed, thereby offering a critique of all ideologies. Even here, as the poem closes, in his list of predecessors Pound allows Propertius to deconstruct the tradition into which they are gathered. For each author in turn in this list is seen as in some way not only affirmed but also superseded by his successors. This is why, just before this, Propertius had spoken of being 'honoured with yesterday's wreaths' – the poet becomes out-of-date at the moment of his recognition and triumph. So Varro, turning from the epic *Argonautica* to celebrate his great passion Leucadia, the 'highly indecorous' Catallus, Calvus, and even now Gallus are all in turn crowded out by the latest incursion, whose living moment confirms their deaths: 'And now Propertius of Cynthia, taking his stand among these'.

That last, indecorous pun, taking up previous lines ('long standing increases all things'; 'Stands genius'; 'Amor stands upon you'), signals the final refusal of a decorum that has been subverted throughout the poem. Significantly, *Homage* ends, not on this movement to closure, momentarily arresting the tradition as it closes around its latest standard-bearer, but with a quite unexpected codicil, a 'Cantus Planus' which hymns that Zagreus or Bacchus who is Lord of sexual as of political Misrule, the sworn enemy of all patriotic pomp and ceremony and pretension, comic, satiric, erotic, carnivalesque. But Zagreus is also the foe of Apollo – the subversive antithesis of the harmony, order and coherence the latter stands for as god of poetry, 'Bringing the Grecian orgies into Italy'.

In a letter to Felix Schelling in 1922 Pound wrote in fury of 'that fool in Chicago' (Harriet Monroe) who 'took the *Homage* for a translation, despite the mention of Wordsworth and the parodied line from Yeats'. Intertextuality here is felt by Pound to be sufficient index of the subversion of discourse in which he is involved. The sonority of Wordsworth and Yeats is invoked in a dissonant recall, a 'resembling unlikeness' like that which Propertius himself attempted, as Pound goes on to indicate:

> MacKail (accepted as 'right' opinion on the Latin poets) hasn't, apparently, *any* inkling of the *way* in which Propertius is using Latin. Doesn't see that S.P. is tying blue ribbon in the tails of Virgil and Horace, or that sometime after his first 'book' S.P. ceased to be the dupe of magniloquence and began to touch words somewhat as Laforgue did.[28]

And, he goes on, switching at once to Provence, 'De Born writes songs to provoke real war, and they were effective. This is very different from Romantic or Macauley–Tennyson praise of past battles.' Clearly, the Provence discussed in *The Spirit of Romance* and the impulse behind

Homage are closely linked in Pound's mind. A much later letter, written to *The English Journal* from Rapallo in 1931, makes the connection clear, and suggests why Pound went into Italian retreat, leaving England in 1921 and taking with him a large part of the argument that Modernism was a specifically English phenomenon:

> As Miss Monroe has never yet discovered what the aforementioned poem is, I may perhaps avoid charges of further mystification and wilful obscurity by saying that it presents certain emotions as vital to me in 1917, faced with the infinite and ineffable imbecility of the British Empire, as they were to Propertius some centuries earlier, when faced with the infinite and ineffable imbecility of the Roman Empire. These emotions are defined largely, but not entirely, in Propertius' own terms. If the reader does not find relation to life defined in the poem, he may conclude that I have been unsuccessful in my endeavour. I certainly omitted no means of definition that I saw open to me, including shortenings, cross cuts, implications derivable from other writings of Propertius, as for example the 'Ride to Lanuvium' from which I have taken a colour or tone but not direct or entire *expression*.[29]

It is precisely then, through the dissonant recall of Propertius and of his fellow poets that Pound attempts, in *Homage*, to make a 'relation to life', to the troubled world of Europe, and specifically of the capital of an Empire at war, in 1917. And the specific stylistic tricks which he played with Propertius' texts, 'shortening, cross cuts, implications', are seen by him as the signs of his subversive intent. As Propertius attempted to undermine the epic assurances of imperial Rome by his cavalier way with tradition, so Pound too attempted to open a fissure in the monolithic rhetoric of contemporary Britain by fracturing that very classical heritage it claimed as its own, the guarantee of its imperial mission, and underwriting of all its profoundest confidences in itself. By opening the monological tradition of the classics to a subversive polyphony, Pound's intent was clear.

In its complex parallels between imperial Rome and contemporary Britain, in its deliberate anachronisms, its impurities and incongruities of style, its rapid shifts of diction, mood and tone, from jocular to serious, bathos to profundity, in its juxtapositions of epic and satiric, love, sexuality and death, *Homage to Sextus Propertius* is a powerful indictment of a monochrome public mood that demanded from its poets 'sonority and resonance, sonority, like a goose' – one single high-minded honk. In that sense, Modernism was a response – itself dialogically bringing together the foreign and the native, as Propertius brings the Grecian measure to Rome – to the crisis of British society in the first two decades of this century, a crisis that in 1914 sought not only resonance and sonority from its heroes, but their 'Young blood and high blood, / fair cheeks, and fine bodies', for a tradition that was nothing more than two gross of broken statues, a few thousand battered books. What was to be done with all that fury of renunciation was another matter.

Chapter Five

The anangke of modernity:
Hugh Selwyn Mauberley

Replacements

In his 1920 essay on de Gourmont, which shares many of the ideas and even the phrasings of *Hugh Selwyn Mauberley*, Pound remarks that Henry James's 'drawing of *moeurs contemporaines* was so circumstantial, so concerned with the setting, with detail, nuance, social aroma, that his transcripts were "out of date" almost before his books had gone into a second edition'. De Gourmont, however, 'is concerned with hardly more than the permanent human elements. His people are only by accident of any particular era.'[1] Pound sees this timelessness as part of de Gourmont's contemporaneity: 'Gourmont prepared our era; behind him there stretches a limitless darkness.' This darkness compounds all the past, from the Counter-Reformation to 'the impeccable Beerbohm'.

In *Hugh Selwyn Mauberley*, published the same year, Beerbohm is barely disguised as Brennbaum 'The Impeccable'. Here, too, Pound collapses all the past into a limitless darkness, briefly transfigured by those moments of illumination which constitute a permanent modernity. The pattern of history and of art which Pound premises in *Mauberley* is one in which his various vignettes, like de Gourmont's, are 'all studies in different *permanent* kinds of people; they are not the results of environments or of "social causes", their circumstance is an accident and is on the whole scarcely alluded to'. For Pound, 'this complicated sensuous wisdom is almost the one ubiquitous element, the "self" which keeps his superficially heterogeneous work vaguely "unified".' What we have here is almost a manifesto for *Propertius* and *Hugh Selwyn Mauberley*, as well as a pointer to the principle of coherence Pound was to work out through five decades of the *Cantos*. The poems aim to generate a 'self' which keeps 'vaguely "unified"' a 'superficially heterogeneous' work.

Apart from its subordinate portraits, however, *Hugh Selwyn Mauberley* actually generates *two* selves, E.P. and Mauberley, to share – or, rather, dispute – its textual territories. The sequence, divided into two by the 'Envoi', appears to set up a clear demarcation between E.P. and Mauberley, only to dissolve it into inconsequence. The whole text becomes a place of contention between two poetic voices. Though critics have continued to allocate different domains to the two attenuated 'selves', we *cannot* know for sure, given the complex overlaid ironies of tone, whether it is the E.P. whose obituary we read at the beginning, or the Mauberley elegised at the end, who presides at any particular point. The whole poem becomes a No-Man's-Land. Pound's delight in Odysseus' punning reply to Polyphemus, that 'No Man did this', is worth bearing in mind when considering the poem's use of Odyssean analogies. What unifies a 'superficially heterogeneous' text is a fractious discourse that transcends individual subjects, whether the various named characters, the eponymous hero, or the 'late' author, relegated at the beginning to initials on a headstone, which, in Odyssean fashion, punningly translate his name into a poetic form ('E.P. Ode': epode). The true subject of the poem, that is, is a discourse: the discourse of Modernity itself.

In explaining to John Drummond in February 1932 the threefold temporal division of the Cantos, Pound's mind slipped back to the time of *Hugh Selwyn Mauberley*. 'The hell cantos', he says, 'are specifically LONDON, the state of English mind in 1919 and 1920' (the two years specifically identified in *Mauberley* in the hinge poems 'Envoi (1919)' and 'Mauberley 1920'). To consider the *Cantos*, Pound proposed in his familiar shorthand, 'Best div. prob. the permanent, the recurrent, the casual'.[2]

The *Cantos* repeatedly return to earlier themes, episodes and obsessions, and in this sense the 'recurrent' is a consistent preoccupation, to be distinguished from the 'permanent', associated with art and the gods. But the 'casual' is a more difficult category to square with Pound's vision. It may be linked, only semi-punningly through the idea of *casus*, chance, with that motif of the 'case' initiated by the opening poem's remark of E.P. that 'the case presents / No adjunct to the Muses' diadem'. The motif is taken up in ' "poor Jenny's case" ' and reiterated of the war dead, who 'fought in any case, / and some believing . . . in any case . . .' Such 'cases' belong to the world of casual circumstance identified as James's forte, 'concerned with the setting, with detail, nuance, social aroma', 'transcripts' which, like so many of the characters and movements in this poem, become 'out of date' before they have registered their presence. *Hugh Selwyn Mauberley* despises 'the casual' in every snide remark about obsolescent fashions in taste, clothing, politics, art. It remains, however, the element in which its figures live and breathe, the very atmosphere of the Modern.

In his early volumes Pound is the inventor as much as the transcriber or translator of recessively nebulous originals. His reflections on *Hugh Selwyn Mauberley* in this letter come, then, as a surprise:

> I wonder how far the *Mauberley* is merely a translation of the *Homage to S.P.*, for such as couldn't understand the latter? An endeavour to communicate with a blockheaded epoch.

Not only the content of *Hugh Selwyn Mauberley* concerns itself with the recyclings of the permanent, the recurrent, and the casual. In its form, too, *Mauberley* becomes for Pound here a reprise, a copy, a secondary adjunct to the Muses' diadem of the *Homage to Sextus Propertius*, indisputably locked in 'the casual', in a history of 'cases'.

It is (in any case) a poem preoccupied with its own origins, an exploration of antecedents (its birth enabled by their deaths), which helps explain the prevailing tone of elegy, obituary, even autopsy. Its moment of origin is also a moment of elegiac return, just as E.P.'s originating impulse is a striving to resuscitate a dead art, proclaimed in a funeral ode which addresses the choosing of the author's sepulchre. Similarly, in 'Envoi', the already-written song of Lawes speaks of a death still imagined when the song was made but long since confirmed, in a celebration which looks forward to future deaths, when their two dusts with Waller's will be laid. It is as much an elegy as an affirmation of art's abiding power, its subtext that most customary of gravestone inscriptions, *ars longa, vita brevis*.

Hugh Selwyn Mauberley is perplexed by the perpetual supersession which renders the up-to-date rapidly 'out of date', a cliché as soon as coined. Its fashionable phrases, like the already out-of-date ' "out of date" ' in the de Gourmont essay or ' "the march of events" ' in the poem, are in quotation marks to show how rapidly the 'contemporary' is ' "replaced" ' by the march of events in a metropolis obsessed with the New. *Mauberley*'s use of quotation marks ironises the clichés it deploys, which, as clichés, have taken on an air of received wisdom, but also, in a metropolitan ethos of permanent updating, of *datedness*. E.P., the provincial from 'a half savage country, out of date', gets his posthumous satisfaction in an obituary which places the metropolitan preoccupation with progress, ' "the march of events" ', in supercilious quotation marks. As the 'familiar compound ghost' of Pound and others was to confide to Eliot in the 1940s London of 'Little Gidding', in a passage full of echoes of the London of 1919–20 and its literary revolutions: 'For last year's words belong to last year's language, / And next year's words await another voice'.

Mauberley also reveals how every text replaces, as it incorporates, its antecedents. Thus the phrase 'the age demanded', casually used at the beginning of poem II, has become ironically framed by quotation marks only two stanzas later, already passing into cliché, and is then picked out, completely compromised by irony, as a title in the 'Mauberley' section. The dead E.P.'s self-regarding epitaph ('His true Penelope was Flaubert') is later embedded with epigrammatic irony in Mauberley's life, the enjambement contracting the prolix lines of the first poem to the engraver's stricter 'art in profile', quotation marks turning the assessment into self-consciously second-hand cliché. The second Mauberley poem repeats but also translates the first line of the whole sequence, turning 'out of key with his time', a dead metaphor linking music and historicity, into a direct musical metaphor which also wakens its own dead theological resonances: 'diabolus in the scale'. Together with the snippets from superseded dialogues and the phrases in French, Latin and Greek, these quotation marks point out the arbitrariness of apparently natural discourses. As Bakhtin observes, 'The word used in quotation marks, that is felt and used as alien', relativises the absolute status of 'the same word ... without quotation marks', creating a 'different degree of distance in relation to the speaker. Words are set on different planes, at different distances, in relation to the plane of the author's words. ... hidden, semi-hidden, scattered, etc'.[3]

Mauberley plays complex games of preservation. It quotes familiar tags from Homer and Villon (high-falutin' epic bard and balladeer of the canaille). And it parades a host of contemporary journalistic clichés to match the tired sententiae of the opinion-forming hacks lampooned in 'Brennbaum' and 'Mr Nixon'. Not only does it immortalise, under their real names or penetrable pseudonyms, a large number of literary and artistic figures such as these; it also preserves as if in amber some of the fashionable phrases of the period. The opening Ode, in fact, is almost entirely composed of them. The ode for E.P. is also an elegy for last year's language, which can think itself only by an accumulation of set phrases and received idioms. But it then turns those empty aphoristic units into something strange and taut and difficult in the fourth stanza, before returning, through the manipulated cliché of the sun-dial, to a pastiche of phrases from a *Times* obituary.

One particularly complex instance is the sneaky overlaying of ironies in 'to maintain "the sublime" / In the old sense', where the enjambement loosens the second phrase's attachment to the preceding noun, allowing it to qualify indeterminately noun or verb. The whole phrase seems to require not one but two sets of inverted commas, making 'maintain

... / In the old sense' itself a self-conscious activity, recessively framing ' "the sublime" / In the old sense'. The sublime was after all a concept of a Romantic era (which had in turn filched it from Longinus) already defunct by the second half of the nineteenth century, upon which Pound in turn looks back as if on an incomprehensibly antique world. There is thus an almost antiquarian element in the attempt to 'maintain', not even the sublime in the new, but 'In the old sense'.

The poem's various narrative fragments span several decades of the recent past, and its key words and phrases constantly retreat down those vistas in a way which suggests the perpetual instability of language and the shiftiness of the retrospective look. But it also collapses those decades. Fitzgerald's *Rubaiyat*, in 'Yeux Glauques' was published in 1859, and Ruskin's *Of King's Treasuries* in 1865, so they are both roughly coeval with the Flaubert invoked in the opening Ode (*Madame Bovary*, 1856, *Salammbo*, 1862). Robert Buchanan's article on 'The Fleshly School of Poetry', which attacked among other things Rossetti's poem 'Jenny' referred to here, appeared in the *Contemporary Review* in 1871; while Burne-Jones's painting *Cophetua and the Beggar Maid* dates from 1884. Yet all these different decades are condensed into the single time zone summed up by the indeterminate phrase 'In those days' – days roughly coterminous with Gladstone being 'still respected'. The historical tagging indicates just how vast a swathe of time Pound is cutting, for Gladstone's eminence extended from 1859 to 1894: thirty-five years of Government, before finally being brought down by the Home Rule question. Whether his 'respect' extended for as long, the poem leaves rudely open.

Pound identifies all these moments as elements of an archetypal unitary Victorianism. Yet the poem which precedes 'Yeux Glauques' confronts the immediate past of the 1914–18 war, and the poem which succeeds it is concerned with memories of the 1890s. And this is precisely the point: the whole poem, like M. Verog, is 'out of step with the decade', detached from contemporaries, neglected by the young, precisely 'Because of these reveries'. Memory, even of the recent past, estranges one from a true temporal location, just as E.P. in the opening poem is 'out of key with his time', 'out of date'.

The poem offers a successive embedding of artistic generations: unexpectedly linking Lionel Johnson and Dr Johnson as London littérateurs; from the latter-day pagan Swinburne, Ruskin the re-inventor of Gothic, and the Victorian Pre-Raphaelites plunging back via Lawes and Waller to the original Pre-Raphaelites (Pier Francesca, 'botticellian sprays'); proceeding beyond Luini and Pisanello's forged Achaia to the original one; past St Paul's Samothrace to that of Dionysus; back via Flaubert to Homer and via Dante to Aeschylus;

seeking always, beyond Attic theatre, Heracleitus and Pindar, those anonymous Homeric sources in the limitless darkness of origins. But that darkness had been revealed in the 1900s as a startlingly 'up-to-date' civilisation, as Sir Arthur Evans uncovered at Knossos three-thousand-year-old frescoes whose figured women had ringlets like those of Parisian café society in the 1890s. The last poem of the whole sequence therefore picks up the image of Circe's elegant hair of the opening poem, and compares the honey-red hair of the female soprano to Botticelli's *Birth of Venus* and then to ancient Minoan braids spun from metal or amber. At this moment of closure the poem vividly invokes remotest origins under the half-watt rays of the truly modern. In the siftings on siftings of oblivion, the 'Beauty alone' of 'Envoi' is 'only by accident of any particular era', permanently contemporary.

E.P.'s excavation of the limitless darkness is not then a return to origins which uncovers earlier and earlier layers of the palimpsest in all their original and alien clarity. On the contrary, each new recovery returns us to the present. The self-conscious pun which speaks of Pisanello's attempt to 'forge Achaia' confirms the process. There is no original impulse to be recovered. There is only a new beginning, in the present, which is nothing like the original it makes its model, a forgery which forges something new. The nineteenth-century Pre-Raphaelites, striving to emulate in the lapsed time after Raphael the prelapsarian vision of the (retrospectively named) Pre-Raphaelites of the Quattrocento, produced something specifically Victorian and contemporary. Luini likewise, in porcelain and medallion, sought the clarity of line of Roman or Greek models. The up-to-dateness of the Minoan frescoes demolished for Mauberley's generation any simple idea of artistic progress. The changes of medium – coin, statue, engraving, porcelain, fresco – only confirm the changes of mode and mood in the perpetual renewals of the fashionable.

Such metamorphoses may create something new, or they may simply parody without replacing something old. The clichés which analogically confound the different arts, indicated by the raised eyebrow of quotation marks in 'the "sculpture" of rhyme', belong to this order. The poem seems to endorse the Gautierian ideal. But the genre confusion of the phrase links with other artistic miscegenations, the mechanical reproductions of the pianola and the 'prose kinema' of film, and other degenerations of narrative in which form and content are sundered or confounded, 'the classics in paraphrase'.

The opening poem had yoked Penelope, a fictive character from Europe's second oldest epic and traditional figure of fidelity, with the author Flaubert whose fictions of modern infidelity (Eliot's '*bovaryisme*') offered a model of artistic good faith for E.P. Many of the generations cited have tried to do the same: to make it new by recreating an impulse read out from an earlier generation. In one sense, this is always 'Wrong from the start'. To start again by going back is the most delusory of quests. For ' "the sublime" / In the old sense' cannot be maintained, only replaced. Such a modern ambition was always-already 'out of date', and, paradoxically, the product of an over-brash newness. For it is because he was born in a half-savage country – one *not yet* civilised, without traditions – that E.P.'s ambition to make it new took an automatically old-fashioned form.

The poem's embeddings are multiple, signalled by that reworking of idioms in which the second E.P. poem begins with a statement that seems its own ('The age demanded an image') only to reveal it retrospectively, in the third stanza, for the meretricious meta-discourse it actually is. An apparently clean idiom, innocently telling us a fact, stands exposed as a shameless rhetoric of expropriation. The age demanded nothing: we were coerced by the suasions of discourse to believe that 'the age demanded'. The 'image' itself is re-presented as a *mis*-representation, not the real thing but a deluding substitute. Poem III calls attention to the device by inserting a subversive 'etc' after its opening *fin-de-siècle* clichés. The repetition of 'tea', playing on shifting associations, underlines the faithlessness of the signifier. But whereas the poem sees this as a real supplanting of the mousseline of Cos, the 'replacement' of Sappho's barbitos by the pianola is a spurious one, put over by a demagogic, co-opting rhetoric. The inverted commas round ' "replaces" ' indicate that replacement itself is not a simple act but a topos in a rhetoric of newness, where casual fashion has substituted for the permanence of art.

Borrowed ladies

In *Mauberley*, individuals are rhetorical *figures*, to be coined and re-coined as instances of a timeless pattern. Capaneus is summoned in a one-word allusion to another text (*The Seven Against Thebes*) to be dropped at once, in measure of how far the poem regards named subjects as mere carriers of signification. But it is the poem's treatment of women which is most revealing. In a note prefixed to the poem 'Na Audiart' in *Personae*, Pound wrote of the technique of the Provençal poet who, to produce a composite woman for his poetic *blasons*, 'begs of each pre-eminent lady of Langue d'Oc some trait or some fair semblance', the glance of one, the 'speech free-running' of another, the hair of a third, 'And all this to make "Una dompna soiseubuda" a borrowed lady or as the Italians translated it, "Una donna ideale" '.[4]

Mauberley is as full of borrowed ladies as it is of borrowed phrases, and women circulate as freely, and are as disposable, as language. Its various 'ideal' women stand revealed as no more than 'borrowed' beauties, their exchange value on a male-dominated market overriding any intrinsic worth. Hugh Witermeyer, in *The Poetry of Ezra Pound*,[5] remarks of 'Envoi': 'In fact it is addressed to a woman who "sang me once that song of Lawes".' In fact it is not: it is addressed to a dumb-born book, as Waller's poem is addressed not to the woman but to the rose that acts as intercessor. The woman who sang that song of Lawes is not only reminded that other mouths once sang it too. She is also told that some other mouth 'Might, in new ages, gain her worshippers'. That is, she has already become a literary figure, incorporated into the text. The opening vocative, 'Go, dumb-born book', addresses the book in which it is written, autoreferentially celebrating its own mute printed origins. And it instructs that book (that is, it instructs itself) to tell *her* (third person) an inset message of which the 'thou' refers ambiguously either to woman or book, before unambiguously returning her to third-person status in the last line of the stanza.

The 'dumb-born book' (dumb only in its origins) is promiscuously vociferous, uttered and known by an infinity of subjects. By contrast, the woman is reduced by the poem to dumb unknowing, as one that goes about 'With song upon her lips / But sings not out the song, nor knows / The maker of it'. Throughout the poem, the apparently first-person knowing subjects of history become third-person unknowing subjects of the discourses they carry. Her mute eloquence is silenced in a sequence of other women here reduced to mere mouths, losing their uniqueness in being passed down a chain of signification in which there is always 'some other mouth' to replace that presently singing. The speaking subject, ostensibly the origin of significance, becomes a mere transmission point of a discourse that depersonalises as it imperson-alises, and moves on without closure.

But if the mouth is thus metonymised, so are other 'traditional' female 'features', parts of the body becoming parts of speech, as in poor Jenny's case.

> The Burne-Jones cartons
> Have preserved her eyes,

says 'Yeux Glauques' of Rossetti's verse pseudonym for his wife, Elizabeth Siddal, the much-misused model of the Pre-Raphaelites. The lines may be taken at face value, like the eyes themselves: Burne-Jones's painting *Cophetua and the Beggar Maid* preserves the image of the woman Pound appears to think modelled for the picture. But Pound is not as ignorant as some critics have suggested, nor is he playing fast and loose with time when he speaks of Elizabeth Siddal's eyes preserved in a painting only completed in 1884, twenty-two years after her death from a drug overdose. The Beggar Maid is another 'Borrowed Lady'. Though the body is that of some other model, the late Elizabeth Siddal's eyes have been preserved in the *cartons*, or preliminary sketches, whence Burne-Jones borrowed them for the later painting. In the transit from 'poor Jenny' to Beggar Maid, preservation involves interruption and repetition across a discontinuous time. Jenny's eyes, like the singer's mouth, become mere components of a composite 'borrowed lady'. The *fin-de-siècle* resonance of 'Yeux Glauques' recalls not only immediate French antecedents but that oldest source of borrowed ladies in *Mauberley*, the *Odyssey*, in which Athene, Odysseus' patron, is described as 'glaukopis', 'owl-eyed'.[6]

There is drollery in that juxtaposition of 'cartons' and 'preserved', though most critics miss the point by making an automatic correction to 'cartoons', against the insistence of both the *Collected Shorter Poems* and the *Selected Poems* in support of the reading in the first edition of *Mauberley*. For if the poem replays the traditional topos of art preserving transient female beauty, it also alludes to modern ways of preserving food which link with the mistranslation of Pindar in 'tin wreath', Verog's pickled foetuses, and the joke about Lionel Johnson, whose autopsy showed no trace of alcohol, though his 'Tissue preserved' might well have been as pickled as the foetuses, and the 'pure mind' which rose to Newman as the whisky warmed reminds slyly of 'pure spirit'.

The word 'cartons' is up-to-date, in 1919. The supplement to the *Oxford English Dictionary* cites the earliest occurrence in the *Daily Chronicle* in October 1906 (amusingly, a reference to a 'a pound carton'). By 1921 it had become an established usage, as in the *OED*'s citation from *Export Packing*: 'Sundry Cartoned Goods'. But Pound's word, linked to 'preserved', has further contemporary resonances, linking the artist's drawings, via the Pharaoh Cophetua, with Egyptologists' accounts of the ancient embalming technique of 'cartonnage', which involved the use of papyrus. An *OED* illustration of this usage dates from 1881:

> The coffins . . . were made of layers of papyrus . . . stuck together so as to form a thick carton, painted within and without with designs and religious emblems. These carton cases were made to fit the swathed body.

A further instance from the *Athenaeum* in 1908 recalls Pound's preoccupation with the text as mask in the most literal manner, speaking of 'The cartonnaged mask which decorated the inner coffin'. Published a year later, *Personae*, in which Pound later claimed he was 'casting off, as it were, complete masks of the self in each poem'[7] contains the poem 'De Aegypto', which testifies to his readings in Egyptian mythology. *Ripostes* in 1912 draws on his Egyptological interests for 'The Tomb at Akr Caar'; and the mock-fragment 'Papyrus' in *Lustra* (1916) carries the idea of a tenuous textual survival to a comic extreme. The passage from the *Athenaeum* suggests something possibly at the back of Pound's mind when he wrote his lines about 'poor Jenny's case': that Rossetti covered his dead wife's half-ruined face with manuscripts of his poems, but subsequently had her coffin exhumed, like some up-to-date 'carton case', to recover the texts.

Poor Jenny is thus a 'borrowed lady' in many senses, her body in life borrowed for sexual as well as artistic purposes by various painters and adulterers, and her represented 'eyes' in death still circulated as an item among their composite images of womanhood. Stilled in death, still at the Tate her still eyes teach not only the pharaoh Cophetua but new generations to 'rhapsodize' (ancient poetic possession converted into modern cliché), her 'vacant gaze' filled, possessed, by many new admirers. Though the face of the original woman is literally as well as metaphorically half-ruined, the painting turns the borrowed 'thin, clear gaze' into a 'faun-like' enchantment, the stillness of the image matching the questing passivity of the gaze. But the idea of permanence ('the same / Still darts out') is subverted by the preceding lines, with their quite different association of 'still' with a movement born dead like the pickled foetuses, 'still-born / In those days'. 'Poor Jenny's case' is precisely that: an illustrative *case*, which, like E.P.'s 'case' earlier, 'presents / No adjunct to the Muses' diadem'. As casually as the casualties of the Great War, she died 'in any case'.

With the phrase 'his true Penelope', another woman is reduced to a mere symbolic figure, subordinate to E.P.'s elegist for whom she stands as a device of figuration, and to the Homer, E.P. and Mauberley who deploy her. The whole sequence constructs a composite female – a figure made up, by name or imputation, of Penelope, Circe and Madame Bovary, the Sirens, the Muses, Sappho, poor Jenny, owl-eyed Athene, La Pia (by way of the title 'Siena mi Fe'), Dowson's harlots, the stylist's placid and uneducated mistress, the 'Conservatrix of Milésien / Habits of mind and feeling' (and her grandmother), Daphne, the society hostess, Lady Valentine, Lady Jane, the nameless she of 'Envoi' and of Mauberley's liaisons, Messalina, Venus Cytheraea and Venus Anadyomene (alluded to also in the 'botticellian sprays'), the sleek head of 'Medallion', and all the nameless models and dedicatees of innumerable works of art. The different social locations these women occupy don't conceal their actual subordination. Penelope and Circe are both abandoned by Odysseus; the apparently deadly Sirens are subdued by his unstopped ear. Even the imperial Messalina is, like the aristocratic La Pia, killed by her husband, thus prefiguring the (more indirect) fate of poor Jenny.

But the men are no better off. Ostensibly patriarchal figures of power and authority, they appear rather as what Canto VII, visiting the underworld, calls 'Thin husks I had known as men, / Dry casks of departed locusts / speaking a shell of speech'. The heaven-defying Capaneus is no more than a burnt-out name, all that is left after the lightning strikes. E.P. is dead and buried before the poem starts, simply a name on a tombstone. Mauberley, an attenuated consciousness throughout the poem, is dead by the end, and his epitaph, unlike E.P.'s, is anonymous and generic: 'Here drifted / An hedonist'. The deadbeats of 'Siena Mi Fe' are defunct, or drag pathetically on in their obsolescence. Verog is a remaindered voice, maundering, in the terms of the same Canto, in 'Words like the locust-shells, moved by no inner being'. Indeed, the poem is full of what this Canto calls the 'rattle of old men's voices'. Its form is a 'mere succession of strokes, sightless narration'. Identity disperses as the narratives within which it is written disappear into drift: 'For the husks, before me, move, / The words rattle: shells given out by shells'.

The critics' desire to pin down precisely who is speaking in each of the two parts, the effort to construct a coherent narrative from the poem's inconsequential succession of vignettes, founder on these obstinate isles. For the poem in both theme and form is concerned with drifting, and itself drifts on to the 'final estrangement', offering in between a 'supervening blankness'. These characters are nothing but hollow discourses, drifting amid phantasmagoria. The men of obvious power, the successful, are equally void: the stiff, unrelaxing Brennbaum has wandered in the desert for forty years, denied entry into the promised land. Mr Nixon, urging the would-be writer 'to advance with fewer / Dangers of delay', abolishes all destinations for that 'advance', which is in the end not a military but a financial one. He invokes an almost tangible 'no one' (Odysseus' pseudonym) as arbiter of merit ('"And no one knows, at sight, a masterpiece"') and turns poetry into mere words over a void ('"There's nothing in it"'). To 'Accept opinion' is to be lost in a welter of clichés, the meaningless circulation of empty signifiers, mouths biting empty air, laughter out of dead bellies, where meaning is transformed into the superficial urgency without substance of an accelerated grimace.

The ultimate victims of this vacuity are the war-dead, whose 'Charm, smiling at the good mouth' succumbs to the siren charms of 'an old bitch gone in the teeth'. The mouth image, contrasting the evanescence of personal voice with the reality of a devouring history, is insistent. The singer of 'Envoi' and 'Medallion' is merely one of a line whose remote ancestors are the sirens themselves. The 'liars in public places' are doubly empty voices, uttering signifiers with no signified. There is no difference between 'old lies' and 'new infamy'. Significantly, however, at this crux the lies of real old men are transformed into the devouring mouth of an iconic old woman, and the fatherland of deceit becomes a feminine *patria*. All the male figures in the poem fall prey to one or another kind of emasculation, real or symbolic, figured metonymically by that circumcision Pound reviled as 'this antique abracadabra ... a degredation [*sic*], an ignominy past all bounds of the comic' in an article called 'The Revolt of Intelligence' in *The New Age* in 1920.[8] If, in this degraded modern world, we have the franchise for circumcision, we exercise our freedom by choosing a knave or eunuch as ruler. It is women who are the agents of this universal emasculation.

Composed and published in the same year as Eliot's 'Gerontion', *Mauberley* misogynistically nominates a scapegoat similar to that poem's castrating female 'History', the old bitch gone in the teeth of a civilisation that demands the ultimate sacrifice from its young men. She resembles Pound's characterisation of Molly Bloom in his 1922 essay on *Ulysses* in *The Dial*[9] which correlates intelligence with masculinity and an oppressive bodiliness with the female. Of Bloom/Odysseus and Molly/Penelope he notes: 'His spouse Gea-Tellus the earth symbol is the soil from which the intelligence strives to leap, and to which it subsides *in saeculum saeculorum*. As Molly she is a coarse-grained bitch, not a whore, an adulteress.' And she resembles, too, that deathly, demanding Cathleen ni Houlihan Yeats had identified with Maud Gonne. The 'stylist' of poem X indeed recalls both Joyce and Yeats, the former with his placid and uneducated mistress, the latter with his withdrawal to a tower with the sagging roof, leaking thatch and creaking latch of 'Innisfree'. Maud Gonne herself strides anonymously through the next poem (XI), in the obscure reference to the ' "Conservatrix of Milésien" / Habits of mind and feeling'.

This phrase can be glossed by a letter Pound wrote to John Quinn the year before, on 15 November 1918, which illuminates many of the preoccupations of *Hugh Selwyn Mauberley*, including its odd equation of franchise and circumcision:

> M.G. (statement from herself) did hold a meeting in Dublin to express sympathy with the Russian Bolsheviks. *If* there had been another rising I fail to see how she would have kept out of it ...
>
> As for the 'revolution,' we have had one here during the war; quite orderly, in the extension of the franchise. Nobody much minds there being several more. But there remains the temperament that wants revolution *with violence*; no special aim or objective, but just pure and platonic love of a row ...

'Conservatrice des traditions Milesienne' [*sic*], as de Gourmont calls them. There are people who have no sense of the value of 'civilization' or public order. . . .

P.S. I think the term 'fanatic' in my cable was the just one. . . . It is a great pity, with all her charm, that the mind twists everything that goes into it, on this particular subject.[10]

Mauberley speaks of poetry as a friend and comforter 'in the case of revolution' for Lady Valentine, a name with erotic connotations. As much as the notes to *The Waste Land* or Yeats's 'Second Coming', written in January 1919, *Mauberley* is haunted by the Russian Revolution and what it prefigures. Such disruptions of the global order are obscurely identified with female sexuality, which subverts a 'civilisation' and 'public order' founded on the masculine intelligence by means of that most conservative of all forces, the body.

Maud Gonne and Molly Bloom, then, join all those other 'Milesian' women out to ensnare the male intelligence. Penelope and Circe seem as one, for both share the sirens' desire to dominate the male. Molly, we might recall, arranges her adultery around an operatic engagement with Blazes Boylan; Yeats frequently paid tribute to Maud Gonne's eloquent voice. If the female voice, like that of the sirens, is not 'Caught in the unstopped ear', it will catch and stop the adventurer. This image of seductive female voices penetrating unstopped male ears (a displaced and inverted troping of sexual intercourse) is repeated in the beautiful voice of 'Envoi', in turn stopped by the poem (for she 'sings not out the song'). Suppression of the female voice is made permanent in the fantasy of her preservation like a rose 'in magic amber laid'. The pun on 'laid' underlines the correlation of art and sexual conquest. Repeated in 'When our two dusts with Waller's shall be laid', its secondary meaning turns Waller's music into pimp and exorcist. Women must be Muses, silently subordinate to the male, or they will be sirens, luring Mauberley to his doom on an unforecasted beach. When Pound in his *Dial* essay speaks of Joyce's debt to Flaubert, we can see why the opening poem of *Mauberley* transmogrifies the female character Penelope into the male author Flaubert as image of the 'true' goal of art.

The obstinate isles by which E.P. sails in the opening poem are those siren islands of the west of which Pound would have read a modern interpretation in Norman Douglas's essay 'Sirens' in *The English Review*. Douglas was one of the first authors to be printed in the six issues of the *Review* from December 1908 which preceded Pound's own first contribution, 'Sestina: Altaforte', in June 1909. Twenty years later Ford Madox Ford (né Hueffer) described Douglas's essay as 'the most beautiful thing we printed', and Pound, who wrote in *Poetry* in December 1912 that 'I would rather talk poetry with [Ford] than with any man in London', almost certainly knew it. With his interest in the motif of metamorphosis, it would have struck a chord. Douglas describes the transmigrations of mythic material in the popular mind over the centuries, so that the Roman *genius loci* becomes the patron saint, the pagan Great Mother the Christian Madonna, and so on. He identifies the Sirens with

> the personification of the sultry dog days when Sirius (whence their name) burns fiercely in the parching firmament; they were vampires, demons of heat, of putrefaction, of voluptuousness, of lust. But Hellas clothed them anew in virginal hearts and garments and sent them westward.[11]

For Pound they are thus effective symbols of that 'miasma' and 'marasma' he encountered in the 'obstinate isles' of Britain, typifying all that prevents the exile's return home to his cultural origins, presided over by emasculating women who are at once revolutionaries and de Gourmont's 'femmes, conservatrices des traditions milesiennes'.

Paradoxically, then, Pound sees 'Woman, the conservator, the inheritor of past gestures' (in the words of the Postscript to his translation of de Gourmont's *Natural Philosophy of Love*) as at once an inertia defusing male intelligence, and a revolutionary, anarchic energy identified with the body and the material world. The Modernist image of woman is full of such contradictions. Maud Gonne, we note, commits a double offence in Pound's letter. Instead of locating herself in the ambience of a beauty braving time, she identifies with the accelerated grimace of the 'modern', the 'up-to-date' events of revolution and 'the Russian Bolsheviks' who threaten to *replace* (we begin to understand the frisson of the word) an attenuated civilisation. Her ancient 'Milesian' licentiousness compounds a modern political licence.

The age demanded

The link between first and last poems of the Mauberley section, and the significance of music in 'Envoi' and throughout the poem, can be elucidated by tracing the suppressed connections underlying the ramblings of *Guide to Kulchur*. Chapter 23 registers Pound's acquaintance with the Frankfurt School (*Frankfurt Institut für Sozialforschung*), which has so far gone unrecorded by critics, though it is clearly vitally important for understanding his 1930s positions, observing that 'The Forschungsinstitut in Frankfurt, thanks largely to Leo Frobenius, drives *toward* a new learning.' Discussing Dowland's and Janequin's music the chapter inadvertently offers a gloss on *Mauberley*'s 'Mouths biting empty air' which links it to the voice/rose correlation of 'Envoi' and the 'profane protest' of the grand piano in 'Medallion'. It also raises the motif of a return to lost origins which involves a specifically modern repetition and replacement:

> If the piano obscures the fiddle, I have a perfect right to HEAR Janequin's intervals, his melodic conjunctions from the violin solo.

> 'I made it out of a mouthful of air'

wrote Bill Yeats in his heyday. The *forma*, the immortal *concetto*, the concept, the dynamic form which is like the rose pattern driven into the dead iron-filings by the magnet, not by material contact with the magnet itself, but separate from the magnet. Cut off by the layer of glass, the dust and filings rise and spring into order. Thus the *forma*, the concept, rises from death

> The bust outlasts the throne
> The coin Tiberius.

> Janequin's concept takes a third life in our time, for catgut or patent silver, its first was choral, its second on the wires of Francesco Milano's lute. And its ancestry I think goes back to Arnault Daniel and to god knows what 'hidden antiquity' . . .

A series of shorthand leaps via Pisanello and Piero della Francesca and two centuries of music (including Lawes and Campion), impel the argument to one of Pound's most important prose statements about *usura* and its relation to general polity, art, and the personal and sexual relations of man and woman:

> For years one has diagnosed the blither of American discussion as in part an ignoring of the demarcation between state and individual. . . . Until the power of hell which is usura, which is the power of hogging the harvest, is broken, that is to say until clean economic conditions exist and the abundance is divided in just and adequate parts among all men, legal enforcements and interjections of the legal finger in relations between man and woman, will be deformation and evil, and no lawgiver will be able to cure the bone disease of society by bits of sticking plaster and paint.[12]

The poem Pound quotes is Austin Dobson's translation of Gautier's 'Ars Victrix', which he anthologised in *Confucius to Cummings*.[13] It also supplies the statement 'All passes' of the second poem in the 'Mauberley' sequence, though Gautier's immediately subsequent statement, 'Art alone / Enduring stays to us', is replaced by Mauberley's bitter 'ANANGKE prevails'. This '*anangke*' is what Pound addresses in the economic and political comments to which he proceeds, inveighing, immediately after this, against 'abortion . . . the last crime any normal and healthy woman wd. commit SAVE UNDER ECONOMIC PRESSURE' (which recalls the 'pickled foetuses' and 'still-born' movements of *Mauberley*) and making this the figure of 'a foetid and sham democracy':

Democracies have for a century failed lamentably to educate the people and keep the people aware of the absolutely rudimentary necessities of democracy. The first being monetary literacy.

For all his qualifications, it is clear that Pound thinks 'a "dictatorship"' is more likely than democracy to bring about 'a civil society . . . where Strength comes with enjoyment. . . . Kraft durch Freude' (pp.157–8). The inverted commas round ' "dictatorship" ' are not reproduced when he cites, apparently straightfacedly, the chilling catchphrases of Hitler's Germany. At this moment, Pound is in deadly earnest, as he is in the next chapter in speaking of 'a Europe not YET rotted by usury', an age of benevolent autocrats where 'a state of mind, of sensibility, of all-roundness and awareness' was still possible, and linking Piero della Francesca once more with Pisanello in an age when 'Intaglio existed. Painting existed. The medal had never been higher'.[14]
The final collocation of these disparate items is in Chapter 25:

> If we reflect on African and oriental vagueness as to time, if we reflect on what is often called 'feminine' lack of punctuality among our more irritating acquaintance, it shd. not unduly astonish us that the idea of a MEASURE of value has taken shape slowly in human consciousness. . . . The degeneracy of the very coin as an object to look at, sets in early in Europe. Greek money is still ornamental. The medal emerges again with Pisanello and co.
>
> An England without. . . . . ['Jews' is to be inferred] wd. or shd. less impel other nations to hoarding. A few usurers in the grand reptilian line make any nation a peril.
>
> A few 'financiers' unjailed are enough in a few generations to pervert the whole press of a nation and to discolour its education.[15]

The idea of 'measure' links geometry, music and painting alike, but it also connects these directly with the realm of value, which for Pound is not divisible, as it is for Brennbaum and Mr Nixon, into aesthetic and utilitarian modes, art and money. A finely produced coin, like the 'Medallion' which gives its name to the final poem, combines utility as a unit of commercial exchange with beauty as a work of art. There is a fitness between object and use, intrinsic and exchange values. Pisistratus, the Athenian benevolent dictator of poem III, from whom democracy 'frees' us merely to elect a knave or eunuch, was responsible not only for having the Homeric cycle transcribed for the first time, but also for introducing a new and 'ornamental' coinage. He represents, thus, that unity of aesthetics, economics and politics Pound thought desirable.
In 'Medallion', however, there is an ill fit between the head of the Empress Messalina on the coin and the value it represents. Like her coinage Messalina circulated a little too freely, and for that she (literally) lost her head. Her power to corrupt was related to the degeneration of

the currency. The image of the coin links women and money in a common and vicious fungibility; both alike are exchanged round the circuits of society, as Jenny was passed around her various 'maqueros'. Woman is replaceable, exchangeable, nothing in herself. Even the song passes from mouth to mouth. The clear soprano of 'Medallion', and the suave bounding-line of the face-oval recall the strait head and the engraver's art in profile of 'Mauberley 1920', which concludes with Pisanello 'lacking the skill / To forge Achaia'. Pisanello, so much admired by Pound, whose work provides the frontispiece of *Guide to Kulchur*, in the end failed to forge Achaia. In the process, the forging turned to mere forgery, one more instance of that false-coining which *The Cantos* indict as Usura, the linguistic inflation of 'usury age-old and age-thick / and liars in public places' identified as causes of the Great War in the first half of the sequence.

Inflation, rife throughout a collapsing post-war Europe in 1919–20, blamed on Jewish capitalists and exploited, it was said, by largely Jewish Bolsheviks, is the figure which stands over all the manifestations of this modern age in *Mauberley*. No wonder, then, that what ' "The Age Demanded" ', in the poem of that name, is the 'down-float / Of insubstantial manna' such as fed the allegedly Jewish Brennbaum during 'the forty years' in the wilderness, that ' "Advance on royalties" ' Mr Nixon proposes as the be-all and end-all of writing. In a world where 'τὸ καλὸν' (beauty) is decreed in the marketplace, intrinsic value is totally overwhelmed by market price. What ' "the age demanded" ', therefore, was not the loving fidelity of the craftsman but a mass-produced mould in plaster 'Made with no loss of time'.

No accident, either, that in ' "The Age Demanded" ' Mauberley's fate is to be struck dumb, 'Incapable of the least utterance or composition, / Emendation, conservation of the "better tradition" ', succumbing instead to any passing 'conservatrice des traditions Milésiennes'. In other words, the artist is in danger of going the way of Maud Gonne, and developing a 'temperament that wants revolution *with violence*'. Pound may have written E.P.'s obituary in the opening poem, but this passage, far from being the postscript on a Mauberley who has also passed away, sounds remarkably like a prescient augury of what Pound himself was to become, his own artistic good sense drowned in the muddy apologia for fascism of *Guide to Kulchur*.

The first half of *Mauberley* had shown us art debased by the tawdry cheapness of a pseudo-democratic modernity, in an age of tin. Aesthetic value is decided in the marketplace à la Bentham, by majority voting or by the laws of supply and demand. The War of Section IV is for Pound a direct consequence of such degeneration, its hysterias and trench confessions intimately related to Mauberley's 'maudlin confession, /

Irresponse to human aggression'. This is one of Pound's most abiding convictions, and predates by two decades the animadversions of *Guide to Kulchur*. In an article in *The Egoist* in February 1917 he blamed 'The hell of contemporary Europe' on 'the lack of representative government *and* . . . the non-existence of decent prose in the German language', just as the writing of the later Roman era was 'the seed and the symptom of the Roman Empire's decadence and extinction'.[16] A couple of years earlier, in *The New Age*, he had written of Renaissance Italy 'destroyed by rhetoric, destroyed by the periodic sentence and by the flowing paragraph, as the Roman Empire has been destroyed before her. For when words cease to cling close to things, kingdoms fall, empires wane and diminish.'[17]

The *ABC of Reading* in 1934 offers the most succinct potting of this particular historical paradigm: 'Rome rose with the idiom of Caesar, Ovid, and Tacitus, she declined in a welter of rhetoric, the diplomat's "language to conceal thought", and so forth.'[18] But this is precisely the kind of language, apparently Mauberley's own, that we find in ' "The Age Demanded" ', just as Pound's subsequent remark, 'It is very difficult to make people understand the *impersonal* indignation that a decay of writing can cause men who understand what it implies, and the end whereto it leads', directly contradicts Mauberley's alleged opinions. Mauberley's aestheticism drives a rift between art and social life. Far from being commended by the poem, it is as much a cause of the current decay of Europe as Brennbaum's and Nixon's philistinism. The downbeat Latinate polysyllables of the Mauberley poem, full of abstractions and thicknesses, state Mauberley's ideas about the separation of art from life in a periphrastic vocabulary (so many words ending in '-ation'), radically at odds with Pound's advice in 'A Few Dont's' to 'Use no superfluous word. . . . Go in fear of abstractions'.[19]

For Mauberley, 'The glow of porcelain / Brought no reforming sense', which is what Pound appears to approve in de Gourmont, dissociating art from 'social inconsequence'. 'Inconsequence', however, is the key word, for it implies a 'social' concern perceived in the superficial terms of fashion and up-to-dateness represented by Lady Valentine. Set against this false sociality is Pound's larger sense, revealed everywhere in his critical writings, of the absolute equation between artistic, economic and political integrity. The flaccidity of Mauberley's language prevents him seeing that his art fails because it is dissociated from social *consequence*. His 'subjective hosannah' thus becomes one of the 'Ultimate affronts to / Human redundancies', reducing him to a powerless subject of power. Such submission is what the age demands; but it leads to that final abnegation, tantamount to spiritual suicide, of the epitaph (replaying E.P.'s) we are instructed to read in the penultimate poem:

'I was
And I no more exist;
Here drifted
An hedonist'.

Tò καλὸν *in the marketplace*

The marketplace was once the *agora* of Athenian civic encounter, where economics, politics, philosophy and aesthetics could all be debated. It is now superseded by the abstract space of the capitalist market, where goods and people and votes are bought and sold. Here too art is degraded into a commodity, for, in the words of Canto XLV in the early 1930s 'with usura . . . / no picture is made to endure nor to live with / but it is made to sell and sell quickly', 'with usura the line grows thick / with usura is no clear demarcation'. This 'line' is punningly that not only of painting or verse but also of inheritance, for, in words which recall the remarks on abortion from *Guide to Kulchur*, 'Usura slayeth the child in the womb'.

In *Mauberley* τὸ καλὸν, printed in its original Greek script, stands out from the debased Roman type around it, like the quotations from Homer earlier and from Pindar two stanzas later, both about heroic endurance and egregiousness. Tò καλὸν, usually translated as 'beauty' or 'the beautiful', presides even in its absence over E.P.'s section, briefly realising itself as 'Beauty alone' in the hinge poem 'Envoi'. Mauberley's section by contrast is dominated by a parallel concept from Greek philosophy, 'TO AGATHON' ('the good', 'virtue'). This word is distinguished by being set in Roman capitals, a kind of imperious linguistic diabolus in the scale of Mauberley's inconsequential, Latinate periphrases and 'verbal manifestations'.

This binary, which divides the two halves of *Mauberley*, finds its intellectual origins in Aristotle. The shift from the original, 'authentic' Greek in the first to the Romanised upper case of the second part reproduces the historical shift of priorities from Greek 'beauty' to Roman 'good', even though the retention of the Greek word for the latter yearns backward to the time when in the philosophy of Aristotle the two concepts were, if not unified, at least conjoined, as *kalokagathia*. Only a later age separated them, as, according to Pound, it separated art from polity, and the marketplace from the whole people. The same separation divides E.P. from Mauberley, compacting aeons of historical time to the brief interval between 'Envoi (1919)' and 'Mauberley 1920'. Here Beauty is set apart, in *italics*, a font neither Roman nor Greek. evoking an early Renaissance culture which is heir of both, and their possible reconciliation.

Pound alludes to Aristotle from quite early in his literary career, beginning at least with *The Spirit of Romance* in 1910.[20] But these tend to be unspecific gestures towards Aristotle's authority as a master of clarification, except when, as here and elsewhere, he is citing Aristotle's description of metaphor as 'a swift perception of relations' (a Greek version of the 'ideogrammic method'). It is not until *Guide to Kulchur* in 1937–8 that he devotes an extended discussion to Aristotle, responding to Harris Rackham's new 1934 edition of the 1926 Loeb text and translation of *The Nicomachean Ethics*.[21]

Some of the key concepts in *Mauberley* can be opened up by reference to this text, and to the *Eudemian Ethics*, which appeared in Rackham's edition in 1935.[22] I have found no explicit acknowledgement in Pound's writings that he had read either book until these translations appeared, and it is unlike Pound not to parade his book-learning.

Possibly he had read an earlier translation during his youthful studies, and returned in 1937 to recruit a text he half remembered as authority for his argument, only to be disappointed. Certainly, though he spends over forty pages of *Guide to Kulchur* on the *Nicomachean Ethics*, he grows increasingly exasperated as he proceeds, as if in working through the book he fails to find what his memories advised him should be there. At one point he dismisses Aristotle as a schoolman, who 'combine[s] such admirable terseness of expression with such shiftiness, such general independability' (p. 311), and whose text is 'heteroclite, a hodge-podge of astute comment and utter bosh' (p. 308), so that it has to be strenuously sifted for grains of meaning – a sifting he is now engaged in. Perhaps the explanation is that Pound encountered Aristotle's concepts at second-hand while reading up for *The Spirit of Romance*, for as Umberto Eco says of the medieval era, 'Its sensibility breathed the spirit of the Greek *kalokagathia*, the good and the beautiful combined'.[23]

As early as 1913, the essay 'The Serious Artist' testifies implicitly to a specific acquaintance with the *Nicomachean Ethics*, whether at first- or second-hand.[24] Its opening paragraphs nominate various arts and sciences as cognate modes of enquiry, as do the opening paragraphs of the *Nicomachean Ethics*. In particular, like that text, it invokes medicine as a model. It explicitly sets as the object of its enquiry precisely that which Aristotle defines as his own: an investigation of happiness ('*eudaimonia*') in terms of the good ('*to agathon*') and the beautiful ('*to kalon*'). The Aristotelian emphasis is apparent in Pound's explicit rejection of utilitarianism:

> It is obvious that the good of the greatest number cannot be attained until we know in some sort of what that good must consist. In other words we must know what sort of an animal man is, before we can contrive his maximum happiness.

Shortly thereafter he refers explicitly to Aristotle's description of metaphor.

If this essay witnesses to a reading of Aristotle as early as 1913, it also gives a first run to several of the topoi of *Mauberley*. The reference to Aristotle, for example, follows directly upon that line from Villon quoted in the first poem of the sequence: '*En l'an trentiesme de mon eage*'; while just before this Pound uses a simile which explains the same poem's miscegenated image of wringing lilies from the acorn – a misguided task because, in the words of the essay, 'ideas, or fragments of ideas, the emotion and concomitant emotions of this "Intellectual and Emotional Complex" ... must be in harmony, they must form an organism, they must be an oak sprung from an acorn'. Another topos shared with *Mauberley* is the image of the Greek statue the 'Victory of Samothrace', 'witness' and 'testimony' to the fact 'that men have desired to effect more beautiful things'. By contrast, says poem III, playing with St Paul's visit to Samothrace:

> Even the Christian beauty
> Defects – after Samothrace;
> We see τὸ χαλὸν
> Decreed in the market-place.

As in Aristotle, intellectual enquiry into 'the good' leads, in essay and poem, into an enquiry about 'the beautiful'. Pound's essay names several writers invoked in the poem. In poetry,

> As there are in medicine the art of diagnosis and the art of cure, so [there is] in the arts. . . . They call one the cult of ugliness and the other the cult of beauty.
> The cult of beauty is the hygiene, it is sun, air and the sea and the rain and the lake bathing. The cult of ugliness, Villon, Baudelaire, Corbière, Beardsley are diagnosis. Flaubert is diagnosis. Satire ... is surgery, insertions and amputations.
> Beauty in art reminds one of what is worth while. I am not now speaking of shams. I mean beauty, not slither, not sentimentalizing about beauty. . . .
> The cult of beauty and the delineation of ugliness are not in mutual opposition.

Unlike the rest of the poem, which is satire and diagnosis, 'Envoi' offers a solitary exemplum of the cure, 'the *forma*, the immortal *concetto*' of Beauty, the 'rose pattern' realised and incarnated in the material substance of art and nature alike. When Pound speaks here of being 'bucked up when you come on a swift moving thought in Plato or on a fine line in a statue', he explicates the contrast *Mauberley* draws between usury age-old and age-thick and liars in public places and the thin-drawn line and thin clear gaze of 'Yeux Glauques'. If *Mauberley* deals in the traffic of imprecisions, it does so with a satiric precision such as the age really needed, though it did not 'demand' it. As the essay says just before this: 'You can be wholly precise in representing a vagueness. You can be wholly a liar in pretending that the particular vagueness was precise in its outline.' If *Mauberley* offers us the 'delineation of ugliness', this is compatible with the 'cult of beauty', which also deals in clean lines, 'not slither.' The estrangement of which the poem speaks is, in fact, the separation of καλὸν from AGATHON.

In another 1913 essay, 'The Tradition',[25] Pound contrasts Greek and Roman culture specifically in terms of a shift from voice and music, 'melody', to the most brutal form of script, an alphabet evolved for chiselling in stone. 'The Romans writing upon tablets did not match the cadences of those earlier makers who had composed to and for the Cythera and the Barbitos.' Replacing the melodic cadences of Sappho's barbitos, the musical score of the pianola, holes punched into paper, carries into the realm of music that incision associated with Roman inscriptions, TO AGATHON's gross, demanding capitals. The distinction between the 'Melic poets' and 'the earnest upholder of conventional imbecility' reproduces the same antithesis. There is making it new, a sung music which is always *the* original, for the art *is* the performance; and there is mechanical reproduction of a pre-existing form according to the Alexandrian rulebooks. Such assumptions lead to the idea of beauty as a mass-produced commodity reviled in *Mauberley* as what 'the age demanded'. (The essay on Arnold Dolmetsch makes a similar point about the pianola.[26])

Τὸ καλὸν becomes, in the Envoi, that 'Beauty alone' which emerges from all time's 'Siftings on siftings in oblivion'. But in the subsequent poem Mauberley is

> Unable in the supervening blankness
> To sift TO AGATHON from the chaff
> Until he found his sieve . . .
> Ultimately, his seismograph.

Mauberley is about the need to sift καλὸν and AGATHON alike from the chaff; but the means for doing this is presented nowhere directly in the poem. Rather it has to be read out from all the blank moments of the text, those gaps and transitions, redundancies and reluctances, the multitude of delays, disjunctions, deferrals and belatednesses with which the poem abounds, in representing a 'consciousness disjunct'. The first poem of the E.P. sequence had used a musical analogy to describe a consciousness 'out of key with his time'. The second poem of the Mauberley sequence develops the musical image more explicitly ('diabolus in the scale') to define that consciousness as an 'overblotted / Series / Of intermittences', drifting to a final estrangement. 'Overblotted' speaks of a written score which is not a palimpsest of meanings but a series of smudged replacements.

The drifting hedonist of poem IV is 'Washed in the cobalt of oblivions', like those into which the siftings of historic dust break down 'All things save Beauty alone'. Such an hedonist Pound considers in *Guide to Kulchur*, discussing Aristotle's attempt 'to get a wedge between two greek words *aesthesis* and *hedone*'. Pound sets out here to reclaim pleasure (*hedu*) for aesthetics, without making it the mere passive sensation it is for Mauberley: 'Put in that form *hedone* is not passive feeling, but concomitant of action' (p. 337). He had remarked earlier that 'The contrast of *kalon* and *hedu* need not be antipodal antithesis. KALON as beauty or order might be an antithesis of *hedu* of certain kinds' (p. 316). The consequence of creating an antithesis between them is neither *hedone* nor *aesthesis* but what Mauberley II calls 'anaesthesis, noted a year late' (belated seeing), leading on to 'retrospect' (belated seeing) and 'epilogues' (belated writing). But, a cryptic note on Book II of the *Ethics* observes, '*Anaisthetos* also cd. contain a thought' (p. 313).

The end of art and of politics for Pound is the union of *to kalon* and *to agathon* as '*kalokagathia*'. In *Guide to Kulchur* Pound commends Rackham's 'perhaps brilliant translation of KALON as nobility' (p. 316). In fact, 'Nobility then is perfect goodness' is how Rackham translates Aristotle's conjunction of '*arete*' and '*kalokagathia*' in the 'Eudemian Ethics'.[27] Beauty detached from the good, a drifting hedonism dissociated from action, leave Mauberley disjunct, out of joint. He is thus a mere 1890s aesthete, for whom 'The glow of porcelain / Brought no reforming sense'. Unlike Pound, whose aesthetics led him on to espouse the Social Credit economics of Major Douglas and the Fascist politics of Mussolini, he is unable to make 'immediate application' of 'this beauty' to 'relation of the state / To the individual'. The 'Impetuous troubling / Of his imagery' implies for once prematurity ('impetuous') rather than belatedness, but he is still 'out of key with his time'. What is at issue here is Pound's concept of 'measure' as a fitness in things, an exact correspondence of end and means in that complex sense he was to give it in *Guide to Kulchur*. In Canto XXXIII, in a meditation on the unbalanced 'despotism of absolute power' in various forms of government, whether 'a popular assembly, an aristocratical council, an oligarchical junto, and a single emperor, equally arbitrary, bloody, and in every respect diabolical', Pound proposes instead 'AGATHOS, eternal and self-existent. . . . That this possessor be kalos k'àgathos, theocrat, baron, bojar or rich man matters very little'. Such a balance offers the right measure whether in music, art or politics. 'Measure' is thus for Pound a complex 'ideogram', the *paideuma* underlying geometry, sculpture, poetry and music alike. It underlies, too, all questions of 'value' and 'price', restoring τὸ χαλὸν to the marketplace by making it the measure, not the index, of order in the state and in the economy.

The anangke of modernity

There is in *Mauberley* a further Greek concept, which seems to decree the divorce of χαλὸν and AGATHON. This is that necessity which is finally named in Mauberley II: 'All passes, ANANGKE prevails.' Where ANANGKE prevails, the sifting of beauty is, it seems, impossible. But what is this 'necessity' that intrudes into human affairs, that delays and detains Mauberley, leaves him 'Asking time to be rid of . . . / Of his bewilderment'? For Pound it is not in the end the ineluctable cosmic force of the Greeks, but the reification of historically created circumstances: in a word, what 'the age demands'.

In *The Little Review* in August 1918, in a context which also alludes to Flaubert and to Gautier's *Emaux et Camées* (stylistic resources of *Mauberley*), Pound defined the modern *anangke* with admirable clarity:

> Balzac gains what force his crude writing permits him by representing his people under the anangke of modernity, cash necessity; James, by leaving cash necessity nearly always out of the story, sacrifices, or rather fails to attain, certain intensities. . . . the factor of money, Balzac's anangke, scarcely enters his stories.[28]

In 1935, *à propos* Henry James, he reformulated this as 'H.J. perceived the *Anagke* of the modern world to be money.'[29] 'ANANGKE prevails' in the very divorce of 'τὸ χαλὸν' and 'TO AGATHON'. To unify them would be to achieve what *Guide to Kulchur* calls 'A word almost an ideogram' which Aristotle may have learnt from 'Plato's gossip of Socrates': '*eudaimonein*'. This

> is not 'well-being' in any ordinary sense, or well-doing or doing well, or happiness in any current use of the word. . . . it is not even 'to be in good spirits'. There is no ready made current English for it. It is not to be among good angels. It is to be possessed of one's good DAEMON. (p. 307)

'*Eudaimonein*' lies beyond the divisions of *Mauberley*, the unattained Ithaca of which the Siren's 'obstinate isles' and the 'scattered Moluccas' of Mauberley's doom are the illusive simulacra. Both sections end with the idea of musical perfection, in 'Envoi' the song which emerges from the siftings of 'oblivion' and a 'dumb-born book'; in 'Medallion' the rebirth of Venus Anadyomene from 'the opening / Pages of Reinach' after the 'cobalt of oblivions' of Mauberley's Moluccan beaches. The amber braids of this poem recall the roses laid in magic amber of 'Envoi'. In each case, the *concetto* is embodied in material form.

Aristotle is severely censured in Pound's final judgement for not holding on to this intuition, in terms which recall *Mauberley*'s critique of the modern age: 'Greece rotted. The story of gk. civilization as we have it, is the record of a decadence. Language had already got down to *Times* leader and *D. Telegraph* level. Arry [Aristotle] wd. have succeeded in the most louche modern milieux.' His books are 'the compost, intelligent enough to serve counterfeiters by providing them means toward the confusion and obfuscation of others' (p. 309). No one, he continues, 'can contemplate the use of *hedu* in Aristotle's whole work . . . without feeling the general slither and slipperiness of the terms used' (p. 316).

Modernity for Pound is, then, a condition of submission to the *anangke* of money. Nevertheless, he commends Aristotle for recognising 'that money is BORN as a MEASURE' (p. 323). In a remark which recalls 'the age demanded', he goes on to observe that

> it makes an infinite difference whether you translate Χρεία as *demand* or USE. Unfortunately Rackham has met somewhere a university professor of economics. . . . He falls into class-room jargon, and translates Χρεία as demand.

But, he continues, in an argument which moves towards the resolution of those antitheses *Mauberley* articulates without reconciling, 'The value of a thing depends on USUS, its price may be distorted by its OPUS' (p. 324). Significantly, in describing the Greeks, he uses an unexpected word that recalls poor Jenny's adulteries in 'Yeux Glauques': 'The greeks, being *maqueros* (happy men) with no moral fervour, left a hole or a sense of lack, and into that hole there poured a lot of crass zeal.'

This happiness is the '*hedu*' of the hedonist, pleasure dissociated from virtue, beauty diminished when separated from the good, creating a lack to be filled by mere zealotry. The Aristotelian decadence is like that in which Mauberley quietly disintegrates, and it explains why the war elegy bulks so large in a poem of 'life and contacts':

> The disgust with the fat faces of politicians, with the slithering sleekness of bishops, the general foulness of monopolists and their educational lackeys conduce to the break-up of orderly institutions, and to temporary losses to culture. (p. 331)

As Aristotle recorded 'the decline of the hellenic paideuma. The Homeric vigour was gone. . . . The splintering had begun' (p. 331), so Mauberley and E.P. between them, in their very division, embody 'the schismatic [who] is a splinterer'. The poem itself constitutes 'an emphasis on something fragmentary and a rejection of the totality' (p. 332).

What can Pound offer to resist this splintering? An earlier section of *Guide to Kulchur*, 'Chaucer was Framed?' (the allusion is to the notorious allegation of rape against Chaucer) suggests an answer: that sensual music which is the true nature of 'measure', intrinsic value set against the infinite fungibility of 'usury':

> Usury is contra naturam. It is not merely in opposition to nature's increase, it is antithetic to discrimination by the senses. Discrimination by the senses is dangerous to avarice. It is dangerous because any perception of any high development of the perceptive faculties may lead to knowledge. The money-changer only thrives on ignorance.
>
> He thrives on all sorts of insensitivity and non-perception. An instant sense of proportion imperils financiers . . .
>
> You have two millennia of history wherein we see usury opposed to the arts, usury at the antipodes of melody, of melodic invention, of design. Usury always trying to supplant the arts and set up the luxury trades, to beat down design which costs nothing materially and which can come only from intelligence, and to set up richness as a criterion. Short curves, etc. 'opulence' without hierarchy. (pp. 281–2)

Mauberley had already made the point. Beauty is associated with woman, with passivity: poor Jenny, prostituted for art, is passed around like money. Messalina becomes a coin. Even Venus, all-powerful goddess of procreation, becomes the passive object of artistic representation. What Pound calls 'usury-tolerance' has led us 'to degrade all moral perceptions outside the relations of the sexes, and to vulgarize the sex relation itself', degrading even the 'Romantic rebellion' to 'luxury-trade advertisements'. But there *is* one alternative image of the female as creative (if secondary) voice: she who sang that song of Lawes, the *concetto* embodied in a creating carnal subject whose voice becomes the very incarnation of melody. In contrast to the Sirens, the clear female soprano sings that song of Lawes, suggesting a proper (fertile but unequal) relation, in Pound's eyes, between gendered creativities.

Pound wrote, in 'The Serious Artist' in 1913, that

> If an artist falsifies his report as to the nature of man, as to his own nature, as to the nature of his ideal of the perfect, as to the nature of his ideal of this, that or the other, of god, if god exist, of the life force, of the nature of good and evil, if good and evil exist, of the force with which he believes or disbelieves this, that or the other, of the degree in which he suffers or is made glad; if the artist falsifies his reports on these matters or in any other matter in order that he may conform to the taste of his time, to the proprieties of a sovereign, to the convenience of a preconceived code of ethics, then that artist lies. If he lies out of deliberate will to lie, if

he lies out of carelessness, out of laziness, out of cowardice, out of any sort of negligence whatsoever, he nevertheless lies and he should be punished or despised. . . .

Yet it takes a good deal of talking to convince a layman that bad art is 'immoral'. And that good art however 'immoral' it is, is wholly a thing of virtue. Purely and simply that good art can NOT be immoral. By good art I mean art that bears true witness, I mean the art that is most precise.[30]

Mauberley could do no more than offer a diagnosis and suggest a cure. *The Cantos* set out, as he observed in his *Paris Review* interview with Donald Hall, to write a *Paradiso*, offer Beauty itself. But 'It is difficult to write a paradiso, when all the superficial indications are that you ought to write an apocalypse. It is obviously much easier to find inhabitants for an inferno or even a purgatorio.'[31] What we see in the failure of *The Cantos* is the consequence, writ large, of that schism represented by the two sections of *Mauberley*. The separation of 'καλὸν' from 'AGATHON', of beauty/order as an aesthetic criterion from virtue/rightness as a moral and political injunction, is what leads to the duplicity and division of the *Cantos*. 'ANANGKE prevails.' When the elegiac, last complete Canto CXVI laments that, though 'the beauty is not the madness. . . . I cannot make it cohere', and contrasts his artefact with Mussolini's, the totalitarian poem against the Fascist state, 'Many errors, / a little rightness, / to excuse his hell / and my paradiso', he is explicitly admitting that divorce which had perplexed E.P. and *Mauberley* on setting out, and for which he had indicted bourgeois democracy in *Guide to Kulchur* and throughout the *Cantos*: the divorce of government, order in the state and in civic morality, from order, nobility, beauty in art.

Wrong from the start, Pound saw that divorce as something which afflicted others, in a complex process of projection which cast on to a variety of scapegoats the fault which was in himself. For the divorce of an abiding, 'eternal' beauty from the living, material world of history, the fetichisation of τὸ καλὸν into a timeless *concetto*, is precisely what allows him to separate the scatological bombast of his most vicious infernal visions from the conceit of a beauty defying time with which it coexists. Pound never recognised the brutally compromised nature of an artistic tradition 'that sheds / Such treasure on the air', its dependence on a long history of violence and violation, though he everywhere celebrates the conjunction of dictatorship and beauty, from Pisistratus, through his despotic Renaissance patrons of art, to Mussolini. On the contrary, it is the democratic knaves and eunuchs who corrupt the beautiful and degrade the good. But Pound's 'live tradition' is not 'gathered from the air'. It is wrung from the labour of countless individuals, the exploitation of whole classes and peoples, an exploitation of which his use of the figure of the female in *Mauberley* is a revealing metonymy. His 'cultural treasures', in Walter Benjamin's famous words, are 'spoils' in 'the triumphal procession in which the present rulers step over those who are lying prostrate'.

When Pound ends *Jefferson and/or Mussolini* with a proclamation of faith in Mussolini's commitment to 'the permanent elements of sane and responsible government', the shift from confident assertion to tremulous question is apparent:

> Towards which I assert again my own firm belief that the Duce will stand not with despots and the lovers of power but with the lovers of
>   ORDER
>   τὸ καλὸν ...
> These things being so, is it to be supposed that Mussolini has regenerated Italy, merely for the sake of reinfecting her with the black death of the capitalist monetary system?[32]

Benjamin's words remain the most eloquent and accurate obituary for such a project, penetrating right to the heart of the origins of Modernism. They indicate why its return to origins is a return not, as Pound envisaged it, to primal beauty, but to a historic brutality, the mixed motives of a world of violence and exploitation. For beauty is not from the gods but from the anonymous labours of millions, who alone are the creators of value. The art of Pisistratus' Athens depended on a slave economy; the art of Pound's Modernist moment, in 1919–20, on those wage-slaves of a Taylorist economy labouring in the new factories to make the mass-produced moulds in plaster, tea-rose tea-gowns, pianolas, tin wreaths and cartons he so reviled, and the half-watt bulbs which illuminate his poem's final vision of Beauty. And in this, not only the origins but the handing-on of the Modernist tradition is sullied:

> For without exception the cultural treasures he surveys have an origin which he cannot contemplate without horror. They owe their existence not only to the efforts of the great minds and talents who have created them, but also to the anonymous toil of their contemporaries. There is no document of civilisation which is not at the same time a document of barbarism. And just as such a document is not free of barbarism, barbarism taints also the manner in which it is transmitted from one owner to another.[33]

The very process which ensures tradition's renewal acknowledges, too, the erasure of what it 'replaces'. The palimpsest of tradition overrides, overwrites. Yet the traces of that originating barbarity show through. In Pound's poetry the dead will not lie down.

Chapter Six

Cunning passages: Eliot's
Poems – 1920

'History has many cunning passages'

Ghost prologue: lost threads

An unpublished poem of Eliot's written in Marburg in 1914, on the eve of the Great War, turned the argumentative streets of 'Prufrock' into 'dialectic ways' down which a restless self 'questioned restless nights and torpid days', only to 'always find the same unvaried / Interminable intolerable maze'.[1] The figure which opens 'Burnt Norton', in another time of crisis and dismay twenty years later, refines that image, seeing time as a maze of subjunctive and indicative moments reflecting endlessly back upon themselves. Time's labyrinth is a maze of words, turning upon a pun on 'passage' which itself reveals how language runs away from its speaker, deceiving us with issues:

> Footfalls echo in the memory
> Down the passage which we did not take
> Towards the door we never opened
> Into the rose garden. My words echo
> Thus, in your mind.
> But to what purpose
> Disturbing the dust on a bowl of rose-leaves
> I do not know.

'Burnt Norton' was written in 1935, the year Hitler repudiated the Treaty of Versailles by marching into the Saar. That Treaty had been imposed on a defeated Germany in June 1919, thereby redrawing the post-war frontiers of Europe and deciding its political agenda for the next three decades. It is not surprising, then, that 'Burnt Norton''s meditation on 'the passage that we did not take' should echo the 'cunning passages' of a sinister History complexly figured in 'Gerontion', which Eliot was working on during June 1919 while compiling reports for Lloyds Bank on the financial implications of the Treaty and its German Debt clauses. 'Gerontion' was the opening text both of *Poems – 1920*, first published in New York by Knopf in late February 1920, and of the erroneously titled *Ara Vus Prec* [*sic*], published in London by the Ovid Press earlier the same month. He wrote to his mother on the twenty-second of this month that he had had

> ·   to struggle through chaos . . . receiving hundreds of reports from branches of the bank, classifying them, picking out the points that needed immediate attention, interviewing other banks and Government Departments and trying to elucidate knotty points in that appalling document the Peace Treaty.[2]

The 'contrived corridors' and 'cunning passages' of 'Gerontion' have been generally seen as an allusion to the 'Danzig Corridor' or 'Passage', that strip of German territory ceded to Poland at Versailles, which was to become the *cause célèbre* of the next twenty years, and its 'wilderness of mirrors' identified with the Hall of Mirrors at Versailles in which the Treaty was signed. *Poems – 1920* is woven on history's shuttles. The equable neutrality of the title – a simple conjunction of heterogeneous texts and a date – is disturbed by a deeper, paranoid cross-referencing which hints at its date with History. If the 'cunning passages' of *Poems – 1920* define the epistemological crisis of the Modern, they also point to the historical crisis that underlies it.

What Eliot wrote of Donne and Chapman in 'Shakespeare and the Stoicism of Seneca' in 1927 applies not only to his own compositional procedures in *Poems – 1920* and *The Waste Land*, but also to the way the minds of his *dramatis personae* function in those poems:

> I found it quite impossible to come to the conclusion that Donne believed anything. It seemed as if, at that time, the world was filled with broken fragments of systems, and that a man like Donne merely picked up, like a magpie, various shining fragments of ideas as they struck his eye, and stuck them about here and there in his verse. . . . [producing] only a vast jumble of incoherent erudition. . . . the 'profundity' and 'obscurity' of Chapman's dark thinking are largely due to his lifting long passages from the works of writers like Ficino and incorporating them in his poems completely out of their context.[3]

It is down such punning passages that we pursue an overwhelming question in 'Prufrock', 'Gerontion' and 'Burnt Norton' – passages rendered obscure and appearing profound because, snatched from their originating contexts, they take on a new and sinister significance in the very moment of their apparently unoriginal repetition. Such is the state of mind of the self in a 'world filled with broken fragments of systems'.

Chapman supplies one of the master passages retrodden in 'Gerontion': that which speaks of being 'whirled / Beyond the circuit of the shuddering Bear / In fractured atoms'. In the 1927 essay 'Seneca in Elizabethan Translation' Eliot refers (in words which stress the uncanny nature of the process) to Seneca's *Hercules Furens* and its

> descriptive passages . . . which haunt us more than we should expect . . . [and] must have lain long in the memory of Chapman before they came out in *Bussy d'Ambois* as
>
> > *fly where men feel*
> > *The cunning axle-tree, or those that suffer*
> > *Under the chariot of the snowy Bear.*[4]

Six years later in *The Use of Poetry*, talking of how a poet transforms a phrase, 'whatever its origins', so that it is 'reborn' in a new context, Eliot took the opportunity to correct the misquotation which had substituted 'cunning' for 'burning'. He had, he says, previously been working from 'an inaccurate text'. Professing ignorance of why this passage should have such significance for him, he deploys a striking metaphor:

> There is first the probability that this imagery had some personal saturation value . . . for Seneca; another for Chapman, and another for myself, who have borrowed it twice from Chapman . . . saturation . . . with feelings too obscure for the authors even to know quite what they were.[5]

The metaphor arises from that idea of 'an emotion which is inexpressible, because it is in *excess* of the facts as they appear' in 'Hamlet and his Problems' (1919),[6] which lies behind much of Eliot's critical thinking. Since it is unlikely that Eliot was using an 'inaccurate' text, it is his 'saturated' memory which had made the substitution, importing 'cunning' into the Chapman text from his own poem 'Gerontion', in which he first made use of Chapman's astronomical image.

The idea strikes an apposite 'Modern' note. The disparate and incoherent scraps of previous discourse, a fragment of Seneca embedded in a fragment of Chapman, are translated into a new meta-discourse, which derives its force precisely from its cunning incoherence, multiplying variety, like that which Eliot discussed in his comments on 'bombast' in 'Seneca in Elizabethan Translation':

> Certainly it is all 'rhetorical', but if it had not been rhetorical, would it have been anything? . . . if new influences had not entered, old orders decayed, would the language not have left some of its greatest resources unexplored? . . . Their subsequent progress is a process of splitting up the

primitive rhetoric, developing out of it subtler poetry and subtler tones of conversation, eventually mingling . . . the oratorical, the conversational, the elaborate and the simple, the direct and the indirect.[7]

The Elizabethan/Jacobean ethos provides many of the discursive contexts for *Poems — 1920*, whose meta-narrative (History) is composed out of a bewildering variety of displaced and disorderly discourses in a world where 'old orders [have] decayed'. Gerontion's riddling, punning assertion that 'History has many cunning passages' provides a link between Prufrock's streets like arguments of insidious intent, the dialectic maze of the Marburg poem, the unentered passages of 'Burnt Norton' and the dark passages of Chapman. History, both here and elsewhere in 'Burnt Norton', is a contrivance, a maze of mirrors where narratives multiply, in which 'The Word in the desert' is assailed by 'Scolding, mocking, or merely chattering. . . . voices of temptation', an hallucinatory wilderness like that in 'Gerontion' where 'The word within a word, unable to speak a word' is 'Swaddled with darkness'. If the house of 'Burnt Norton', like Gerontion's rented house, has many cunning passages, it is because it fuses memorably the idea of the labyrinth with that of a history which is all text (among others, those 'hundreds of reports' Eliot had read for Lloyds), tempting to false conclusions, taunting with foregone opportunities which probably would not have been worth it, after all, disturbing with memories of the untaken passage, the door left unopened.

The subject of these poems eludes itself in the passages of history, slipping away from both origins and ends as it moves between too soon and too late, ambitions and vanities, belief and unbelief, giving and famishing, refusal and fear, fear and courage, caution and impudence. It is perpetually volatile and yet fixed forever in an empty craving where authentic original passion is always crowded out by something second-hand and reconsidered. The site of the self is that place of distraction in which 'attention' (always waiting upon) becomes 'memory only, reconsidered passion', already too late. This is the 'place of disaffection' spoken of in 'Burnt Norton', 'Neither plenitude nor vacancy', where we are 'Distracted from distraction by distraction', the word itself distractingly refusing to stay in place, at once empty and overfull, 'Filled with fancies and empty of meaning', so that men and women become 'bits of paper', fragments of texts, blown about the gloomy hills of London.

The footfalls of 'Gerontion' in 1919 are those of Middleton, Chapman, Donne, Webster and Shakespeare, brilliantly mimicked by Eliot. But they also tread those 'dark passages' which lead from Keats's 'Chamber of Maiden Thought' (with its innuendo of a sexual initiation).[8] That Eliot was thinking about Keats at the time is confirmed by the reference to the Nightingale Ode in 'Tradition and the Individual

Talent', along with Dante's Ulysses and Paolo and Francesca, *Othello* and *Agamemnon*. The latter is also recalled along with Keats's poem in 'Sweeney Among the Nightingales', where Keats's transcendent poetic bird is translated into a slang term for prostitutes.[9] But there is nothing maiden-like about the Keatsian echoes in 'Gerontion'. Like Keats's 'belle dame sans merci', history is a diseased and deadly whore, cunning etymologically rooted in *cunnus*, her contrivances and 'issues' sticky and polluted secretions. She deceives, whispering back to us our own whispered ambitions, as Keats's beldam betrays the pale kings and princes with their own desires. She takes advantage of our distraction, gives only to confuse and to increase the craving.

History, the ultimate signifier, dominates and eludes us in 'Gerontion'. Its 'cunning passages' are punningly those of a female sexuality which is also a female *textuality*. The figure of Theseus in the Labyrinth stands behind the poem (a figure evoked without being named in 'Sweeney Erect'). Gerontion wanders like Theseus the corridors of a textual maze, the echoing passages of a history which is also a 'concitation / Of the backward devils': a *citing together* as well as a *stirring up* of diabolical narratives. History is duplicitous and multiplicitous: we do not know which thread to pick up as 'vacant shuttles weave the wind'. The poem trails the threads of many other texts: lives of minor nineteenth-century writers, a Christmas Day sermon of 1618, the Authorised Version of the New Testament, histories of the Persian Wars and of eighteenth-century piracy, Elizabethan and Jacobean drama, dissertations on Bradleyan philosophy, Lloyds' Register, astrological charts, textbooks of contemporary physics.

'Being read to by a boy', Gerontion is also being read into a narrative. This constituting moment of the poem is not original, but as Eliot himself later observed, 'lifted bodily from a Life of Edward Fitzgerald' (in fact an almost word-for-word transcription of a passage in A.C. Benson's 1905 biography).[10] We enter a discourse which is already, from its inception, adulterated by the traces of earlier texts, unable even in starting out to make a new start. Gerontion himself thus becomes 'The word within a word, unable to speak a word, / Swaddled with darkness'.

This last is perhaps the darkest corner of the most contrived passage in the poem. The name given to the earliest printed books, 'incunabula', originally meant swaddling clothes, and by transference came to mean 'childhood, beginning, origin'.[11] The old man, being read to by a boy, is returning to the origins – to that moment of inception which remembers the Jew's spawning and prefigures all the poem's subsequent propagating, fathering, bearing and multiplying – only to find that print has already installed itself where the speaking voice should be, so that that voice is 'unable to speak a word'. In this swaddled textual darkness, 'a vast jumble of incoherent erudition' that points only to itself, no word finds itself at home.

'Gerontion' was originally intended as a prologue to *The Waste Land*, though it claims 'I have no ghosts', possibly an instance of the 'Senecan ghost-prologue form' of which Eliot's essay speaks.[12] It was Pound who suggested a separate printing of *The Waste Land* and Pound who first noticed echoes of Joyce's *Ulysses* in his marginalia to the latter's drafts, in particular writing 'Penelope J.J.' against a passage in 'A Game of Chess'.[13] Eliot and Pound had been responsible for the publication of *Ulysses* in serial extracts in *The Egoist* and *The Little Review* between March 1918 and December 1920, and Eliot was profoundly impressed by the book. Through the mediation of the novel, the image of adulteration in 'Gerontion', illicitly linked with adultery, combines with that of 'vacant shuttles' which 'weave the wind'. The Penelope of the *Odyssey* remained faithful to her husband, fending off her suitors by weaving and unweaving, without ever finishing, a shroud for his father. In *Ulysses*, by contrast, Bloom and Dedalus (the latter named after the Labyrinth's inventor), find themselves woven on the shuttles of history by the wiles of women (mother, wife, daughter, queen, enchantress, whore), in treacherous liaisons with the larger discourses of church, state and sexuality. 'Weave, weaver of the wind', Dedalus says of that same History Gerontion reviles, and shortly after speaks of 'a riddling sentence to be woven and woven on the Church's looms' (a riddling sentence: a cunning passage).[14] *Ulysses* unites Penelope and Circe in echoing Blake's song of the harlot's cry which weaves old England's winding sheet, which Mr Deasy identifies with the power of 'the jew merchants'. The same 'jew' squats, the owner, on Gerontion's window-sill.

From cradle to grave, swaddling-clothes to winding-sheet, such powerless figures are woven on History's looms by a cunning, rapacious female linked to the devouring tiger, to Grishkin and her 'sleek Brazilian jaguar' and to the murderous Jewish paws of Rachel née Rabinovitch in other poems of the volume. As in *Mauberley*, it is not as Ariadne or Penelope, distaff supports of the male enterprise, but as Circe, beldame, siren, enchantress, *femme fatale* linked to an insidiously alien, sub-human subversion, that these texts imagine the female.

Old men, ex-men and con-men

In a world of 'adulterated' discourses, signs are taken for wonders; but they are merely unstable places where beauty is lost in terror and terror in inquisition. The reader, like the unbelieving Jews of Matthew 12:38, belongs to 'an evil and adulterous generation [that] seeketh after a sign' – a meaning to be read out from the dark passages of the poem itself. But the poem's great Modernist insight is that the subject of history is not in control, is in fact merely an agent and carrier of its signs. To live in history is to live perpetually in arrears. To have the experience is to miss the meaning; to find the meaning is to lose the experience, fixing it 'In memory only, reconsidered passion'. The signified (experience) and the signifier (the meaning) change places, so that *meaning* becomes the signified, and experience merely the signifier, betraying pretext to meaning. The demand, inviting betrayal, ' "We would see a sign!" ' is always heretical as well as apocalyptic, for it assumes that meaning and experience can be joined in some primal fullness of signification. Their relation on the contrary is always transitive, sliding between memory and desire. Displaced from the start, Gerontion takes second place to a text we never hear which interpellates him as one 'read to', just as Prufrock's 'Love Song' is never uttered. And, as in 'Prufrock', at the centre of the text is an absence: all the exploits and adventures in which the sedentary, bookish Gerontion has *not* engaged.

Among these is the oddly anachronistic narrative of Thermopylae ('the hot gates'). The allusion is explained by two texts which also elucidate the poem's title. We know from his 1920 essay 'Euripides and Professor Murray' that Eliot was well acquainted with Gilbert Murray's work on the origins of Greek tragedy.[15] It is unlikely that he would not have known Murray's *Euripides and His Age*, which appeared in a mass-production format in the *Home University Library* series in September 1913, and reprinted in August 1914, June 1918 and May 1919.[16]

Euripides, Murray informs us there, was by popular repute born in the year the Persians suffered their naval defeat at Salamis (the same year as the battle of Thermopylae) (p. 104). On the evidence of his plays, 'Euripides was considered in antiquity a bookish poet', Murray says. But like all Athenian citizens, Euripides had seen his share of military service, a commitment only ended when he reached the age of 60:

A man everlastingly wrapped round in good books and safe living cries out for something harsh and real – for blood and swear-words and crude jagged sentences. A man who escapes with eagerness from a life of war and dirt and brutality and hardship to dwell just a short time among the Muses, naturally likes the Muses to be their very selves and not remind him of the mud he has just washed off. . . .
Forty years of military service finished: as the men of sixty stepped out of the ranks they must have had a feeling of mixed relief and misgiving.

> They are now officially 'Gerontes,' Old Men: they are off hard work, and
> to be at the end of hard work is perilously near being at the end of life.
> (pp. 102–6)

Murray has more to say about the *gerontes* in another book, the
Columbia University Lectures of April 1912 published as *Four Stages of
Greek Religion*. Murray's opening chapter, 'Saturnia Regna', a motif
that is to appear in the Ovid quotation in the notes to *The Waste Land*,
adverts to the fertility religions that poem evokes by way of Ovid, and
speaks of a threefold division of the generations in Greek society:

> We . . . think of an old man as a kind of man, and an old woman as a kind
> of woman; but in primitive peoples as soon as a man and woman cease to
> be able to perform his and her tribal functions they cease to be men and
> women. . .: the ex-man becomes a *geron*.[17]

Gerontion is not only an old man but an ex-man, as his catalogue of
losses makes clear, a precursor of 'the Old Guy' for whom a penny is
sought at the beginning of 'The Hollow Men' in 1925. For Murray, the
old man has to be replaced by a new man, or Saviour, as in the ancient
Athenian fertility ritual in which the 'Year-Daemon' is resurrected, 'a
spirit that in the first stage is living, then dies with each year, then rises
again from the dead, raising the whole dead world with him – the
Greeks called him in this phase "The Third One" or the "Saviour" '
(p. 47). This pagan Saviour Murray links with St Paul's New Man,
Christ, with whom 'we may walk . . . in newness of life': 'And this
renovation must be preceded by a casting out and killing of the old
polluted life – "the old man in us must first be crucified"' (p. 47).

The crucifixion/rebirth motif focuses for Murray the crisis of a culture
which has run out of answers, and now asks only questions the Old
Men cannot answer. All that they can do, it appears, is reiterate obsolete
axioms from 'the old polluted life'. The Old Men were repositories of
knowledge about the past, and the Greeks went to them in emergencies:

> But from time to time new emergencies arise, the like of which we have
> never seen, and they frighten us. We must go to the Gerontes, the Old
> Men of the Tribe; they will perhaps remember what our fathers did. . . .
> And suppose the Old Men themselves fail us, what must we needs do? . . .
> If the Old Men fail us, we must go to those older still, go to our great
> ancestors . . . the Chthonian people lying in their sacred tombs. (p. 51)

'Tradition and the Individual Talent' also speaks of not 'following the
ways of the immediate generation before us in a blind or timid adherence'
but of finding originality where 'the dead poets, his ancestors, assert
their immortality most vigorously'.

Murray's 'Chthonian people' rule over the oracles, like Eliot's
'ancestors'. But his explication of the duplicitous word Χραν opens up a

whole range of associations in Eliot's poetry – in particular, *The Waste Land*'s linking of dubious prophecy with confidence tricksters and extortionists, horoscopes read by charlatans with exotic, probably spurious Greek names. ('Madame Sosostris' might well derive hers from a conflation of Murray's 'dying Saviour, the Sosipolis, the Soter' (p. 50) as well as from Aldous Huxley's novel *Crome Yellow*.) It also provides the unremembered link between Gerontion's personal emergency and that of Europe in 1919, fractured into atoms by the post-war settlement, racked by monstrous inflation, with the ubiquitous 'jew', whether capitalist or Bolshevik, squatting everywhere on the windowsill, the owner:

> The word Χραν means both 'to lend money' and 'to give an oracle', two ways of helping people in an emergency. . . . You go to the Chthonian folk for guidance because they are themselves the Oldest of the Old Ones, and they know the real custom. . . . And by an easy extension of this knowledge they are also supposed to know what is. (pp. 51–2)

'After such knowledge, what forgiveness?' Gerontion asks, before his excursus on History. The emergency confronting Greece in the fifth century was an Asiatic invasion like that Bolshevik insurgence which Eliot evokes fearfully in the Herman Hesse note to *The Waste Land*. Into the closed universe of the 'Prufrock' poems has irrupted 'the new (the really new)', in the form of European revolution. Gerontion can only lament loss; he cannot cope with the accession of 'the really new'. Any power the Old Men and the oracles preserve depends upon their refusal of clarity, despite the proclaimed desire to 'meet you upon this honestly'. The crisis of which Murray speaks is precisely Gerontion's condition:

> But of necessity the oracles hated change and strangled the progress of knowledge. Also, like most manifestations of early religion, they throve upon human terror: the more blind the terror the stronger became their hold. (p. 52)

In the unforgivable state after knowledge, he has lost beauty in terror, terror in inquisition – the inquisition of oracles that cannot speak true, that, like history, deceive with ambitions, guide by vanities. Gerontion's interlocutors demand a sign. But, like the prophet Tiresias, in gaining knowledge he has lost his passion, an old man with wrinkled female dugs, an ex-man, no longer warrior, worker, begetter, but one 'read to by a boy', unable to answer the new questions. Gerontion, identified with in the poem as the repository of tradition, is at the same time brutally disowned as the representative of an aetiolated and inadequate status quo. Eliot's poem hovers precariously between embracing all and rejecting all.

By the end of 'Gerontion', many different tales have been summoned up and dismissed. The final return of the nautical motif touched on in the opening allusion to piracy is perhaps most significant. The sweep of the world's oceans and winds, from Belle Isle in the North Atlantic to Cape Horn in the extreme south, call up, by way of Joyce's *Ulysses*, other textual ghosts. According to Eliot what lay behind the original lengthy narrative of a doomed sea-voyage in *The Waste Land* (reduced to a mere handful of lines in 'Death by Water') was Ulysses' account of his last voyage in Dante's *Inferno*.

In fact, echoes of Tennyson's 'Ulysses' are stronger than Dantescan ones in the cancelled passages. The excised opening section ironically misquotes Tennyson, whose Ulysses says 'all times I have enjoy'd / Greatly, have suffer'd greatly. . . . / Much have I seen and known', while Eliot's mariner's more passively has ' "much seen and much endured" '. His crew are a sullen race, while Tennyson's Ithacans are 'a savage race, / That hoard, and sleep, and feed, and know not me'. Tennyson's 'deep / Moans round with many voices', while Eliot's crew joins in the moaning in weather which recalls Tennyson's 'rainy Hyades':

> So the crew moaned, the sea with many voices
> Moaned all about us, under a rainy moon,
> While the suspended winter heaved and tugged,
> Stirring foul weather under the Hyades.

Tennysonian parallels are stronger than has been acknowledged in 'Gerontion' too. Gerontion himself could well be an exhausted remake of Tennyson's hero, ironically refuting all his Victorian values. There are strong correspondences of situation between the two poems: an aged Greek man beside a dying hearth, an old woman, a boy, possibly his son, the imagining of voyages in the beyond. But there are marked differences in each persona's relation to the narrative order. Tennyson's hero recalls hearing, on his travels, tales of his own adventures, for he has already become a part of all he saw. What the boy reads is certainly not tales of Gerontion's adventures, for Gerontion's past is empty of repute. Ulysses has 'drunk delight of battle with [his] peers'; Gerontion offers a potentially endless list of where he has *not* fought. Ulysses envisages one final voyage in which 'It may be that the Gulf will wash us down'. Gerontion, however, has been *driven* to this sleepy corner by the trade winds. 'The Gulf claims' other victims. As Dedalus reflects in *Ulysses*, 'The void awaits surely all them that weave the wind.'

'Much have I seen and known', claims Tennyson's Ulysses. He will 'follow knowledge like a sinking star, / Beyond the utmost bound of human thought'. For Gerontion, knowledge interdicts action, and 'After such knowledge, what forgiveness?' Ambition promises a new start, but

it 'Guides us by vanities'. Virgil and Baedeker are alike redundant here.
Ulysses considers it 'dull . . . to pause, to make an end, / To rust
unburnish'd'; Gerontion consoles himself that 'We have not reached
conclusion, when I / Stiffen in a rented house'. For Ulysses 'It little
profits' to sit by a dying hearth. He wishes for 'Life piled on life'. For
Gerontion 'a thousand small deliberations / Protract the profit of their
chilled delirium'. For Ulysses "'Tis not too late to seek a newer world';
but Gerontion knows that the world is already lost, that history 'Gives
too late' or 'Gives too soon', that knowledge lags behind experience 'in
memory only, reconsidered passion'. While Tennyson's hero grandi-
loquently pronounces himself still 'strong in will', prepared 'To strive, to
seek, to find, and not to yield', Gerontion can only lament a passion
rendered passé in the passages of history. The Victorian hero seeks 'To
sail beyond the sunset, and the baths / Of all the western stars, until I
die'. His idea of the infinite, the 'beyond', is of a full universe to be
mastered by a hungry ego. Gerontion's is an empty infinity of
dispossession, hurled 'Beyond the circuit of the shuddering Bear', where
all human motive is fractured into atoms.

Presiding over this disenchantment is the 'jew', that insidious syllable
which returns insistently in unexpected places, in 'juvescence' and
'flowering judas', who controls even 'the Trades'. Critics who play
down Eliot's anti-Semitism to a few explicit remarks, here, for example,
and in *After Strange Gods*, miss the point. The tenor of this whole
volume is announced in Gerontion's opening denunciation of the
usurper who squats on his windowsill, the owner. This is even more
apparent if we look at the order in which the poems originally appeared
in *Ara Vus Prec*, a sequence disguised by the order adopted in the
Collected Poems. In their original sequence the linking of the Jew,
female sexuality and the usurpatory plebeian is even more apparent:
'Gerontion' (with its lower case 'jew'), 'Burbank' (ditto; Bleistein and
Klein; Princess Volupine), 'Sweeney Among the Nightingales' (the lady
in the cape and Rachel née Rabinovitch's 'murderous paws'), 'Sweeney
Erect' (the hysteric woman, 'ladies of the corridor', etc., in what seems
like the brothel of the previous poem), 'Mr Eliot's Sunday Morning
Service' (with its parasites from *The Jew of Malta*, reflections on sex and
Sweeney's hams), 'Whispers of Immortality' (death, sex and Grishkin's
'rank feline smell'), 'The Hippopotamus', 'A Cooking Egg' (Pipit,
Lucretia Borgia and the fraudulent Madame Blavatsky; the Jewish
financier Sir Alfred Mond 'lapt / In a five per cent Exchequer Bond'; the
red-eyed scavengers creeping from Golder's Green), 'Lune de Miel' ('La
sueur aestivale, et une forte odeur de chienne'), 'Dans le Restaurant'
(with its impertinent waiter and 'Phlébas, le Phénicien'), 'Le Spectateur'
(whose 'petite fille . . . crève d'amour'), 'Mélange Adultère de Tout',

'Ode' (with its 'Succuba eviscerate'). After this *Ara Vus Prec* reprints the *Prufrock* poems as a separate section in the sequence found in *Collected Poems*, the sneering citation from *The Jew of Malta* in 'Sweeney Among the Nightingales' recalled in the dead wench of the epigraph from the same play in 'Portrait of a Lady'.

Joyce's Leopold Bloom had recently set a precedent for casting the Greek wanderer Odysseus as a Wandering Jew, an idea derived from contemporary speculations that Homer's 'cunning Odysseus' was Phoenician in origin.[18] The subterranean link between 'Gerontion' and 'Phlébas le Phénicien' in 'Dans le Restaurant', who returns as the 'drowned Phoenician sailor' of *The Waste Land*, is reinforced by the odd conflation of Greek and Semite in the latter's 'Mr Eugenides, the Smyrna merchant'. But it is the voracious Jewish Maenad, Rachel née Rabinovitch, reiterating the opening figure of a siren History, who brings a sense of closure to the book's themes.

Norman Douglas proposed in *Siren Land* in 1911 that the cannibalistic Sirens of the *Odyssey* were 'probably of Phoenician origin'.[19] Prufrock had prefigured the link in his half-identification with John the Baptist, who lost his head for another Greco-Jewish *femme fatale*. If Prufrock's Lazarus is that of Luke 16, he links the Pharisees seeking a sign in 'Gerontion' with the image of Sir Alfred Mond in heaven in 'A Cooking Egg'. In Luke's parable, the rich Jew Dives, suffering in hell, wants to send Lazarus, resting in Abraham's bosom, to warn Dives' brothers of their fate, if they do not repent. Abraham refuses, because 'if they hear not Moses and the prophets, neither will they be persuaded, though one rose from the dead'. Lazarus' prophetic knowledge will be ignored, even though he returns a 'new man'.

In tune with the wave of anti-Semitism which swept through Europe after 1918, the mood of *Poems* is similar to that which animates *Hugh Selwyn Mauberley*: anger at the 'old men's lies' which had led a generation to walk eye-deep in hell. And the culprit is not hard to find: 'usury age-old and age-thick / and liars in public places'. 'Burbank with a Baedeker, Bleistein with a Cigar' is integrally linked to 'Gerontion' by means of this disgraceful grace-note.

Painted deserts: tourists in the wilderness

The rats are underneath the piles and the 'jew' underneath the lot in 'Burbank', but what are these piles of? The compound epigraph with which the poem opens tells us: piles of used words, of rotting discourses, all in this case about Venice. There is no need to reconstruct their sources: I.A. Richards supplied most of them early, in an appendix to *The Principles of Literary Criticism*.[20] More important to know that every word in this epigraph is from some other text, torn out of context, dumped down in this poem as rubbish is dumped in the Grand Canal, but not washed out of sight. It sits, instead, at the head of the poem, forever deterring entry with the bewilderment which asks: what has this to do with Venice, Burbank, Bleistein, Baedeker?

Baedeker offers the clue. For if this poem is a puzzle, like the streets of a foreign city in which we have arrived for the first time, which lead like an argument of insidious intent to an overwhelming question, we do not need to ask, 'What is it?' We can go and make our visit, armed with, on the arm of, our cultural cicerone. If Dante had Virgil, we moderns have Baedeker, assuaging our anxiety by substituting for a maze of unfamiliar streets the safe text of an authoritative knowledge.

Tourist guides construct a homogeneous history, charting the slow accumulations of cultural capital by which a city grows, in an unproblematic evolution where nothing is superseded, everything re-articulated in some 'organic whole' of harmony and significance, very like Eliot's model of 'Tradition'. Baedeker's narrative makes Venice safe and significant for the tourist – safe in being significant. But who are these tourists? Bleistein himself seems to be little more than an accumulation of cultural debris from three continents – 'Chicago Semite Viennese'. There is nothing homogeneous or structured at all here, no integral selfhood, merely an accretion of contexts, like the epigraph which takes bits and pieces from a heterogeneous bunch of texts linked only by place, and makes a sentence of them.

This is an odd sort of sentence, certainly, but one which nevertheless *works*. It is not just a pile of junk, 'a vast jumble of incoherent erudition'. It makes sense, though the narrative it constructs, like the identities of these tourists, is a mish-mash which bears little relation to the contexts from which it and they have sprung. Significantly, these citations do not lead us out to all the contexts from which they derive. Rather they sit inertly, displaced signifiers uprooted from their origins like those displaced persons wandering aimlessly in 1919 through a rewritten Europe, their textual patronymics erased, struggling to make a new life and meaning in unpropitious circumstances.

If we do enquire into their origins we discover that these are not simple, homogeneous citations in a syntagmatic whole composed of extracts from equally linear narratives. They are, rather, fragments recycled from earlier repetitions. The opening refrain, from the traditional song 'The Carnival of Venice', is actually taken at second-hand from the first line of Gautier's poem 'Sur les Lagunes'. The Latin quotation appears, not in a book of its own, but as a fragment of

unknown provenance in Mantegna's painting of St Sebastian's martyr-
dom which Eliot had seen in Venice, inscribed on a scroll wrapped
round a guttering candle. The story of Niobe is recirculated by way of a
masque by Marston. Mark Antony is here courtesy of Shakespeare's
reworking. The gondola extract, though it derives from James's *The
Aspern Papers* (a text which questions the retrievability of texts), is
actually cited at second-hand in the condensed form it took in Ford
Madox Ford's *Henry James, A Critical Study* (1913, p. 141), which on
nearby pages (pp. 140, 143) also twice cites *Othello*'s 'goats and
monkeys' which James adapted as the final words of another story,
'Cats and monkeys, monkeys and cats – all human life is there!' If all
human life is here, it is only as human life experiences itself in a
disordered and disorderly world, whirled round the shuddering circuits
of language and of commerce alike.[21]

These signifiers, ripped untimely from their contexts, cannot be linked
by diachronic delving into their origins. Rather, like the Modern subject,
they struggle to create a new synchronic configuration out of what their
surfaces supply, a provisional coherence shored against time's ruins.
'Venice' is not so much a place as a discursive practice (like
'Michelangelo' in 'Prufrock'), in which each item offers itself as
metonymy for the whole, so that one can say, 'Ah, Venice; on the Rialto
once . . .'. The Rialto is indeed the nub. The Merchant of Venice plied
his trade as a money-lender there because it was the hub of Venetian
capitalism, where, constantly circulating, nothing in itself, money
substituted for all intrinsic, use values the exchange of empty signifiers.
If nothing stays in place in this text, if no sentence can be pinned down
to an originary context and every phrase is just passing through,
language functions like money in the capitalist economy. As do the
tourists themselves.

Before arriving here, Bleistein had passed through Vienna and
Chicago, but his origins lie veiled in that displaced signifier – that
Wandering Seme – 'Semite'. Bleistein is one of Shylock's many
spawnings. Even the parts of speech are fungible: the noun 'Chicago' (a
native American name appropriated into English) becoming here an
adjective, 'Semite' loitering indeterminately between noun and adjective,
'Viennese' an adjective formed from a noun which aspires to return to
full noun status. The suspect title of Princess Volupine may well
combine suggestions of vulpine voluptuousness with literary echoes of
Jonson's *Volpone*. But it also has more immediate resonances, recalling
that Count Volpi widely reputed for restoring prosperity to post-war
Venice, whose achievement was not without its seamier side.[22] Rachel
née Rabinovitch's loss of her maiden name, we recall, probably obscures
her suspect origins.

Mercantile expansion made Venice for a time the trade capital of Europe, the first 'capitalist' economy. Now, the economic motor moved elsewhere (to Shakespeare's England, to Bleistein's modern Chicago), it is no more than a museum of dead achievements, living parasitically off its past. As the god Hercules left Antony, his credit with his troops in irreversible decline, so in the post-war collapse of the European economy finance capital quits Venice, returning only in the form of voyeuristic American tourists. Venice now battens on these déraciné capitalists as it once battened on the Mediterranean and the (Semitic) East. The barge that burns on the water is no longer the candle-bearing boat which celebrated Venice's marriage to the sea, guarantee of its trading power, but an image of marginality and decline like that which afflicted Cleopatra's Egypt before it.

There is in reality no national, native continuity, only the perpetual migrations of a nomadic Capital symbolised by the stateless 'jew' underneath the lot, who squats on the windowsill throughout Europe, turning the whole continent into a rented house, in Antwerp, Brussels, London, Vienna, Venice. Like Venice's Lions of St Mark, Britain's imperial lion has had its wings clipped by the ubiquitous alien, in this case the dubiously knighted Sir Ferdinand Klein. Imagery of castration runs through the poem, reinforced by enjambement: 'The smoky candle end of time / Declines', a declension by homophony and position rhymed with 'She entertains Sir Ferdinand / Klein'. Time is ruined in this interplay of predation ('Descending at' – or on? – a small hotel) and spiritual, financial or sexual collapse, *Paradise Lost* mediated by Tennyson's 'The Sisters' ('They were together, and he fell'). The passing bell rings everywhere on this world. As Venice floats on a fragile raft, so the whole western economy has no secure foundations.

This unedifying but powerful poem, like Baedeker, is an anthology of soiled goods and second-hand opinions. It is the reader who stands at the smoky candle end of time, contemplating time's ruins like any tourist. The lustreless protrusive eye of a dying sun looks at an over-familiar prospect. But if the eye stares at us *out of* a picture, it is also true that we are that eye, staring *into* the prospect. We see not a place, but 'a perspective of Canaletto', the 'real thing' forever pre-empted for us by the neo-classical geometry of Canaletto's canvases. If our perspectives are shaped by the cool rationality of the painter, there are other, more modern influences on the way we see this collapsing world, revealed in the dislocated perspectives and angular collisions of the text. That 'lustreless protrusive eye' recalls a decidedly more up-to-date perspective: an 1898 oil painting by the Symbolist and Decadent Odilon Redon, illustrator of Baudelaire, whom Eliot may have come across through his mentor on Symbolism Arthur Symons, who wrote about Redon as 'A New French Blake' in *The Art Review* in July 1890.

Redon's 'The Cyclops' depicts a single eye at the centre of a conspicuously phallic head and neck drooping like a declining candle end over a desolate landscape, staring down upon a naked and recumbent female body. Bleistein's 'saggy bending of the knees / And elbows' prefigures the 'Gesture of orang-outang' of the next poem, 'Sweeney Erect', in which Sweeney rises from the bedclothes like Polypheme above an ironically named Nausicaa. The poem opens with the commissioning, in a stiff bombastic style, of a painting which as described would properly belong to the late Italian Renaissance. But when the scene finally coheres, it could have been painted by Redon, for Sweeney here is a Polypheme, whose 'withered root of knots of hair / Slitted below and gashed with eyes, / This oval O cropped out with teeth', resembles strikingly Redon's third lithograph in *Les Origines* (1883), 'Le polype difforme flottait sur les rivages, sorte de Cyclope souriant et hideux'.[23]

Sweeney cannot perform against a backcloth provided by the artists of the Italian tradition. The poem's stage-setting 'Paint me a cavernous waste shore / . . . Paint me . . . / Display me . . .' extends the instructions of its epigraph to 'Make all a desolation' (a desolation relieved by 'wenches'). For his first appearance on the staged wilderness of contemporary history, Sweeney, who is to have the final say in *Poems – 1920* and to bulk large in Eliot's subsequent verse, through *The Waste Land* to the unfinished melodrama *Sweeney Agonistes*, must find an appropriately Modern *mise-en-scène*.

The recurrence of Sweeney at key points in this volume provides a shadowy meta-narrative to the apparently heterogeneous vignettes it collects – a meta-narrative which casts the lengthened shadow of history over all the subordinate stories the poems tell. If 'Gerontion' is one of the 'old men' of an order now finally bankrupt, Sweeney is the 'new man', brutal, plebeian, cynical, a marauder who seizes what he wants without any of Prufrock's prevarications. But if he is a 'new man' he is also a throwback. The title 'Sweeney Erect' recalls the 'pithecanthropus erectus' ('apeman erect') of contemporary palaeontological debate. The designation 'Apeneck', like the 'Gesture of orang-outang', cast him as the 'missing link', a topical concern in the wake of the Dutch archaeologist Eugène Dubois' fossil discoveries in the jungles of Java in the 1890s,[24] his very physique presaging a reversion to origins. And it is indeed origins of one kind or another, intellectual or biological, which are foregrounded by the parenthetical insertion in 'Sweeney Erect' which mocks the high talk of tradition with the coarse stance of Sweeney, confidently straddling the present:

(The lengthened shadow of a man
Is history, said Emerson,
Who had not seen the silhouette
Of Sweeney straddled in the sun.)

Writing of 'Senecan bombast' in 'Seneca in Elizabethan Translation', Eliot quotes a passage about Polyphemus which calls on the sea to 'swallow me into her wat'ry gulf', linking this poem and 'Gerontion'. Both poems are centrally concerned with bombast, dressing up a brutal reality in a variety of discourses, the overwrought diction of Elizabethan drama, or, for that matter, the fine phrases of New England Transcendentalism. Parodic periphrases are repeatedly exposed by sudden switches to the literal and demotic, as Sweeney's broad-bottomed bulk reminds that history is more than the shadow-play of cultured traditions. Sweeney's companions in this poem, the ambiguous 'ladies of the corridor' in a dodgy lodging-house, point back to the 'contrived corridors' of 'Gerontion' and forward to the 'suspect' women of 'Sweeney Among the Nightingales'. But they also relate to the remarkable double discourse sustained in 'Whispers of Immortality', another meditation on Elizabethan and Jacobean literature.

The first four stanzas of this poem speak with a vivid necrophily of corporeal lust and mortality, but they are at the same time critical reflections on an immortal corpus, on precisely those authors (Webster, Donne) Eliot was concurrently trying to establish in various essays as the core of a new tradition. These texts, like Eliot's own, and like all three authors, are 'possessed by death' in a multiple sense (preoccupied with, sexually or spiritually possessed by, owned by), and death puts an end to whispers, turning the organ of speech into 'a lipless grin'. Like Emerson's history, such texts constitute a diachronic dimension contrasted with the synchronic modernity of the second half, presided over by a Grishkin whose feline power (compared to 'The couched Brazilian jaguar') recalls the tiger of 'Gerontion'.

The poem 'whispers of immortality' in its very title, speaking metonymically for all poems which substitute for the senses of dying bodies the sense of their own immortal lines. Thoughts and words do what bodies do, at least within the dead metaphors of a punning etymology: they 'cling' and 'tighten', 'seize and clutch and penetrate'. But though the same signifiers define both functions, the poem opens up an ironic and enormous gap between the two signifieds.

'Sense' is both senses here, physical and semantic, the sensory organs and the 'sense' of words. But the one undermines the other, is 'no substitute' for it. Together with 'No contact possible to flesh', the phrase points back to the opening poem, where Gerontion asks, 'How should I use them [the senses] for your closer contact?' Textuality and female sexuality converge in the second half of the poem in Grishkin's cosmetics, her eye 'underlined for emphasis' like any text. The pneumatic bust (real or inflated) recalls 'breastless creatures', but also stirs a theological wind: that divine spirit (Greek *pneuma*) of which Pentecost 'Gives promise of pneumatic bliss'. The poem really comprises two juxtaposed discourses: an eroticised, grossly corporeal Jacobean death, and a fleshy modern sensuality, each subverting the other. But what emerges from the very vocabulary they share is the irreducible plurality of language, which diverges, bifurcates, multiplies in a wilderness of mirrors.

The poem ends with a reduction of the diverting and diversely physical to the verbal abstractions of that 'metaphysics' which dominates the next poem, 'Mr Eliot's Sunday Morning Service'. But for all its abstruse language, this poem is centrally concerned with the relations between sexuality and textuality. It begins, at this late stage in the book, by speaking of beginnings, quoting an originary statement about origins: 'In the beginning was the Word'. But the opening words of the Gospel according to St John, recalled here, are not themselves original. They merely repeat the opening formula of the first book of the Bible, Genesis, which begins, 'In the beginning. . . .' The words recall, too, 'The word within a word, unable to speak a word,' already spoken for at the beginning of *this* volume. As if to underline its point about the oddity of beginnings, the phrase from St John is repeated at the start of the second stanza, undermining originality. Ironically, the first time the phrase is used it functions to put a summary end to the lines which precede it. When it is repeated, unoriginally, at the start of the second, it acts as a prelude to what is to come.

The transformations of language in this poem expose the unreliability and evasiveness of origins. The opening word, 'Polyphiloprogenitive', is a neologism. It originates with this text, so that it could itself be described as *the* word which is 'In the beginning'. (It is certainly 'in the beginning' of the poem.) But in another sense its total originality means that it is the *last* word, uttered *ex nihilo* as the poem begins. It is not, however, completely original, for it is a hybrid composed from existing semantic units. 'Polyphiloprogenitive' is an adulterated, bastard word, combining (in its first two semes) Greek and (in its second two) Latin roots. It is also not the first neologism in the book, though 'juvescence', in the opening poem, contracts rather than expands on its root 'juvenescence' (both neologisms address sexual potency). 'Polyphiloprogenitive' combines (and enacts its meaning by hyperbolically exceeding) two quite different concepts, which point to origins and ends respectively: 'polygenetic', having more than one origin, and 'philoprogenitive', having many offspring (OED).

Both meanings are combined in the deliberately obscure 'Super-fetation of το'εν', a plural impregnation in which a superabundance is begotten upon the One. Plurality overwhelms unity, overflowing and disrupting the One with an endless proliferation. This is precisely what happens in the text, where a multitude of meanings dissolve the syntagmatic, narrative unity of the Word, breaking it down into paradigmatic sub-narratives that diverge, bifurcate, spawn, will not stay still. The Greek 'το'εν', differentiated even as script, reminds us that the New Testament narratives of the Jewish, Aramaic-speaking Jesus are told in Greek. In the same way the Greek word 'Paraclete' (an intercessor) intercedes between the Aramaic and the English.

Throughout the poem there is this mutual multiple impregnation of semes. While the 'wilderness' (which in 'Gerontion' multiplies variety) is described in straightforward Anglo-Saxon words, the theological terms ('presbyters', 'penitence') have been detached from their Greek and Latin origins by two millennia of hermeneutic schisms. Like 'piaculative pence', language passes unfaithfully through numberless hands. We can see how labile it is by noting how the apparently referentless 'sapient sutlers' becomes clear in retrospect as a stately periphrasis for humble bees. Linguistic excess breeds its opposite, that Origen who denies procreation by castrating himself in the name of a chaster Word.

Before this theme can be developed, however, the poem seems utterly to change direction, embodying its abstract speculations about divine paternity in the concrete images of a painting. On earth as in heaven, authorship is problematised. The Son of God who is the Word incarnate is coeval with his progenitors, 'the Father and the Paraclete', in the 'Superfetation of το'εν'. The painting is a generic product of the 'Umbrian school', identified not by a single authorising patriarch ('school of Raphael'), but as a collective practice which is multiple from the beginning. Even the poem itself, if Lyndall Gordon and Christopher Ricks are to be believed, dissembles its origins, for the 'Mr Eliot' named in the title may well refer not to the poem's author but to the poet's cousin Fred, whose Sunday morning services Eliot 'evidently resented'.[25] The 'subject' (theme) of the poem turns out to be different from its 'subject' (speaker). He is not, it appears, what he seems. The same is true of the painting so fully and familiarly described, in a volume full of pictorial reference.

For all the familiarity of the topos, this 'Baptism of Christ' is not that by Piero della Francesca in the National Gallery which it usually calls to mind. It corresponds almost exactly to a 1470 painting by Andrea Verrocchio which Eliot would have seen in the Uffizi Gallery in Florence.[26] Here the feet are clearly visible through the water (not the case in Piero's painting), and Father and dove are visible in the clouds.

But Verrocchio is not Umbrian but Florentine (though the picture is hung in the room of the Florentine and Umbrian Schools), and his picture is a framed canvas, whereas the poem's is upon a gesso ground – that is, the plaster ground of a mural. This indeterminacy of attribution in what is so specifically described is reproduced in the language of description itself, which refers simultaneously to the content of the painting, read as a true story, and to the material ground on which it is painted. For if the 'wilderness' depicted is 'cracked and browned', so also is the actual 'gesso ground' on which it is painted. In unsettling retrospect we realise that 'ground' itself has a double significance, that the water 'pale and thin' is actually thin paint, and that the feet which *appear* to shine through it are, like the water, marks on the same flat surface, their relations of depth and dimension mere *trompe-l'œil*.

The depths of the picture become all surface, just as the depths of history in which the many tellings of Christ, their many fifteenth-century depictions, and the proliferating theologies derived from and interpreting those tales, are all collapsed into the depthless present of the speaker. (In a similar double-take in 'Lune de Miel', the tourists find Leonardo's Last Supper and their own in one levelling zeugma.) If the unnamed painter in 'Morning Service' once 'set / The Father and the Paraclete' above the image of Christ (enthroned, set in place, as paint sets), he also becomes the real father (and mediator) of the Father and Paraclete he depicts. Paternity, authorship, the multiplying Logos as only-begotten, is the recurrent insinuation of the poem, giving a sexual twist even to the word 'service'.

Like the Paraclete (the intercessive Word), the patristic interpreters including Origen intercede between us and the original narratives, but in the process multiply variety in a wilderness of mirrors, some of which, like the painting, are cracked and brown. There is no ur-narrative, only an endless proliferation of versions, readings, interpretations. Mr Eliot's Sunday Morning Service is not the same as other people's, even Fred Eliot's, even though they share the same service. The Word is 'polyphiloprogenitive': it swarms and drifts like the bees. And as the bees pass between the staminate and the pistillate, themselves epicene neuters pollinating others, so the interpreters of scripture pass between us and the original texts, the 'sapient sutlers' become 'subtle schools', the first word already adulterated by the unflattering reference to Grishkin's 'subtle effluence of cat', the second harking back to the 'Umbrian school' of painting.

If 'school' shifts from icon to hermeneutics, art to theology, concrete to abstract, the idea of the 'masters' also shift from that of creativity (the painter) to that of criticism, pedagogy, even pedantry (the schoolmen of medieval theology become schoolmasters, wielding disciplinary power).

Throughout the transmigrations of language in this poem, the last word lies with discourse, with controversy, argument and disputation, an excess and diversity of learning, not agreement. It lies, that is, with the plurality of knowledges, not a unifying wisdom. 'Poly-', that morpheme that opened the poem, returns at the end to set the seal on an irresistibly plural universe. Here, in the much or varied learning of the polymath, interpretations breed as prolifically as the birds, bees and flowers, and the one Word in the desert disintegrates into broken fragments of systems, a vast jumble of incoherent words, 'attacked by voices of temptation'.

Ghost epilogue: loose ends

Pound wrote in the *Criterion* in June 1932 that the tightly formal poems in this volume were a reaction against 'general floppiness [which] had gone too far' and the 'Remedy prescribed "Emaux et Camées" (or the Bay State Hymn Book). Rhyme and regular strophes'. But their formal tautness of rhyme and stanza belies the incoherence of their narratives. They occupy an incoherence which is just waiting to be called to order, and their Saviour, their 'new man' duly makes his (re-)appearance, thrusting his shifting hams into the high-flown discourse, with a coarse knowingness more fundamental than that of enervate Origen. This return of the repressed prepares for Sweeney's ceremonial enthronement as lord of misrule and eponymous hero of the poem which now concludes the sequence, 'Sweeney Among the Nightingales'.

In this poem's brutally forced quatrains, Sweeney has the last laugh on all the treasured items of Tradition which have gone before. The tradition itself has its origins in violation and brutality, in those bloody Greek tales figured in the alien script of the opening epigraph from Aeschylus' *Agamemnon*, the cry of a dying victor, home from massacre at Troy only to be stabbed in his bath by an adulterous wife. It is, indeed, the 'stiff dishonoured shroud' of the *geron*, reversing the swaddling clothes of the first poem, with which the whole volume concludes. In the *Ara Vus Prec* version of this poem, an epigraph from *The Raigne of King Edward the Third* declares that 'The nightingale sings of adulterous wrong'. The theological abstractions of 'Mr Eliot's Sunday Morning Service' are here degraded into the profane and incoherent rituals of a drunken orgy, the pollutions of a 'bloody wood' where whorish nightingales serenade 'The Convent of the Sacred Heart', and all stands 'dishonoured'. In this world swaddled in language, where a drunken collapse can be rephrased as becoming 'Reorganised upon the floor' (like Tradition after the supervention of novelty), all meaning is 'veiled', 'hushed', 'shrunken', stained, shrouded. Clouds drift over a muffled world, where even the characters are 'indistinct'. The volume as finally constituted closes with this occlusion.

'Sweeney Among the Nightingales' is not casually placed. It reverts to many of the motifs of 'Gerontion', but in contrast with his empty house, this one overflows with drunken revellers. The whole poem operates through narrative displacements, as we drift from one sensual vignette to another. It seems to begin in the sordid interiors of 'Sweeney Erect', but moves at once, at least metaphorically, to the same far sea-passages we read of in 'Gerontion' (the River Plate is on the Cape Horn passage, swept by the South East Trades). The shifts not only in space but in time recall the violent centrifugal motions of the last section of 'Gerontion'. These are 'Time's ruins', and when the man with heavy eyes 'Declines the gambit' of the lady with the cape, a new meaning is given retrospectively to the same verb in 'Burbank with a Baedeker'. We see throughout this volume a narrative evacuated of its agents, in the doldrums all the way from Gerontion's 'sleepy corner' (not 'running on the Horn') to this poem's 'hornèd gate' of dream. The odd image of the 'maculate giraffe' picks up a motif from that equally odd French insert, 'Mélange Adultère de Tout', whose title in a sense describes the whole volume: an adulterated (and adulterous) mix of everything. Not unity but plurality; not τὸ'εν, the One, but multiplicity, a promiscuous and incoherent mélange. Sexual promiscuity becomes then the model of a textual promiscuity, the transient passages of ships in the night.

In a post-war world breaking down into a centrifugal modern heterogeneity, the 'fractured atoms' of 'Gerontion', *Poems – 1920* intervenes with an unequivocal political indictment. The old men of the antebellum order have failed. They have abdicated in the face of a new configuration of malignant social forces which undermines the whole idea of Tradition and order. Throughout the book an unholy alliance of rapacious female sexuality, plebeian brutality and Jewish rapacity, whether capitalist or Bolshevik, conspires to subvert a civilisation represented by the great works of a Renaissance culture now, like Venice, in terminal decline. History, the presiding figure of the volume, is not that eloquent muse Clio but a voracious and deceitful beldame who reappears in many guises but nowhere more explicitly than in that Rachel *née* Rabinovitch who 'Tears at the grapes with murderous paws'. The rats are underneath the piles and a Jewish *Conservatrice des traditions Milésiennes* is underneath the lot.

In that famous encounter in 'Little Gidding' many years later between a night-walking poet and a familiar compound ghost, Tradition speaks to its most honoured individual talent in terms which recall these early poems. 'East Coker' had spoken of the lies of 'the quiet-voiced elders' and the folly of old men, 'Their fear of fear and frenzy, their fear of possession'. But now the poet himself is one of those old men, about to learn from 'some dead master. . . / Both one and many' the gifts reserved for age. These 'disclosures' in fact reveal nothing new, merely reiterate the already known and repressed, ' "rehearse / My thought and theory which you have forgotten" '. Such *rehearsal* (which is also a re-burial) of what has always-already been said reproduces the dilemma of Prufrock on starting out.

Echoes of both the vacillating Hamlet and of that ghostly father whose words prompt his acts ring through the passage in 'Little Gidding' as they haunted Prufrock's imagination. A ghost is the proper figure to bring such faded news, since like the neurotic it is doomed for a certain term to walk the night, condemned to revisit the scene of its sorrow, to repeat compulsively the deed which signifies its own unreality. It is here a ghostly language which takes precedence over the various voices that speak its words, as if the script were predictable from the beginning. Quitting a 'disfigured street' (among other things, a street without figures), the ghost acknowledges its artificial status, a merely *textual* figure, interceding, carrying a message we already know, in a *passage*, cunning, dark, dissatisfied, between two worlds, that body abandoned on a distant shore as Gerontion is driven to a sleepy corner, Sweeney to the desolate beach.

What the disembodied figure speaks of in this ghostly epilogue to the Modernist project is the same dull crisis of recurrence that exasperated Prufrock, 'the rending pain of re-enactment / Of all that you have done, and been' – or, for that matter, left undone, failed to be:

> For last year's words belong to last year's language
> And next year's words await another voice.
> But as the passage now presents no hindrance
> To the spirit unappeased and peregrine
> Between two worlds become much like each other,
> So I find words I never thought to speak
> In streets I never thought I should revisit
> When I left my body on a distant shore.

Chapter Seven

Broken images: *The Waste Land* and the European crisis

Benighted readings, mutual friends

The original title of *The Waste Land* is well known, and its polyphonic implications often remarked: 'He do the Police in different voices'. What has been less well noted is the relation of this polyphony to the question of *power*. Being read to by a boy like Gerontion raises questions of power in both the structure and content of the reading, even when the analogy is with Betty Higden hearing Sloppy 'do' the police reports from the newspapers in chapter XVI of *Our Mutual Friend*. Related questions of autonomy and dependence are raised by the émigrée lady at the start of *The Waste Land*: 'I read, much of the night, and go south in the winter'.[1]

If Eliot's poem is polyphonic, and all the men and women meet in Tiresias, where they meet is a locus of power. Speaking through all the different voices is the *police*. 'What Tiresias *sees* . . . is the substance of the poem': he invigilates all the inhabitants of *The Waste Land*, subjecting them all to his contemptuous prophetic scrutiny. Yet impotence, political as well as physical and spiritual, pervades him and them alike. Agents as well as victims, emperors, monarchs, archdukes and millionaires among their number, they seem powerless and ineffectual, as if they lacked the code of commands that would give them authority, though that contemplated at the end ('Give, Sympathise, Control') might well do. *The Waste Land* is a poem full of deposed powers, in a Europe ravaged by a continental civil war turning to revolution, where all the icons of authority have been toppled. Its heaps of broken images recall Milton's *Iconoclastes* during an earlier Civil War. These are graven images of power overturned, bringing a

126

disorientation of vision such as that 'dissociation of sensibility' Eliot saw flowing from such an historical watershed. These may well be the broken images of a Modernist poetic. They are primarily, however, those spoken of by that Ezekiel who heads the poem's list of citations, not in the chapter and verse Eliot cites, but in Chapter VI, where interpellated as 'Son of man', he is urged by the Lord to 'set [his] face toward the mountains of Israel, and prophesy against them', to warn, in words which for Eliot must have rung with contemporary resonance, that 'your altars shall be desolate, and your images shall be broken: and I will cast down your slain men before your idols'.

If the context in *Our Mutual Friend* is significant, so is the aporetic play of identity signalled by Dickens's title: a third person in a series of manifestations widely spoken of as 'our mutual friend' only in the end to stand revealed as a case of mistaken identity. All the speech acts in *The Waste Land*, whether lament, persuasion, prophecy, indictment, seduction, conversion, hailing, insult, reproach, complaint, confession or whatever, involve such a third party, a mutual friend referred or deferred to, whether Mrs Equitone, Lil, or Christ. Even the nightingale, symbol of pure poetic utterance overheard in solitude, denounces in her song her violator Tereus. In 'What the Thunder Said', this 'mutual friend' is named explicitly as 'the third who walks always beside you', though, 'When I count, there are only you and I together'. This mutual friend, like Tiresias, is of indeterminate gender, constituted discursively by the very act of asking after him/her: 'I do not know whether a man or a woman / – But who is that on the other side of you?'

This 'third' has his precedents in Gilbert Murray's *Four Stages of Greek Religion*, the language of which lies unmistakably behind the conflation of pagan and Pauline dying gods in *The Waste Land*:

> At the great spring Dromenon the tribe and the growing earth were renovated together: the earth arises afresh from her dead seeds, the tribe from its dead ancestors; and the whole process, charged as it is with the emotion of pressing human desire, projects its anthropomorphic god or daemon. A vegetation-spirit we call him, very inadequately; he is a divine Kouros, a Year-daemon, a spirit that in the first stage is living, then dies with each year, then thirdly rises again from the dead, raising the whole dead world with him – the Greeks called him in this phase 'the Third One', or the 'Saviour'. . . . It is this range of ideas, half suppressed during the classical period, but evidently still current among the ruder and less Hellenized peoples, which supplied St. Paul with some of his most famous and deep-reaching metaphors. 'Thou fool, that which thou sowest is not quickened except it die'. 'As He was raised from the dead we may walk with Him in newness of life'. And this renovation must be preceded by a casting out and killing of the old polluted life – 'the old man in us must first be crucified'.[2]

When Stetson is hailed at the end of the first section, the corpse buried in the garden is such a 'Third One', who in Murray's words 'comes the next Year as Avenger, or as the Wronged One re-risen' (p. 47). The reader likewise is hailed as an accomplice in some similar crime of suppression and deceit, as 'Hypocrite lecteur, mon semblable, mon frère'.

Eliot's reading on what he calls 'vegetation ceremonies' has been exhaustively sourced, and I do not cite Murray simply to add one more item of baggage to an already-overladen text. Certainly, Murray makes explicit the parallel between pagan and Christian, so central to the poem, that Frazer hints at but always avoids, and he makes connections with the anthropological origins of tragedy of a kind which Eliot's 1920 essay on 'Euripides and Professor Murray' acknowledges to be of interest. But Murray's real significance is that he relates such otherwise merely quaint anthropological data to crucial questions of social and political power, and, by implication at least, particularly in his chapter on 'The Failure of Nerve', he touches nerves which are specifically modern.

Eliot's notes to *The Waste Land*, with one significant exception, point consistently away from the modern world, like the mock-scholarly citation of Ovid's tale of Tiresias. When pursued, such sources frequently open, nevertheless, on to contemporary concerns. Other, clearly relevant sources are not cited at all. Tiresias, we read, has walked among the dead. Indeed, though we are not told, he is specifically consulted by the eponymous heroes of the classical epic for advice on the burial of the dead appropriate to the first section of the poem. His role in *Oedipus Rex*, where he warns Oedipus against seeking to know too much (to know, specifically, the primal crimes of parricide and incest), is clearly relevant to a poem which speaks of dangerous knowledge and dangerous ignorance, dead fathers and murmurs of maternal lamentation. Thebes, like modern London or Vienna, is an unreal city under a curse. The play's new topicality because of Freud's speculations on the incest taboo in *Totem and Taboo* (1913) was well known to Eliot: 'Euripides and Professor Murray' notes that Murray 'is very much of the present day', in which 'we have read books from Vienna ... and we have a curiously Freudian-social-mystical-rationalistic-higher-critical interpretation of the Classics and what used to be called the Scriptures ... and it is this phase of classical study that Professor Murray ... represents'.[3] But, though the poem refers to his walking by the walls of Thebes, Tiresias' role in *Oedipus Rex* is not annotated.

Eliot's allusions rarely return us to the origin without the mediation of intervenient readings. Tiresias is no exception. He comes, by way of

Ovid, from the originals in Sophocles and Homer, only at several removes, the most significant of which is the most recent. A clue to Eliot's purpose in using the figure of Tiresias is offered by the poem's echoes of Wagner's *Tristan und Isolde*. Friedrich Nietzsche's *The Birth of Tragedy from the Spirit of Music* (1872), a text only recently translated into English in Eliot's postbellum world, was dedicated to Wagner, whose *Tristan und Isolde* it describes as a voice crying in 'the wilderness of our exhausted culture' in Dionysian revolt against the tyranny of a 'knowledge-craving Socratism'.[4]

A passion for Wagner is one of the few things Eliot shared with Nietzsche, whose work he disparages in several places, and most damningly in 'Shakespeare and the Stoicism of Seneca'.[5] Nevertheless, Nietzsche's seminal study, newly fashionable in the first decades of the century, provides a key to the locked rooms of *The Waste Land*. Expounding Act III of *Tristan*,[6] where the individual figure of 'the hero wounded to death and still not dying' emerges abruptly from the 'thundering stream' of the music, Nietzsche explains how the Apollonian principle intercedes between the audience and the 'orgiastic self-annihilation' to which the music invites it:

> All of a sudden we imagine we see only Tristan, motionless, with hushed voice saying to himself: 'the old tune, why does it wake me?' And what formerly interested us like a hollow sigh from the heart of being, seems only now to tell us how 'waste and void is the sea'.

Not only does Eliot deploy this same phrase to end the second movement of 'Burial of the Dead', after quoting 'the old tune' which opens the opera; he also adapts Nietzsche's phrasing ('a hollow sigh from the heart of being', the music opening a view into 'the heart chamber of the cosmic will') in creating the context abruptly terminated by the inruption of German:

> I was neither
> Living nor dead, and I knew nothing,
> Looking into the heart of light, the silence.
> *Oed' und leer das Meer.*

Nietzsche's account of the struggle between the Apollonian principle of 'individuation' and the Dionysian impulse to 'absorb the entire world of phenomena' is based in a discussion of Euripides' *Bacchae*. Here, it mediates between the poem's Wagnerian elements and its range of classical and anthropological allusion. Dionysus, he says, 'appears in a multiplicity of forms', 'a god experiencing in himself the sufferings of individuation', and he undergoes a 'dismemberment . . . a transformation into air, water, earth and fire',[7] elements which preside over the first four sections of *The Waste Land* ('A Game of Chess' is full of the wind). The final section brings all four together at a moment of possible rebirth where Christ merges with Dionysus among the 'tumbled graves' of a ruined chapel which is 'only the wind's home', 'In a flash of lightning. Then a damp gust / Bringing rain'. Dionysus, in the *Bacchae*, is known as the Thunderer, and as the first lines of the play tell us he was conceived, in the exact formula of Murray's translation, 'In a flash of lightning'.[8]

Dionysus, in Murray and Frazer an archetypal dying god, becomes in Nietzsche's definitive modern reading the transformative, orgiastic life-energy which offers renewal for a desiccated, over-intellectualised culture. In this, he stands in sharp contrast to Tiresias, who epitomises for Nietzsche the Socratic intellectual will-to-know:

> In a myth composed in the eve of his life, Euripides himself most urgently propounded to his contemporaries the question as to the value and signification of this tendency. Is the Dionysian entitled to exist at all? Should it not be forcibly rooted out of the Hellenic soil? Certainly, the poet tells us, if only it were possible: but the god Dionysus is too powerful. . . . The judgment of the two old sages, Cadmus and Tiresias, seems to me also the judgment of the aged poet; that the reflection of the wisest individuals does not overthrow . . . the perpetually propagating worship of Dionysus, that it in fact behoves us to display at least a diplomatically cautious concern in the presence of such strange forces.[9]

Nietzsche's Socratic man is one 'disintegrated by the critico-historical spirit of our culture', a culture 'without myth' which has lost 'its healthy creative natural power'. He is a wandering figure, for 'it is only by myth that all the powers of the imagination and of the Apollonian dream are freed from their random rovings'. 'The mythless man', Nietzsche says, 'remains eternally hungering among all the bygones, and digs and grubs for roots, though he have to dig for them among the remotest antiquities.' One symptom of this 'unsatisfied modern culture' is 'the gathering around one of countless other cultures, the consuming desire for knowledge'.[10] He is, in fact, a *geron* who asks like Gerontion, 'After such knowledge what forgiveness?' or is like Eliot's Tiresias, punished with blindness and sterility for having known too much, seeking 'the roots that clutch', the branches that might 'grow out of this stony rubbish', a 'heap of broken images' which is all that remains of Tradition, of 'all the bygones'.

As the Thunder proclaims in the last section of the poem, the waste land over which Tiresias presides can be redeemed only by surrender to a life-giving force found in the heart of destruction, which will reunite the sundered fragments, set the lands in order with a new originating myth. It is not difficult to see Nietzsche's valorisation of myth behind Eliot's advocacy of the 'mythical method' in his review of *Ulysses* in

1923.[11] Through the 'mythical method', he says there, the 'immense panorama of futility and anarchy which is contemporary history' will be transformed into a new order, made 'possible for art'. The last section of *The Waste Land* wills a similar resolution upon a desolated Europe. The glimpse into chaos offered by Hermann Hesse's *Blick ins Chaos* focuses on a Russian Revolution both loathsome and fascinating, which 'drives drunkenly in spiritual frenzy along the edge of the abyss, sings drunkenly ... as Dmitri Karamazov sang', while 'The offended bourgeois laughs at the songs; the saint and seer hear them with tears'.[12]

The fertility cult allusions in *The Waste Land*, far from being antiquarian paraphernalia, a mere mythic framework, return us right to its most pressing engagements with contemporary history. When, a decade later, in even more urgent times, Eliot came to publish his 1933 lectures at the University of Virginia in the pamphlet *After Strange Gods* (1934), he chose as epigraphs two passages, in untranslated Greek and German, which hark back to the configuration here. One is a passage from Theodor Haecker's *Was ist der Mensch?* about 'chaos in "literature"' in 'sick, chaotic times', reflecting 'every disorder in human affairs'. The other, on the title page, is Tiresias' assertion of prophetic accuracy in *Oedipus Rex* (lines 460–2), which Murray translates: 'Cool thine ire / With thought of these, and if thou find that aught / Faileth, then hold my craft a thing of naught'.[13]

The Waste Land is the site of a hermeneutic crisis. That crisis is located in the text's various voices, but also in the reader, whose identity is problematised in the act of reading. Looking into the heart of light, the silence, the reader also knows nothing, remembers nothing, only a heap of broken images in a text which has to be respelt from sibyl's leaves at every reading. Like the Thames-daughter in Section III, the reader at first can 'connect / Nothing with nothing', though the text's hints and echoes stir and mix memory and desire in a perpetual delaying of meaning. The Fisher King's question, 'Shall I at least set my lands in order?', is the reader's problem also. The waste land is a barren tract of meaning, where connections lose themselves in trailing sentences, lapse into silence, incantation or gibberish, ultimately into animal noises and the mad discourse of Hieronymo, Hamlet or Ophelia.

The Old Testament voice of the opening mocks with questions that it knows the reader cannot answer, for 'You cannot say, or guess, for you know only / A heap of broken images'. Such incompetence arises in great part because the reader cannot know who is speaking, but, even more importantly, who the reader is supposed to be. The vocative, whether as command, summons or indictment, is ubiquitous. This is a poem full of insistent buttonholings. Rhetorical questions cast the reader as that generic 'Son of man' interpellated by obsolete discourses to an unexplained historical guilt. If the reader resists, he or she is rudely forced by the direct hailing at the end of Section I, scandalously conflated with the murderer Stetson named, in direct vocative, as 'You! hypocrite lecteur! – mon semblable, – mon frère!' Ostensibly fixed in a subject-position here, the reader is then at once dispossessed as the narrative shifts, plunged into the same volatility as all the other 'personages' in the poem.

When Eliot calls Tiresias 'not indeed a "character"' but 'the most important personage in the poem, uniting all the rest', he is playing on the etymology of *persona* as one who 'speaks out' ('personare') through an actor's mask. The various 'I's of the poem are no more 'characters' than Tiresias: they are simply a medium (in a spiritualist as well as literal sense, like Madame Sosostris) through which the poem speaks. But so is the 'hypocrite lecteur'. In retrospect, the hyacinth girl's sudden rebuke is aimed straight at the reader. The reader is the Gentile or Jew invited to 'Consider Phlebas', commanded to 'Come in under the shadow of this red rock' by the prophet Ezekiel, commanded, like some silent oracle, to 'Speak' by the 'neurotic woman', commissioned by the latter-day sibyl Madame Sosostris to take her message to Mrs Equitone. The plaintive vocative even casts the reader as the 'Sweet Thames', urged to bear with its narrative, 'run softly till I end my song', and as the 'O City city' (line 259) invited to share another confidence. The poem's opening line initiates this interpellation: April itself calls the poem's characters and readers into existence, the transitive participles at the line ends, like memory and desire, beckoning the subject to that which is not yet or awakening regret for what is no more, initiating with that 'forgetful snow' a continuous counterpoint of forgetfulness and recognition.

But if the voice of the text sometimes speaks with vatic authority, it can also disclaim all title to being *the subject supposed to know*. Told at the very beginning by an ostensibly omniscient voice that 'you know only / A heap of broken images', sharing a visionary askesis in which 'I was neither / Living nor dead, and I knew nothing', drawing the blank tarot card signifying 'something . . . / Which I am forbidden to see', by the time of 'What the Thunder Said' it is the reader/addressee who has become the subject-supposed-to-know 'Who is that third who walks always beside you?' Inability to answer becomes an index of guilt, just as ignorance of the right question at the Chapel Perilous condemns the quester to failure.

Hermeneutic anxiety is both form and content of the poem. Everywhere the concept of *knowing* is called in question. Madame

Sosostris may be 'known to be the wisest woman in Europe', but the text treats the claim with ironic disdain. Stetson is 'one I knew'. The woman in 'A Game of Chess' claims 'I never know what you are thinking'. Albert will 'want to know what you done with that money he gave you'; and Lil will 'know who to thank' should Albert desert her. The speaker in 'What the Thunder said' does 'not know whether a man or a woman'. The reader is interpellated to an ignorance like that of Oedipus who exclaims in Murray's 1911 translation, 'Oh, riddles everywhere and words of doubt!' – to which Tiresias replies in bitter reproach, 'Thou wast their best reader long ago' (lines 439–40).

Tiresias is the most appropriate personage to unite all the rest because, as Murray writes in the Preface to his translation of *Oedipus Rex,*

> The character of the professional seer or 'man of God' has in the imagination of most ages fluctuated between two poles. At one extreme are sanctity and superhuman wisdom; at the other fraud and mental disease, self-worship aping humility and personal malignity in the guise of obedience to God. There is a touch of all these qualities, good and bad alike, in Tiresias.[14]

Uniting at one pole Ezekiel and Buddha, at the other the 'famous clairvoyante' Madame Sosostris and the pub's unnamed Cassandra ('if Albert makes off, it won't be for lack of telling'), Tiresias figures forth the poem's definitive aporia, signifying at once too much and too little, leaving the reader to construct a narrative by selection and excision, blindness and insight. Both *lecteur* and *lexis*, reader and read, addresser, addressee and object of the address, implicated in the poem's smooth transitions between 'I', 'you' and 'we', the reader in the end is confirmed in the prisonhouse the text has wrought for him or her.

In its closing moments, however, the poem extricates itself from this new-found complicity, reverting to an 'I/you' relation which leaves the voice of the text the subject-who-knows and the reader the manipulated victim, prevented by the subjunctive from ever entering into full intercourse with power: 'your heart would have responded, when invited' (if invited), 'beating obedient / To controlling hands'. A poem which has shrunk indecisively from any kind of certainty and assurance, which progresses by continually deferring semantic closure, promising to 'end my song' and then sidestepping in displacement after displacement, suddenly, in this quiet dissociation, closes the whole question of mastery, obedience, and control. The last question of a poem overflowing with questions seems addressed not so much to the reader as to itself: 'Shall I at least set my lands in order?'

Unheard words, wasted women

The voice of the Fisher King here has no more status than that of the 'neurotic woman' in 'A Game of Chess'. Both direct hopeless enquiries to some external authority which will endow them with a narrative in which to live. They thus repeat the first unsatisfactory exchange of a poem full of frustrated questions, in the epigraph from Petronius' *Satyricon*. The originating voice of prophecy in *The Waste Land* is not Tiresias at all but the caged Cumaean sibyl. Her confinement is echoed in the closing lines of the poem as we each hear, blindly, the key turn on our own isolation. Not what Tiresias sees but what the sibyl says, then, becomes the context within which all the other utterances of the poem should be interpreted. What she says, however, enters the text only at second-hand, doubly distanced as Greek script within a Latin text, her mediator an unidentified male voice of authority. Even here, at the beginning of this new text, there is then a recessionary citation of other texts, which in their fragmentariness raise questions of power in the very act of citation, and not 'a new start'.

The epigraph may, if we choose, call our attention to a usually unnoticed fact: that the preponderant voices in this poem are the voices of *women*, from Marie, through the hyacinth girl, Madame Sosostris, the 'neurotic woman', the pub gossip, the secretary, the three Thames-daughters, to the murmur of maternal lamentation at the end.[15] The sibyl, supposedly the source of authoritative answers, is asked not what *we* should *do*, but what *she wants*. Each of these female voices, however, is put in its place by a male voice which reports it at second-hand, as the Petronius extract brackets the sibyl's *cri de cœur*. There are no narratives left in which to inscribe memory or desire. The voice of power, of authority, is missing. The voice of the Thunder is not that power: its commands merely provoke a further series of inadequate answers. But the Tiresias who has foresuffered all, for all his bisexuality, remains a stubbornly masculine reporter.

In *Oedipus Rex* the primary role of Tiresias is not to reveal but to withhold meaning, advising Oedipus not to pursue his enquiries. He stands for that dumbfounded trancelike beatitude of which, in the opening sequence of *The Waste Land*, an unidentified but clearly male voice speaks, 'Looking into the heart of light, the silence'. There is a confusion of plenitude and emptiness here, the arms full, the heart full (it would seem), the clarity of 'heart of light' set against the impenetrability of 'the silence':

> Your arms full, and your hair wet, I could not
> Speak, and my eyes failed, I was neither
> Living nor dead, and I knew nothing.

But the dumb blind stupefaction is all retrospective, a kind of indirect reported speechlessness after the male voice has recovered articulacy and control. This the poem does by switching, through the Wagnerian quotation, to the garrulous female chatter of the charlatan Madame Sosostris.

In a poem so much concerned with voice, this silence is significant, and not isolated. There are other stories to be told at this silent heart of the poem, which press upon utterance in that eminently talkative sequence, 'A Game of Chess'. Here, the so-called 'neurotic woman' addresses her companion as she might address an unspeaking seer, a source of power and authority, asking him to 'Speak'. His reply, when it comes, is spoken with all the gnomic ponderous obliquity of an oracle. I have used the phrase 'neurotic woman' because this is how this figure, usually thought to be modelled on Eliot's wife Vivienne, is commonly described. But this designation itself reveals the closed circle of interpretation within which the text moves. The woman is diagnosed, and in the process dismissed, as 'neurotic' in an act of presumptive critical shorthand which prejudges her behaviour from the viewpoint of her morose male companion. The only evidence for such a 'diagnosis' is her echoic, repetitive talkativeness confronting an uncharacteristically silent male. But her 'empty' repetitive speech is actually overburdened with psychic meaning, the index of an anxiety which is the generic condition of a poem where agitated and urgent questionings regularly remain unanswered. Her partner's sinister-toned reply explicitly rejects conversation, his reiterated 'Nothing' picked up by a woman desperate for contact, in a negative reprise of the ecstasy in the Hyacinth garden: 'Do / You know nothing? Do you see nothing? Do you remember / Nothing?'

'Nothing' is the most significant negative uttered by any female literary character, the terse reply of Cordelia in *King Lear*, paternally reproved with the (as it turns out) grossly incorrect prophecy: 'Nothing will come of nothing'. But it is also how the sibylline discourse of another Shakespearian woman repressed by male discourse is dismissed in *Hamlet*. The words of the mad Ophelia are recalled overtly at the end of 'A Game of Chess', in the pub's closing farewells: 'good night, sweet ladies'. But echoed without recognition here and elsewhere, Ophelia's sibylline madness meets in *The Waste Land* the same cavalier dismissal that greets it in *Hamlet*: 'Her speech is nothing'. Like that of Philomel, the sibyl, or any other oracle, or the poem itself, it is also capable of being properly interpreted by the right 'hypocrite lecteur':

> Yet the unshaped use of it doth move
> The hearers to collection; they yawn at it,
> And botch the words up fit to their own thoughts,

> Which as her winks and nods and gestures yield them
> Indeed would make one think there might be thought,
> Though nothing sure, yet much unhappily.
>
> (IV, v, 7–13)

Which is a fairly good description of how the poem also works, inviting the reader to inscribe his or her own thought upon the nods and winks of the text, where nothing is sure and only 'nothing' *is* sure. When one of the Thames-daughters concludes 'On Margate Sands. / I can connect / Nothing with nothing', echoes reverberate in a readerly *mise-en-abyme*. Women are either mute in this poem or (like the chatter in the pub which seems intended primarily simply to say 'I am here') speak in such a way that their language is not authoritative and authorising, leading on to action, but performative, uttering primarily itself. As such, it can be easily dismissed by the voice of power as a 'neurotic' call for attention.

The questions, ' "What shall I do now? What shall I do?. . . . / What shall we do tomorrow? / What shall we ever do?" ', echo Eliza Doolittle's recriminations, 'What am I fit for? What have you left me fit for? Where am I to go? What am I to do? What's to become of me?', in Act IV of Bernard Shaw's *Pygmalion* (1912). This intertext has not, to my knowledge, ever been observed, though as the figure of female speech totally controlled by male authority it is clearly of crucial significance for the poem. (Pygmalion's Galatea, of course, is originally all body, a marble statue.) In *The Waste Land* women are listened to only when they use a carnal discourse heavy with sexuality, like the woman who 'drew her long black hair out tight / And fiddled whisper music on those strings'. This explains, perhaps, the odd crossover in 'A Game of Chess' from the physical (and for Eliot always erotic) act of a woman brushing her hair to the idea of speech:

> Under the firelight, under the brush, her hair
> Spread out in fiery points
> Glowed into words, then would be savagely still.

The formulae here develop the immediately preceding allusion to Ovid's fable of 'the change of Philomel, by the barbarous king / So rudely forced'. After her rape by Tereus, and his tearing out of her tongue to prevent her telling of his crime, Philomel was translated into a nightingale which 'Filled all the desert with inviolable voice', a perennial symbol of the disinterested, referentless discourse of poetry. Emptiness and fullness converge as the nightingale fills all the desert – the waste and desolate space – with a voice which says nothing and says everything. Far from being pure utterance empty of semantic content, which cannot be violated by *meaning*, however, the nightingale's voice like the 'neurotic woman''s is overfull. It perpetually names, in its inviolacy, the agent of its violation, 'Tereu'.

If discourse is power, what *The Waste Land* repeatedly offers is the identification of the female with a mute, incommunicable atrocity, a suspension of discourse which calls all into question, like the sibyl who knows too much and wishes only to die – the terminal condition, for Nietzsche, of an over-intellectualised civilisation. The women of this poem all foregather round the concept of voice and its repression. The sibyl, like the uncredited prophetess Cassandra, is promptly dismissed; so is Madame Sosostris, by a text that casts her as a charlatan, even though her prediction is fulfilled in 'Death by Water'.

These female voices are disembodied, undescribed, pure utterance. They emerge abruptly from the text and sink back into it. They crave, and lack, audiences, like the wind that crosses the brown land 'unheard' in III. They have no addresses, like the departed nymphs, though, like the Thames-daughters, they may remember the names of the places where they were born and undone. The silence descends again in Section V after all the shouting and crying and prison, palace and reverberation and amidst the 'murmur of maternal lamentation'. These are not women at the centres of discursive power, but witnesses and victims of it, standing on the margins, looking on, being read to and narrated. Philomel's mute, mutilated tongue is quite literally a 'withered stump of time'. When women speak, like the 'neurotic woman' they merely echo the discourse of the male.

The story of Tiresias' bisexuality in the passage from Ovid Eliot cites is followed immediately by the story of Echo and Narcissus (earlier drafts of 'Death by Water' were called 'The Death of St Narcissus'). The male Narcissus drowns in his own reflection. The nymph Echo, wasting away in love for him, turns into mere echo and repetition, a secondary and fading copy of the originating male voice.[16] In the last section, the word 'empty' is used three times, in each case of places where voices echo without significance, singing out of empty cisterns, wind singing in an empty chapel, obituaries and memories which reveal nothing when the seals are broken in empty rooms, and Echo makes her final appearance as the 'aethereal rumours' which briefly revive a broken Coriolanus. At the heart of light lies the silence of an empty signifier. At the very moment that the subject tries to grasp significance, it slips elsewhere, leaving the chapel empty, the prison confirmed. Even as the lean solicitor breaks the will's seal in our empty rooms, a subtext out of Webster slanders the female legatees who will 'remarry / . . . ere the spider / Make a thin curtain for your epitaphs' (a double instance of men having the last word).

To read this poem against its phallogocentric grain is to see Eliot's misogyny not as a personal grumble but as an historic contestation of voices in the very fabric of his text. The liberation of the female voice, as in those lyric, erotic vignettes that precede the poem's final disintegration into the rags and scraps of discourse, offers the real and original 'new start', for all those dissatisfied questions and frustrated narratives from which it is constructed. We encounter the suppression of speech everywhere in Eliot's poetry, from the epigraph of 'Prufrock' onwards. It is deeply intertwined with an idea of female sexuality, whether in the unuttered love song of that poem or the tongue-tied tergiversations of 'Portrait of a Lady'. In retrospect, the 'word within a word, unable to speak a word' of 'Gerontion' can be seen to presage the (positively valorised) repressed discourse of the female in 'Ash Wednesday', where the 'Word . . . unspoken, unheard' is that of a woman who 'bent her head and signed but spoke no word'. 'Little Gidding' explains how the oracles of the dead converge with this theme in *The Waste Land*, for 'what the dead had no speech for, when living, / They can tell you, being dead'.

Mythical methods and narrative communities

The Waste Land constructs an empty space where the perpetual recession of echoes, quotations within quotations, refuses the reader any *point d'appui* in discourse. Petronius' sibyl sets the agenda. Marie recalls the command of her cousin the archduke, in the process identifying herself simply as the object of male address, as does the hyacinth girl. Lil and Albert are named, but not the speaker or her audience. Madame Sosostris' seance hovers between direct and indirect reported speech. It ends by commissioning a future conversation which may or may not occur. Stetson is hailed only in recollection, as are those improbable questions which report only one side of the dialogue. Tiresias quotes the secretary's one dismissive line on her encounter with the house agent's clerk. Mr Eugenides' proposition is recounted in indirect summary. The second Thames-daughter embeds within her story an isolated and telling phrase from a past encounter: 'After the event / He wept. He promised "a new start". / I made no comment. What should I resent?' The rhetorical question expects no comment from us either. The 'promise' is a futile performative act to which she is indifferent, merely words promising an imaginary future he, she and now we know it cannot deliver.

In the pub one woman speaks to another of their mutual friend. But the real signifier is 'Lil's husband', a soldier returning from the old men's war, to become once more the centre of discourse. Like the nightingale, the speaker seems almost to be talking to herself, in a monologue which merely masquerades as a dialogue and offers a précis of several earlier conversations, direct reported speech within direct reported speech. The half line 'He did, I was there' leaves unclear whether it is said now to her immediate audience, or is reported from a past conversation with Lil. What we overhear is a narrative in which we have to supply the missing links, as in the larger poem. Original events disappear in their perpetual discursive recycling, reported speech swallowing up the moment reported and the moment of reporting alike in its auditory *mise-en-abyme.*

Just as we do not know from one moment to another who is speaking, until they announce themselves either directly ('I Tiresias', over-insistently, three times) or by quoting others ('He said, "Marie, / Marie"'), so, here, we do not know from one moment to the next what we are hearing direct and what at second- or third-hand. The reader must disentangle what exchanges are the *content* of the conversation, and what the *form* of it. Narrative suffers from a radical indeterminacy. From moment to moment we find ourselves slipping in and out of subject positions, unsure of whether the voice we identify with is that of the subject of the *énonciation*, the narration, or of the *énoncé*, the narrated. It is in the empty space between the two that the waste land is located.

Madame Sosostris is at least clairvoyant in this. 'If', she says in a careful conditional of their mutual friend, 'you see dear Mrs Equitone, / Tell her I bring the horoscope myself: / One must be so careful these days'. Between the commission and the act, falls the shadow. It falls precisely in that area where speech is reported, asks to be reported, and gets transformed on the way from 'I', 'you', or 'we' to a collective impersonal pronoun, 'one'. 'One' consorts with the conditional again in the final section, flickering fitfully out of a series of 'we's at a moment when the subject seems about to succumb to the hypnotic impersonality of the repeated 'there is not'. The personalised, communal 'we' exists only in the conditional, and it is only here that we encounter agency. The indicative in which 'one' exists, by contrast, is dominated by the negation of all acts and presences:

> If there were water we should stop and drink
> Among the rocks one cannot stop or think
> Sweat is dry and feet are in the sand
> If there were only water amongst the rock
> Dead mountain mouth of carious teeth that cannot spit . . .

The narrative draws 'us' on in a place where 'one' cannot stop or think. The text becomes that compelling desert in which the subject has no time to recollect, re-collect, itself. 'We' becomes 'one' before dispersing into a bundle of features, sweat, feet, mouth, impulsion. 'Dead mountain mouth' seems to be a surreal metaphoric description of the landscape, its rocks like dead teeth in a dried mouth. But it could just as well apply literally to the dry mouth of the speaker. 'Mouth' and 'mountain' metaphorise each other in both directions, each becoming in turn the tenor for the other's vehicle.

The subject disappears into an hallucinatory sense of place. The reader, absorbed into that 'we', shares in the distress of this dissolution; shares, too, in the paradox that, as the narrative proceeds, it speaks of not being able to speak, of a mouth that cannot utter. Yet, as the text says, there is no silence here. In the beatific silence of Section I a voice recalled: 'I was neither / Living nor dead, and I knew nothing'. Here, by contrast, 'He who was living is now dead / We who were living are now dying'. 'The shouting and the crying' were utterances that, gerunds without agents, broke free of their utterers as empty noise. Now language degenerates into sneers and snarls, mere contortions of the face. Finally, language as meaning gives way to a fantasy that it is the landscape rather than the human subject that sings: cicada, dry grass, water and hermit-thrush, empty cisterns and exhausted wells.

Nevertheless, this section *is* about utterance. It is called 'What the Thunder said'. There will be speech, but it will issue not from the narrating subject but from the landscape, as, in the opening, it was April which initiated action, to which human subjects reluctantly responded. At the end, the poem returns to the question raised in the opening accumulation of sibyls, prophets, clairvoyants. The interpretation of omens such as thunder and the flight of birds has been the role of the seer or shaman, as Frazer reports, from the beginning of things. In this section, which Eliot wrote, almost as a piece of automatic writing,[17] the subject is reconstructed as the medium through which a series of questions reopen onto the world of discourse. Voices begin to sing out of empty cisterns and exhausted wells. Meaning is reconstituted on the other side of meaninglessness. The whispers which picked the bones of Phlebas become the 'whisper music' fiddled on a woman's long black hair, before passing on to become the 'ethereal rumours' that revive for a moment a broken Coriolanus.

Tiresias' association with the voice of the Thunder may be explained by a review Pound wrote in *The New Freewoman* (15 November 1913) of Allen Upward's *The Divine Mystery*, an anthropological study of a Nigerian 'wizard' known as the 'Lord of the Thunder'. In a time of drought, Pound wrote, he will be seen travelling to a place apparently to summon the thunder, though in fact the thunder has summoned him, for he possesses a preternatural sensitivity which can read from the atmosphere when and where the thunder is coming. Pound's lengthy quotation from Upward is a possible mediation between the Tiresias of *The Waste Land*, journeying towards Emmaus or the Chapel Perilous, and the idea of the artist in 'Tradition' as a catalyst, the inert agency of change:

> The secret of genius is sensitiveness. The Genius of the Thunder who revealed himself to me could not call the thunder, but he could be called by it. He was more quick than other men to feel the changes of the atmosphere; perhaps he had rendered his nervous system more sensitive still by fasting or mental abstraction; and he had learned to read his own symptoms as we read a barometer. So, when he felt the storm gathering round his head, he put on his symbolical vestment, and marched forth to be its Word, the archetype of all Heroes in all Mysteries.[18]

Tiresias has cultivated his sensitivity in foresuffering all, and journeys to that mysterious place where the oracular thunder will speak, releasing meaning like a flood. He is called, though he appears to be calling. Like the individual talent of 'Tradition', he has made his mind 'a receptacle for seizing and storing up numberless feelings, phrases, images, which remain there until all the particles which can unite to form a new compound are present together', depersonalising himself until he is 'a more finely perfected medium in which special, or very varied, feelings are at liberty to enter into new combinations'. His impotence then is the necessary condition for the role of 'catalyst', itself 'apparently unaffected . . . inert, neutral and unchanged' by what it changes. The word 'medium', though here predominantly scientific, carries with it a shamanistic resonance of the sense in which Madame Sosostris is a 'medium', the channel through which supernatural communications flow, a sense more obviously present in Eliot's second use of the term:

> The point of view which I am struggling to attack is perhaps related to the metaphysical theory of the substantial unity of the soul. . . . the poet has, not a 'personality' to express, but a particular medium, which is only a medium and not a personality, in which impressions and experiences combine in peculiar and unexpected ways.

If Tiresias is a medium, a prophet or diviner, it is because his own life is a compendium of all those ordinary men and women whose mute or garrulous hysteria confronts us at every turn in the text. 'The Metaphysical Poets' proposes that 'the ordinary man's experience is chaotic, irregular, fragmentary', while 'in the mind of the poet these experiences are always forming new wholes'. Tiresias' doubleness lies in his being simultaneously the man who suffers and the artist who creates. Foresuffering all, a rootless victim of the modern wilderness, he is also that Lord of the Thunder who can focus and deliver the whole of the past, not as a heap of broken images, but as the synchronic, 'ideal order' from Homer until now. His 'significance' arises from 'his relation to the dead poets and artists', and 'You must set him . . . among the dead'. Tiresias himself of course has 'walked among the lowest of the dead'.

In the *Upanishads*, 'DA' is the oracular answer the Creator as lord of thunder gives to three groups of questioners, each of which interprets it differently, according to the three readings the poem offers: 'Give, Sympathise, Control'. Grover Smith has suggested[19] that the repeated 'Da' recalls the Dadaism which Eliot had called 'a diagnosis of a disease of the French mind' early that year in the essay on 'The Lesson of Baudelaire'.[20] Eliot also spoke of Dadaism, however, in his essay on 'Ulysses, Order and Myth' in 1923, refuting the idea that Joyce was 'a prophet of chaos', releasing a 'flood of Dadaism . . . at the tap of the magician's rod'. Instead Joyce restores the 'classical' mode in the face of 'chaos', which is not the same as 'selecting only mummified stuff from a museum'.

In its equivocation, like all true oracles, the Thunder's 'DA DA' can be interpreted in any way the questioner is predisposed to desire. It is in fact both chaos and cure, invoking not only the cultural bolshevism of Dada, but the Name of the Father, to which all the children's voices of *The Waste Land*, 'chantant dans la coupole', must finally be subordinated, if order is to be restored. Control, setting in order, are the priorities dictated at the end of the poem. Joyce's method has the same end in view, according to Eliot. It has recognised that, in the modern world, the old narrative forms are obsolete. For these, it substitutes 'the mythical method':

> in manipulating a continuous parallel between contemporaneity and antiquity. . . . simply a way of controlling, of ordering, of giving a shape and a significance to the immense panorama of futility and anarchy which is contemporary history. . . . a method for which the horoscope is auspicious.

The poem repeatedly tries to return us to the origins, imagining in its overlaying of myths an ur-narrative that will take up these fragments and make them branches of a single root that clutches. In the reversion to Sanskrit, language itself promises an infolding of meanings, as all the varied Indo-European dialects uttered in the text return to that ancient root, 'DA' as if to the original mother-tongue. Sanskrit, however, is not a living tongue at all, but a fossilised sacred script. An archaic *writing*, always-already subsequent to and substituting for an originary event, takes precedence over all the desperately transient *voices* with which the poem closes. It is not polyphony which prevails, but the spiritual Police of a monologistic if variously interpreted scripture. The vision of a heart 'obedient / To controlling hands', the wish to 'set my lands in order' in *The Waste Land* then express a call to order which is both aesthetic and political, timelessly traditional and urgently contemporary: 'Instead of narrative method, we may now use the mythical method. It is, I seriously believe, a step toward making the modern world possible for art, toward that order and form. . . .' The 'narrative method' has failed us. The 'mythical method', even as it reverts to the origins, is the 'modern' way of coping with a world in which the grand narratives of bourgeois civilisation have gone down in the mud of Flanders and disappeared into the wilderness of mirrors at Versailles.

In an essay in *The Dial* in January 1921, Pound makes the same relation between traditional narrative and a superseded social order, and describes the modern approach in terms which elucidate Eliot's overlaying of parallels:

> The life of a village is narrative . . . you have not been there three weeks before you know that in the revolution et cetera, and when M. le Comte et cetera, and so forth. In a city the visual impressions succeed each other, overlap, overcross, they are cinematographic.[21]

Pound's reworking of Eliot's manuscript repeatedly truncates and dislocates classical narrative, excising the account of a drunken night on the town, the description of the lady's toilet, the tale of a sailing expedition and the death of St Narcissus. Pound's cuts created from Eliot's raw material an overlapping, overcrossing of discourses sundered from their narrative contexts. *The Waste Land* takes various narratives of transformation and development and disrupts them. It opens with a refusal of one narrative momentum, that of Chaucer's *Canterbury Tales*, rejecting the invitation to a pilgrimage of tale-telling such as that collection offers. The story of Tiresias offers, not an Ovidian frame for a sequence of tales, but a context in which various narratives fail to reach their conclusion – even, at times, to make themselves heard. Similarly, the Grail Quest loses it way, circling back on itself like all those other circling figures of the text. The poem ends where it started, always about to begin, with a question which has no more authority and dignity in the text than those earlier, desperate questions, ' "What shall I do now? What shall I do?" ', generalised into a collective anxiety: ' "What shall we do tomorrow? / What shall we ever do?" ' All the voices of *The Waste Land* are uprooted from a narrative community which would make sense of and give substance to their personal narratives. This is the modern wilderness Nietzsche decried, redeemable only by a return to the origin, to that Dionysiac flood from which the individuated subject is a belated extrusion. At the end of 'Tradition and the Individual Talent', Eliot observes that the poet 'is not likely to know what is to be done . . . unless he is conscious not of what is dead, but of what is already living'. The desperate refrain that runs through *The Waste Land* asks repeatedly that urgently modern question: 'What is to be done?'

Foxes in waste places

An aside in 'Ulysses, Order and Myth', citing Thackeray's comment that thinking of Swift 'is like thinking of an empire falling', indicates what meta-narrative community *The Waste Land* seeks to manufacture from the materials at hand. The vision of empires falling is ubiquitous in the poem. Eliot himself, in citing Hesse, points us towards this vitally contemporary theme, which is also, as the poem's many allusions indicate, a perennial one. It is now many years since David Craig, in a seminal essay, first and briefly called our attention to the poem's fraught relation with the Russian Revolution.[22] I do not intend here to rerun that argument, but rather to extend the connection, in the light of what we now know of the poem's origins from the original draft and Eliot's letters, to show how integrally related it is to the whole emotional and referential infrastructure of the poem.

Eliot's notes tell us that one of the themes of Part V is 'the present decay of eastern Europe', and the quotation from Hesse elucidates the lines about maternal lamentations and hooded hordes swarming over endless plains. The original lines in the *Waste Land* draft asked 'Who are those hooded hordes swarming / Over Polish plains'. When these lines were written in 1920–1, there was only one answer: the Red Army, which had swept across the Ukrainian and Polish steppes right to the gates of Warsaw, and was only turned back there by Pilsudski's national army in a counter-offensive that led in February–March 1921 to a peace settlement at Riga. In November 1920, the Civil War in Russia came to an end with a qualified victory for the Bolsheviks. An early draft of the lines just before this, ending with the voices chanting out of cisterns and wells, contained an equally explicit contemporary reference:

> A man lay flat upon his back, and cried
> 'It seems that I have been a long time dead:
> Do not report me to the established world.
> The world has seen strange revolutions since I died.
> It has seen strange revolutions: let me bide.'[23]

These 'revolutions' are literal as well as metaphoric translations, transmigrations of power. That list of unreal cities towards the end of *The Waste Land* tells a series of historical downfalls, in which city after city is deposed from power, reduced to servitude by its successor states. Jerusalem was destroyed in that Babylonish Captivity evoked in the echo of the first part of the poem, and destroyed again by the Romans a few years after that journey to Emmaus the poem recounts. Athens decayed after the Peloponnesian war and the rise of Alexander, becoming the backwater of several empires. Alexander's Alexandria, built on the remains of a conquered Egypt, was a cosmopolitan, polyglot capital, a 'cauldron' or melting-pot of Greek, Jewish and Egyptian cultures, before it became a provincial outpost of Rome.

The drowning of Phlebas the Phoenician may be a repeated, mythic act, but it can also be given an accurate historical date, for we can reasonably assume that he was a casualty of that battle of Mylae in which Stetson and the speaker also fought. In the synchronic order of this poem it may be a battle that took place last year. In fact it was fought in 260 BC off the north coast of Sicily – hence the reference to Phlebas entering the whirlpool, for classical sources identified Odysseus' Charybdis with the treacherous currents of the straits of Messina, over which Mylae stands guard.[24] This was no ordinary naval encounter, but the first sea victory of an expanding Roman Republic over the seagoing Carthaginians (originally Phoenicians), a victory in which the future destruction of Carthage – burning, burning – was already inscribed. Four years later, the Roman legions came for the first time to the very gates of Carthage, thereby laying the foundations of their Mediterranean empire. Phlebas dies in 260 BC therefore so that Augustine, whose words close 'The Fire Sermon', might come in 370 AD to a thoroughly Romanised Carthage, lustfully burning. Augustine was himself to address the issue of burning cities in a more literal sense, imagining in his *Civitas Dei* a heavenly Eternal City after Alaric the Goth had sacked the earthly city of Rome in 411 AD.[25]

Vienna, capital of a polyglot Austro-Hungarian Empire dismantled at Versailles, from which Jewish capital in the figure of Bleistein, 'Chicago Semite Viennese', has already fled, is the latest metropolis to fall in this succession of strange revolutions. As we have seen in Chapter 1, in a letter to his mother in December 1919 which mentions his new year resolution 'to write a long poem I have had on my mind for a long time', Eliot wrote of the current collapse of Central Europe: 'the destitution, especially the starvation in Vienna, appears to be unspeakable. I suppose Americans realise now what a fiasco the reorganisation of nationalities has been: the "Balkanisation" of Europe'.[26] Less than three weeks later (6 January 1920) he returned to the theme:

> I wonder if America realises how terrible the condition of central Europe is. I can never ~~forget~~ quite put Vienna out of my mind. And I have seen people who have been in Germany and they are most pessimistic about the future, not only of Germany, but of the world.[27]

With revolution sweeping through a crumbling Europe, even London, the heart of an Empire broken but not defeated by the Great War, may not long remain exempt. On 27 April 1921, with the poem already under way, Eliot wrote reassuringly to his mother, who was planning to visit him from the United States, to confirm that one 'cruellest month' had weathered its crisis, and 'The danger of a general strike is over. So do not be apprehensive. . . . The temper of England is not revolutionary – it is only in Scotland that we see some manifestations of that spirit.'[28] *The Waste Land* itself is much less sanguine about the prospects of this latest unreal city, racked by social and political discontent, its crowds already ghostly. London last appears in the poem, immediately after the Fisher King's desperate question, not as Spenser's or Shakespeare's vital city, but in the ragged inauspicious incoherence of a playground chant from the lower orders: 'London Bridge is falling down falling down falling down'.

Eliot's text carries in its allusive interstices an apostolic succession of imperial discourses, to be recovered from the heaps of broken images which mark the end of every particular empire. Its metempsychoses, its fugues and flights of the soul, parallel Ovid's tales of metamorphosis with a multitude of emigrations, departures, migrations, evacuations, demobbings, exiles, restless voyagings over land and sea, nymphs and loitering heirs of city directors who have departed, leaving no addresses. A ghostly crowd flows over London Bridge. Tiresias walks among the lowest of the dead, not only in many cities but through many texts, Homer, Sophocles, Euripides, Virgil, Ovid, Dante. Augustine comes to Carthage, the speaker to Lac Leman, his very words to describe this journey migrating across millennia and languages to recall an ancient exile in Babylon.

Texts also migrate. Lines of Spenser or Shakespeare or Marvell or Goldsmith mutate into Eliot's lines in 'The Fire Sermon', as ballads and popular songs migrate from England to Australia and back again, and ideas and myths flip from language to language. Music creeps by on the water, in a phrase which itself has crept in from elsewhere, as oil and tar and rubbish drift on the river. Augustine's words are displaced by those of another spiritual pilgrim, Buddha. Eliot's notes, by insisting on *translation*, return this now linguistic concept into a spatial and political one, *trans-latio*, carrying from one place to another, a crossing of frontiers.

As with the Grail, if we know what questions to ask, a flood of contemporary reference can be struck by the magician's rod from the rock of *The Waste Land*. 'Mr Eugenides, the Smyrna merchant' has a pure Greek name ('well-born') which mocks his suspect ethnic roots in that cosmopolitan entrepot and 'cauldron of unholy lusts', Smyrna. Smyrna, in 1920–1, is more than an ancient Greek trading colony on the coast of Asia Minor. A Turkish city with half a million Greek inhabitants (about half the population) it was in 1920 ceded to Greece for a trial five years at the Treaty of Sèvres. The 'Young Turk' successors to the Ottoman Empire began military operations against the Greeks in

June. By the time *The Waste Land* was published in October 1922, Ataturk's armies had thrown the Greeks into the sea, and Greek Smyrna had become Turkish Izmir.[29] Not only is Mr Eugenides, then, another displaced person, but the city of 'Smyrna' is itself 'dis-placed', another unreal city.

One of the most cryptic, because apparently inconsequential, citations of the poem is unusual in lacking a literary source. A solitary, contextless German sentence stands, isolated by full stops and by its own linguistic egregiousness, foursquare in the opening sequence as a foretaste of all the confusion to come: 'Bin gar keine Russin, stamm' aus Litauen, echt deutsch.' The line foregrounds the relation of language to political power, in a threefold fragmentation of linguistic identity which problematises nationality. Assiduous researchers have traced a source in the memoirs of Marie Larisch (cousin of Archdukes and of the mad, drowned Wagnerian, Ludwig II of Bavaria), whom Eliot had met, possibly in Lausanne.[30]

Marie's closeness to the centres of pre-war imperial power is significant; but the significance is supplied by the poem itself, and hardly needs further elucidation. The sentence remains essentially sourceless, without resources, displaced like its speaker from the linguistic and social context that would give it meaning. These are words plucked from the air of a wintry Lausanne, the passing breath of trivial conversations, without literary resonance. Nevertheless, they speak with the true voice of post-war Europe. What they announce is a double dispossession parallel to that of the 'well-born' Mr Eugenides. As Marie proclaims her class, ethnic and linguistic purity she simultaneously reveals her real deracination, belonging to no community, sundered triply by language, race and politics: 'I am not Russian, I am from Lithuania, pure German.'

'A real aristocracy is essentially of the same blood as the people over whom it rules: a real aristocracy is not a Baltenland aristocracy of a foreign race', Eliot wrote in 1923.[31] Lithuania gained its independence from the Russian Empire along with Poland and the other Baltic states at Versailles in 1919. Its 'Baltenland aristocracy', administrative and middle classes, however, were neither Russian nor native Lithuanians but largely descended from medieval East Prussian colonisers: *echt deutsch*. Richard M. Watt describes the situation in the Baltic lands at the time of the Treaty of Versailles thus:

> In these impoverished lands the Germans controlled the bulk of all wealth and constituted the majority of the educated population. Like the old Teutonic Knights, the Baltic Germans jealously preserved their racial strain. They would enter the service of the Russian tsars, and they eagerly accepted Russian titles of nobility, but they regarded the native Baltic

peoples with disdain. The Germans married among themselves, spoke their own language. . . . The German landowners . . . held their peasantry in ravenous bondage.[32]

Confronted by nationalist movements and an insurgent Communism, and 'Fearing the native populations, these Baltic Germans now wrapped themselves tightly in their national cloak and became, if possible, more German than before' (p. 417). The insistence on being 'echt deutsch', then, is not an innocent pride in nationality but an assertion of social and racial superiority over both Slav and Lett. The speaker is a member of that 'Baltenland aristocracy of a foreign race' which fled in droves before the advancing Red Army in 1919, whom Watt describes gathering in such cities as Munich, 'embittered refugees [who] set themselves up as experts on the "Judaeo-Bolshevik menace" from the east' (p. 419).

One brief enigmatic sentence, a sibylline utterance in its own right, raises the whole issue of ethnicity, nationality and language at the heart of European politics for the next two decades, and augurs that revolutionary disintegration described by Hermann Hesse. The context of such statements is supplied, not by tradition, but by the futility and anarchy of contemporary history. When the Fisher King speaks of setting his lands in order under the banner of Parsifal his dream differs little from that, for example, of The Hamburg *Freikorps*, who pillaged under the banner of the medieval Hanseatic League, warriors of a new order recruited throughout Germany after 1918 to put down an insurgent working class which looked to Petrograd for its political models. As Watt records:

> The age-old lure of the Baltic was reinforced by the tale of free 'estates' to be had for the taking. And for those to whom this did not appeal there was the role of the modern-day Teutonic Knight forcing back the pagan forces of Slavic Bolshevism which menaced Germany's borders. Recruiting posters showed a pack of ravaging wolves, their jowls dripping blood, racing across a map of Germany's eastern frontiers. The message beneath read, 'Germans, defend the Fatherland from Russian Bolshevism'. (p. 423)

The Waste Land was finalised in Lausanne in December 1921, though it appears to open in April – at the latest, April 1921, during which, as Eliot's letter to his mother records, Britain had faced 'the danger of a general strike'. Lil's husband was probably demobbed in early 1919. The Baltic Germans fled from Lithuania to Munich with the retreating German Eighth Army in January 1919, before an advancing Red Army. If it is Marie who speaks the lines about April, then she spent at least the previous summer (1920) in Munich and on the Starnbergersee in Bavaria, before moving south for the winter. The April which led this émigrée Baltic German to regard it as 'the cruellest month' is likely, however, to be a year earlier, in 1919.

After the Armistice in November 1918, revolution swept through the armies and working classes of the defeated nations, sweeping away the *anciens régimes* overnight. In the spring of 1919, a second wave of Bolshevik-style soviets sprang up throughout Germany and the former Austro-Hungarian Empire. In early 1919 the tide had turned in the Civil War which followed the Russian Revolution and, despite one or two reverses, from then on through to the summer of 1920, the Red Army swept victoriously westward, entering Poland in late July, halted only at the gates of Warsaw in mid-August, when it still seemed possible that the eastern and western wings of Bolshevism might meet up. The first Bavarian Revolution had begun in November 1918. On 4 April 1919, a second revolution, proclaiming direct allegiance to the newly instituted Third International, erupted on the streets of Munich (the city where Eliot had completed 'Prufrock' in 1911). In the winter of 1921 in Lausanne, the 'city over the mountains' that had recently 'cracked and reformed and burst in the violet air', could well be Munich, the capital of a Bolshevik Soviet which was crushed on May Day, 1919 by the same *Freikorps* battalions who had been laying waste the Baltic states.

As the émigrée Baltic German lady knows, political frontiers, linguistic maps and national allegiances do not coincide in the Europe relocated by Versailles and its successor treaties. In 1928 Eliot was to note in his essay 'Religion Without Humanism' that 'The problem of nationalism and the problem of dissociated personalities may turn out to be the same'.[33] This is the 'continuous parallel' which the mythical method allows *The Waste Land* to effect, converting a prolonged personal grumble into the requiem for a civilisation. Overlaying and merging Carthage, Rome (by implication), Jerusalem, Athens, Alexandria, Vienna, London, all at one time or another imperial metropoles, in the modern Lausanne of 1921, the poem reproduces at the political level that frightening volatility suffered by its dissolute 'personages'. If cities and selves merge into and slide through each other in this poem, this only reproduces the shifting, malleable, interpenetrating frontiers of a Europe in post-war flux. No more than narrative communities do speech communities have a common political identity. 'The Function of Criticism' in 1923 remarks that what is at issue in the whole debate about tradition is 'essentially a problem of order', of ' "organic wholes", as systems in relation to which, and only in relation to which, individual works . . . have their significance'.[34] The text's critical preoccupations directly transpose political imperatives of the day about the need to reconstruct, in a fragmenting Europe, 'organic' national and cultural identities.

What *The Waste Land* laments is the loss of that cultural–political homogeneity which Eliot was to advocate in his lectures at the University of Virginia in 1933, published as *After Strange Gods*.[35] Eliot's desiderata here consciously spell out the implications of 'Tradition and the Individual Talent' (p. 15), and they identify precisely what is absent from the modern waste land: 'at least some recollection of a "tradition", such as the influx of foreign populations has almost effaced' (p. 15), 'the re-establishment of a native culture' only possible for a people 'less industrialised and less invaded by foreign races' (p. 16), 'in which the landscape has been moulded by numerous generations of one race', traditional forms, including taboos, 'which represent the blood kinship of "the same people living in the same place"' (p. 18). For 'The population should be homogeneous; where two or more cultures exist in the same place they are likely either to be fiercely self-conscious or both to become adulterate' (p. 19). This last word, wakening echoes of the adulteration and miscegenation dreaded in *Poems – 1920*, leads on to his final prerequisite, recalling the anti-Semitic spleen of that volume: 'unity of religious background; and reasons of race and religion combine to make any large number of free-thinking Jews undesirable' (p. 20).

The personages of *The Waste Land*, however, are not so 'quixotic' as to make 'a hopeless stand for a cause which was lost long before they were born' (p. 17). The poem speaks not of reconstruction and restoration but of disintegration and decay, emerging from that moment in which time and space, history and geography, were rewritten and redrawn at Versailles, and post-war frontiers fabricated new and factitious 'organic wholes' and instant national 'traditions' out of Europe's heap of broken images. Against the 'Judaeo-Bolshevik menace from the east' perhaps only some Nietzschean thaumaturge could take a stand, presaged by those 'aethereal rumours' which, in the dying moments of the poem, 'Revive for a moment a broken Coriolanus'. But the overtly Fascist 'Triumphal March' of Eliot's unfinished poem *Coriolan* in the 1930s only half-heartedly remembers that nebulous promise of 'a new start'.

Still paused at the frontier of action in his American lectures ten years later, Eliot remains a morbid, disregarded Tiresias, impotently calling at the end of *After Strange Gods* for the restoration of order in the words of that same Ezekiel who spoke at the beginning of *The Waste Land*. As if offering his last words on that poem, the passage recalls some of its most desperate and familiar moments, in which a rebellious people, beguiled by false prophets, in a waste place full of broken images/idols, know and see nothing, and all enquiries are vain:

'Woe unto the foolish prophets, that follow their own spirit, and have seen nothing! O Israel, thy prophets have been like foxes in the waste places. . . . And the word of the LORD came unto me, saying, Son of man, these men have taken their idols into their hearts, and put the stumbling-block of their iniquity before their face: should I be inquired of at all by them?'[36]

Chapter Eight

Writing a will: Yeats's ancestral voices

Rough beasts

W.B. Yeats wrote to George Russell (AE), probably in April 1919,

> What I want is that Ireland be kept from giving itself (under the influence of its lunatic faculty of going against everything which it believes England to affirm) to Marxian revolution or Marxian definition of value in any form. I consider the Marxian criterion of values as in this age the spearhead of materialism and leading to inevitable murder. From that criterion follows the well-known phrase, 'Can the bourgeois be innocent?'[1]

'The Second Coming', written in January 1919, is, according to Yeats, a poem about 'The end of an age, which always receives the revelation of the character of the next age.' The present era is approaching a cataclysmic reversal, so that

> All our scientific, democratic, fact-accumulating, heterogeneous civilisation ... prepares not the continuance of itself but the revelation as in a lightning flash, though in a flash that will not strike only in one place, and will for a time be constantly repeated, of the civilisation that must slowly take its place.[2]

But if this lightning flash is like that which heralds the birth of Dionysus in *The Bacchae* and *The Waste Land*, Yeats's new age has other, more earthly midwives. According to Yeats's widow, the poem grew from his 'apprehensions about the socialist revolutions in Russia, Germany and Italy during and after World War I'.[3] In the first drafts of the poem, the opening lines are succeeded by the raw statement: 'The Germany of Marx has led to Russian Com[munism] / There every day some innocent has died'.[4]

'The Second Coming' embodies the idea of history as repetition at the level both of language and event. The repetition with which it opens,

152

'Turning and turning', sets up a linguistic routine which continues through the poem, revealed in a parallelism both within and between lines. For all the abstraction with which they are formulated, the key lines still inscribe their particular origin:

> Things fall apart; the centre cannot hold;
> Mere anarchy is loosed upon the world,
> The blood-dimmed tide is loosed, and everywhere
> The ceremony of innocence is drowned.

The first two pithy clauses describe the same event from different points of view (the falcon's and the falconer's respectively). But they also attribute a kind of simultaneous causality to the process: things fall apart *because* the centre cannot hold; the centre cannot hold *because* things fall apart. The next line of a loosely rhyming couplet parallels and repeats the idea, but also carries it forward, translating the active 'cannot hold' into the passive 'is loosed upon'. What can be seen from one perspective as three ways of phrasing the same event can, from another, be seen as a sequential history of imperial collapse, as the metropolis succumbs to its peripheries: first the internal disintegration, then the relinquishing of power at the centre, and finally the loosing of insurgent violence upon an undefended world.

'Mere anarchy' is an abstraction which hovers between cosmology and politics. It becomes more tangible as the emotive 'blood-dimmed tide'. The two processes are revealed to be a single one in the repetition of 'is loosed upon', which converts a metaphor of political control (the feudal, aristocratic grasp of the falconer) into the impersonal image of loosened flood waters, culminating in that powerful 'drowned'. The passive voice, here and throughout, gives the impression of a process in which human agency is no more than a hapless instrument of impersonal, cosmic forces – centripetal forces which in the first four lines seem to equate political rebellion (the falcon's disobedience) with the collapse of gravity itself.

There is a certain rhetorical insistence to the poem, which only half conceals the deep uncertainty in which it is founded:

> Surely some revelation is at hand;
> Surely the Second Coming is at hand.
> The Second Coming! Hardly are those words out
> When a vast image out of *Spiritus Mundi*
> Troubles my sight: somewhere in sands of the desert
> A shape with lion body and the head of a man,
> A gaze blank and pitiless as the sun,
> Is moving its slow thighs, while all about it
> Reel shadows of the indignant desert birds.

The repeated 'Surely' lays claim to more conviction than it warrants. The repeated phrase 'the Second Coming' itself magically calls up the 'vast image' which appears to resolve the status of an utterance poised between question and assertion; but there is nothing in the poem which actually gives this image objective status. The contrast between the blank and pitiless *gaze* of the beast, objective, unseeing, and the subjectively troubled but visionary *sight* of the poet emphasises that revelation is a disturbance of vision. This image which 'Troubles my sight' emerges from *Spiritus Mundi*, the collective unconscious, in Yeats's words 'a general storehouse of images which have ceased to be a property of any personality or spirit'. Though Yeats wishes us to see this 'vast image' as an objective thing, the poem acknowledges that it is something subjectively *imagined* before it can be objectively external- ised, a revelation before it is a coming. Despite the apparent confidence of the assertion 'but now I know', we see that the whole supernatural vision is sustained by a mere rhetorical question which *presumes* that which it merely in fact *posits*: the actual existence of the 'rough beast'.

In the same way, we cannot pin the event down to a real place and time. Its location is vague: '*somewhere* in sands of the desert'. The phrase in the original version in *Michael Robartes* was 'a waste of desert sand'. Its relation to Eliot's wildernesses and waste lands suggest that both poets were drawing on a common apocalyptic theme from Revelation given new meaning by Europe's post-war collapse into anarchy and revolution. 'Is moving its slow thighs' turns into the powerfully physical verb 'slouches', a word which, like 'rough beast', calls up the suppressed class feelings in which the poem originated: proletarians slouch.

The same is true of the reeling desert birds: they are low-class collectivist vultures, set in antithesis to the stately turning of the (aristocratic and solitary) falcon. Carrion not hunting birds, they converge with thankless plebeian indignation upon the beast that will supply their dinners. Though Yeats clearly loathes birds and beast, there is too a sinister attraction in their brutish vitality, concentrated in the verbs, 'reel', 'vexed', 'slouches'. The abstract Latinate vocabulary of the first section, a language of power associated with the Anglo-Norman hegemony which had built Yeats's own tower at Ballylee, 'centre', 'anarchy', 'ceremony', 'innocence', 'conviction', 'passionate', 'intensity', palls beside the immediacy and concreteness of the second. This, the poem tells us, is the brutal reality. In the context in which it was first published in *Michael Robartes and the Dancer* in 1921, the nature of that reality is clear. The poem follows a sequence about the Easter Rising which begins with the annunciation, in 'Easter 1916', that 'A terrible beauty is born', and proceeds, via 'On a Political Prisoner', with its picture of Constance Markiewicz become 'a bitter, an abstract thing, / Her thought some popular enmity', to 'The Leaders of the Crowd', with its revulsion at gutter politicians who 'Pull down established honour; hawk for news / Whatever their loose fantasy invent'. It is immediately preceded by 'Demon and Beast', with its gyring seagull and final dismissal of imperial power, 'What had the Caesars but their thrones?' and followed by 'A Prayer for My Daughter', with its fears of the future the 'roof-levelling wind' brings 'Dancing to a frenzied drum / Out of the murderous innocence of the sea'. The volume concludes with an inscription to be carved on a stone at Thoor Ballylee, recording Yeats's restoration of the tower and his wish that 'these characters remain / When all is ruin once again'.

If the rough beast then represents the 'filthy modern tide' of a proletarian century which will overthrow all custom and ceremony, it possesses too the inhuman archaic majesty of those fabulous beasts Yeats would have passed regularly in the Assyrian Room of the British Museum. The phrase with which the poem ends emphasises that this is a new beginning as well as a (possibly deserved) end, and Christ's rocking cradle, vexing stony sleep to nightmare, is not a positive image of the order about to be overthrown. Yeats's antithetical imagination here reveals what Patrick J. Keane in *Yeats's Interactions with Tradition*[5] calls 'the notoriously conflicted tone of the speaker, his mingled anguish, terror, and exultation'. Yeats's rough beast is the figure of a proletarian insurgency which both terrifies and enthrals; but it also endows 'mere anarchy' with the monumental grandeur of ancient imperial statuary. This is the 'savage god' Yeats predicted would come into his own at the turn of the century. Both halves of the oxymoron have to be given equal weight. Between them they define the ambivalence of Yeats's own politics. As with that shudder in the loins, half divine, half bestial, which violates Leda and fathers Helen of Troy in 'Leda and the Swan', destruction and creation are intimately entwined. Knowledge cannot be separated from power. Time goes on. Unable to help itself, the modern age gives itself to its brutal lover, the rough beast of Marxian revolution and civil war.

Nations formed from least beginnings

Hugh Kenner has pointed out the 'tip to the reader' in the 'parody' of Wordsworth's diction which opens 'The Tower', indicating, he suggests, Yeats's fear and defiance of 'the formula of Wordsworth's decline'.[6] Richard Ellmann, too, stresses the defiance with which Wordsworth is evoked in the closing lines of 'Meditations in Time of Civil War', the poem which immediately follows it in *The Tower*.[7] Neither, however, comments on the double incidence of Wordsworthian echoes, nor considers why Yeats should evoke this most inimical of English poets at the opening and close of these two intricately linked poems, though the occurrence almost places a kind of Wordsworthian parenthesis around the Yeatsian texts. Harold Bloom is equally silent on the matter, simply noting the appropriateness of the second echo.[8]

Since both poems are centrally concerned with the idea of inheritance, with the writing of a will and with writing as that which is willed, the legacy itself, these transactions with the ghost of their Romantic predecessor call for closer scrutiny. The opening section of 'Meditations' is called 'Ancestral Houses'; but what equally preoccupies both poems is the 'ancestral voices' of a literary and political tradition, of which Wordsworth is only one instance. Yeats in these poems conducts what Julia Kristeva has called a 'hidden interior polemic' with the voices of this tradition, in a cunning and complex intertextuality where, 'It is the writer who "speaks", but a foreign discourse is constantly present in the speech that it distorts.'[9]

For Yeats, this 'foreign discourse', like the ancestral voices of Coleridge's opium fragment, is 'prophesying war' – in 1928, the year *The Tower* was published, wars that are 'past, or passing, or to come', in what had increasingly come to seem an era of permanent war and permanent revolution. To be able to read the signs without like Coleridge sinking 'unmanned / Into the half-deceit of some intoxicant', the poet in 'Nineteen Hundred and Nineteen' seeks in the 'ghostly solitude' of 'The half-imagined, the half-written page' a fullness denied him by the 'coming emptiness' of a violent age. 'Any text', says Kristeva, 'is constructed as a mosaic of quotations; any text is the absorption and transformation of another'; thus all 'poetic language is read as at least double'.[10] The text does not merely imitate, allude to, or register the influence of other texts: it exploits the speech of others for its own purposes, following their direction while 'relativising' it.[11] To look closely at these poems of Yeats's is to see how this relativising doubleness plays off the ghostly voices of the past against his own ghostly solitude, the 'ecstasy' of 'tradition' against the forgotten bitter crusts of personal memory.

The last allusion brings us back to Wordsworth, and that passage in *Per Amica Silentia Lunae* where Yeats distinguishes the quarrel with others which makes rhetoric from the quarrel with ourselves which makes poetry. *The Tower* combines both quarrels, pitting the practical man, concerned about the entail of property, against the poet, owing allegiance to that larger, intangible heritage, 'smitten even in the presence of the most high beauty by the knowledge of our solitude'. The sentimentalists, among whom he nearly always numbers Wordsworth,[12] are practical men: 'They find their pleasure in a cup that is filled from Lethe's wharf, and for the awakening, for the vision, for the revelation of reality, tradition offers us a different word – ecstasy.' Such forgetfulness is never more of a temptation than when the poet thinks his vision is achieved:

> A poet, when he is growing old, will ask himself if he cannot keep his mask and his vision without new bitterness, new disappointment. . . . Surely, he may think, now that I have found vision and mask I need not suffer any longer. He will buy perhaps some small old house where like Ariosto he can dig his garden, and think that in the return of birds and leaves, or moon and sun, and in the evening flight of the rooks, he may discover rhythm and pattern like those in sleep and so never awake out of vision. Then he will remember Wordsworth withering into eighty years, honoured and empty-witted, and climb to some waste room and find, forgotten there by youth, some bitter crust.[13]

By tone and rhythm and image this links with *The Tower*, particularly in its celebration of idyllic natural acquiescence in decline. Yet the unexpected juxtaposition of Ariosto and Wordsworth hints that the minatory image of the latter is evoked not simply, as Kenner might suggest, in defiance of his destiny. For Wordsworth and Ariosto have something more in common than, latterly, a desire to cultivate their gardens, and that something they share with many of the other poets evoked in *The Tower*: epic ambitions, the urge to repeat the achievement of Homer, to be the poets of some national political and cultural revival. The obverse of this – that, like Homer, they become the poets of internecine warfare, recording that violence out of which national unity is actually constructed – is the double discourse of all the poems in *The Tower*.

Edward Engelberg has seen the epic ambition as central to Yeats's poetry:

> Yeats's imagination – if not his talent – was primarily neither lyric nor dramatic but epic. Had he lived in another time he might have been a great epic poet. Regardless of how many dreams possessed his life, the earliest and the greatest was to become a modern Homer of Ireland, its mythmaker.[14]

And certainly Yeats's desire to 'get back to Homer', away from 'the literature of the point of view' and his obvious glee at Wilde's comparison of his story-telling to Homer's,[15] reinforce this impression. Yet what characterises the long poems of *The Tower* is the steadfast refusal of the epic mode. The Wordsworth invoked is the author of an autobiographical poem which precisely fails to be an epic: its very title admits to that failure, offering itself as *The Prelude* to a greater work which did not come. Thomas Whitaker hears an echo of Tennyson's 'Ulysses' in Section III of 'The Tower',[16] but, strangely doesn't remark on the even more apposite allusion to 'Morte d'Arthur', and its 'full-breasted swan / That, fluting a wild carol ere her death, / Ruffles her pure cold plumes'. In this poem, the passing of the aged British hero signals 'the end of an age', closing an epoch of prosperity in defeat and civil war. This is a theme much more relevant to the poems of *The Tower*, as, too, is the *Idylls of a King*'s reputation as a failed epic. Similarly, the Milton invoked in Section II of 'Meditations' is the author of 'Il Penseroso', the meditative poet whose own epic of civil war in heaven is still, in 1632, thirty years in the future. In between lies that earthly Civil War which in 'Nineteen Hundred and Nineteen' Yeats saw echoed, for his own generation, in the Great War and the violence of the Black and Tans:

> All teeth were drawn, all ancient tricks unlearned,
> And a great army but a showy thing;
> What matter that no cannon had been turned
> Into a ploughshare? Parliament and king
> Thought that unless a little powder burned
> The trumpeters might burst with trumpeting
> And yet it lack all glory. . . .
> Now days are dragon-ridden. . . .

There is little chance that the Yeats of 1919, or 1923, or 1926, will emulate his blind predecessor: such hopes are 'mere dreams' for men 'Who are but weasels fighting in a hole.' It is the reality of civil war, and not the hope of forging some unitary national image from division, that haunts these poems, and deflects their epic pretensions.

This perhaps explains why *The Prelude* is so repeatedly and perhaps unconsciously echoed in them. For *The Prelude* too is a poem of the 'Imagination . . . impaired and restored', of a man divided in himself, riven by 'outward troubles,' and 'his own uneasy heart' (*The Prelude*, 1850 text, Bk XII, ll. 22–9), giving way 'to overpressure of the times / And their disastrous issues' and fleeing them 'upon the barren sea, / My errand . . . to sail to other coasts' (1805 text, Bk XI, ll. 42–56), as Yeats envisages for himself in 'Sailing to Byzantium', the opening poem of *The Tower*. And for Wordsworth too this self-division is cast in terms derived from that pressing political world: 'Thus strangely did I war against myself; / A bigot to a new idolatry', labouring 'to cut off my heart / From all the sources of her former strength' (1805, Bk XI, ll. 74–8). Initially, Wordsworth had seen in revolutionary France 'a risen people' (the slogan of *Sinn Fein* and the Irish Republican Army):

> How quickly mighty Nations have been formed
> From least beginnings; how, together locked

> By new opinions, scattered tribes have made
> One body, spreading wide as clouds in heaven.
> To aspirations then of our own minds
> Did we appeal; and finally beheld
> A living confirmation of the whole
> Before us, in a people risen up
> Fresh as the morning star.
> (1805, Bk IX, ll. 383–91)

But this vision of a people 'from the depth / Of shameful imbecility uprisen' (1850, Bk IX, ll. 83–4) turned for Wordsworth, as for Yeats later, into a nightmare of 'domestic carnage' (1805, Bk X, l. 330). Wordsworth had greeted this first dawn as Yeats later was to respond to Thoor Ballylee:

> Why should I not confess that Earth was then
> To me what an inheritance, new-fallen,
> Seems, when the first time visited, to one
> Who thither comes to find in it his home?
> He walks about and looks upon the place
> With cordial transport, moulds it and remoulds,
> And is half pleased with things that are amiss.
> 'Twill be such joy to see them disappear.
> (1805, Bk X, ll. 729–36)

Initially 'Not caring if the wind did now and then / Blow keen upon an eminence that gave / Prospect so large into futurity' (1805, Bk X, ll. 751–3), despising those who

> by the recent deluge stupefied,
> With their whole souls went culling from the day
> Its petty promises, to build a tower
> For their own safety
> (1805, Bk X, ll. 620–3)

the rapidly disenchanted Wordsworth could escape from 'the weary labyrinth' of a murderous politics only by recovering that 'office' of Poet, 'no further changed / Than as a clouded, not a waning moon' (1805, Bk X, ll. 916–30), which restored him to the 'converse strong and sanative' of 'The noble Living and the noble Dead' (1850, Bk XI, ll. 394–6). In such company, he recovered a different birthright, for

> Poets, even as Prophets, each with each
> Connected in a mighty scheme of truth,
> Have each for his peculiar dower, a sense
> By which he is enabled to perceive
> Something unseen before.
> (1805, Bk XII, ll 301–5)

Yeats too, of course, seeks consolation for the depravities of politics, the 'blood-dimmed tide' of that stupefying recent deluge, amidst 'changeless work[s] of art', in the bosom of tradition. That the Wordsworthian example is present in his mind is suggested by perhaps the most remarkable, if unremarked, source for 'Meditations' in *The Prelude*, itself an evocation of earlier poets, and most directly, Theocritus:

> I hear thee tell how bees with honey fed
> Divine Comates, by his tyrant lord
> Within a chest imprisoned impiously;
> How with their honey from the fields they came
> And fed him there, alive, from month to month,
> Because the goatherd, blessed man! had lips
> Wet with the Muse's nectar.
>
> (1805, Bk X, ll. 1007–28)

For the later poet, closed in 'the empty house of the stare', with the key turned on his uncertainty, such images, coming all the way from the originary 'fountain' of 'pastoral Arethuse', calling in their train many a 'philosopher or Bard' (including, by name, Empedocles and Archimedes, and by echo and implication, Milton and that Coleridge who had fed on honey-dew to whom *The Prelude* is addressed) constitute an alternative discourse to the ancestral voices prophesying war. Intertextuality here becomes, not only a literary device, but a political strategy, confirming to the isolated Yeats of 'The Stare's Nest by My Window', cut off by local fighting, that he is 'not a captive pining for his home' but a 'gladsome votary' by 'some other spring' than the extinct Arethuse (1805, Bk X, ll. 1029–39). The 'other spring' is, of course, that stream by his door upon which, in the previous section, he has watched the moor-hen guide her young, before turning towards his room, 'caught / In the cold snows of a dream'.

Full and empty men

The ways in which Yeats summons his voices are various. Wordsworth, for example, is never named, merely swims into our mind as an unspecified resonance, a siren cadence signalling difference, danger. Milton is subtly different: unnamed, he is appropriated to the discourses which constitute him: the text of 'Il Penseroso', and Neoplatonism. Chaucer is negated as he is mentioned, half-erased in a historical and comparative placing ('Chaucer had not drawn breath / When it was forged'). Shakespeare enters courtesy of one of his characters, the 'heavily-built Falstaffian man' suggesting a web of contradictory allusions to earlier civil wars resolved to unitary myth by the imagination of the national poet. Raftery, whose song of Mary Hynes invites comparison between him and the equally blind Homer in Section II of 'The Tower', remains anonymous.

Only Homer himself, about whom nothing is known, who may, as Yeats knew, be merely a name for a multitude of anonymous bards, is dignified with the status of a name and a biography. At the same time, Homer is no more than a myth of origins, figuring some originary epic purity from which all subsequent poems are declensions ('the tragedy began / With Homer that was a blind man'). Homer, that is, becomes the primal father, against whom subsequent attempts at epic are a kind of oedipal revolt. For him, imagination and reality were spontaneously consonant, in a primal fullness and self-presence, 'certain beyond dreams', the 'self-delight' from which springs 'The abounding glittering jet'. For his successors, however, the legacy is absence, emptiness, unfulfilment, the 'marvellous empty sea-shell flung / Out of the obscure dark of the rich streams', no more than a 'shadow' of this inherited glory.

Homer is always an ambiguous figure in Yeats's work. He may be the figure of some lost plenitude, but he is also the author of loss ('the tragedy began' with him). In Yeats's observations on the Greeks in *A Vision* the same doubleness obtains.[17] The insurgent Greek tribes, 'after a first multitudinous revelation – dominated each by its *Daimon* and oracle-driven', broke up a great Empire and replaced it with 'intellectual anarchy'. (The verbal parallels here with 'The Second Coming' are instructive.) Yet despite this heterogeneity, usually, for Yeats, linked with the world of 'casual comedy', the Greeks are here seen as 'hurling upon some age of crowded comedy their tragic sense'.

Homer, far from being the bard of an original fullness, comes belatedly, linked with containment and closure: 'Then came Homer, civil life, a desire for civil order dependent doubtless on some oracle, and then . . . for independent civil life and thought'. What follows is 'personality', 'intellectual solitude', and separation from 'the general mass', the moment of the 'solitary soul' in which the poems of *The Tower* are founded. Elsewhere, Homer is linked with a 'fulness' that simultaneously prefigures an imagined future and draws upon a memoried past, calling up a 'dream time' beyond normal temporal succession altogether:

> All great poets – Dante not less than Homer and Shakespeare – speak to us of the hopes and destinies of mankind in their fulness; because they have wrought their poetry out of the dreams that were dreamed before men became so crowded upon one another, and so buried in their individual destinies and trades, that every man grew limited and fragmentary.[18]

Three years after writing this, in 1901, Yeats visited Stratford-on-Avon, to see Shakespeare's history plays performed 'in their right order, with all the links that bind play to play unbroken'. His comments, in essays first published in *The Speaker*,[19] expand upon the conflict of plenitude and emptiness by developing a series of antitheses, of which the implicit, framing opposition is that of Ireland and England. Shakespeare, he suggests, has been appropriated by a 'utilitarian', 'imperialistic' criticism which makes Henry V 'Shakespeare's only hero' and Richard II his useless antithesis:

> It did not occur to the critics that you cannot know a man from his actions because you cannot watch him in every kind of circumstance, and that men are made useless to the State as often by abundance as by emptiness, and that a man's business may at times be revelation, and not reformation.

Shakespeare 'cared little for the State', he says, 'apart from its shows and splendours, its turmoils and battles, its flamings-out of the uncivilised heart', though he did think it wrong to 'over-turn a king, and thereby swamp peace in civil war'. But in Richard II he offered a figure of 'the defeat that awaits all, whether they be artist or saint, who find themselves where men ask of them a rough energy and have nothing to give but some contemplative virtue, whether lyrical fantasy, or sweetness of temper, or dreamy dignity'. That 'rough energy' had become embodied, by 1919, as a 'rough beast' slouching to centre-stage, but he is already figured in the insurgent Fortinbras, contrasted with the contemplative Hamlet, in a series of observations which clearly look forward to the preoccupations of *The Tower*:

> The Greeks, a certain scholar had told me, considered that myths are the activities of the Daimons, and that the Daimons shape our characters and our lives. I have often had the fancy that there is some one myth for every man, which, if we but knew it, would make us understand all he did and thought. Shakespeare's myth, it may be, describes a wise man who was blind from very wisdom, and an empty man who thrust him from his place, and saw all that could be seen from very emptiness. It is in the story of Hamlet, who saw too great issues everywhere to play the trivial game of life, and of Fortinbras, who came from fighting battles about 'a little patch of ground' . . . and who was yet acclaimed by Hamlet and by all as the only befitting king. And it is the story of Richard II, that unripe Hamlet, and of Henry V, that ripened Fortinbras.

The sentiments here are very close to those which close 'Meditations', where the poet wonders 'how many times I could have proved my worth / In something that all others understand or share', only to conclude that success would have generated its own lack ('It had but made us pine the more'); but they also recall the pride and faith which are the legacy in Section III of 'The Tower'. Hamlet is the true heir. In his visionary blindness, he shares the fullness associated with Homer. But he is thrust from his place by an empty man who is nevertheless 'the only befitting king'. The empty man of violence is not the agent of 'mere anarchy', in the end, but the restorer of order, not cause but cure, slouching towards the centre to claim his own, in a world swept by 'this filthy modern tide'.

These antitheses open right up into the central contradiction of Yeats's poetry in the 1920s. For *The Tower*, which Yeats spoke of as 'evidence to show that my poetry has gained in self-possession and power'[20] nevertheless carries with it, as a kind of subversive verso, a message of failure and defeat. When Yeats speaks of Henry V abandoning his friends (without mentioning Falstaff by name), of his 'coarse nerves, of one who is to rule among violent people', and of his rhetoric, contrasted with 'that lyricism which rose out of Richard's mind like the jet of a fountain to fall again where it had risen', we should be alerted to the premonitions of the poetry. In 'Meditations' it is Homer who had found it 'certain beyond dreams / That out of life's own self-delight had sprung / The abounding glittering jet'. Now, however, the empty sea-shell rather than the overflowing fountain seems to be 'the symbol which / Shadows the inherited glory of the rich'.

'To pose character against character,' says Yeats, 'was an element in Shakespeare's art.' In *The Tower* he poses discourse against discourse, turning the echoes and reminiscences of his poetic predecessors into moments in the drama of the poems. Shakespeare's antithetical sense resolves contradiction only through a 'tragic irony' which proclaims that 'all men great and little fail', 'in the end', no matter what their momentary success. Shakespeare's own story too is one of only partial success. He wrote at a time 'when solitary great men were gathering to themselves the fire that had once flowed hither and thither among all men, when individualism in work and thought and emotion was breaking up the old rhythms of life'. Thus, afflicted by 'the great famine, the sinking down of popular imagination, the dying out of traditional fantasy, the ebbing out of the energy of the race', he was compelled to seek in 'foreign tales', in 'the natural history and mythology of the classics', a source of inspiration not to be found in English history alone:

> English literature, because it would have grown out of itself, might have had the simplicity and unity of Greek literature, for I can never get out of my head that no man, even though he be Shakespeare, can write perfectly when his web is woven of threads that have been spun in many lands.

By the same token, the very presence in Yeats's text of these alien voices, of Homer, Shakespeare, Milton, Wordsworth, is an acknowledgement

ledgement of failure. The text has failed to recover 'simplicity and unity'; the inheritance it transmits is thus a partial one, inscribing in the very fullness of its packed allusiveness the lack of a spontaneous self-sufficiency and 'self-delight'. The 'half-read wisdom of daemonic images' may suffice, but it does not recover the originary plenitude of Homer and the Greeks. It is, as Yeats says in this essay, 'doubtless a necessity also that something might be poured into the emptiness. Yet how they injured the simplicity and unity of the speech!'

Yeats's ancestral voices thus constitute a paradox. On the one hand, they are an inheritance, to be passed on to his heirs. On the other hand, they dispossess him the moment they are cited, for they represent a past he has not transcended, a patriarchal authority and power he cannot supersede. Set against them, his creations, whether the fictional Hanrahan, or the Mrs French reclaimed from oral tradition, or his son and daughter, or Thoor Ballylee itself, pall into insubstantiality, in 'natural declension'. As Yeats observed of 'That strange procession' of Shakespearian characters he had seen at Stratford:

> The people my mind's eye has seen have too much of the extravagance of dreams, like all the inventions of art before our crowded life had brought moderation and compromise, to seem more than a dream, and yet all else has grown dim before them.

Emblems of adversity

Catherine Belsey, comparing *The Prelude* and 'Meditations', remarks that 'The "I" of these poems is a kind of super-subject, experiencing life at a higher level of intensity than ordinary people and absorbed in a world of selfhood which the phenomenal world, perceived as external and antithetical, either nourishes or constrains.'[21] Yet what, on reflection, is most striking is the belatedness of the 'I' in the later work. It doesn't appear at all in the opening poem, 'Ancestral Houses', which remains stubbornly third-person until the questioning (and called-into-question) 'ours' of the last lines in each of the last two stanzas; and, here, there is a peculiar sense of a first-person plural repeatedly deferred by a syntax that seems reluctant to acknowledge its presence. The same movement is reproduced in the second poem, 'My House', which initiates the insistent possessiveness that runs through all the subsequent titles, until 'I' finally appears in the last title. But in 'My House' the 'I' is again delayed and, when it finally does appear, it is only to be supplanted almost at once by its successors. The poet, first of all deferring to his estate in all its ancientness, and then to his predecessor ('Two men have founded here'), already 'Forgetting and forgot', is effaced almost at once by his heirs, his labours robbed of their immediacy and personal urgency by becoming simply 'emblems' in a spiritual bequest:

> And I, that after me
> My bodily heirs may find
> To exalt a lonely mind,
> Befitting emblems of adversity.

Similarly, that other, *literary* predecessor, Milton, is displaced by the discourses which produced him and which he in turn produced. He is present to Yeats only as a trace, a written page. But even as a living man, he was visible only as an effect, a sign to benighted travellers who saw 'his midnight candle glimmering'. Himself 'shadowing forth / How the daemonic rage / Imagined everything', he is shadowed forth in turn, his toils, in all their physical ferocity, now vanished away, to be replaced by the calm 'written page' which is his only residue. Despite the repeated 'my' of this poem what such passages propose is the evanescence of the toiling and possessing subject. It is the objects men create which take possession: we hear, not of Milton's poem, but of '*Il Penseroso's* Platonist'.

This pattern of usurpation is everywhere in the poem, if once we look for it. It is the gardens and the lawns which are the sly agents of 'Ancestral Houses', which 'But take our greatness with our violence'. That 'taking', in all its redolent ambiguity, has the force of an expropriation. In 'My Table' it is Sato's sword that 'may moralise / My days out of their aimlessness', while another poetic predecessor, Chaucer, is invoked only to be brutally banished by the emphatic presence of the sword, whose own maker is equally expunged by the passive voice ('Chaucer had not drawn breath / When it was forged'). Similarly, it is the 'marvellous accomplishment' which runs unchanging through the centuries, merely using fathers and sons as its successive carriers, leaving 'the most rich inheritor' with the emptiness of an 'aching heart', dispossessed in the midst of plenty. Little wonder, then, that in this poem it is the peacock that has the last word, and not the 'waking wits' of a man who has already become merely the object of some other discourse: 'a country's talk'. 'My Descendants' enacts the same supersession with even more insistence, inserting the 'I' at the pivot of a sentence which moves from ancestors to heirs, erasing the subject as it goes:

> Having inherited a vigorous mind
> From my old fathers, I must nourish dreams
> And leave a woman and a man behind
> As vigorous of mind, and yet it seems
> Life scarce can cast a fragrance on the wind,

> Scarce spread a glory to the morning beams,
> But the torn petals strew the garden plot;
> And there's but common greenness after that.

'Life', the desired fullness of the moment, turns into 'mere dreams' like that imaginary plenitude associated earlier with Homer. Mere 'common greenness' inherits, a plebeian nationalism trampling on the scattered petals of tradition. Repeatedly, throughout 'The Tower' and 'Meditations', Yeats stresses man as the 'maker'; yet this making with equal repetitiveness is seen as a merely secondary, shadowing activity, reproducing the authentic and originary powers of 'The Primum Mobile that fashioned us'.

In 'The Road at My Door' the political dimensions of this eviction of the subject become more apparent. For what Belsey calls the 'super-subject' has been put in his place, marginalised, by the pressures of a transgressive, violating history. The Irregular and the National Army Lieutenant crowd out the lyric subject, displacing his discourse with 'jokes of civil war', leaving him to 'complain / Of the foul weather', finally reduced to silence and envy, turning away once more to the inadequacy of dream. Such casual comedy, the prerogative of Falstaffian lords of misrule, presages the new order of things. In the refrain of the next poem, 'The Stare's Nest by My Window', the possessing poet has already been evicted by starling and emptiness. The world is no longer arranged around him in careful hierarchies, and this breakdown of values is reproduced in a fragmentary syntax whose discrete details are all jumbled together, the killing of a man and the burning of a house interchangeable, bees building homes while men build only barricades, birds feeding their young while hearts are fed only on empty and destructive fantasies, space itself dislocated into a collection of uncertain 'somewheres'.

By the time the last poem in the sequence is reached, the subject can present itself with an insistent foregrounding of the 'I' (placed first in the title and in first and last stanzas). But this is an illusory dominance, for what happens in the rest of the poem is the swamping of this 'I' by external appearances and inner phantoms, leaving it with 'wits astray / Because of all that senseless tumult', almost swept up in the irrational cries which seem about to take over the poem. What we see here once again is the dominant discourse invaded, dislocated, turned aside by foreign voices, by frenzies that bewilder and reveries that perturb, which nevertheless are *family* ghosts: 'Monstrous familiar images'. The clangour of an 'indifferent multitude' fixated on negation ('plunged towards nothing . . . / For the embrace of nothing') over-whelms the vision of a self-delighting fullness and originary presence represented by the magical ladies. Such plenitude of self-presence, the Arethusan spring ('their minds are but a pool / Where even longing drowns under its own excess'), is mocked by the sheer negativity, the empty 'complacency' of these alien discourses. The poem turns away from this 'multitudinous revelation', this 'barbaric and Asiatic' anarchy, where men are 'crowded upon one another . . . limited and fragmentary', as the poet turns away into mere empty speculation ('Wonder'), into a redoubled negation (that which has not happened would simply have 'made us pine the more') and finally into contemplating 'The half-read wisdom of daemonic images'.

There is an odd and apparently incidental motif that recurs throughout the three long poems that open *The Tower*, articulated through various compounds based on 'half': the idea of sufficiency. It is there in the 'old, necessitous, half-mounted man' of 'The Tower', the lieutenant and his men 'Half-dressed in national uniform', the 'half-deceit of some intoxicant' and, most appositely in 'Nineteen Hundred and Nineteen', 'What my laborious life imagined, even / The half-imagined, the half-written page'. In the last poem, Yeats can say, of some moralist or mythological poet's image of the solitary soul as a swan: 'I am satisfied with that'. Yet it is clear that this *sufficiency* is quite different from the self-delighting *self*-sufficiency of Homer, the beautiful ladies and the 'abounding, glittering jet'. It carries with it the sense not of totality and completeness – that 'Unity of Being' spoken of in *The Trembling of the Veil* as his goal in poetry and politics alike[22] – but of lack, accommodation, the 'limited and fragmentary'. To be *satisfied* is not to be 'full / Of [one's] own sweetness', as the persistent use of the comparative and superlative, of rhetorical questions and such limiting formulae as 'but', 'mere', 'it seems' and of the conditional and subjunctive throughout these poems all indicate.

In a world which is merely sufficient, haunted by fullness and emptiness alike, experience is essentially double, everywhere inscribing otherness in its presences. The subject has to learn to 'read the signs', decipher the 'emblems of adversity', without sinking unmanned into half-deceit. But the opportunity for misreading is always there, in the gap between the 'half-read wisdom' and the 'half-imagined, the half-written page'. The subject, that is, partakes of the doubleness of discourse, cast adrift amidst memory and imagination, those twin absences he systematically interrogates:

> I send imagination forth
> Under the day's declining beam, and call
> Images and memories
> From ruin or from ancient trees
> For I would ask a question of them all.

Yeats's permanent tendency is to refuse dislocation, to incorporate schism, as in 'Easter 1916' the transgressive moment of insurrection is re-appropriated, sealed over within a seamless totality which makes terror into 'a terrible beauty'. But it is within these interstices that the wisdom of the daemonic images resides. It is there that the answers to his questions can be 'half-read'. 'All creation is from conflict, whether with our own mind or with that of others', Yeats observed, and 'the historian who dreams of bloodless victory wrongs the wounded veterans.'[23] In *The Tower* the conflict for Yeats is ultimately between the drive for unitary utterance and the recognition of real discord, of conflict itself. Everywhere, the subject struggles to hammer a unity out of disparate discourses, to forge a single, unfragmented narrative out of the multiplicity and violence of Ireland. The epic simplicity is lost forever. What the poet may achieve, however, is a *sufficient* unity, imposing the 'fantastical imagination' upon all those warring elements, to achieve that 'polyphonic' unity that Kristeva sees located in an alternative tradition.[24]

Bankrupt masters

The 'I' is everywhere in 'The Tower' – from the first impatient question, through the obsessive reiterations in the body of the poem – 17 instances in the next 116 lines – to the ringing declarations of the last section: 'it is time that I wrote my will', 'I choose upstanding men', 'I declare', 'And I declare', 'I mock', 'I have prepared my peace', 'I leave both faith and pride', 'Now shall I make my soul'. This is a subject in control of its life, arrogantly setting its estates in order, confident of its mastery. The omnipresence of this 'I' is underestimated by a simple word-count, since in many cases it occurs at the beginning of a sentence which contains several main verbs, so that stanza after stanza exists and moves only as the articulation of this all-embracing ego. And yet this is not the whole story.

Julia Kristeva's development of Bakhtin's two narrative modes, 'epic monologism' and 'dialogical discourse', offers an appropriate distinction here. In the former:

> The dialogue inherent in all discourse is smothered by a *prohibition*, a censorship, such that this discourse refuses to turn back upon itself, to enter into dialogue with itself. To present the model of this censorship is to describe the nature of the differences between two types of discourse: the epic type (history and science) and the Menippean type (carnivalesque writings and novel), which transgressed prohibition.[25]

'Monological discourse' is expressed through 'grammatical affirmation and negation'; 'the utterance of a subject ("I")' is self-sufficient. 'The speaker (subject of the epic) does not make use of another's speech'; 'the two aspects of enunciation remain limited by the narrator's absolute point of view, which coincides with the wholeness of a god or community. Within epic monologism, we detect the presence of the "transcendental signified" and "self presence" as highlighted by Jacques Derrida'.

Yeats's whole discourse in 'The Tower' is posited on a kind of interior dialogue, a question-and-answer structure in which 'The writer's interlocutor . . . is the writer himself, but as reader of another text. The one who writes is the same as the one who reads. Since his interlocutor is a text, he himself is no more than a text rereading itself as it rewrites itself.'[26] Such self-questioning is a disruption of the epic monologism of Homer, Milton, Wordsworth, whose univocal utterance expresses some kind of metaphysical conviction of a transcendent *fons et origo* of meaning. But it is difficult to see how Yeats, with his steadfast hatred of 'gregarious humour' – that 'bitter comedy' which arose because 'fragments broke into even smaller fragments' and issued in hatred, the snatching away of accomplished beauty, and 'the growing murderousness of the world'[27] – could be identified with the 'carnivalesque' as Kristeva describes it.

Kristeva's account of the carnivalesque dialogue, 'composed of distances, relationships, analogies, and non-exclusive oppositions', in which 'two texts meet, contradict, and relativise each other' has, nevertheless, striking resemblances to Yeats's own pronouncements:

> A carnival participant is both actor and spectator; he loses his sense of individuality, passes through a zero point of carnivalesque activity and splits into a subject of the spectacle and an object of the game. Within the carnival, the subject is reduced to nothingness, while the structure of *the author* emerges as anonymity that creates and sees itself created as self and other, as man and mask. . . . The carnival first exteriorizes the structure of reflective literary productivity, then inevitably brings to light this structure's underlying unconscious: sexuality and death. Out of the dialogue that is established between them, the structural dyads of carnival appear: high and low, birth and agony, food and excrement, praise and curses, laughter and tears.[28]

It is the 'polyphonic' nature of the carnivalesque, and not the 'parody' of established forms, which is its essential feature: 'it is no more comic than tragic; it is both at once, one might say that it is *serious*' and this makes it 'politically and socially disturbing'. The presence of the fantastic and the mystical, 'pathological states of the soul', madness, dreams and daydream 'destroys man's epic and tragic unity as well as his belief in identity and causality; they indicate that he has lost his totality and no longer coincides with himself'.[29]

There is a drive towards epic monologism in 'The Tower', towards unitary being, to the tragic mastery of the 'solitary and proud . . . anti-self'.[30] But subverting that, cutting across it, is another discourse, revealed in the opening phrases by a language that points towards 'bitter comedy': 'this absurdity', 'this caricature', 'Decrepit age that has been tied to me / As to a dog's tail', 'derided by / A sort of battered kettle at the heel'. This note of derision persists throughout the text, undermining the 'passionate' and the 'fantastical' with sudden plunges into bathos, into 'low' imagery (signalled by that Wordsworthian 'humbler worm'), deflecting the masterful coherence of the syntax with sudden breaks and anacolutha, as in the caprice which cuts short the story of Hanrahan in mid-flight:

> Hanrahan rose in frenzy there
> And followed up those baying creatures towards –
>
> O towards I have forgotten what – enough!

Though this seems to insist on the absolute mastery of the author over his creations – over the Hanrahan he created in *another* story, and arbitrarily summons up and dismisses here, and over the direction of *this* narrative itself – the next line tells a different tale, suggesting that he has been cut short by some external and more pressing necessity: 'I must recall a man'. And this man, mirroring Yeats, is 'so harried' that no stories can cheer him, though he too, like Yeats, has already been translated into the realm of fable: 'A figure that has grown so fabulous / There's not a neighbour left to say / When he finished his dog's day'. The author, far from being an authority over his 'figures', himself becomes one of them, surreptitiously, through that repeated canine analogy, linked with them, his mastery reduced to an empty farce: 'An ancient bankrupt master of this house'.

Yeats, absorbed and absolved in his characters, comes to share in their tragicomic doubleness. The story of Mrs French, for example, combined grandeur with mere grandiosity, as that wicked *double entendre* 'Gifted with so fine an ear' indicates, contrasting genteel accomplishment with the scandalous and absurd literal meaning (the insolent farmer's clipped ear, brought 'in a little covered dish'). Farce likewise turns into tragedy without losing its bathos in the story of the drunkards, 'maddened by those rhymes', who sought 'To test their fancy by their sight' but 'mistook the brightness of the moon / For the prosaic light of day'. Here, a confounding of genres is both content and form of the narrative, and the blindness of the characters leads on to the two blind poets who are authors of imaginary and of real misfortunes, Raftery and Homer. For the 'tragedy' that began with Homer, like that caused by Raftery, has issue in the real world as well as in fiction, and

Yeats sees himself too as the possible author of future madness, presumably in his readers. (He is probably thinking of his writings' responsibility, *inter alia*, for sending out 'Certain men the English shot'.) If 'Helen has all living hearts betrayed', she is the figure not only of some mythical originary betrayal but of the betrayals inscribed in Yeats's text itself, betrayals of that authorial voice which aspires to epic monologism, but is constantly undercut by his own textual inventions.

Yeats may claim that 'I myself created Hanrahan', that 'I thought it all out twenty years ago'; but, twenty years later, he shares some of the comic vulnerability of his character, with 'only broken knees for hire / And horrible splendour of desire'. Though he is the historical author who 'drove him drunk or sober through the dawn' there is within the story another author of Hanrahan's misfortunes: 'Caught by an old man's juggleries / He stumbled, tumbled, fumbled to and fro'. Yeats in old age shares in the clownish clumsiness of Hanrahan and in the saturnalian license of the 'juggler'. Like the 'ancient ruffian' he too can 'so bewitch [. . .] the cards under his thumb' that, whether as magic or sleight-of-hand, he can transform himself into his characters, start a story as he starts a hare and then with the abrupt impatient impulse leave it perpetually suspended. Such a compacting of the poet with his characters prepares the way for the semantic confusion of Yeats with the 'Old lecher with a love on every wind' in the final stanzas of Section II, where it is not clear whether Yeats addresses his vocatives to Hanrahan, or to himself as his own phantasmagoria.

Like his characters, Yeats too is bewitched by the subversive discourses of his own text, which call up voices beyond his immediate ordinance. He too is the victim of 'mocking Muses', who invert all established values by choosing a country wench for queen, in an act of deliberate misrule, and who turn Yeats's epic pretensions in old age to the tragicomic rage of 'all old men and women, rich and poor' against their destiny. It is in the context of this anarchic levelling – the effect of carnival, which reveals and revels in the fact that death and sexuality are shared by all, irrespective of hierarchy – that the concept of *pride*, which Yeats is to make the arrogant positive of his bequest in the last section, is brought down to earth by the company it keeps in the last stanza of Section II:

> Does the imagination dwell the most
> Upon a woman won or woman lost?
> If on the lost, admit you turned aside
> From a great labyrinth out of pride,
> Cowardice, some silly over-subtle thought
> Or anything called conscience once;

And that if memory recur, the sun's
Under eclipse and the day's blotted out.

Yeats 'needs' all Hanrahan's 'mighty memories' because only in this
seance-like communion with his own invention, this double discourse of
question and half-answer, can he negotiate those absences summoned
up by memory and imagination alike, that 'forgetting' which is a
repeated motif. The poem, which set out to bring all to mind, to gather
its properties in to some primary plenitude of creation, finds itself
'turned aside' from self-presence into absence, darkness, death: under
erasure. It is on the grounds, then, not of aristocratic mastery, but of
'cowardice' and 'silly' self-defeat (both of Yeats's words, as he would
know, with feudal class resonances), that Yeats comes to terms with his
finitude, recognises the reality of supersession implicit in writing a will.

Climbing to the source

Yeats, himself the victim of mockery, like his characters betrayed by
'mocking Muses', comes to mock in Section III of 'The Tower'. That
mockery is implicitly associated with carnival is confirmed by that bitter
sarcasm which in 'Nineteen Hundred and Nineteen' turns mockery
against itself. There he ironically invites the reader to join him in
mocking the great, who 'toiled so hard and late / . . . Nor thought of the
levelling wind'; and the good, 'That fancied goodness might be
gay, / And sick of solitude / Might proclaim holiday'. But it is to 'Mock
mockers after that' that he finally invites us, and the statement that
'we / Traffic in mockery' is a rhetorical reproach which really invites the
reader to share in a different communion, with good, wise and great. It
is in this spirit, and not the spirit of carnival 'holiday', that the will is
'read' in 'The Tower'.

Yet in a real sense, 'The Tower', like 'Meditations' with its Falstaffian
jokes and its evocation of a 'polyphonic' Chaucer, is a poem where
motley is worn. It is, in Kristeva's words, 'a pavement of citations',
whose 'structural signification is to denote the writer's distance from his
own and other texts'. It is not what elsewhere she calls a 'bounded
Text', but 'a permutation of texts, an intertextuality: in the space of a
given text, several utterances, taken from other texts, intersect and
neutralize one another'.[31] From this neutralising, however, Yeats tries to
produce a unitary, bounded text. From the 'multi-stylism and multitona-
lity of this discourse' he tries to construct a will which balances all,
brings all to mind.

He does this through that very self-conscious preoccupation with the
act of writing which Kristeva sees as a feature of the carnivalesque: 'Its

language seems fascinated with the "double" (with its own activity as graphic *trace*, doubling an "outside").'[32] A concentration on the act of writing carries with it a parallel emphasis on the process of reading. The 'half-imagined, the half-written page' becomes 'the half-read wisdom of daemonic images'. To 'read the signs' is to return to that nexus where the *image* brings together the *imagination* and the *imaged* world, offering us 'befitting emblems'. That phrase itself, in 'Meditations', comes at the end of a sequence which begins with the 'symbolic rose' but moves on to that 'candle and written page' which simultaneously alludes to Yeats's present and Milton's past labours, doubling the poets and making each in turn a shadow of that 'daemonic rage' which in reality 'Imagined everything'. It is by simultaneously reading and re-writing the texts of his predecessors, of history itself, that he writes his own.

Yeats could speak of getting 'great pleasure' from remembering that Homer was sung,[33] and Homer's singing is alluded to in the preceding section of 'Meditations'. Yet despite this preoccupation at the conscious level with the identity of voice and self-presence (compare 'Chaucer had not drawn breath' with its assumed identity of utterance and breath), the deepest impulse of Yeats's poetry is away from *voice*, to the hieratic solitude of *writing*. In 'Easter 1916', for example, the discordant voices of history are stilled and reborn in a perpetual present ('Now and in time to be . . . / A terrible beauty *is* born') only when Yeats comes to 'write it out in a verse'. Writing is extra-territorial, part of the 'artifice of eternity'. As the young Stephen Dedalus in *Portrait* considers that 'the language that we speak is his before it is mine', in his encounter with the English dean, so Yeats too finds the primal betrayal of nationality in speech, which is infiltrated, *ab initio*, by alien discourses. Speech lives in that dimension of *history* which for Dedalus is nightmare. But writing in its materiality constitutes the *synchrony* of *dream*. In writing, all texts coexist, as objects, in an absolute present which overthrows time and sequence (and hence supersession). Speech is diachronic, illusive and elusive, living in memory and expectation, imagination and reverie, and thus in forgetfulness – the tyranny of a time which is always elsewhere. When Yeats writes 'It is time that I wrote my will' there is a paradoxical play of potential and actual in the resolve. The intention to translate personal 'will' (subjective being, wish, purpose) into a written 'will' (objective text) brings diachrony and synchrony into ironic conjunction.

In Wordsworth's and Milton's epic texts there is a tension between articulating voice, the self-constituting and therefore always deluded subject, the autobiographical poet, and the author as textual presence, as the always-already-written, the self as writing. In saying 'It is time that I wrote my will' the text also says, 'here is the will already'. The subsequent pronouncement, 'Now shall I make my soul' cannot be separated from this earlier declaration. The soul is made in the act of writing itself, the transfer to the page which for the reader of the poem (and we are required to posit Yeats himself as the imaginary primal reader) has always already taken place, leaving him to decipher that *trace* which, it seems, is all the text is. The past self who 'created Hanrahan' takes on the same status in this new text as his recreated character, a textual figure, perpetually present in this discourse of the poem. This is how 'Death and life were not / Till man made up the whole' and this is the meaning of those mystical pronouncements:

> And further add to that
> That, being dead, we rise,
> Dream and so create
> Translunar Paradise.

It is the 'mirror-resembling dream' of writing, the graphic trace, that abolishes death, and makes the writing of a will unnecessary by the very act of writing. The 'I' who speaks here can never be superseded, though he speaks only of supersession. On the 'half-imagined, the half-written page' the axes of diachronic and synchronic intersect. Section III of 'The Tower', as if to emphasise this, runs through the whole gamut of the tenses to absorb them all into the perpetual present of writing. Yeats's heirs 'shall inherit my pride' but this is 'the pride of people that were / Bound neither to Cause nor to State'; and they are linked together in the impressive present tense of utterance: 'I declare . . .'. The will unfolds from its originating utterance in a remarkable decrescendo:

> It is time that I wrote my will;
> I choose upstanding men
> That climb the streams until
> The fountain leap, and at dawn
> Drop their cast at the side
> Of dripping stone; I declare
> They shall inherit my pride,
> The pride of people that were
> Bound neither to Cause nor to State,
> Neither to slaves that were spat on,
> Nor to the tyrants that spat,
> The people of Burke and of Grattan
> That gave, though free to refuse −
> Pride, like that of the morn,
> When the headlong light is loose,
> Or that of the fabulous horn,
> Or that of the sudden shower
> When all streams are dry,

Or that of the hour
When the swan must fix his eye
Upon a fading gleam,
Float out upon a long
Last reach of glittering stream
And there sing his last song.
And I declare my faith . . .

The words themselves float out upon the long last reaches of the
sentence; yet at the same time, in a peculiar contrary movement they
climb back to the source, seeking their lost lineage. 'My pride' is
immediately qualified, in a recessive movement, as 'The pride of people
that were . . .', and 'people' is in turn qualified in a tracing of ancestry
which takes us back to the patriarchal fountainhead. Yet, in what could
be an interruptive curtailing rather than a natural close to the
parenthesis, we are returned to 'Pride' in a way which merges what
Yeats wills to his heirs and what 'The people of Burke and of
Grattan / . . . gave, though free to refuse'. The latest and the oldest
generations here combine in an act which is momentary and perpetual,
as the 'upstanding men' forever climb, in a kind of perpetual present,
towards an 'until' which is never reached. 'Pride' then, in what is almost
a Homeric simile, takes the sentence off once more, this time into fable
rather than history, in pursuit of that lost originary plenitude; and then
both these recessive movements are rounded off by that closure in which
writing turns back upon song, incorporating it within its declarations as
death encompasses the breathing creature. In the lines that follow, many
other discourses – Plato and Plotinus' thought, 'learned Italian things',
'Poet's imaginings / And memories of love, / Memories of the words of
women' – are all likewise subsumed within this writing/reading of a will,
including, in the end, the poet's own 'imaginings / And memories'.

In a recursive movement, the poem turns back upon itself, constituting its own boundaries. 'It is time that I wrote my will', with its strange
subjunctive mode that seems to take up past, present and future into one
transcending tense, a kind of absolute present, thus returns the poem to
its primal moment, at which, in some lost original world, the boy Yeats
set out to climb Ben Bulben's streams. Returning to the source, the
Arethusan fountain, the text also returns to its own origins, to that
moment when 'it seem[ed] that I must bid the Muse go pack'. Both
source of inspiration and river of forgetfulness ('Lethe's wharf') the
poem inscribes a double relation to tradition. These half-read images
'Suffice the ageing man as once the growing boy' because the child is
father to the man, in strange inversion of Oedipal relations, as Dedalus
argued of Shakespeare in *Ulysses*. And indeed we see Yeats acting out
both parts of that Shakespearian myth of Oedipal supplanting he

describes in 'At Stratford-on-Avon', both the 'wise man who was blind from very wisdom, and an empty man who thrust him from his place, and saw all that could be seen from very emptiness'. The insistently oral world of history – argument, song, toast, mockery, raging, gossip, jokes, complaint, rumour, Masonic incantation – has its last gasp in the 'bird's sleepy cry', but has already acceded to the 'sedentary trade' of writing. Supplanter and supplanted, he both frets in the shadow of ancestral voices, and takes those voices – one might almost say emasculates them, robbing them often of their very names – to become his own children, actors in his own texts.

If then, in Kristeva's words, the doubleness of these poems speak of a subject who 'has lost his totality and no longer coincides with himself', the act of writing a will can take these sundered fragments and reconcile ageing man and growing boy, present speaker and ancestral voices, within a polyphonic narrative. In this sense, these texts both aspire to and refuse the condition of epic. In his notes, Yeats speaks of the oral 'legend, story and tradition' of which the text are reworkings, and of 'unconsciously' echoing Sturge Moore and of having 'forgot' how we misperceive Plotinus. This 'forgetting' in a sense constitutes the unconscious of the text. Here, 'forgetting and forgot', the text invokes and revokes simultaneously its ancestral voices, the discourses which are the very condition of its writing.

Chapter Nine

Porphyry's cup: Yeats, forgetfulness and the narrative order

I have taken 'the honey of generation' from Porphyry's essay on 'The Cave of the Nymphs,' but find no warrant in Porphyry for considering it the 'drug' that destroys the 'recollection' of pre-natal freedom. He blamed a cup of oblivion given in the zodiacal sign of Cancer. (Note to 'Among School Children', *The Tower*, 1928)

A figure grown so fabulous

Halfway through 'The Tower', Yeats's masterful voice appears to stumble, tripping over some half-buried thought that prevents him from completing his sentence. He has been remembering Hanrahan, 'created' and 'thought out' by himself twenty years ago – specifically, that moment in the story 'Red Hanrahan' when the ancient ruffian in the barn bewitches the playing cards into a pack of hounds and a hare, which Hanrahan rises as in a trance to follow:

> Hanrahan rose in frenzy there
> And followed up those baying creatures towards –
>
> O towards I have forgotten what – enough!
> I must recall a man. . . .

And then Yeats too is off, compelled, like Hanrahan, to follow some new trace, forgetting where he started, wandering as if *off* the subject onto the *new* subject that becomes his theme for the rest of the stanza.

This new, unnamed subject is also a figure of fable, 'A figure that has grown so fabulous / There's not a neighbour left to say / When he finished his dog's day'. Yeats shifts, that is, from his own *invented*

character, whose tale he now claims to forget, to another, originally
historical individual, whose transfiguration into 'fable' in the popular
imagination has subjected him to an even more radical forgetting.
Because, in the re-telling, this man's story never ends, it has no need to
remember any actual biographical conclusion. And yet Yeats knows that
the man ended – as the poet elsewhere fears he or his heirs may – in
emptiness and dereliction, his fullness reduced to bankruptcy, mastery
disclosed as an insecure tenure, 'An ancient bankrupt master of this
house'.

This double forgetting, this curtailing of the fiction in the course of its
repetition, and the perpetual unfinishedness of the narrated subject,
provide the subtext of the whole poem. Yeats himself suffers from it, in
the final stanza of this section, when thought of the 'woman lost' who
compels the imagination more than the 'woman won' brings the
admission of another faltering, in which 'you turned aside / From a
great labyrinth out of pride, / Cowardice, some silly over-subtle
thought'. In a deliberately ambiguous vocative, poet and character,
Yeats and Hanrahan are confused here, their fictional and 'real' fates
overlaid in a way which produces a *new* fiction. Yeats too has become a
figure of fable, entering his own phantasmagoria as an invented
character. Memory, retelling once again the story of that actual turning
aside, involves at the same time a forgetting, a momentary extinction of
the prosaic light of day in which the actual self walks abroad, as the
section's abrupt closure itself cuts short that 'dog's day' which is now
the poet's own:

> And that if memory recur, the sun's
> Under eclipse and the day blotted out.

It is to avoid such another eclipse that, in the final section of the
poem, Yeats sets out to write his will, to guarantee that inheritance
which both as a lineage and as a set of poetic lines will preserve him
from being blotted out (the almost dead metaphor, one might note, is
also from writing). He will thus 'Mock Plotinus' thought / And cry in
Plato's teeth', proclaiming that even death and life are themselves
human inventions, transfigured in their turn into the fabulous dimension
of 'mirror-resembling dream' and 'translunar paradise'.

There are reasons why Yeats should want to forget Hanrahan's story.
The poem claims that he needs all Hanrahan's 'mighty memories'. But
the story itself is about a prolonged forgetting and a series of turnings
aside in which a woman, a house, an inheritance and, ultimately, a
'translunar paradise' are all forfeited, first by an act of trance-like
forgetfulness and betrayal in the mortal world, in which Hanrahan fails
to answer a call for help from his lover, and then by a failure of courage

and will to ask the right questions at the right time of the supernatural women in the world of the Sidhe, whither he is led by the old man's enchantments. Returned to the mortal world, Hanrahan the scholar and great songmaker has forgotten all his stories, even looks at his Virgil 'like a man that had never learned to read'. Finally remembering all, he is told: ' "there are many go wandering and forgetting like that . . . when once they have been given the touch." '[1]

This is not the place to interpret this story, but its tenor is clear. A narrative full of displacements, where authority and authorship shift as in a dream and characters merge and are reduplicated, prefigures that process in 'The Tower' whereby the author Yeats is doubled by his own fictive persona, by his character Hanrahan, and by the old man whose juggleries ensnare him, so that the uttering author is confused with the uttered, imaginary characters he narrates or addresses. Hanrahan and Yeats alike are 'lured by a softening eye' to plunge into the 'unforeknown, unseeing'. But 'The Tower' is full of similar fabled and reported instances of devotion compounded with seduction and betrayal. Each of these is an instance of *narrative*, told stories, betraying individuals into practical acts, with practical consequences, which confuse the real and the imagined: the insolent farmer shorn of his ears, drunkards maddened and ultimately drowned by a song which confers glory on a peasant girl, blind Homer himself, whose *story* of Helen betrays far more than Helen ever did. The 'tragedy began', after all, with him, not her. It is his *narrated* Helen who 'has all living hearts betrayed'.

Through to 'The Man and the Echo', Yeats expressed the fear that his own narratives, as with his play *Cathleen ni Houlihan*, may have compelled men to acts and errors in the real, historical world. In 'The Tower' likewise he fears that, successfully taking up Homer's and Raftery's mantle, he too in creative triumph 'must make men mad'. The transformations of art, that is, are closely bound up with betrayal. Hanrahan was betrayed in the very moment that Yeats conceived of him, and drove him drunk or sober through the dawn by his authorial jugglings (disguised as those of his surrogate, the old man). He is betrayed again into narrative being as Yeats defly summons him up and then dismisses him once more with the masterful authority of a necromancer.

But Yeats too is now in the same plight, both betrayer and betrayed, caught by his own 'old man's juggleries', author and victim of his own text, brooding over the ruin of a house and lineage as of a body, compelled it seems to 'bid the Muse go pack, / Choose Plato and Plotinus for a friend', to reject the sensuously embodied images of art for the ghostly paradigms of philosophy. Yeats himself, in this poem, is a 'figure grown so fabulous' that his own *real* dog's day, in the realm of history, will be eclipsed by the textual eternity in which his figurative double lives for ever. For Yeats then, entry into the narrative order, being 'reborn as an idea, something intended, complete', carries with it a loss of freedom like that of the new-born child betrayed by Porphyry's 'cup of oblivion'. The connection between certain Neoplatonic motifs, forgetfulness, and the narrative order lies close to the heart of Yeats's Modernist project.

To go where Homer went

Yeats's footnotes are full of forgettings, and forgetfulness for him seems the very condition of narrative. A footnote to 'The Hosting of the Sidhe', for example, remarks: 'I do not remember where I have read this story, and I have, maybe, half forgotten it.'[2] Again he annotates 'Aedh hears the Cry of the Sedge', with an extreme casualness towards his readers, 'I have read somewhere that a stone engraved with a Celtic god . . . has been found somewhere in England; but I cannot find the reference, though I certainly made a note of it.'[3] This can also become a casualness towards the story itself, as in his observation: 'I find that I have unintentionally changed the story of Conchobar's death',[4] where the innocuous adverb almost exculpates the author for distorting the myth without the reader even remarking it. The casualness can extend to a certain capriciousness in the handling of his sources, as in the note to 'The Secret Rose': 'I have founded the man . . . upon something I have read. . . . I am writing away from most of my books, and have not been able to find the passage; but I certainly read it somewhere.'[5]

As this last remark reveals, the casualness is studied, even arrogant. The poet is affirming his authorial authority to do what he likes with his sources, his characters, his readership. His relation to each of them is a double one: he is disarming in his humble admissions, and cocksure in his dismissal of any concern for accuracy and veracity. Thus, in another case, he seeks in the authority of a putative source a precedent not for fact but simply for his casualness towards fact: 'But maybe I only read it in Mr Standish O'Grady, who has a fine imagination, for I find no such story in Lady Gregory's book.'[6]

The strategy is revealed most clearly in the note on the prefatory poem to *Responsibilities*:

> Some merchant in Villon, I forget the reference, was 'free of the ten and four'. Irish merchants exempted from certain duties by the Irish Parliament were, unless memory deceives me again, for I am writing away from books, 'free of the eight and six'.

Or as he also phrases it: 'again – I cannot remember my authority.'[7]

Forgetting his authority is not a casual act for Yeats. It is a deliberate act of rebellion in which he affirms his independence of all that might restrict his narratorial freedom, reader, source and text alike, insisting instead on the self-delighting, self-creating power of the imagination to invent its own imagined world, without benefit of history. Yet at the same time, his constant nervous deferring to these authoritative presences reminds that he is not in fact 'free of the eight and six', but has to pay his taxes to the realities of a pressing and contingent history. Story-telling for Yeats is a way of repressing that history, and forgetfulness is an essential element in this repression.

Yeats's various remarks about story-telling in his essays on Lady Gregory's collections of Irish folklore make explicit and implicit connections between the idea of narrative and certain Neoplatonic motifs. The central connection is, perhaps, that characteristically late nineteenth-century assumption, revealed in work as diverse as Sir James Frazer's *Golden Bough*, Max Müller's solar theories, Cecil Sharp's collections of English folk songs, and Biblical exegesis, that all extant narratives are degenerations, corrupt variants, of primal narratives which can be restored by the imaginative reworkings of the scholar. Yeats's *A Vision* is itself an instance of the same intellectual activity, seeking to reconstruct the unifying 'secret history' that underlies the surface confusions and proliferating heterogeneity of the historian's chronicles. For Yeats, this means disclosing that eternal return within the ostensibly open-ended moments of historical time, revealing, in Neoplatonic terms, the paradigms that are forgotten in the fall into history, but which remain accessible to the eye of the imagination.

In an essay in Lady Gregory's *Visions and Beliefs in the West of Ireland* he argued that 'Much that Lady Gregory has gathered seems but the broken bread of old philosophers, or else of the one sort with the dough they made into their loaves', and didn't doubt that much could be found there that corresponded to the arcana to be found in Greek, Renaissance and Medieval Latin sources, 'old writers on medicine', and 'the seventeenth-century Platonists [who] quote much from Plotinus and Porphyry and Plato and from later writers, especially from Synesius and John Philoponus in whom the school of Plato came to an end in the seventh century'.[8] His Preface to Lady Gregory's collection *Cuchulain of Muirthemne* in 1902[9] admires her artistic imagination in reconstructing, or constructing for the first time, the narrative paradigm from a plethora of debased variants. Translators from the Irish have previously, he says, 'retold one story or the other from some one version', using 'the best and fullest manuscripts they knew'. 'But few of the stories really begin to exist as great works of the imagination until somebody has taken the best bits out of many manuscripts', and

It has been necessary also to leave out as to add, for generations of copyists, who had often but little sympathy with the stories they copied, have mixed together versions in a clumsy fashion ... and every century has ornamented what was once a simple story with its own often extravagant ornament. We do not perhaps exaggerate when we say that no story has come down to us in the form it had when the story-teller told it in the winter evenings.

Lady Gregory's achievement is to have 'put a great mass of stories, in which the ancient heart of Ireland still lives, into a shape at once harmonious and characteristic'. But to appreciate her work fully, we must ourselves recover a primal authenticity of response, 'if we are to recall a time when people were in love with story, and gave themselves up to imagination as if to a lover'. There has been a degeneration, then, in imaginative wholeness since those days. Yet the degeneration had already occurred for those original listeners, too, for whom the stories were no more than the platonic shadows of earlier ones, figuring forth an already lost plenitude. Such hearers

> delighted in arranging their Kings and Queens, the shadows of forgotten mythologies, in long lines that ascended to Adam and his Garden. Those who listened to them must have felt as if the living were like rabbits digging their burrows under walls that had been built by Gods and Giants, or like swallows building their nests in the stone mouths of immense images, carved by nobody knows who.

The recessive movement here, in which an original fullness of imaginative response is always projected further and further into the past, corresponds to that ascent to the ancestral source which occupies the last section of 'The Tower', and its correlative in 'Meditations in Time of Civil War', the 'obscure dark of the rich streams' which flow from Homer, now degenerated to nothing but some 'marvellous empty sea-shell', singing of the lost sea and its fullness. In his introduction to Lady Gregory's *Gods and Fighting Men*, Yeats stresses both this perpetual declension in the restless sublunary realm of history and the need to find renewal in a return to origins:

> Was it not Aeschylus who said he but served up dishes from the banquet of Homer? – but Homer himself found the great banquet on an earthen floor and under a broken roof. We do not know who at the foundation of the world made the banquet for the first time, or who put the pack of cards into rough hands; but we do know that, unless those that have made many inventions are about to change the nature of poetry, we may have to go where Homer went if we are to sing a new song. Is it because all that is under the moon thirsts to escape out of bounds, to lose itself in some unbounded tidal stream, that the songs of the folk are mournful ... ?[10]

The chronicles of this sublunary realm are the *disjecta membra* of an original truth which can be apprehended now only through myth. The Irish story-teller, Yeats says in 'Cuchulain of Muirthcmne', 'only feels himself among solid things, among things with fixed laws and satisfying purposes, when he has re-shaped the world according to his heart's desire. He understands as well as Blake that the ruins of time build mansions in eternity.' Authentic story-telling involves a release from, a forgetting of history, so that the imagination can enter into the freedom of myth:

> [T]he Irish stories make us understand why the Greeks call myths the activities of daemons. The great virtues, the great joys, the great privations come in the myths, and, as it were, take mankind between their naked arms, and, without putting off their divinity. Poets have taken their themes more often from stories that are all, or half, mythological, than from history or stories that give one the sensation of history, understanding, as I think, that the imagination which remembers the proportions of life is but a long wooing, and that it has to forget them before it becomes the torch and the marriage bed.[11]

A note to the early poem 'Michael Robartes bids his Beloved be at Peace' makes it clear that Yeats is not using the Neoplatonic imagery of river and sea, time's ruins and eternity's mansions idly in these observations. He writes with a characteristic forgetful insouciance:

> Some neo-platonist, I forget who, describes the sea as a symbol of the drifting indefinite bitterness of life, and I believe there is like symbolism intended in the many Irish voyages to the islands of enchantment, or that there was, at any rate, in the mythology out of which these stories have been shaped.[12]

Yeats overlooks not only his source here but also his own narrative poem of 1889, *The Wanderings of Oisin*, in which Oisin is seduced away by the beautiful Niamh to the Island of Forgetfulness, to join 'all who are winter tales'. Throughout the poem Oisin and his interlocutor St Patrick are aware of their actual single lives being translated into multifarious narratives. Yeats's version is of course only one more variation, yet in its very capriciousness of invention it implies that it is returning to the originary paradigm. Entering the narrative order on the Island of Forgetfulness, dying into the text, the forgetful Oisin is reborn as an unremembering idea. For as Yeats remarks in 'The Tables of the Law', 'the world only exists to be a tale in the ears of coming generations'. Yet this also involves a loss. The subject is dissolved into innumerable conflicting tales, falls away from his originary plenitude into a multitude of forms and functions, what that story calls 'the refuse of creation'.[13]

Narrative, then, is a paradoxical dimension. On the one hand, in its very nature, it involves a falling-away from unity of being, the dispersal of the narrated subject into innumerable variants. But as Lady Gregory has shown, it is possible to regain access to that 'Great Memory' in which the ur-text, the originary myth, is stored. The *Spiritus Mundi* is the place fullness and simplicity are unified, instead of at odds. But it can be apprehended now only through the intuitions of myth and dream. These can restore an image of that unity of being which in the fractured world of history has fallen away into multiplicity. Homer is the figure of this originary plenitude of self-presence from which all subsequent poets are a degeneration. In 'Discoveries' Yeats writes of a time when 'there was little separation between holy and common things . . . the one song remembering the drunken miller and but half forgetting Cambuscan bold', so that

> The occupations and places known to Homer or Hesiod, those pure first artists, might . . . have changed before the poem's end to symbols and vanished, caught up as in a golden cloud into the unchanging worlds where religion alone can discover life as well as peace. A man of that unbroken day could have all the subtlety of Shelley, and yet use no image unknown among the common people, and speak no thought that was not a deduction from the common thought. Unless the discovery of legendary knowledge and the returning belief in miracle . . . can bring once more a new belief in the sanctity of common ploughland . . . we may never see again a Shelley and a Dickens in the one body, but be broken to the end.[14]

Earlier, speaking of the fall as something which occurred 'as men came to live in towns and to read printed books and to have many specialised activities', he had seen the ethereal Shelley as the multiplying modern type and the oral tradition as the repository of wholeness:

> In literature, partly from the lack of that spoken word which knits us to normal man, we have lost in personality, in our delight in the whole man − blood, imagination, intellect running together − but have found a new delight, in essences, in states of mind, in pure imagination, in all that comes to us most easily in elaborate music. There are two ways before literature − upward into ever-growing subtlety . . . or downward, taking the soul with us until all is simplified and solidified again. That is the choice of choices.[15]

It is the same antithesis we have encountered with Homer and Irish myth earlier: between endless devolution into greater and greater heterogeneity and elaboration, or renewal in a return to some original simplicity and unity of being. A note to 'The Host of the Air' suggests that the 'magical sleep, to which people have given a new name recently' (he clearly means the collective unconscious) may offer access to truths denied to the historical waking consciousness. Irish folk tales may then be veiled and censored versions of such a vision: 'These tales are perhaps memories of true awakenings out of the magical sleep, moulded by the imagination, under the influence of a mystical doctrine which it understands too literally, into the shape of some well-known traditional tale.'[16] For Yeats this is not a negative process. Misrememberings and forgettings of events in the realm of history may well offer access to a larger truth in the realm of imagination. The 'magical sleep' of the imagination may offer direct access to that realm where opposites are reconciled, unity of being actual, and all degenerate variants of the one tale are reintegrated into their primal unity. This is the significance of the young girl's dreams in 'The Gift of Harun Al-Rashid', a poem centrally concerned with Neoplatonism, story-telling, and the relations between them.

Truths without father

'The Gift of Harun al Rashid', Yeats tells us in a note, is 'founded on [a] passage in a letter of Owen Aherne's, which I am publishing in *A Vision*'.[17]

It is thus 'founded' on the fictitious text of an imaginary character. By attributing his story, and its critical apparatus, to an invented character, Yeats compounds that narrative recession which is part of the poem itself. For, as its opening lines announce, this is a story not intended for us, written by a named and imaginary author, Kusta Ben Luka, for a named and imaginary reader, Abd Al-Rabban, 'And for no ear but his'. Part of Ben Luka's delivery then becomes a proleptic narrative of how this letter we are overhearing *may* be preserved in a copy of the Treatise of Parmenides in the Caliph's library, so that

> When fitting time has passed
> The parchment will disclose to some learned man
> A mystery that else had found no chronicler
> But the wild Bedouin.

This antithesis, between the story as it is preserved in script, and as it is dispersed in the oral tradition among those who will 'In after time . . . speak much of me / And speak but fantasy', is then complicated by Aherne's own exegetical comments. These all emphasise that no original text now survives, and that all we know is based on variants of variants. Thus this fictive product of Yeats's own imagination lectures us on the unreliability of *all* narrative, while perpetrating a more fundamental imposture upon us. Yet this imposture is no more than the 'poetic license' Yeats subsequently lays claim to when he ostensibly comes clean with us and explains that he has 'greatly elaborated this bare narrative'.[18] Since the only 'source' he has for the narrative are the words of his own invented character, it is clear that the honest poet is being less than ingenuous here. Aherne's own identity as a fiction, then, adds a further twist to the play with narrative transmission of which Aherne supposedly writes:

> According to one tradition of the desert . . . but according to another . . . one version of the story says . . . while another story has it that. . . . The only thing upon which there is general agreement is that he was warned by a dream to accept the gift of the Caliph, and that his wife, a few days after the marriage, began to talk in her sleep, and that she told him all those things which he had searched for vainly all his life in the great library of the Caliph, and in the conversation of wise men. One curious detail has come down to us in Bedouin tradition. . . . All these contradictory stories seem to be a confused recollection of the contents of a little old book, lost many years ago with Kusta-ben-Luka's larger book in the desert battle which I have already described. This little book was discovered, according to tradition, by some Judwali scholar or saint between the pages of a Greek book which had once been in the Caliph's library. The story of the discovery may however be the invention of a much later age, to justify some doctrine or development of old doctrines that it may have contained.[19]

The narrative deliberately drowns us in a profusion of sources and recensions, so that we cannot in the end be sure whence Aherne derives his narrative, or even whether the story which provides the narrative frame for Yeats's poem — the story, that is, of how the letter is hidden inside a great book in the Caliph's library — is part of the original narrative or a later 'invention', for some ulterior and unconnected motive. Thus, while all these 'contradictory stories' seem to be a 'confused recollection' of some originary text, that text is itself in turn re-inserted into a story-telling tradition where, for the scrupulous scholar, it might well disappear up its own tale. But this is not the end of it. Ostensibly 're-producing' the authoritative narrative of Aherne's, and then allowing its authority to dissolve in a welter of speculative readings and reconstructions, Yeats then adds a further dimension of narrative elaboration, with remarks that introduce into the story his own scholarly pretensions and philosophical preoccupations, as if he too, with his anecdotal additions, intended 'to justify some doctrine or development of old doctrines'.

All the stories we hear, then, are degenerations from some now inaccessible primal source. Even the poet who sets out to re-invent that source ends up by elaborating greatly. And yet right at the centre of this whole story, in all its variants, is the account of an unimpeded access to a truth that resides beyond all its degenerate tellings, available to discourse only in the dream utterances of the young girl Kusta has taken for bride. The whole text reduplicates this antithesis between authentic, unmediated revelation and the distortions of report. Thus, of one remark of the Caliph's we are told: 'That speech was all that the town knew', and without true knowledge speculation, rumour and intrigue, the 'traitor's thought' spawned. The antithesis can be found even in the reiteration of Heraclitus' belief that, in the world of historical event, no one 'does the same thing twice' – reiteration itself becomes a new act. This in turn provokes the question of whether poetry itself is merely the mimicry of some remote, original act of utterance – a question that goes right to the heart of this poem's concern with the nature of narrative:

> And so a hunter carries in the eye
> A mimicry of youth. Can poet's thought
> That springs from body and in body falls
> Like this pure jet, now lost amid blue sky . . .
> Be mimicry?

This not only recalls 'the abounding glittering jet' of Homer's originary fabulous plenitude, it also connects poetry with the unmediated revelation of the girl's dreams, for she shares a 'thirst for those old crabbed mysteries / . . . strains to look beyond our life . . . / And yet herself can seem youth's very fountain, / Being all brimmed with life'. In the world of public report, we hear, she 'Had heard impossible history of my past; / Imagined some impossible history / Lived at my side; thought time's disfiguring touch / Gave but more reason for a woman's care'. Ordinary love ('a man's mockery of the changeless soul') belongs to this dull sublunary world of report, set against 'the stark mystery that has dazed my sight' – a mystery which we are still not (or ever) vouchsafed. Whatever it is that has 'Perplexed her fantasy' about him, the girl is moved to enquire into his books, staring 'On old dry writing in a learned tongue'. The 'disfiguring touch' of time upon his mortal human features is then picked up in a paronomasia which contrasts it with the abiding, unchanging text of 'writing or the figured page', touched by *her* hand as if it were 'some dear cheek'. Moved by this passion she finally expounds from sleep, as if possessed by some great Djinn, the arcane wisdom that underlies all the changing forms of history and its troubled narratives:

> Truths without father came, truths that no book
> Of all the uncounted books that I have read,

> Nor thought out of her mind or mine begot,
> Self-born, high-born, and solitary truths,
> Those terrible implacable straight lines
> Drawn through the wandering vegetative dream,
> Even those truths that when my bones are dust
> Must drive the Arabian host.

With this idea of the 'Truths without father, truths that no book ... begot', 'Self-born, high-born, and solitary truths' to be set against the 'wandering vegetative dream' of history, we return right to the heart of Yeats's Neoplatonic ideas of narrative.

To alter Plato's parable

A note to 'An Image from a Past Life' refers to another fictive letter Robartes wrote to Aherne in 1917 about Kusta's vision of a woman's dream-face in sleep, whom he considered to be a woman loved in another life, and whose likeness, 'without being identical', he also found in a painting and in a woman he subsequently loved. This real woman then 'left him in a fit of jealousy' because he preferred the painting to her. Yeats goes on, with solemn specificity, to note that 'In a dialogue and in letters, Robartes gives a classification and analysis of dreams which explain the survival of this story among the followers of Kusta-ben-Luki.' 'They distinguish', he says, 'between the memory of concrete images and the abstract memory, and affirm that no concrete dream-image is ever from our memory.' This he found hard to believe, he says, since it belied his experience and all he had read in books of psychoanalysis. When he studied his dreams, however, he found that 'the image seen was never really that of friend, or relation, or my old school, though it might very closely resemble it':

> A substitution had taken place, often a very strange one, though I forgot this if I did not notice it at once on waking. The name of some friend, or the conceptions 'my father' and 'at school', are a part of the abstract memory and therefore of the dream life, but the image ... being a part of the personal concrete memory appeared neither in sleep nor in visions between sleeping and waking. I found sometimes that my father, or my friend, had been represented in sleep by a stool or a chair, and I concluded that it was the entire absence of my personal concrete memory that enabled me to accept such images without surprise. . . . Were these images, however, from the buried memory? had they floated up from the subconscious? had I seen them perhaps a long time ago and forgotten having done so? ... But Robartes denied their source even in the subconscious. . . . Robartes traces these substitute images to different

sources. Those that come in sleep are (1) from the state immediately preceding our birth; (2) from the *Spiritus Mundi* – that is to say from a general storehouse of images which have ceased to be a property of any personality or spirit.[20]

Only a 'counterfeit' image of the beloved enters dreams. The living lover is 'but a brief symbol forgotten when some phase of some atonement is finished' of one loved in earlier life (which of course sets up that infinite regress to some lost original and source which we have already encountered in his remarks on Homer). Entering dream, this 'Over Shadower' or 'ideal form becomes to the living man an obsession, continually perplexing and frustrating natural instinct'. The actual, given and unsatisfactory image is then simply a substitution for that which is forgotten, or repressed.

The entire note illuminates, and complicates, the discourse about the nature of images in 'Among School Children'. In particular, it throws light on that juxtaposition of three images of Maud Gonne: the image of a Ledaean body endlessly renewed in dream (almost, it seems, an image out of a past life), her 'present image', floating into the mind as an old woman subject to time, looking like a Quattrocento painting, and finally, the timeless image in which she stands before him as a living child, reproduced in that concrete likeness which, without being identical, is offered by 'one child or t'other there'. But it is perhaps an almost gratuitous item in this passage which sets off the most interesting associations.

Kusta ben Luka had spoken of such dream revelations as 'Truths without father', 'high-born' and 'solitary'. These are the images which 'Among School Children' speaks of as 'self-born mockers of man's enterprise', akin to but different from the images which nuns and mothers worship. Just before this the poem had spoken of the shape upon the lap of a youthful mother, 'betrayed' by 'Honey of generation'. Both mother and child are implicated, by the ambiguous syntax, in the betrayal. But what is missing from all these references to conception and child-bearing is the idea of a *father*. Yet when Yeats comes to speak of the images that present themselves in dream, it is the father (along with school and a friend of unspecified sex but presumably Maud Gonne) that comes at once to mind. The sheer gratuitousness of the father's presence here emphasises his crucial absence in 'Among School Children'. As we shall see, this is a significant omission.

The story told in Yeats's note (in the epigraph above) about the 'honey of generation' is actually more complex than he allows, and subject to its own forgettings. Yeats, too, it seems, has drunk of the cup of oblivion, and suffers a defect of memory. It is not Porphyry who says all this, but Macrobius, who creeps into Yeats's memory of Porphyry's text through the mediation of Thomas Taylor, the classical scholar in whose edition Yeats read him.

Thomas Taylor's edition of Porphyry's essay 'On the Cave of the Nymphs, in the thirteenth book of the Odyssey' lies behind much of the imagery and thought of Yeats's poetry, and is recurrently referred to in his prose.[21] Porphyry glosses the honey which in Homer's account is deposited in stone amphorae in the Cave of the Nymphs as 'subservient to many and different symbols, because it consists of many powers; since it is both cathartic and preservative'. Bees, he says, are a symbol of 'souls . . . proceeding into generation' through a rebirth which (in Wordsworth's Neoplatonic terms) is 'but a sleep and a forgetting', 'who, after having performed such things as are acceptable to the Gods, will again return [to their kindred stars]'. For 'since this insect loves to return to the place from whence it came', it signifies too the soul's desire for reunion with the primary perfection and fullness of the divine principle, from which the sublunary realm of generation is a falling away, an overflowing in which unity is fragmented into diversity, loss, dispersal.

It is Porphyry's comments on this 'descent into generation' as symbolised in the Greek theogony, where Saturn overthrows Uranus ('Heaven'), to be overthrown in his turn by Jupiter, and so on, which are most significant here. For Porphyry, the descent of the eternal into the sublunary world of time corresponds to that succession of Oedipal struggles in which a rebellious son betrays and emasculates his father, enthrones himself as the patriarch, and is in turn betrayed, dethroned and emasculated. The act of generation itself is the moment of betrayal, the seminal fluid the vehicle of that process in which both father and mother are self-betrayed to their supersession, and the newly conceived child in turn betrayed to the curse of time. The unformed 'shape' upon the mother's lap is already trapped in that cycle of generation in which it will soon have 'sixty or more winters on its head'. Taking on the burden of the father, displacing its predecessor, each individual soul is in turn betrayed into that realm of generation to which belongs, in the words of 'Sailing to Byzantium', 'Whatever is begotten, born, and dies'. All history is then the history of supplantings. Porphyry is quite explicit about this:

> In Orpheus . . . Saturn is ensnared by Jupiter through honey. For Saturn, being filled with honey, is intoxicated, his senses are darkened . . . and he sleeps. . . . Saturn being bound, is castrated in the same manner as Heaven; the theologist obscurely signifying by this, that divine natures become through pleasure bound, and drawn down into the realms of generation; and also that, when dissolved in pleasure, they emit certain seminal powers. Hence Saturn castrates Heaven, when descending to earth, through a desire of coition. But the sweetness of honey signifies,

with theologists, the same thing as the pleasure arising from copulation, by which Saturn, being ensnared, was castrated. . . . But Saturn receives the powers of Heaven, and Jupiter the powers of Saturn. Since, therefore, honey is assumed in purgations, and as an antidote to putrefaction, and is indicative of the pleasure which draws souls downward to generation; it is a symbol well adapted to aquatic Nymphs, on account of the unputrescent nature of the waters over which they preside, their purifying power, and their co-operation. For water co-operates in the work of generation.

There can be few likelier candidates for the title of aquatic nymphs than the 'daughters of the swan' of 'Among School Children'; while in 'A Prayer for my Daughter' Yeats's anxiety about being supplanted finds issue in the image of an irresponsible, foam-born Aphrodite, 'that great Queen, that rose out of the spray, [who] / Being fatherless could have her way / Yet chose a bandy-legged smith for man'. At the same time, the correlation of honey and water (the 'generated soul' of 'Coole Park and Ballylee') supplies the otherwise unapparent link between the 'honey of generation' of stanza V and the sublunary 'spume that plays' over the 'ghostly paradigm of things' in stanza VI (the ghostly word-play on 'spume/sperm' supplying the essential link).

The remark about divine natures emitting 'certain seminal powers', however, elucidates a major crux in 'Leda and the Swan', and one directly relevant to the idea of the father here: 'Did she put on his knowledge with his power . . . ?' The power of Jupiter descends through Leda to Helen at this moment of violation, bringing into existence, according to *A Vision*, those warring antithetical forces out of which the modern era has been shaped: 'I imagine the annunciation that founded Greece as made to Leda . . . and that from one of her eggs came Love and from the other War.'[22] The patriarchal principle enters history, that is, as a disruptive force of sexual and political violation, shudderingly propagating a new annunciation from which it then withdraws, all passion spent. Taylor's notes confirm this interpretation:

> the genital parts must be considered as symbols of prolific power; and the castration of these parts as signifying the progression of this power into a subject order. So that the fable means that the prolific powers of Saturn are called forth into progression by Jupiter, and those of Heaven by Saturn; Jupiter being inferior to Saturn, and Saturn to Heaven.

Such an annunciation sets not only histories but stories under way, initiating, as the next paragraphs of *A Vision* indicate, not only Helen but Homer, with whom the tragedy began. The question again raised here is focused on that ambiguous word 'author': who is Helen's 'author': Jupiter, or Homer, the god or the poet? History is here doubled into story which then becomes in turn a power in the subject order of history. There is, in fact, a curious paralleling between this paradigm for history's declensions and what happens in Yeats's relation to his own 'sources'. The crucial forgetting in Yeats's footnote to 'Among School Children' has all the qualities of a repression. Mis-remembering the source of the 'cup of oblivion', which actually derives from Macrobius' commentary on Scipio's Dream, Yeats imagines himself drawing inspiration at a purer source than in fact he does. The ideas are muddied with their transmission. But if he has 'no warrant' at all from Porphyry, by the same token he has every warrant to trust to his own creative forgetfulness, to do what he likes with the supposedly sacrosanct tradition.

The process by which Yeats's fleshed material ideas are derived here is like that by which the soul descends into matter. As Taylor says, Macrobius 'has derived some of the ancient arcana which it contains from what is here said by Porphyry': Taylor derives from Macrobius, and Yeats from Taylor. In the process, the ideational primal father is castrated into textual being, culminating in the material body of Yeats's text, in the same way that the sequence of castrations derives from Heaven to Jupiter. We have, here, an analogy between literary, spiritual and sexual succession, and at their epicentre is that repression of the idea of an earthly, heavenly or literary father (the paternal authority from which the text derives) which lies at the heart of 'Among School Children'.

The divine in the guise of a bird is the only real father this poem allows. At the same time, the two surrogate parents, impotent 'sixty year old smiling public man' and sterile 'kind old nun' preside over the children *in loco parentis* in the same way that the pedagogue Aristotle lorded it over a 'king of kings'.

In the end, stories rule history, myths determine politics. In the fallen world of history, the children are constantly re-inscribed within the narrative order – 'learn to cipher and to sing, / To study reading-books and histories, / In the best modern way'. Everywhere, according to Macrobius in Taylor's footnote, there is this eddying and overflowing of being from its primal source down into the sublunary realms of generation, and it is in this rushing out of demiurgic energy that the turbulence of history originates and the multiplicity of opinion and dissension is spawned:

> Pythagoras thought that the empire of Pluto began downwards from the milky way, because souls falling from thence appear to have already receded from the Gods. . . .
>   'As soon, therefore, as the soul gravitates towards body in this first production of herself, she begins to experience a material tumult, that is, matter flowing into her essence. And this is what Plato remarks in the

Phaedo, that the soul is drawn into body staggering with recent intoxication; signifying by this, the new drink of matter's impetuous flood, through which the soul, becoming defiled and heavy, is drawn into a terrene situation. But the starry *cup* placed between Cancer and the Lion, is a symbol of this mystic truth, signifying that descending souls first experience intoxication in that part of the heavens through the influx of matter. Hence oblivion, the companion of intoxication, there begins silently to creep into the recesses of the soul. For if souls retained in their descent to bodies the memory of divine concerns, of which they were conscious in the heavens, there would be no dissension among men about divinity. But all, indeed, in descending, drink of oblivion; though some more, and others less. On this account, though truth is not apparent to all men on the earth, yet all exercise their opinions about it; because *a defect of memory is the origin of opinion.* But those discover most who have drank [sic] least of oblivion, because they easily remember what they had known before in the heavens.

If even the 'paddler's heritage' has its own descent into being, betrayed by the honey of generation, the text too has its paternity, not only in the world of other texts but in the realm of autobiography, which is itself a constellation of stories, a 'phantasmagoria'. The poem is generated, in its onward movement, by an act of redoubled recall which also involves a forgetfulness. Distracted by dream from the actual presence of these children in this schoolroom, the poet tells a story of another, long-distant act of story-telling which, like that of Scheherezade, seized the imagination of its auditor and drew him into a subject order in which his own being was transformed, thereby transforming not only that past moment but the present in which this poem repeatedly comes into existence. And this transformation is described in terms which immediately recall that primal Neoplatonic perfection from which all trivial events in the realm of history are degenerations, just as 'tale' and 'tragedy' are degenerated versions of that paradigmatic 'parable' which, as in 'Harun al-Rashid', may still be recovered in the immediacy of 'dream'. Plato's parable too is altered in its falling away from origins, becomes defiled and heavy, as an egg in its oval materiality is an imperfect copy of a sphere:

> I dream of a Ledaean body, bent
> Above a sinking fire, a tale that she
> Told of a harsh reproof, or trivial event
> That changed some childish day to tragedy –
> Told, and it seemed that our two natures blent
> Into a sphere from youthful sympathy,
> Or else, to alter Plato's parable,
> Into the yoke and white of the one shell.

In the poem 'The Choice', subsequently retitled 'Chosen' and printed sixth in the sequence 'A Woman Young and Old', the woman speaks of learning that 'The lot of love is chosen' while 'Struggling for an image on the track / Of the whirling zodiac'. She speaks, too, of finding that post-coital 'stillness', 'Where his heart my heart did seem / And both adrift on the miraculous stream / Where – wrote a learned astrologer / The Zodiac is changed into a sphere'. Yeats's original footnote observed, with characteristic vagueness, 'In some Neoplatonist or Hermatist [*sic*] – whose name I forget – the whorl changes into a sphere at one of the points where the Milky Way crosses the Zodiac.'[23] The footnote to the retitled poem makes it clear that his forgotten source here is the passage in Macrobius that occurs in the gap between the two paragraphs on Scipio's Dream above. Yeats observes:

> The 'learned astrologer' . . . was Macrobius, and the particular passage . . . is from Macrobius's comment upon 'Scipio's Dream' . . .: '. . . when the sun is in Aquarius, we sacrifice to the Shades, for it is in the sign inimical to human life; and from thence the meeting-place of Zodiac and Milky Way, the descending soul by its defluction is drawn out of the spherical, the sole divine form, into the cone.'[24]

The primal unity of being symbolised by the union of man and woman in Plato's parable, then, is for Yeats a direct analogy with that unitary original source, in all its fullness of self-presence, from which all particular tales are fallings-away, and both in turn figure forth what Macrobius, in Taylor, calls 'the soul of the world . . . without division'. This 'soul of the world' is that *Spiritus Mundi* out of which emerge the vast images of apocalypse in 'The Second Coming', to create in their overflowing turbulence 'a material tumult'. It is just this tumult which, in a comment on 'The Stare's Nest By My Window', Yeats grasped amidst the newsless, decentred anarchy of civil war, realising that 'Men must have lived so through many tumultuous centuries', and setting against this the strange experience of coming 'to smell honey in places where honey could not be'.[25]

The poem which precedes 'Chosen' in 'A Woman Young and Old', 'Consolation', takes comfort in the wisdom of 'what the sages said', and this comfort lies precisely in the act of forgetting that accompanies drinking of Porphyry's cup, the entry into history:

> How could passion run so deep
> Had I never thought
> That the crime of being born
> Blackens all our lot?
> But where the crime's committed
> The crime can be forgot.

In the realm of story-telling the same forgetfulness occurs. The honey of generation is simultaneously a cup of oblivion, both beneficence and curse, crime and forgiveness. All stories originate in the crime-blackened realm of generation, the fallen world of history. But the act of narration then creates a 'mirror-resembling dream' which, like the dream of the young bride in 'Harun al-Rashid', forgets its origins, creating 'Truths without father', 'self-born' – those images which, in 'Among School Children', are 'self-born mockers of man's enterprise'. Drinking Porphyry's cup, the author, like the soul, may die, but being dead, will 'rise, / Dream and so create / Translunar paradise', reborn as 'an idea, something intended, complete', as, that is, his own self-born textual double.

Mine author sung it me

Yeats is particularly prone to forgetfulness in the vicinity of Neoplatonism, especially as it relates to the carnal, sublunary world of history and politics. In 'Nineteen Hundred and Nineteen', for example, he may be thinking of the revolutionary Neoplatonist Shelley's *Prometheus Unbound* (II, 5, 72–4) when he remarks, casually, 'Some moralist or mythological poet / Compares the solitary soul to a swan', before going on to repeat the same formula in a reference which Norman Jeffares, *inter alios*, suggests is to Taylor's 'Cave of the Nymphs':

> Some Platonist affirms that in the station
> Where we should cast off body and trade
> The ancient habit sticks,
> And that if our works could
> But vanish with our breath
> That were a lucky death,
> For triumph can but mar our solitude.

The poem had opened with the image of 'golden grasshoppers and bees' of the Acropolis destroyed in the Peloponnesian War. But its real theme is closer home, in the many ingenious lovely things that are gone in the current Troubles, a sublunary struggle under 'the circle of the moon / That pitches common things about'. Such a conflict has destroyed the shallow confidences of the preceding decades, and has caught man 'lost amid the labyrinth he has made / In art or politics'.

But perhaps the most interesting forgetting is in a note to those lines in 'The Tower' where he speaks of having to bid the Muse go pack:

> When I wrote the lines about Plato and Plotinus I forgot that it is something in our own eyes that makes us see them as all transcendence. Has not Plotinus written: 'Let every soul recall, then, at the outset the

truth that soul is the author of all living things, that it has breathed the life into them all, whatever is nourished by earth and sea, all the creatures of the air, the divine stars in the sky; it is the maker of the sun; itself formed and ordered this vast heaven and conducts all that rhythmic motion – and it is a principle distinct from all these to which it gives law and movement and life, and it must of necessity be more honourable than they, for they gather or dissolve as soul brings them life or abandons them, but soul, since it never can abandon itself, is of eternal being'?[26]

The rhetorical question, as if accidentally, catches a characteristic link of authorship, authority, and paternity in Yeats: soul as author of the universe, of the text, of the human creature. The ambiguity of the word 'author' has a lineage running back through Chaucer to antiquity. It is this which is centrally focused in that poem where Yeats's literary and philosophical progenitors are brought into conjunction with his own fictive creations, Robartes and Aherne, 'The Phases of the Moon'. It is no accident that this poem, in all its narrative obliquity, occupies a key position in that mysterious text where Yeats's own philosophy of history is translated into story-telling, *A Vision*.

Yeats's 1922 note complicates the relation between author and fictive characters in this poem, by attributing to Robartes and Aherne a putatively 'actual' existence in a text where they speak of their author as if *he* were a story they are telling. The unseen omnipresence throughout the text of this imaginary 'Yeats', on whom the whole dialogue between the two characters is posited, then duplicates the absence/presence of the invisible author himself, present everywhere in his effects, apparent nowhere *in propria persona*.

> Years ago [he writes] I wrote three stories in which occur the names of Michael Robartes and Owen Aherne. I now consider that I used the actual names of two friends, and that one of these friends, Michael Robartes, has but lately returned from Mesopotamia, where he has partly found and partly thought out much philosophy. I consider that Aherne and Robartes, men to whose namesakes I had attributed a turbulent life or death, have quarrelled with me. They take their place in a phantasmagoria in which I endeavour to explain my philosophy of life and death. To some extent I wrote these poems as a text for exposition.[27]

Much depends on that 'now', and whether it means 'now, in actuality', or 'here, in this poem'. And this indeterminacy is deliberate, for it calls into question the whole status of the fiction. The strange doubling in that reference to their 'namesakes' compounds this questioning. The 'namesakes' to whom a turbulent life or death have been attributed in the past are in one sense the fictional characters of Yeats's three original stories. By contrast, the characters referred to now are the supposedly real-life 'originals' of those stories. This of course only compounds the paradoxical interplay of 'real' and 'imaginary', by incorporating the earlier fictions as interior distances of the poem's claim to actuality here and now. These ostensibly more 'actual' characters, the Aherne and Robartes of the poem, are simply new fictional extensions of those earlier fictions, taking their place, at the poet's masterly authorial direction, in a text which is even more literary and unreal than the earlier stories, a 'text for exposition' which is also a bucolic dialogue.

Yeats's presence in his own phantasmagoria is no more than that of a Platonic shadow on a windowpane; yet in the end he can extinguish the whole elaborate fiction he has constructed by the simple act of concluding the narrative. In the process, he also terminates the existence of his own textual double, for at the same moment that the poem is completed, 'The light in the tower window [is] put out'. The impersonal framing narrative which surrounds the dialogue between the two characters then becomes the 'objective' source of authority for their existence, constituting and then dismissing them into the fabulous formless dark where they will remain in latency until again summoned up to provide some of the framing paraphernalia of *A Vision*, which includes in one version, an introduction by Aherne which alludes to the (supposed) genesis of this poem. By reverting to and developing his earlier inventions, and mingling them with a textual double of himself, the poet creates a paradoxical new dimension, in which strange cross-overs occur between real and imaginary. It is in this context that the poem explores the central ambiguity of 'authorship'.

This is most apparent in the attitude which the characters themselves take towards their author. Within the framed dialogue of the poem, Robartes exposits mysteries of which his author, he tells us, remains in ignorance, seeking 'in book or manuscript / What he shall never find'. Aherne in turn plays with the idea of ringing at his door, to 'speak / Just truth enough to show that his whole life / Will scarcely find for him a broken crust / Of all those truths that are your daily bread'. But it is not in fact these characters, but the poem itself that plays with these various narrative possibilities, toying with the idea of bringing the author directly into the foreground of its story, only to reject that opportunity. Yet of course this is profoundly paradoxical, and relates to a larger paradox of the text. For both these characters feel superior to their author, mocking him in their conversation for his exclusion from that which they know, when, in reality, the joke is on them. They are, after all, not the self-directing, knowing subjects they believe themselves to be, but simply effects of the text, carriers of an 'exposition' which is not theirs but Yeats's, textual demiurges, in Neoplatonic terms, of his own creative authority. All that they know must, by definition, be known to him. But he knows in addition what they can never know: that they are his creatures, that every step of their discussion is not a moment of freedom and choice in which they can do this or the other, but a moment of foreclosure which locks them in the very temporal cycle of which they speak, no more able to escape from the twenty-eight phases of the poem than the characters they speak of, their end pre-determined by this already-written text.

In the closing return to the narrative frame, Aherne may laugh at the idea of Yeats cracking his wits without ever finding the meaning. But his true, unnoticed intuition had come earlier, in his recognition of that bondage in which the text holds them, as, in the larger philosophy which is the text's *theme*, they are also bound on the wheel of history: 'But the escape; the song's not finished yet'. It is the mocked 'laborious pen' of the poet which will decide when their song is finished. The story has authority over its characters and its tellers. What for Aherne seems merely an empty narrative formula actually conceals the secret of their subjection to the narrative: 'The song will have it'.

That this is the case is revealed at the beginning of the poem when Robartes has to establish even the most simple facts of their *mise en scène* which are brought into existence by the very act of utterance: 'We are on the bridge; that shadow is the tower, / And the light proves that he is reading still'. These are two souls newly emerged from limbo, constituted, along with their context, by the writing of the poem. Their nervousness at a strange sound conceals a deeper insecurity, and they make obeisance to their source and author in the very moment that they dismiss him as the finder of 'Mere images', not realising that they are two of the images he has found. When Robartes congratulates his companion on the clarity of his thought, there is a complex irony at play: 'Because you are forgotten, half out of life, / And never wrote a book, your thought is clear'. He despises the ideas of author, book and writing. But in fact he is himself their creature, only an empty written figure. The forgottenness they share, their being half out of life, arise from this very fictiveness. They have, since those three early stories, been forgotten by Yeats, and now they are revived by him. And they are not revived to life but only to that peculiar mode of existence enjoyed by textual figures (to alter Yeats's parable) 'Estranged amidst the strangeness of themselves'.

The paradoxical nature of this problematic textuality is raised at the beginning of the poem, in that exchange which sets Robartes off on his exposition of the phases of the moon:

> ROBARTES: He wrote of me in that extravagant style
> He had learned from Pater, and to round his tale
> Said I was dead; and dead I choose to be.

AHERNE: Sing me the changes of the moon once more;
True song, though speech: 'mine author sung it me.'

The character acknowledges his own earlier textuality. But he sees this as merely a secondary distorting copy of which he, the speaking subject, was the real source. But in fact the 'subject' who speaks in this poem now, is merely a derivative of that earlier text, which in turn was a derivative, not just of Yeats's authorial energy, but of a style of *writing* which has its own paternal, and Paterian, lineage elsewhere. The free will of the fictive character is then ironically 'affirmed' in an act which simply chooses to confirm that which the author has already conferred upon him. It is deliberately unclear who has the final say, and who derives from whom, for text and figure are of course, in reality, coterminous and coincident: we cannot tell the dancer from the dance.

As Robartes looks backwards to a perpetually recessive textuality in the past, Aherne looks forward to a text yet to come, which is nevertheless simply a repetition of some earlier telling. What's more, this is a text within a text: Robartes' song becomes not only the main *theme* of the rest of the poem, but also the main *body* of the text itself, thus collapsing the distance between form and content as it sets it up, only to reopen that gap through the antithesis of writing and song. For Robartes' text is 'True song, though speech'; whereas Yeats's text (the same words, redefined by that larger narrative frame) is quite definitely *writing*. But in case this is not enough, Aherne adds a final complexity to this overlaying of texts with that unattributed quotation, which itself feels the lack of an author at the moment that it speaks of authorship.

Yeats uses this tag on several occasions, and always with the same apparent assumption that his readers will recognise it. When this chapter appeared in an earlier form, the nearest analogy was a series of such uses in Chaucer's *Troilus and Criseyde*, of which the closest is 'For as myn auctour seyde, so seye I'. A.N. Jeffares[28] had suggested that 'the changes of the moon' motif 'may be traced to Yeats's interest in Chaucer. In 1910 he was "deep in Chaucer" and extremely interested in "the eight and 20 mansiouns / That longen to the moon" of *The Frankelyn's Tayle* (lines 1115 ff)'. Certainly, too, Chaucer telescoped the word 'author' to mean both 'writer' and 'author of one's being', either father or God, and sometimes seems to imply both. Warwick Gould, in an essay on Yeats and the *Arabian Nights*, had linked this source with a passage in the *Arabian Nights* Yeats alludes to in *Per Amica Silentia Lunae* which underwrites the Oedipal dimension here: 'Answered Wird Khan, "True, O my son, but whence learnedst thou geomancy and thou young of years?" Quoth the boy, "My father taught it me . . ." '[29]

But Yeats's tag seemed too specific to be a misquotation, and since then an important article by Wayne K. Chapman has revealed a direct source in, significantly, Milton's *The Doctrine and Discipline of Divorce* (1644). The passage is concerned with the false doubles which substitute for Love and subvert his power, so that the

> original and fierie vertue giv'n him by Fate, all on a sudden goes out and leaves him undeifi'd, and despoil'd of all his force. . . . Thus mine author sung it to me.[30]

Milton's author is Plato, and the recessive embedding of a tradition is highly apposite to the context. When Aherne says 'Mine author sung it me' in quotation marks he himself compounds the embedding. Yeats's text itself becomes another double discourse, a self-delighting utterance in which the imagined text cites the author who created it, as he in turn is constituted by an unbroken narrative order stretching back to Plato. In a poem where form and content merge into a single text which has a double utterer and, therefore, a double author, 'Mine author' for Aherne, using one of that author's favourite tags, is Yeats himself, and what he sang him is everything that the poem contains, including that very tag. The text, that is, is 'twice born, twice buried', and 'die[s] into the labyrinth of itself'. Aherne and Robartes seem to have access to a great truth, but like those souls 'cast beyond the verge' in Robartes' last servile crescent, 'they speak what's blown into the mind', and, since they are not substantial figures but figures of speech, 'They change their bodies at a word'.

What climbs the stair?

In 'J.M. Synge and the Ireland of his Time' Yeats has some interesting things to say about the representativeness of the parricide motif in Synge's *Playboy*, which he links without noticing with its inverse, the desire of Chronos to devour his children before they supplant him:

> It is the strangest, the most beautiful expression in drama of that Irish fantasy which overflowing through all Irish literature that has come out of Ireland itself . . . is the unbroken character of Irish genius. In modern days this genius has delighted in mischievous extravagance, like that of the Gaelic poet's curse upon his children: 'There are three things that I hate: the devil that is waiting for my soul; the worms that are waiting for my body; my children, who are waiting for my wealth and care neither for my body nor my soul: O, Christ, hang all in the same noose!' I think those words were spoken with a delight in their vehemence that took out of anger half the bitterness with all the gloom. An old man on the Aran

Islands told me the very tale on which *The Playboy* is founded, beginning with the words: 'If any gentleman has done a crime we'll hide him. There was a gentleman that killed his father, and I had him in my own house six months till he got away to America'.[31]

Such a cursing might not seem far from one aspect of the mood in which Yeats comes to write his will in 'The Tower' or consider the possible degeneration of his line 'Through natural declension of the soul' in 'Meditations in Time of Civil War'. But if we bear in mind the implicit link he assumes between 'author' as father and as poet, between hereditary lineage and poetic lines, the almost inadvertent juxtaposition of 'authority' and 'honey' in his immediately subsequent remarks on art's chilly estrangement from the warm, fluid 'realms of generation' acquires a deeper resonance:

> Great art chills us at first by its coldness or its strangeness, by what seems capricious, and yet it is from these qualities it has authority, as though it had fed on locusts and wild honey. The imaginative writer shows us the world as a painter does his picture, reversed in a looking-glass, that we may see it, not as it seems to eyes habit has made dull, but as we were Adam and this the first morning.[32]

This mirror-resembling dream creates the world anew, then, in its prelapsarian fullness. But this for Yeats is related to another return, in which the whole descent into generation is turned back, in an ascent to the source like that which in the final section of 'The Tower' has him in imagination climbing the streams until the fountain leap, seeking the pride and plenitude of 'the fabulous horn':

> To speak of one's emotions without fear or moral ambition, to come out from under the shadow of other men's minds, to forget their needs, to be utterly oneself, that is all the Muses care for. Villon, pander, thief and man-slayer, is as immortal in their eyes, and illustrates in the cry of his ruin as great a truth, as Dante in abstract ecstasy, and touches our compassion more. All art is the disengaging of a soul from place and history, its suspension in a beautiful or terrible light to await the Judgment, though it must be, seeing that all its days were a Last Day, judged already. It may show the crimes of Italy as Dante did, or Greek mythology like Keats, or Kerry and Galway villages, and so vividly that ever after I shall look at all with like eyes, and yet I know that Cino da Pistoia thought Dante unjust, that Keats knew no Greek, that those country men and women are neither so lovable nor so lawless as 'mine author sung it me'; that I have added to my being, not my knowledge.[33]

Art's authority derives from eating the honey of forgetfulness, which wipes out the shadow of other men's minds, leaving the Muses' favourite 'self-born', a soul 'disengaged from place and history', and returned, therefore, in story, to its proper home. Yet this return rounds off time into eternity by combining prelapsarian Eden and post-apocalyptic Heaven in one timeless 'translunar paradise', just as in 'The Tower' Yeats writes his will by merging heirs and ancestors in a single time-defying 'Pride, like that of the morn'. The Luciferian associations here suggest that for Yeats art's proper place is that moment of suspension where it is always awaiting judgement for its rebellion against the Father, and always-already judged, poised between Dante's 'abstract ecstasy' and Villon's 'ruin', between, that is, the 'artifice of eternity' and the 'sensual music' of nature. Yet at the same time, the poem deceives as it transfigures: the author who sings it to us adds to our being, not our knowledge, and his authority is founded, in the end, on our subjection to his authorial power. Entering a realm where we free ourselves from the patriarchs of history, the heirs of Chronos, we are re-inscribed under the anonymous song which claims a self-begotten authority over us.

Yeats uses the Miltonic tag once again in the Introduction he wrote for the poems of Dorothy Wellesley. Her poem 'Matrix' he identifies as

> a long meditation that seemed the most moving philosophic poem of our time, and the most moving because its wisdom bulked animal below the waist. In its abrupt lines, passion burst into thought without renouncing its dark quality. I had a moment's jealousy, I had thought of expending my last years on philosophic verse but knew now that I was too old. Only men and women in vigorous vigour can have such hatred of the trivial light. Here was something new or very old, the philosophy of the Vedanta or Plotinus with a terror not of their time before human destiny; yet its author had never read Plotinus or the Indian thinkers. I was certain of that because of omissions, or an emphasis impossible had she some logical system in mind. No, that terror itself had made poem and philosophy. If man ever had knowledge, or wisdom, it was in the dark of the womb, so 'mine author sang it me', or before he was conceived; in the hush of night are we not conscious of the unconceived. There must be an escape, death is no escape because the dead cannot forget that they have lived and dread to enter into the body once more through the elements, finding there 'the reiteration of birth.'[34]

Beneath the occult rhetoric, Yeats here works a variation on the characteristically Modernist perception of history as a making new through repression and repetition. One point, however, should be noted. Yeats writes of 'passion burst[ing] into thought without renouncing its dark quality'. It brings a knowledge which derives from some pre-natal freedom which is forgotten and yet carried everywhere as an unconscious surplus, a terror investing all conscious acts and utterances. In 'Speaking to the Psaltery'[35] Yeats wrote of the role of music in poetry as just such a hidden discourse, informing the conscious verbal one 'the music was an unconscious creation, the words a conscious, for no beginnings are in the intellect, and no living thing remembers its own birth.' In his poem 'To Dorothy Wellesley' he focuses centrally on this relation.

The whole poem is premised on a series of commands which call up, from nowhere, a hypothetical narrative. This essential fictiveness is reinforced by the repetition of 'As though' and a series of negative constructions, as well as by the rhetorical question which, like those in 'The Second Coming', 'The Statues' and elsewhere, summons an unspecified and formless terror out of the fabulous dark to stalk into the realm of history. As with 'And what rough beast . . . ?' and 'What stalked through the Post Office?' the question 'What climbs the stair?' gives neither answer nor circumstantial detail. The terror remains unspoken, unspecified, and terrifies us all the more, as in all tales of the supernatural, by leaving everything to our imagination. It lets our unconscious work on supplying its particular images to the empty imageless signifiers of conscious discourse. It is enough for Yeats to ask the question to allow some of that nameless surplus to spill over, for the 'sensuous silence' of consciousness is 'rammed full' with a passion that cannot be spoken, as those two words themselves are charged with a sexual intensity that must be withheld. Yeats's answer, then, is no mere empty 'Nothing', but an unspeakable excess of meaning that is latent everywhere in the poem, which can be contemplated only obliquely, in the same way that the Furies are spoken euphemistically of as 'the Kindly Ones', and that Yeats avoids naming his authorising source in Aeschylus and Sophocles:

> Rammed full
> Of that most sensuous silence of the night . . .
> Climb to your chamber full of books and wait,
> No books upon the knee, and no one there . . .
> What climbs the stair?
> Nothing that common women ponder on
> If you are worth my hope! Neither Content
> Nor satisfied Conscience, but that great family
> Some ancient famous authors misrepresent,
> The Proud Furies each with her torch on high.

Such 'misrepresentation', then, is part of the authorial patrimony, art's way of warding off by containing that vision of terror that would otherwise shatter the soul. Writing of the role of the unconscious in this poem in a letter to Dorothy Wellesley, Yeats uses terms which recall both the image of Maud Gonne in 'A Bronze Head' and his vision of Hamlet and Lear in 'Lapis Lazuli':

We have all something within ourselves to batter down and get our power
from this fighting. I have never 'produced' a play in verse without showing
the actors that the passion of the verse comes from the fact that the
speakers are holding down violence or madness – 'down Hysterica
passio'. All depends on the completeness of the holding down, on the
stirring of the beast underneath. Even my poem 'To D.W.' should give this
impression. The moon, the moonless night, the dark velvet, the sensual
silence, the silent room and the violent bright Furies. Without this conflict
we have no passion only sentiment and thought.[36]

'About the conflict in "To D.W.,"' he goes on, 'I did not plan it
deliberately. That conflict is deep in my subconsciousness, perhaps in
everybody's', a conflict, he suggests, with an erotic or sexual base.
Elsewhere, in response to her account of a highly sexually charged
dream, he writes to her: 'Often in spiritual dreams there is something
one cannot say – a deeper part of the dream is hidden from a more
superficial part.'[37] While in another letter he relates this to his own
philosophy as a body of knowledge emerging from latency, half-
forgotten, to inform the very texture of his poetry: 'I am finishing my
belated pamphlet and will watch with amusement the emergence of the
philosophy of my own poetry, the unconscious becoming conscious. It
seems to increase the force of my poetry.'[38]

The question Yeats might then ask of his own poetry would be that he
asks of Wellesley's in his Introduction, 'murmuring, with better reason
than Coleridge knew, "Where learnt you that heroic measure?"' To
which the written text might reply: 'Mine author sung it me'. But this
author would not be the biographical Yeats who writes; rather it would
be the singing voice of 'the great memory, the memory of Nature
herself'[39] of which he wrote in the essay 'Magic' in 1901:

I must commit what merchandise of wisdom I have to this ship of written
speech, and after all, I have many a time watched it put out to sea with
not less alarm when all the speech was rhyme. We who write, we who
bear witness, must often hear our hearts cry out against us, complaining
because of their hidden things, and I know not but he who speaks of
wisdom may sometimes, in the change that is coming upon the world,
have to fear the anger of the people of Faery, whose country is the heart of
the world. . . . And surely, at whatever risk, we must cry out that the
imagination is always seeking to remake the world according to the
impulses and the patterns in that Great Mind, and that Great Memory?
Can there be anything so important as to cry out that what we call
romance, poetry, intellectual beauty, is the only signal that the supreme
Enchanter, or some one in His councils, is speaking of what has been, and
shall be again, in the consummation of time?[40]

Nearly forty years later, in 1937, having just finished *A Vision*, he
wrote to Wellesley of reading Roger Fry's translation of Mallarmé:

I find it exciting, as it shows me the road I and others of my time went for certain furlongs. It is not the way I go now, but one of the legitimate roads. He escapes from history; you and I are in history, the history of the mind. . . . I begin to see things double – doubled in history, world history, personal history. At this moment all the specialists are about to run together in our new Alexandria, thought is to be unified as its own free act, and the shadow of Germany and elsewhere is an attempted unity by force. In my own life I never felt so acutely the presence of a spiritual value and that is accompanied by intensified desire. Perhaps there is a theme for poetry in this 'double swan and shadow'. You must feel plunged as I do into the madness of vision, into a sense of the relation between separated things that you cannot explain, and that deeply disturbs emotion. Perhaps it makes every poet's life poignant, certainly every poet who has 'swallowed the formulas.'[41]

The continuity between Yeats's early formulation and this late one is clear, if complex. Central to both is the conviction that some return to a primal unity and plenitude of being is on the cards – the tarot cards perhaps – for this moment in history where all things are doubled. And poetry, with its visions of 'translunar paradise', is what sings, from the textual unconscious, of this 'change that is coming upon the world'. The Great Enchanter, or some one in His councils, may now be Hitler, but this 'sense of the relation between separated things that you cannot explain' is nevertheless going to issue in 'an attempted unity by force'.

The discourse that is repressed in every poem and philosophical vision is, then, the discourse of history itself, that history which is a series of parricides and slaughters of the innocents, in which Chronos/Saturn devours his children and is in turn castrated and deposed by them. We would rather forget this discourse, but it emerges as a vision of terror, a terrible beauty, to stalk through every translunar paradise that art creates. This Oedipal dimension explains the otherwise enigmatic endnote to *A Vision* in 1936, with its link between the discords that 'will drive Europe to that artificial unity – only dry or drying sticks can be tied into a bundle – which is the decadence of every civilisation', and the arcane rhyme, 'Should Jupiter and Saturn meet, / O what a crop of mummy wheat!'[42] It explains, too, the equally enigmatic ending of 'The Gift of Harun Al-Rashid'. Here the sudden unprepared-for vision of violence and war, storm-tossed banners and armed men speaking from the fabulous dark of the concluding sentence is made more mysterious by the cryptic candour of the declaration which precedes it:

> And now my utmost mystery is out.
> A woman's beauty is a storm-tossed banner;
> Under it wisdom stands, and I alone –
> Of all Arabia's lovers I alone –

Nor dazzled by the embroidery, nor lost
In the confusion of its night-dark folds,
Can hear the armed man speak.

In 1910 Yeats thought he was outside history. Over a quarter of a century later, he admitted to Dorothy Wellesley that he was well and truly in it. What climbs the stair is the same 'terrible beauty' that speaks out of the night-dark folds of all Yeats's texts. Like Coleridge's damsel with a dulcimer, linked so intimately with ancestral voices prophesying war, these furies bind a woman's beauty to the armed man of a transgressive history which, like Hamlet's father's ghost, will insist, finally, on being remembered.

Chapter Ten

The living world for text: Yeats and the book of the people

Ancient sects and filthy modern tides

'A woman's beauty is a storm-tossed banner', Yeats says in oracular tones at the end of 'The Gift of Harun al Rashid', and the 'armed man' of an insurgent history speaks through her acts of transgressive super-natural invasion of the sublunary world. It is a remarkable collocation, with a Romantic lineage back to the damsel with a dulcimer and the ancestral voices prophesying war of 'Kubla Khan'. It points forward, too, to the implacable Furies who climb the stair in 'To Dorothy Wellesley'. The biographical origins of this motif in Yeats's work have been well explored. They are, however, usually misunderstood, which is to say interpreted in the terms Yeats himself proffered, which are in the most literal sense a repression of their historical significance.

Biographical accounts of Yeats's relations with Maud Gonne rarely address her actual signification in his texts, as opposed to the role he overtly assigns her. To do so would require taking the history in which they were both involved as more than the mere 'background' for a timeless poetry. In all these readings Gonne fulfils one of several traditional roles in male fantasy. She is Helen of Troy, a type of the dangerous beauty which drives men to historic acts of brutality and shame. She is the *fin de siècle femme fatale* who withholds her favours, driving him to distraction, and then turns the screw by marrying a fool – a scenario straight out of Sacher-Masoch. Or she is the figure of Ireland, representing a 'Traditional sanctity and loveliness' which has to be recreated in a world where heroic reverie is mocked by clown and knave.[1]

Yet throughout these narratives another story speaks, and it is the strength of Yeats's poetry that it everywhere utters this alternative history, even as it tries to marginalise and transform it. The *meaning* of his texts is often just this contention between conflicting readings of contemporary history, a struggle for hegemony within the poem itself. For the historical Gonne, like those other women appropriated by Yeats, Constance Markiewicz, Eva Gore-Booth, Dorothy Wellesley, was a type of woman quite different from the poet's mythologies. Her resistance to his impostures figures a clash of discourses which she put to good use, eliciting from his 'unrequited love' a poetry *of use* to the struggle for national liberation. Her response to importunity, that rejection gave Yeats something to write about, sounds remarkably like the words his spirit instructors put into the mouth of that equally shrewd woman, Yeats's wife Georgie Hyde-Lees: 'We have come to give you metaphors for poetry.' Gonne, however, would not subscribe to that secondary inscription. Yeats might do what he liked with his fantasy of her, but unless it served the cause of Ireland she had come to give him nothing, as Yeats himself acknowledged in 'Words' in *The Green Helmet*, noting that, though words obeyed his call, she didn't, adding that if she had he 'might have thrown poor words away / And been content to live'.

Eliot spoke of Yeats as a belated Modernist and it is generally argued that it was Ezra Pound who in 1913 effected Yeats's transit from Celtic Twilight to Modernism. This places the volume *Responsibilities* in 1914 as the first work under the dispensation of Modernism. There are reasons why transatlantic critics should want to foreground this moment. But Yeats's transformation predates Pound's arrival on the scene, and it owes much more to the crisis of modernity Yeats confronted in contemporary Ireland, at the centre of which lay the question of nationality. It is the poems of *The Green Helmet* in 1910, whose combative nationalism is indicated by the title, which mark the major breakthrough in his style, heralding a new, tough, argumentative dialogism, confronting 'the fascination of what's difficult' in 'the day's war with every knave and dolt', rather than retreating to the twilight's glimmer. Modernism in Yeats, that is, was generated by the pressure of contemporary history in a moment of compulsive modernisation, mediated by the revolutionary nationalism of Maud Gonne.[2]

The Maud Gonne of history is a more representative figure than the Maud Gonne of Yeats's imagination: a New Woman, expressing a new and at times wilful autonomy through the discourses of feminism, revolutionary socialism and nationalism, advocating the 'physical force' solution to the national question. She was, along with Gore-Booth and Markiewicz, one of those women whose voices, according to Yeats, 'grew shrill with argument', turning into 'an old bellows full of angry wind'. She took an active part in organising support for the prolonged

Dublin Transport Workers' strike of 1913 (which Yeats, under her influence, campaigned in support of).[3] Yeats's poetry acknowledges but mystifies all this. In it, she is the mindless militant, redeemed only by her storm-tossed beauty, who in 'No Second Troy' in *The Green Helmet*

> would of late
> Have taught to ignorant men most violent ways,
> Or hurled the little streets upon the great,
> Had they but courage equal to desire.

But he can forgive this, as he can forgive her filling his days with misery, because these are the mere froth of history through which a deeper meaning is expressed. Her 'nobleness' is 'not natural in an age like this'. It is, ultimately, a supernatural force linking her to the great mythic archetypes,

> What could have made her peaceful with a mind
> That nobleness made simple as a fire,
> With beauty like a tightened bow, a kind
> That is not natural in an age like this,
> Being high and solitary and most stern?
> Why, what could she have done, being what she is?
> Was there another Troy for her to burn?

'Being what she is' is not described except in terms of a metaphor which calls up other classical and mythological analogues, the virgin huntress Diana and Penthesilea and her Amazons.

'What she is', as a historical figure, however, is precisely *not* this. 'What she is' is a very Modern agitator, a stirrer-up of class hatred, seeking to bring down the very 'nobleness' Yeats in imagination attributes to her and to the 'great streets' she wishes to burn. Yeats's ennobling metaphors and analogies do violence to the actual historical figure, by casting the origins of all her activity precisely in the Ascendancy power she pits herself against. She is 'high and solitary and most stern', and thereby reappropriable to traditional cultural–political discourses and fantasies. The mythologising diminishes as it claims to aggrandise, making her actual courage and tenacity into one more instance of an effortless supernatural energy.

The literary means by which this is effected is simple. The whole poem is a series of rhetorical questions in the subjunctive mood. The first two questions insinuate a subjective motivation to external acts, and cast the external world as a mere stage for the expression of 'inner' power. 'Why should I blame her . . .?' from the start gives priority to Yeats's viewpoint; 'What could have made her peaceful?' suggests that it is the inadequacy of the age which drives her to desperate acts. The second sentence moves away from the historical specificity of the first, which links the poet's misery with ignorant men and mean streets, to a realm speculatively in the interior of Maud Gonne's mind, a site remarkably like the *Anima Mundi*. Both of these sentences engage in, as they dissemble, acts of historical interpretation, as do the two one-line questions with which the poem ends.

The penultimate sentence repeats in miniature the doing and being antithesis of the first two questions. For such great figures, being issues directly in action, without prevarication. Grammatically a subordinate, participial qualification of deeds, 'being' in Yeats's rhetoric actually displaces deeds, which the past subjunctive reduces to a mere emanation of 'being'. Yet the tautological emptiness of the phrase 'being what she is' indicates how Yeats substitutes a hollow signifier for an actual signified. That signified in turn is pushed out of its historical particularity by the use of a merely conditional and speculative form of the verb. Gonne 'would have taught', 'would have . . . hurled' – *if* there had been a matching historical force in the masses. And, given her nature, what else 'could she have done' but what she did? The poem denies the possibility of historical agency and choice, with all its uncertainties and anxieties, to instate instead a kind of mythic determinism. It presents, in traditional terms, a woman driven by her nature, rather than by a sense of historical urgency and choice, existentially compelled to do what she has done. But if this is in her nature, then she is in a strange sense not responsible for it. The poet exonerates her of her grotesque politics. As another, later Amazon might have declaimed, there is no alternative.

Yeats's last question then answers itself. Gonne's problem – one of how tactics relate to strategy in a class struggle – is not that her *actual* projects found no matching correlative in the balance of class forces in Irish society. The problem instead becomes a *tragedy*: that the age was unworthy of her. Her 'real' being for Yeats is not her historical contingency at all, but that of a historically displaced mythic force.

Nevertheless, though the question answers itself (the answer is 'No'), it remains rather puzzling. What have Irish class and national politics in the 1900s got to do with Troy? And did Maud Gonne burn the first Troy? For that matter, did *Helen*, rather than her affronted cuckold husband and his gang of brigands? Or does Yeats simply mean that unfortunately in this degenerate world there are no more Troys and so Maud must degrade herself to put up with second-best, burning only an inferior Dublin? Behind this lies a further implication: that she is forgiven her vulgar actual politics on the grounds that she was driven, not by the urge to right injustice, abolish poverty and inequality, but by a *femme fatale*'s desire to see civilisations burning. The eternal female gets her kicks from goading men to fight for her. Whatever else is going on in this poem, Yeats is engaged in a major act of ideological recuperation. It is a form of taming and domesticating at the very moment that it speaks through a fantasy of wildness.

We can see the same process at work in one of Yeats's last poems, 'A Bronze Head', about the bust of Gonne in old age in the Dublin Art Gallery. Here, the phrase 'not natural in an age like this' is replaced by an invocation of a supernatural linked, as in 'Leda and the Swan', to the bestial. The bust presents a head 'Human, superhuman, a bird's round eye'. Gonne is in some way *uncanny*, for such a concept alone can explain the intensity and persistence of her commitment. Once again, the rhetorical question allows Yeats to slide surreptitiously from history to myth, speculatively summoning up supernatural forces ostensibly to explain but actually to mystify the nature of historical agency. The plenitude of being he attributes to Gonne in youth, 'her form all full / As though with magnanimity of light', turns easily into an emptiness – one founded in 'terror'. This emptiness, as if in desperation, seeks relief in the *hysterica passio* of deeds, in a world which is also empty, for it 'finds there nothing to make its terror less'. The bronze bust catches in Gonne's old age the 'terror' that Yeats detected in her youth, though then she was a 'form all full', not empty, and 'a most gentle woman'. But youth and age, fleshly and bronze images are only superficial forms of a 'substance' that exists outside of history. The rhetorical question once more raises the relation between eternity's noumena and the mere phenomena of history. Gonne is subjected to the poem's authorial power in the very question, 'Which of her forms has shown her substance right?' This male interpreter can, in this present of retrospect, see her true substance, has a special insight:

> But even at the starting-post, all sleek and new,
>
> I saw the wildness in her and I thought
> A vision of terror that it must live through
> Had shattered her soul.

That terror can only be the 'terrible beauty' of contemporary Irish history, supposedly envisioned by Gonne but actually retrospectively attributed to her by the poet who is trying to remake her as an image, something intended, complete. That this is actually domestication is confirmed by the overt patriarchal appropriation which closes the stanza. Infected by her wildness, himself grown wild, he 'wandered murmuring everywhere, "My child, my child!"' 'Among School Children', almost two decades earlier, had performed the same recuperative act, summoning up as a mythical archetype the unapproachable Ledaean body of a Maud Gonne now, in the order of history, transformed into a crone, and then projecting her before him as a 'living child' who drives his heart 'wild'. There too he had spoken of how the merely 'trivial event' of some 'childish day' in the realm of personal history could be transformed by the power of emotion into 'tragedy', and then transformed once again into a Neoplatonic, transhistorical pattern through the mediation of story-telling.

By the opening of the final stanza of 'A Bronze Head', he can offer an alternative interpretation of Gonne which endows her explicitly with 'supernatural' power, because it is only in his memory of how he 'thought her' that she possesses it. Masochistic admiration for the 'stern' female makes her a captive of an historical teleology. She is a scourge of god, the carrier of some darker agency whose sterner eye looks through her eye, contemplating the massacre necessary to purge a modern world in decline and fall. No longer a free agent, her image (its metallic hardness part of the meaning) is recruited from the actual politics she espoused to a quite contrary cause, embodying that aristocratic disdain for democracy which in the 1930s Yeats sought in Fascism. If Yeats here thinks only massacre can save this world where heroic reverie is mocked by clown and knave, he in turn engages in mockery of the real historical subject whose memory is summoned up only to be misrepresented. He does not admit to such ruthlessness of motive, nor attribute it directly to Gonne. Instead, he envisages a power that works through and sometimes against the grain of the actual human intentions, rather like Hegel's 'cunning of Reason'. It is not Gonne but some supernatural power that looks through her eye and wonders what is left for massacre to save.

'Hound Voice', which comes shortly after 'A Bronze Head' in both arrangements of *Last Poems*, makes the connection explicit, not by dissociating the sweetness of the woman's voice from violence, but by linking it to the baying of the wild hunt of Irish and English legend. Its second stanza spells this out, evoking the concept of terror he associates with Gonne in 'A Bronze Head':

> The women that I picked spoke sweet and low
> And yet gave tongue. 'Hound Voices' were they all.
> We picked each other from afar and knew
> What hour of terror comes to test the soul,
> And in that terror's name obeyed the call,
> And understood, what none have understood,
> Those images that waken in the blood.

But these are not images out of the Great Memory. They rise up from a specifically modern source, a Nietzschean modern myth of a blood wisdom driving to tear up 'the settled ground' of civilisation. The poem itself summons the hound voices, a call to violence, 'Stumbling upon the blood-dark track once more', delighting in awakening from quotidian lethargy. After this poem 'High Talk' speaks contemptuously of those 'modern' people who lack high stilts, for some Promethean 'rogue of the world' stole them to 'patch up a fence or a fire'. The poem ends with a vision of the 'terrible novelty of light', a nightmare vision as 'night splits' of great sea-horses which bare their teeth and laugh at a dawn which heralds the really new: a postmodern era of ruthless predation. This new dawn is a Fascist one. 'Why Should not Old Men be Mad?' gives as reason for the poet's madness the degenerations of this filthy modern world which see:

> A girl that knew all Dante once
> Live to bear children to a dunce;
> A Helen of social welfare dream,
> Climb on a wagonette and scream.

Old men and old books alone possess a knowledge founded in and leading to madness. Women cannot keep their beautiful voices, once they venture into what for Yeats is a realm of male discourse, the order of politics and of history. Their scream then is not just demagogy but hysteria.

What these last poems of Yeats's speak of is the negation of all human agency. As in *A Vision*, human acts will fail or succeed insofar as they advance the intentions of some ferocious, transhistorical force, founded in wildness and terror with its own ideas of hierarchy and authority, foul and fair, gangling and great, ancestral pearls and modern sties. Yeats casts on to the universe a paradigm of ancient authority which has a brutally up-to-date aetiology. The supernatural is the site of a disturbance in the surface of Yeats's rhetoric, an attempt to contain within established forms historical forces which threaten to overwhelm and destroy them. But the poems repeatedly half admit that which they are repressing. 'The Statues', dated 9 April 1938, looks back in commemoration of the month in which the Easter Rising occurred to forge a direct link between the moment of modernity and the independence struggle. But it is a contradictory linkage, only redeemed by a supernatural intervention which transfigures squalid event into mythic archetype. The supernatural, itself a question dialogically awaiting an answer, enters history through the back door of the rhetorical question:

> When Pearse summoned Cuchulain to his side,
> What stalked through the Post Office? What intellect,
> What calculation, number, measurement, replied?
> We Irish, born into that ancient sect
> But thrown upon this filthy modern tide

> And by its formless spawning fury wrecked,
> Climb to our proper dark, that we may trace
> The lineaments of a plummet-measured face.

The origins of Modernism may be sought by enquiring into those ancient sects and sources, and everywhere in the poetry of Yeats as of Eliot and Pound we are encouraged to seek them there. But what we find, on enquiry, is an 'address not known' that returns us to the 'filthy modern tide' of contemporary history. If the posthumously published *Last Poems* address the historical emergency of the late 1930s, they repeatedly return us to those originary moments of the century in which this crisis of the Modern was forged. In its new-found modernity, *The Green Helmet* in 1910 was the first bitter revelation of what was to come.

Our modern preoccupation

'Reconciliation', the poem which follows 'No Second Troy' in *The Green Helmet*, is a particularly complex version of this crisis. Also of twelve lines and in the same measure, it begins like the preceding poem with the concept of blame, but statement rather than question projects the blaming on to others. 'Some may have blamed you', he says, for taking away the verses that could move them. One of Yeats's last rhetorical questions, in 'The Man and the Echo' in *Last Poems*, would remind us what that 'moving' involved: 'Did that play of mine send out / Certain men the English shot?' But Maud Gonne not only silences poetic discourse. She also magically imposes on the historical man a sensory blackout as extreme as Gerontion's, 'the ears being deafened, the sight of the eyes blind / With lightning', in a supernatural annunciation like that of Dionysus. The figure of the female ostensibly replaces that which in actuality she everywhere signifies. Gonne is supposed to represent Venus rather than Mars, but in reality she figures forth the violence of war and patriarchal power: 'kings, / Helmets and swords, and half-forgotten things / That were like memories of you'.

Anything that Yeats says about memory is full of contradictions, but this is a peculiarly convoluted utterance. He is deafened and blinded by her departure – but not dumb. Instead he sings about new topics which are actually old topics, topics she in her newness and modernity is supposed to have replaced. These 'half-forgotten things' of a time (his Celtic Twilight verse, the Keatsian inheritance) before he knew her seem also like memories of her. Before the full implications of this can be grasped, the poem shifts tack with an interruption which puts the world back in its irrelevant place and, calling up their shared hysteria, a laughing and weeping fit, hurls the imagery of war into the pit. She is 'gone', but the poem's final couplet appeals to her as if she were present, and speaks of a symbolic loss not of male potency but of female fecundity:

> But, dear, cling close to me; since you were gone,
> My barren thoughts have chilled me to the bone.

The final rhyme names her fullness ('gone' / 'Gonne') in contrast to his emptiness. Maud Gonne in her very name becomes the figure of lack, a gap in being who exercises power by virtue of her absence, opening a breach through which the ancestral voices prophesying war pass and repass. She is the site of that central contradiction indicated in the very title of the next poem of the sequence, 'King and No King':

> 'Would it were anything but merely voice!'
> The No King cried who after that was King,
> Because he had not heard of anything
> That balanced with a word is more than noise;
> Yet Old Romance being kind, let him prevail
> Somewhere or somehow that I have forgot,
> Though he'd but cannon — Whereas we that had thought
> To have lit upon as clean and sweet a tale
> Have been defeated by that pledge you gave
> In momentary anger long ago;
> And I that have not your faith, how shall I know
> That in the blinding light beyond the grave
> We'll find so good a thing as that we have lost?
> The hourly kindness, the day's common speech,
> The habitual content of each with each
> When neither soul nor body has been crossed.

The poem opens with the mysterious cry of the No King who afterwards was King, a lack which contains its fullness *in potentia*. But the cry suggests a discrepancy between the fulness of history and the emptiness of voice. Even the half-rhyme with 'noise' reinforces this sense, though the No King's lack arises in part from his inability to grasp that 'anything / That balanced with a word is more than noise'. He misses, that is, the speech as signification, reducing it to meaningless noise. It is precisely meaning that turns 'anything' into something, gives the potential body and fullness. Narrative gives context and body to event. But the language is strangely indeterminate here, as if taunting with the empty volatility of signifiers never fixed to time and place and significance. 'Old Romance', the cliché enacting the obsolescence to which it refers, allows the No King to prevail in his signifying void, and the poet's own forgetfulness leaves him dangling there, 'Somewhere or somehow that I have forgot'.

Out of this forgetfulness the armed man strides. Words are empty before the reality of power, the poet's tale defeated. But these words are defeated only by other words that suddenly take on a new and terrifying substance, in part because though spoken in momentary anger long ago they seem a pledge that cannot be broken. Cut short in an impotence figured as blindness, the speaker's rhetorical question rises to the full height of loss, which, at first unspecified, then emerges as the loss of a shared discourse in which solidarity also involves an invidious levelling, 'The hourly kindness, the day's common speech', where 'kindness' takes up the idea of Romance 'being kind', but also has resonances in that 'King and No King' Hamlet, another empty man (see pp. 162–4 above) dispossessed by one 'a little more than kin and less than kind'.

'Common' is a word at a crossroads here. Yeats links it with insufficiency, 'mere' common speech, 'habitual content', mundane kindness, and the negation of the last line reinforces this. Yet this is also 'so good a thing . . . that we have lost'. The word focuses the central class contradiction in which the Modernist impulse originates. On the one hand, 'common speech' implies linguistic unification under the sign of power (King). On the other, it suggests the reduction of authority to the meanness of the mean (No King). The poem is strange in its refusal of specification. What it does however specify is linguistic insufficiency as the figure of an historical lack. Heir and usurper are simultaneously Kings and No Kings, the fullness of the referent and the emptiness of the signifier, self-negating in the play of mere voice, cry, word, noise, Old Romance, tale, pledge, common speech, conspiring to cancel each other out in a historical deadlock where only deeds and cannons can claim meanings unto themselves. Where words are deadlocked, that is, the discourse can be changed only by acts of violence.

Richard Ellmann has called our attention to the source of the poem's title in Beaumont and Fletcher's 1611 play, *A King and No King*.[4] Here, falling in love with the woman he believe to be his sister, Arbaces rages against the idea of kinship, whose bonds are mere linguistic fetters on behaviour. The speech that gives rise to Yeats's opening line questions the relation between words and swords. Systems of kinship are authorised it seems not by nature but by a consensus of common assumptions. But if the flesh rebels against these common values, where is the source of authority? How *can* discourse, mere voice, construct power?

> I have lived
> To conquer men, and now am overthrown
> Only by words, brother and sister. Where

Have those words dwelling? I will find 'em out
And utterly destroy 'em; but they are
Not to be grasped: let 'em be men or beasts. . . .
Let 'em be anything but merely voice.

If they were substantial things, Arbaces says, he could seize and destroy them. But they have ineluctable power precisely because they are 'merely voice'. Discourse is more irresistible than any physical force, because it cannot be fixed and extirpated. It is everywhere and nowhere, as Arbaces is King and No King, slipping from the grasp only to surround the troubled subject with bans and remonstrances.

The play finally reveals Arbaces to be an adopted child, and therefore not lineally king or brother. By marrying his supposed 'sister' he can become husband and king, entering into *real* relations not through inheritance but through contract. It is a profoundly significant myth for Yeats, combining the personal anguish, of a compulsory 'fraternal' relation with Gonne, with the whole question of legitimacy and succession, authority as both the signifier and the signified. Words are not to be grasped, yet they set the common limits and define the powers of authority, shaping the whole discourse within which acts become thinkable. Arbaces' normal solution would be violence, but this peculiar deadlock of words cannot be resolved by action because it is in the very nexus of ideological and material relations, of kinship and kingship, that the contradiction is most effectively transfixed.

The Green Helmet is obsessed with the relation between solitary individuals and crowds, from its very first poem, 'His Dream', which announces the painful transit from Celtic twilight at sea to the turbulent crowds of history on the shore. This baying crowd draws the poet into its agitation, so that he too takes up the song. But the mysterious figure in his boat is that of Death, the destiny to which poet and crowd alike are drawn. 'A Woman Homer Sung' tries to return Gonne to dream, detached from history, transformed into an image which 'shadowed in a glass / What thing her body was'. But 'thing', as elsewhere, dehistoricises and dehumanises. Similarly, in the image of her walking on a cloud, interpretation and event, history and story merge into a myth where 'life and letters seem / But an heroic dream'. 'Peace' likewise is about the wish that art might transform the historical 'storm' Gonne symbolises into a form of 'noble lines', combining delicacy, sternness and charm, sweetness and strength. The use of Homeric analogy as vehicle of reappropriation is exposed here in the wish that 'Time could touch a form / That could show what Homer's age / Bred to be a hero's wage'. The commodification of the woman as wage is the hidden agenda of all the romanticising, dreamy glorification. The troubadour motif of poetry as courtly tribute in 'Against Unworthy Praise' reveals its true face in the idea of a dreaming which 'Earned slander, ingratitude, / From self-same dolt and knave'. Gonne's life becomes a labyrinth 'That her own strangeness perplexed' because in part of the need to mystify her historical agency into strangeness, rhetorically transforming her into a mythical archetype combining the wildness of the lion and the vulnerability of the child, reinstating patriarchy as an act of loving kindness.

Three twelve-line poems linked together in this volume spell out the political undertones of this whole negotiation: 'Upon a House Shaken by the Land Agitation', 'At the Abbey Theatre', and 'These Are the Clouds'. The first speaks of Lady Gregory's house as one threatened by popular agitation. Its rhetorical question (How would the world benefit if this house were ruined, no longer a home for greatness?) answers itself negatively and in passing in a concessionary clause which dismisses the answer as trivial: 'Mean roof-trees' would be 'sturdier for its fall'. What is interesting, however, is the way this leads at once to the relation between language and power, between 'The gifts that govern men' and 'gradual time's last gift, a written speech / Wrought of high laughter, loveliness and ease'. That 'written/Wrought' combination relates to Gonne in 'A Woman Homer Sung', but is here applied to Lady Gregory, the disputed territory across which a debate is conducted with Gonne's politics. The argument assumes that the identification of traditional sanctity and loveliness with a life of leisured ease, that is, of culture with class privilege, cannot be refuted.

The oxymoron 'written speech', referring to Lady Gregory's transcriptions of Irish folk tales, attempts rhetorically to resolve a political division between a popular oral culture and the authoritative writing of those who govern men. In 'These Are the Clouds', also addressed to Gregory, the clouds are the crowds that mob a declining power, reducing all things to 'one common level'. But a syntactical Freudian slip confers 'The majesty that shuts his burning eye' (intended to be in apposition to the kingly 'sun') on the clouds (by implication the masses), complicating the poem's allegiances.

'At the Abbey Theatre' expands on the dilemma of this dual allegiance. The closeness of the imitation to its original in Ronsard, elegist of a declining aristocracy, adds a peculiar frisson to the up-to-dateness with which it speaks of contemporary Ireland. Ostensibly it addresses the idea of a new writing for a new nation, represented by the Gaelic verse of Douglas Hyde (under his Gaelic pseudonym). Yet in reverting to Ronsardian precedent Yeats undermines the very idea of originality: it is all a matter of fashion. He remarks that 'we' (it is not clear whether Hyde is included in the pronoun) have been attacked for being 'high and airy' and then contrarily mocked 'Because we have made our art of common things'. Hyde has dandled and fed his public from the book. Yeats asks for the secret, in an insulting request for 'a new trick to please'. But the way forward is not to trick or bridle this Proteus, the volatile, fickle crowd, as changeable as the sea, like the mob in Shakespeare's Roman plays. His two questions imply an excluded middle:

> Is there a bridle for this Proteus
> That turns and changes like his draughty seas?
> Or is there none, most popular of men,
> But when they mock us, that we mock again?

'Popular' is clearly, like 'common', at a semantic crossroads here, suggesting both 'of the people' (good) and 'demagogic' (bad). The ambivalent jeering tone speaks straight out of the vulnerable heart of Yeatsian ideology, and prepares the way for that carnivalesque counter-mocking which, in 'Easter 1916', 'Nineteen Hundred and Nineteen' and 'Meditations', contrasts the 'high laughter' of the genteel with the 'casual comedy', 'motley', 'jokes of civil war' of the low. Yeats's comments on Hyde, who became first president of the New Republic, as 'the cajoler of crowds'[5] are revealing. Of the charm of Hyde's Gaelic, 'all spontaneous, all joyous, every speech born out of itself', he wrote elsewhere in *Autobiographies*:

> Had he shared our modern preoccupation with the mystery of life, learnt our modern construction, he might have grown into another and happier Synge. . . . He had the folk mind as no modern man has had it, its qualities and its defects, and for a few days in the year Lady Gregory and I shared his absorption in that mind. . . . Nothing in that language of his was abstract, nothing worn-out; he need not, as must the writer of some language exhausted by modern civilisation, reject word after word, cadence after cadence; he had escaped our perpetual, painful, purification.[6]

The word 'modern' wears itself out by repetition here. By contrast with the complexity, exhaustion and self-subversion of the Modern, Hyde's Gaelic writings represent an impossible spontaneity and clarity associated with 'the folk mind' which cannot be depleted because it does not live in the temporal order of supersession which is the very site of the Modern. These poems seem to be about 'art' and its relations to society, to a public, a tradition. But they are actually about authority, about what discourse authorises action, whether in writing or politics. In a prose draft and comment to 'A House Shaken by the Land Agitation' Yeats argued explicitly that the traditional loveliness fostered by Coole Park was more important than the improvement to a hundred rooftrees for the poor, 'for here power has gone forth, or lingered giving energy, precision'. The poet cannot reconcile two allegiances of equal importance to his art and politics. He tries dialogically to impose a binary ordering on a disorderly world. But his antitheses spawn other antitheses, images beget fresh images in a sea which swamps all the dikes on which order struts.

Elsewhere in Yeats's verse it is precisely the violence of the independence struggle which overcomes the clash of allegiances in the word 'common' by specifying two parallel or convergent sources of linguistic power, a new legitimation of poetry and politics which reconciles the opposed forces of popular and elite traditions. One of his *Last Poems*, 'The Municipal Gallery Revisited', offers a retrospect on the images of thirty years of Irish history which, in the founding of a new order out of insurrection and terror, had raised the most fundamental questions about legitimacy in politics and culture alike. The intersection of the common and the elite determines the whole course of the poem, for its 'images of thirty years' record a struggle conducted not only by great men like Casement, 'Griffith staring in hysterical pride', O'Higgins's 'gentle questioning look' ('pride' and 'gentle' both carry class connotations), but also by the anonymous masses, represented by the nameless 'revolutionary soldier kneeling to be blest', with a humility that in the next stanza is cast as the complement of pride. Since both egregious individual and obedient masses are essential to the struggle, Yeats accommodates them in an image which has a similar dual authority, 'An image out of Spenser and the common tongue'. He has prepared the way for this metaphor by casting himself in the (unlikely) posture of humility, kneeling in imagination before the image of Augusta Gregory. Here too emptiness is transfigured to plenitude under her roof, in a strange incomplete sentence where noun and verb enter into problematic relationship – 'all lacking found'. The verse sweeps on to another act of obeisance to the common people, speaking of the shared belief of Yeats, Lady Gregory and John Synge, 'our modern preoccupation' setting them apart from ordinary modernity, that –

> All that we did, all that we said or sang
> Must come from contact with the soil, from that
> Contact everything Antaeus-like grew strong.
> We three alone in modern times had brought
> Everything down to that sole test again,
> Dream of the noble and the beggar-man.

Mere historical accuracy is marred by a characteristic Romantic displacement. The final rhyme would more appropriately read 'working-man', since it was from the working classes radicalised by Connolly's and Larkin's near-general strike of 1913 and then by the Easter Rising and its aftermath that the revolutionary soldier will have been drawn, as his leaders came from the professional strata and from those lower-middle classes mobilised by the earlier national struggle. But Yeats cannot allow to that explicitly modern class, the proletariat, a proper role in Ireland's history, displacing onto the marginal beggar-man the linguistic vitality Joyce found in the Dublin pubs and work-places. Hence 'soil' and the classically distancing literary-mythological allusion to Antaeus deflect us from seeing where that struggle should have led, restoring us instead to the ordered hierarchical world to which Yeats's 'medieval knees' belong. Thus, we are not surprised to find that Synge's greatness arose in part from ' "Forgetting human words" ', despite his rootedness. Forgetfulness, we have seen, is always an *interested*, partisan act in Yeats's work, the repression of an otherwise insoluble dilemma.

The whole poem is cast in the light of retrospect. Its only future is that of unspecified consumers of the images to be found in the Gallery and in Yeats's verse. Those who come after will want to judge 'This book or that'. They will focus not on a future but on the traces of a past: 'Ireland's history in their lineaments trace'. Understanding history is a matter of seeking lineaments and lineages of the past in the present. Such an act seems to preclude an openness to any future beyond the moment of judging and tracing. History is all retrospect, even when it is still in prospect. Future seekers are urged to 'Think where man's glory most begins and ends'. It begins and ends here, in the timeless works of art. It is here, too, that Yeats seeks to place the origins of Modernism. A divisive, continuous, always incomplete history, the merely 'contemporary' in which the Modern is perpetually updated, is set against the finality of epitaphs: 'And say my glory was I had such friends'. Retrospection is the final horizon of Yeats's historical vision. This 'saying' is projected into the future only to round off the pastness of it all. The imagined epitaph pre-empts any other response, inscribing the refractory historical self in a unitary and 'common' textuality, the Book of the People, where the poet himself has, though dead, literally the last word, though he requires others to speak it. Yeats and his friends will thus be placed, not in the actual contingency and turmoil of their *histories*, ' "The dead Ireland of my youth" ', but in that imaginary tradition which mystifies discordant voices to a common significance, founded in a single principle of power, forging, from 'Approved patterns of women or of men', the phantasmagoria of ' "An Ireland / The poets have imagined, terrible and gay" '.

Nothing but a book

The alternative titles of a 1916 poem called at different times 'The Phoenix' and 'The People' reveals Yeats's own vacillation between the personal (and exceptional) and the public (and common). Couched as a dialogue, the poem contrasts his own and Maud Gonne's responses to the national liberation struggle. Though he hankers after a life among 'The unperturbed and courtly images' of Renaissance Ferrara or Urbino, where (he alleges) artist, aristocrat and people shared common values, mixing 'courtesy and passion' as the Duchess and her people mingled on terms of respect, he himself inveighs against 'The daily spite of this unmannerly town' in an idiom which ironically links him to the despised, mercenary Paudeen – a language of buying and selling, profit and loss, 'earned', 'charge', 'trade'. Gonne's reply, consummately endorsing yet refuting all that the poet has said, is not that of a politician but of a dedicated revolutionary. She had driven away the dishonest crowds, but 'When my luck changed and they dared to meet my face' they crawled out to set upon her, even people she had served and fed: ' "Yet never have I, now nor any time, / Complained of the people" '.

Her reply draws on Yeats's distinction (ultimately derived from Wordsworth) between a people and a mob – the one ideal and potential, the other actual. Stung, he responds with a distinction between his living in thought and hers in deed, and then (having spoken of her as 'my phoenix'), addresses her as one with 'the purity of a natural force'. He claims for himself what he despises elsewhere, 'the analytic mind'. The 'eye of the mind' cannot be closed to reality, nor the tongue kept from speaking truly by faith in a speculative renewal. But the final three lines, with their strategically placed repetition of 'abashed', speaking of nine years ago and of today, tell a different story. The poem is a powerful little drama of conflicting political interpretations, the more effective because although the poet has the last word in terms of the narrative, it is clear that that narrative does no more than concede defeat, acknowledging her rebuke because his heart, leaping at her words, rather than his head, tells him she was right. The very changes of title testify to this continuing struggle of interpretation, making the poem an unstable terrain. Maud Gonne is not here associated with traditional sanctity and loveliness. She implicitly rejects her identification with the Duchess of Urbino. Nor does she romanticise the people. As a revolutionary, rather than a fawning politician or foolish romantic, she has no illusions about their venality and reprobation. But complaint will change nothing. Committed to completing a task, she has to find a way round, or a way of transforming, all these negatives. This poem casts as dramatic dialogue the conflict of elitism and populism, the eternal Book and the passing history, at the heart of Yeats's Modernism. That conflict is summed up likewise in the opening and closing poems of *Responsibilities* (1914), which define between them the conflicting responsibilities of the writer.

Introductory and envoi poems point in opposite directions. But this is not an antithesis of past and future, as one might assume at start and finish of a volume, but of two different pasts and two different futures. The opening poem addresses an actual patriarchy, begging pardon of those 'old fathers', his genealogical ancestors. The poem (and the volume) opens by speaking of them waiting already 'for the story's end'. The pardon he seeks is for reaching 49 without any heirs, because of 'a barren passion', an admission delayed in its enormity until the last two lines of a twenty-two line poem which is all one sentence:

> I have no child, I have nothing but a book,
> Nothing but that to prove your blood and mine.

Syntactically, it is a tour de force of delaying syntax, in which the poem enacts that deferral of significance of which it speaks, which has left his lineage incomplete, as here, his poetic lines are attenuated to the point of extinction.

The envoi of the volume by contrast turns from real to imagined fathers, the textual fathers of the literary tradition, for whom this book is a real child. The poem enacts the same delaying syntax, but it begins this time not in a vocative address to others, but in a foregrounding of the speaking subject, and its verb comes in three-and-a-half lines, surmising companions from the literary tradition, in particular naming and quoting Ben Jonson as a voice which authorises his contempt for the populace. The voice is newly confident here, having moved in the course of the volume from seeking pardon to venturing forgiveness. Even in its degraded and degrading final image the book asserts mastery. The very ability to speak thus suggesting calm defiance, the surety of 'a sterner conscience' which can overcome the 'undreamt accidents' that have made him 'Notorious'. 'Fame', 'Being but a part of ancient ceremony', has long perished, leaving his 'priceless things' as 'a post the passing dogs defile'. But the artist survives all this in solitary, tragic grandeur.

This is the mood of a poem such as 'Fallen Majesty', a product of 1912, a year in which the Third Irish Home Rule Bill was introduced in the House of Commons. Pound proposed various changes to the poem. One Yeats accepted involved dropping 'as it were' from the final lines:

> A crowd
> Will gather, and not know it walks the very street
> Whereon a thing once walked that seemed, as it were, a burning cloud.

But he refused Pound's alternative 'A crowd / Will gather and not know that through its very street / Once walked a thing'. C.K. Stead says this was pride, refusing to get rid of the repetition and the awkward 'Whereon'.[7] Yeats, however, was right. The repetition emphasises the discrepancy of knowledge and power, knowing and doing. They walk now, she walked then; but, unlike him, they lack the magical knowledge of the connection, which transforms the mundane street. There is continuity between then and now, but also loss. The repetition is of a parcel with the others in the poem which juxtapose sameness and difference through time: 'Although crowds gathered once . . . A crowd will gather'. Stead is also wrong to object to the 'awkward' word 'thing' applied to Gonne, and to quibble about whether she was a 'burning cloud' or merely 'seemed' one. Yeats's language is quite clear: it specifies uncertainty. The poet doesn't know what status he attributes to Gonne. She is a 'thing' in the sense that in 'A Bronze Head' she seems both more and less than human. The strange, uncomfortable word relates her to the thing that climbs the stair and slouches towards Bethlehem, more historical agency than individual human being. As a 'burning cloud' she has the same determinate indeterminacy: like Jove visiting Io, she is a supernatural intervention in the material world; but like a cloud, she is also a vapid and vaporous natural process, lacking in contour and substance, with neither beginning nor end but a vague nebulous diffusiveness.

But this is not quite all, for there is another key repetition, which foregrounds the role of the poet as chronicler, and elucidates the title. The hand which writes, he says,

> Like some last courtier at a gypsy camping-place
> Babbling of fallen majesty, records what's gone.

Lineaments (external features) and a heart made sweet (internal effect) remain; but the poet repeats, 'I record what's gone', and rhyme and reiteration of that punning participle reinstate presence as it proclaims absence: 'I record what's Gonne'. Yeats's image is revealing. Its tenor is obvious: he survives to speak of a fallen majesty. But the vehicle – the metaphor itself – is as vague as the cloud to which Gonne is compared ('seemed', like the simile, a weaker device than metaphor, reinforces this sense of unsureness). His social status in this analogy is unclear. Is he a courtier surviving from the *ancien régime* now fallen, cast upon the gypsy camp to seek his bread by recalling a better world, playing on the nostalgia of the low for the greatness they have replaced? Or has he always been a 'courtier' – the term suffering terminal inflation – at the court of a gypsy 'king', rousing that 'king' to delusions of grandeur with tales of a fallen majesty he would like to think he shared? Yeats's own class-ambiguity as an artist is here defined. Does he survive from an older order of custom and ceremony, in which he had a small but valued place? Or did he always belong to this vile world in its decline and fall, to the raggle-taggle gypsies of the modern, democratic era, to be saved only by massacre?

There is then a further contradiction: his hand records, presumably by writing. Yet in the analogy the recorder is compared to one 'babbling of fallen majesty'. The contrast of script and voice (and incoherent voice) overthrows the usual hierarchy. The oral tradition is heroic, Homeric, goes back to the primal hierarchies of history. Writing belongs to the modern, democratic world of shared literacy. But here the simile confounds the whole contrast. Babbling is associated with the transiency of the gypsy camp, as opposed to the fixed order of majesty, yet it is a survivor of that era who is reduced to a babbling then redefined as writing. The metonymy 'this hand', depersonalising, distancing, becomes, by repetition, the focused subject of 'I record', almost as if the recorder had grown to fullness in his responsibility to link crowds in present and future, *without their knowing it*, to those in the past.

Crowds will gather now for an unspecified purpose which we might suspect to be a political meeting, in this year when Nationalist and Unionist forces grouped and regrouped at the prospect of Home Rule. But, though Yeats would wish us to believe that they once gathered simply to observe Gonne's beauty, wasn't the real reason, even then, the same? Didn't she draw crowds not because she was beautiful – though this may have contributed to her charismatic effect – but because she was a powerful orator arguing a sympathetic case? But to admit this would be to concede that there is some historical substance to that which Yeats regrets as merely loss and emptiness – a beautiful voice growing shrill with argument. The old men whose eyes grow dim are like those old men who looked on Helen at Troy. Yeats, that is, represses the whole historical dimension of Gonne's being-in-the-world, substituting an appropriating myth. Yet the poem registers the uncertainty of his interpretation in its use of the verb 'seemed' and in the way it reduces her to nebulousness, dissipating her actual concentrated agency into a diffuse and unstable presence. If the poem juxtaposes knowledge and ignorance, elite individual and raggedy crowd, it also in its confusion of script and voice opens up another schism in the text of history. It is one to which Yeats returned in his two Coole Park poems, in 1929 and 1931.

'Coole Park, 1929' was not published until 1931, and the date in the title implies a deliberate historical placing, calling our attention to this year of capitalist crisis and collapse. It centres its melancholy defiance of endings in the ambiguous image of 'a swallow's flight'. This flight is both that of the bird actually before his eyes, a figure of material presence, and the more abstract idea of the bird's migratory flight, a figure of loss and absence. In the fourth stanza, the writers associated with Lady Gregory are spoken as coming and going like swallows, but the sense of transience throughout is qualified by the consolation of return. The swallows are ambiguous figures in that they represent both the fleetingness of things and a constancy of repetition, returning to the same nest year after year. So the opening antithesis, between the stability of meditation, of the world of thought, and the transiency of the world of nature, is belied by the unfolding of the image.

This consolatory doubleness in the image of time is everywhere in the poem. The poet himself migrates in thought from swallow to 'an aged woman and her house', equally vulnerable to mutability. But in the human world, 'Great works constructed there in nature's spite' persist for new generations, 'For scholars and for poets after us'. Though history unravels, thought is knitted together into a unity and fullness. But this 'distaff' image – like the equally feminised images of dance and begetting – is then succeeded, in the second stanza, by a peculiar, complicating variation on a proverbial cliché. As scholars and poets will come after Yeats, so others preceded him. Foremost among these was Douglas Hyde, whose transcription of the old Irish legends did so much to prepare the ground for the cultural renaissance in which Yeats shared. But Hyde is seen as beating, not the sword into a ploughshare (or a pen), but rather as beating into (plebeian) prose 'That noble blade the Muses buckled on'.

As in 'The Gift of Harun al Rashid' and 'To Dorothy Wellesley', poetry is associated with the arts of war, not peace. The implicit class antithesis here reproduces itself in a series of other antitheses – Yeats's own 'manly pose' versus his 'timid heart', John Synge's 'slow' and 'meditative' nature contrasted with the impetuosity of Shawe-Taylor and Hugh Lane – before joining them all in a 'company' which reaffirms the corporate image of class collaboration between aristocratic and plebeian virtues encountered elsewhere, 'pride established in humility'. 'Established', like 'constructed' earlier, indicates how much effort is required to effect this combination. The linking of order and authorship in art with order and authority in society is the preoccupation of the next stanza.

Compared with the transient swallows, it is the constancy and continuity of 'a woman's powerful character' that maintains order. Lady Gregory's aristocratic power lies in her ability to 'keep a swallow to its first intent', to represent that primary fullness, that identity of purpose and act which makes half a dozen birds 'in formation . . . whirl upon a compass-point'. The air is dreaming, but 'certainty' can be found within it. As the birds can be held to their purpose across all the distractions of space, so a culture can be maintained, by resolution of purpose, in 'lines / That cut through time or cross it withershins'. The ambiguity of that word 'lines' – lines of verse, lines of genealogy – is continued in the last stanza, which speaks of a time 'When all those rooms and passages are gone' – 'passages', as in Eliot's 'Gerontion', linking the material and verbal forms of the culture. But other elements in this last stanza suggest a third meaning to 'lines' – battle lines – which points back to the Muses' 'noble blade' as a figure of art founded in violence, gives a martial twist to the image of 'half a dozen in formation there', and suggests that 'cut through time' carries over the image of the sword.

The poem envisages a time when this stately house is no more than a shapeless mound and broken stone, topped by nettles and saplings. The image recalls, perhaps, the mound at Hissarlik which is all that remains of Troy – apart from Homer's lines. But the appeal to the itinerant traveller, scholar, poet who will view this inheritance of rubble adds other, more martial echoes. For he does not appeal to them to 'stand' here and view the desolation, but to 'take your stand'. The address recalls the epitaph of the Spartan three hundred at Thermopylae, 'Go stranger, tell the Spartans that we lie here, obedient to their command'. But 'take your stand' suggests that the future generation must also share in that last stand, not simply meditating upon but dedicating themselves to the idea of survival the image offers us. If the Spartans were the last defence of western 'civilisation' against Asiatic tyranny (and in 1929 this meant, of course, Bolshevism), that defence was founded not on democracy but on a slave-owning oligarchy. But so too was that other genteel order, the Confederate States of America, for which many a man in another era of civil war declared himself ready to 'take my stand for Dixie'.

It is unclear whether when writing this in September 1929 Yeats already knew of the projected manifesto of the 'Agrarian School' of Southern US writers, *I'll Take My Stand*, which was to appear in 1930.[8] But he was certainly aware of the Agrarians, who had transferred his organicist myth of rural Ireland, with its imaginary alliance of peasant, poet and aristocrat, to the antebellum South. There is here a similar battlecry of a rearguard action against an incursive modern barbarism, in the name of traditional sanctity and loveliness. When, then, Yeats calls on future visitors to this spot to 'dedicate . . . / A moment's memory to that laurelled head', the imagined bays combine martial and poetic honours. For Yeats, the lines of poetry, genealogy and battle belong to the same complex. Order in art is the same as order in society and in war. Authorship and authority, creative and political power, derive from the same source. It is in the stress that such an identification generates that the second of these two poems, 'Coole Park and Ballylee, 1931', finds its richness and its difficulties.

Yeats wrote in 'In Memory of Major Robert Gregory' that John Synge 'dying took the living world for text'. That, in a sense, is what Yeats is doing in 'Coole Park, 1929', reading off the significance of swallow, house, writers, aged woman, taking a stand in each case against the erosion of the meaningful into meaninglessness. Even as a pile of stones, he indicates, perhaps remembering Wordsworth's 'Michael' as much as Homer's Troy, that debris can be restored to significance by a mind able to meditate on the past. The 'luminous' western cloud in the first stanza recalls Coleridge's 'Dejection: An Ode', both in its opening scene-setting at evening and in its forced conviction that the imagination can recreate the dead world of material things like 'a fair luminous cloud'. Coleridge's poem too makes a distinction between the superior isolate mind and the dull dense crowd. 'Coole Park and Ballylee, 1931' makes explicit this Romantic lineage in the concluding stanza of the poem, at the very moment that it seems to admit its insufficiency. But before that, much has been prepared for. The poem takes the living world for text, but it moves conspicuously from the book of nature to 'what poets name / The book of the people'. The text that Yeats reads here defines the trajectory of Modernism in the 1930s.

The poem opens in the living world, with an item by item delineation of the material reality under his window. But, as in Coleridge's 'Kubla Khan', with its river that also rises from and returns to measureless underground caverns, the landscape is transformed into a symbolic terrain. By the end of the first stanza, the real river of otters and moorhens and Raftery's cellar has become, if only in a rhetorical question, a figure for the 'generated soul' out of Porphyry's essay on the Cave of the Nymphs. Yet this racing, running, rising, dropping and spreading does not cease to be a tangible process, the sense of reality enforced by that unpoetic 'hole' which prepares the final couplet.

The lake and woods, depicted in mid-winter banality, are also transfigured by a sense of nature's histrionics: 'For Nature's pulled her tragic buskin on / And all the rant's a mirror for my mood'. This theatricality may not simply mirror but may in Coleridgean fashion be created by the poet's mood, which projects onto the book of nature a text that is only there to his interpreting gaze. The thunder of the swans' wings compounds this ambivalence. It is something out there which actually interrupts his internal reverie, making him turn about and look. But it is also immediately incorporated into discourse, acclaimed as 'Another emblem there!' The third stanza unfolds the full complexity of such an intuition.

We know from other poems some of the emblematic significances Yeats attributes to the swan. In 'Nineteen Hundred and Nineteen', with his usual deliberate insouciance about sources, he remarks that 'Some moralist or mythological poet / Compares the solitary soul to a swan'. But though he says 'I am satisfied with that', the amplification of the image goes beyond mere comparison, to a point at which the actual creature overwhelms its emblematic significance. His description of its flight makes the image stand before us as 'a living thing', flesh and blood and muscle in action, so that the soul takes second place to that which is supposed to signify ('cygnify') it. Soul and swan fuse, so that the syntax acquires a double subject, 'it' ambiguously referring to either, making each the mirror of the other:

> Satisfied if a troubled mirror show it,
> Before that brief gleam of its life gone,
> An image of its state.

The soul is then considered in a formula ('Some Platonist affirms') which repeats the construction of the opening analogy before returning to the physical, embodied image of the swan. The return totally transforms the argument, cutting it short with a powerful, corporeal rebuke to all this abstraction. The 'image' takes on a life of its own, a real creature out there in the wind and water, not a mere emblem of something else. In its very substantiality it bursts into the argument, refuting the 'desolate heaven' of thought with the display of a force that interrupts discourse, threatening to cut short the acts of writing and imagining themselves:

> The swan has leaped into the desolate heaven:
> That image can bring wildness, bring a rage
> To end all things, to end
> What my laborious life imagined, even
> The half-imagined, the half-written page.

The wildness here, interrupting discourse, is like that wildness he detected in Maud Gonne or the bestially divine Zeus invading the body of history in 'Leda and the Swan', a supernatural irruption into the ordered language of philosophy, writing, society itself. In 'Coole Park and Ballylee, 1931' the same dramatic reversal occurs:

> Another emblem there! That stormy white
> But seems a concentration of the sky;
> And, like the soul, it sails into the sight
> And in the morning's gone, no man knows why;
> And is so lovely that it sets to right
> What knowledge or its lack had set awry,
> So arrogantly pure, a child might think
> It can be murdered with a spot of ink.

The bird is first of all constituted in discourse, a signifying emblem. But, though it still functions as a signifier of the signified 'soul', its signification disrupts that discourse, appearing and disappearing beyond knowledge. Knowledge and its lack are curiously fused in unity as sources of disorder, compared with what the loveliness sets right. The bird seems merely 'a concentration of the sky'; but that abstract noun hovers between mental and physical – between thinking concentratedly and making denser, more concentrated. The bird remains as if a written sign in that sky, concentrated white on white, so that a child, uninitiated into the difference between mind and world, imagination and reality, might think of it as no more than a sign, a mark on paper, easily overwritten. The word 'murdered', however, establishes the distance between erasing a sign and killing a living thing. The whole stanza insists on the discrepancy between discourse and reality in a world in which, nevertheless, the real can be apprehended only through discourse.

When in the fourth and fifth stanzas Yeats turns to the human scene, the same interplay occurs between what people and places *are* and what they *signify* – between the sound of a stick on the floor and the old woman who wields it, between that old woman and the Ascendancy tradition she metonymically embodies. The poem works through a series of expanding metonymies, in which each item indicates a set which then becomes the metonymy for another set. The sound of the stick suggests an undefined 'somebody that toils from chair to chair'; but the chair becomes part of the furniture of rooms in which age does not diminish but enhances value; the rooms become the haunts of the generations who found content or joy here; and then, in the final concentration of the tradition, like the swan in the sky, Lady Gregory emerges as the 'last inheritor' of all that richness, a richness set against 'lack' and 'folly'.

That the parallel between woman and swan is not fortuitous is suggested by the recurrence of the words 'lack' and 'spot' (again associated with survival and extinction) immediately after. This house is 'A spot whereon the founders lived and died', and the place becomes a metonymy for a succession of marriages, alliances, families. The whole living world, that is, is constructed like a text the meaning of which can be read off by the initiated eye from each instance and particular. For the interpreting imagination, it is impossible to distinguish the trees from the 'ancestral' lineage they evoke, the gardens from the memories in which they are rich, the inheritance they 'glorified'. But this spot only 'Seemed once more dear than memory', as the swan only seems a concentration of the sky, and only in a child's thought can be murdered with a spot of ink. The discourse can be expunged, the poem suggests, and indeed is in process of being expunged. Coole Park and all it stands for can be erased as easily as a sentence on the page. A spot of ink can do it all, the signing of a will, or a builder's contract.

What animates Yeats here, then, is the memory of an emptiness. This is the repository of all that has been evacuated of meaning, lost to history. We know that there is much that has been forgotten. We know that whole civilisations have disappeared from the historical record. For millennia, we thought that Troy was just a story, but Schliemann revealed it to be history. Before this could be assimilated, however, we had seen the fictive certainties of Homer disappear, leaving us with a mound of rubbish. Archaeology, which seemed to vindicate Homer as history, then problematised him, by offering us a different, more parochial and local Troy, just as textual scholarship dissolved the unitary patriarch 'Homer' into several generations of anonymous bards handing on tales collected belatedly in the age of Pisistratus. As Yeats noted dispassionately in 'Lapis Lazuli', whole civilisations are put to the sword, their wisdom vanishes, 'No handiwork of Callimachus ... stands' (that word again), and no one remembers. Why, then, should this little local phenomenon, the Ascendancy culture, be privileged? The memory of an absence generates the expectation of an absence – a future in which this so substantial present has vanished without trace, translated into debris for the archaeologist to reconstruct.

It is here, then, that Yeats forges a link with earlier poems, with that 1910 image of himself as the recorder of fallen majesty, the last courtier in a gypsy camp, and with the 1923 'Gift of Harun al Rashid', with its idea of a knowledge partially recovered by patient reconstruction, putting together from scattered and surviving fragments a story that is always in danger of being misattributed, misinterpreted, turned into fantasy. This story may be discovered in one surviving parchment, hidden in another book from a library long dispersed, or it may be culled from its many variants in the oral tradition, with 'no chronicler / But the wild Bedouin'. In *Per Amica Silentia Lunae*[9] Yeats had set up an antithesis very similar to that expounded here, between high tradition and folk memory, speaking of the Arab boy become Vizier, whose wisdom has ' "taken stock in the desert sand of the sayings of antiquity" '. In 'The Gift of Harun al Rashid', the young bride and her aged scholar husband pursue 'old crabbed mysteries', 'old dry writing in a learned tongue', in a perpetual recession and recension of interpretings, straining 'to look beyond our life'. What speaks at the end of all this labour is a Djinn, voicing truths beyond the written tradition:

> Truths without father came, truths that no book
> Of all the uncounted books that I have read,
> Nor thought out of her mind or mine begot,
> Self-born, high-born, and solitary truths,

> Those terrible implacable straight lines
> Drawn through the wandering vegetative dream,
> Even those truths that when my bones are dust
> Must drive the Arabian host.

Yeats's simile in the closing lines of 'Coole Park and Ballylee, 1931' compounds intertextual references to his own past writing. It may be that, losing this rich inheritance, the modern imagination too is dispossessed, shifting about 'Where fashion or mere fantasy decrees ... / Like some poor Arab tribesman and his tent'. Neither fashion nor fantasy recognises any integral relation between the sign and what it signifies, perpetually and lightly fashioning transient correspondences between a shifting succession of objects, as Yeats himself successively offers water and then the swan that swims on it as emblems of the soul. The synecdochic 'emblem', suggesting a transitory succession of one-for-one correspondences between sign and signified, sunders that unity of thing and meaning contained in the metonymic symbol, where 'Old marble heads, old pictures everywhere' both symbolise and *are* the inheritance, the 'great glory' they figure forth.

The modern world is one in which the chronicler shifts like an Arab nomad about a desert stripped of meanings, packing up his purely personal and arbitrary symbols every dawn. But we know from 'The Gift of Harun al Rashid' that it is among just such that the truth has been preserved, in an oral, not a written tradition. The final stanza of 'Coole Park and Ballylee, 1931' makes a stand against desolation by reaffirming 'Traditional sanctity and loveliness' at the very moment that it laments their passing, indeed, concedes that they have passed. The ambivalence is focused in an uncertain shifting between song and writing. The elegiac voice concedes its own supersession, concedes that 'all is changed, that high horse riderless'. But at the very moment that the lost order is mourned, the dead theme is resurrected as the new theme of a poem whose very date proclaims its modernity as the latest thing, even more up-to-date than 'Coole Park, 1929':

> We were the last romantics – chose for theme
> Traditional sanctity and loveliness;
> Whatever's written in what poets name
> The book of the people; whatever most can bless
> The mind of man or elevate a rhyme;
> But all is changed, that high horse riderless,
> Though mounted in that saddle Homer rode
> Where the swan drifts upon a darkening flood.

Yeats achieves his effect by insisting on the interdependence of interpreting mind and interpreted world. That world is not simply a thing in itself: it is also a 'theme' for poetry, an already written compendium of narratives, and a source for other, yet to be written texts. The reflections on literary history are less important than the poem's strange condensations of perspective. These last romantics, at the end of things, were not like their Romantic predecessors, impelled by some irresistible urgency of utterance. They could *choose* their themes, and what they chose was a past already 'traditional'. Yet they also chose whatever *is* written, a past act of *writing* now become, in the present, an always-already *written*. The shift into the present tense is extended in that rebellious auxiliary 'can'. This 'book of the people' is not simply the oral tradition. Rather it is 'what poets name / The book of the people': it has to be constructed, called into being by writers who choose whatever most can bless and elevate. The book of the people looks not backwards but towards a future, both blessing the mind of man and 'elevating', in the sense of both ennobling and building, a *new* rhyme, a newness not undercut by the archaisms which echo first Wordsworth ('elevated thoughts', 'in the mind of man') and then Milton ('build the lofty rhyme'). And these unnamed poets of epic, Neoplatonic and Romantic voices, one chronicling the loss of paradise, the other of glad animal movements, lead back to the origin of things as they lead forward to the poem's conclusion, to that first voice of the European tradition, named in the very moment that his absence is acknowledged, Homer.

The 'rode'/'drifts' antithesis suggests a history without direction, yet moving inexorably on a darkening flood. The impersonal terse 'But all is changed' reinforces this sense of the loss of human control. But there is an odd contrary current in the phrase 'that high horse riderless'. This is Pegasus, certainly, crossed with an Arab stallion, and we should not stop to ask too many questions about a blind man riding a horse, or about taking a horse to water. But a 'high horse' is something presumptuous, a false pride. Is Yeats saying that it was right to get down from that high horse, right to abandon the pretensions of 'traditional sanctity and loveliness'? Is there more than a hint of dismissal in that opening proposition: we were hopelessly romantic, like Pound's E.P., out of key with our time?

In the very moment that he writes an elegy for a lost tradition, Yeats defiantly recreates and continues it, making of his poem a new embodiment and emblem of what it mourns, itself cast upon the darkening flood. At the beginning of the 1930s, as Modernism entered the decade in which all its projects foundered, Yeats's intertextual echoes call up, not a dead history, but a living one, which is neither progress nor decline but a series of successive shocks and confrontations in which changing social forces clash upon a darkling plain. As part of that continuing history, Wordsworth and Coleridge in the 1790s had sought to open up the book of the people in *Lyrical Ballads*, as an act, as Eliot recognised in *The Use of Poetry* of political as well as cultural revolution. A century-and-a-half earlier, Milton had written as a participant in a popular revolution aimed at rewriting the book of the people. Yeats's allusions, far from returning us to the origins, bring us back to the very world where Homer is no longer in the saddle. The solitary soul, which has been compared to a swan, finds itself drifting rather than riding upon the darkening flood of what has always been a collective history.

The last stanza, that is, sets up but then effaces a contradiction which is at the centre of Yeats's work and at the heart of Modernism itself: between 'traditional sanctity' and 'the book of the people', between the leisured culture of the Gregories and the Hydes, genteel collectors of folk tales, and the polyphony of a 'people' that refuses the monological authority of tradition. The poem records the dilemma of Modernism at its most endangered and desperate extreme, adrift on the filthy modern tide of a history no longer, if it ever was, in capable hands, a riderless horse. 'At the Abbey Theatre' in 1910 had asked what seemed like mocking rhetorical questions of a new century:

> Is there a bridle for this Proteus
> That turns and changes like his draughty seas?
>
> Or is there none, most popular of men,
> But when they mock us, that we mock again?

Already by 'Nineteen Hundred and Nineteen' that century had given hard and mocking answers, telling those who had 'planned to bring the world under a rule' that they were 'but weasels fighting in a hole', its 'levelling wind' mocking an age where 'we / But traffic in mockery'. In 1919, there is 'Violence upon the roads: violence of horses' but at least 'Some few have handsome riders'. By 1931, it is clear that there is neither bridle nor rider.

Chapter Eleven

Postmodern postmortem

Historians and magicians: the ends of modernism

Near the beginning of Act II of Samuel Beckett's *Waiting for Godot* there is a moment of repetition and recapitulation which brings Vladimir and Estragon into sharp contrast. Vladimir insists on holding on to memory. For him, it's the foundation of identity. It's important that 'things have changed since yesterday', that Estragon remembers their shared experience in the Macon country, that he should recall Lucky and Pozzo and the suicide attempt.

All this is unreal for Estragon. The past lives on in his present only as bruised shins, and the rest is something Vladimir has dreamt: 'Another of your nightmares'. For Estragon, an early postmodernist, the subject is a momentary being, its past and future imaginary. He is not interested in origins. 'You can start from anything', he notes in passing. For Vladimir, a classic Modernist, finding something to start from means returning to the origin once again:

VLADIMIR: What was I saying, we could go on from there.
ESTRAGON: What were you saying when?
VLADIMIR: At the very beginning.
ESTRAGON: The beginning of what?
VLADIMIR: This evening . . . I was saying . . . I was saying . . .

And Estragon cuts him short: 'I'm not a historian'.

For Vladimir the future can be constituted only in the reclamation of the past. Our origins tell us who we are and who we will be. But for Estragon the past is suppositional, primarily a figment invented to keep others happy: 'I suppose we blathered', he says, his supposition at once taking on a spurious certainty, 'Blathering about nothing in particular. That's been going on now for half a century.'[1]

Waiting for Godot, published in French as *En attendant Godot* in 1952, looks back upon the half-century of Modernism which precedes it with a jaundiced eye. Vladimir's nightmare is that to which twenty centuries of stony sleep were vexed in 'The Second Coming', which 'Rides upon sleep' in the dragon-ridden days of 'Nineteen Hundred and Nineteen', the 'numb nightmare' which, Yeats says, 'rides on top' in 'The Gyres'. It is the nightmare of history from which Stephen Dedalus is trying to awake in *Ulysses*. By the time Beckett pens the lines, a half-century of blathering about nothing in particular has brought about the massacre of hundreds of millions. But for Estragon, trying on a new pair of boots has greater significance than all the ideological blather:

ESTRAGON: We always find something, eh Didi, to give us the impression we exist?
VLADIMIR: (*impatiently*) Yes, yes, we're magicians. But let us persevere in what we have resolved, before we forget.

Beckett sets in antithesis here two modes of historical interpretation which struggle for dominance throughout the course of Modernism. If Estragon decries the role of historian, Vladimir with equal impatience dismisses the improvisatory existentialism of Estragon as mere conjuring. Both approaches, however, share a common ground in discourse, as is revealed when a fallen Pozzo calls for help and Vladimir sees it as the opportunity to make a speech about doing something, rather than simply making speeches. Estragon begins 'And suppose he —' but is cut off by an impatient Vladimir:

Let us not waste time in idle discourse! Let us do something, while we have the chance! It is not every day that we are needed. Not indeed that we personally are needed. Others would meet the case equally well, if not better. To all mankind they were addressed, those cries for help still ringing in our ears! But at this place, at this moment of time, all mankind is us, whether we like it or not.

Estragon represents that 'Imagiste' impulse in Modernism which detaches its luminous moments from any historical continuum and contemplates them in their isolate intensity. Vladimir has the world-historical ambitions of the Pound who set out to write a poem including history, the conviction of the activist that doing, rather than merely supposing, is the only authentic thing. Both alike, however, waste their time in idle discourse. Godot, the ultimate signifier, *fons et origo* of meaning, is precisely *not here*, and his determinate absence determines the vacuity of everything else. The promise of a new start (when he finally arrives) proposes a future, but fixates all meaning on an authorising, originating past; it is now always 'after the event'.

Vladimir's song at the beginning of Act II catches the paradox of an historical consciousness that lives only in retrospect, embedding its antecedents within a recursive discourse which endlessly chases its tail/ tale, where every dog has its day only as the subject of a narrative which renders it always-already posthumous:

> Then all the dogs came running
> And dug the dog a tomb
> And wrote upon the tombstone
> For the eyes of dogs to come:
>
> A dog came in the kitchen. . . .

And so on, *ad infinitum*. Such is the way in which the intertextual returns on itself in the whole self-repeating history of Modernism, opening an infinite and uncrossable distance between origin and end, event and writing, the 'new start' promised and reported and the return to old ways which it actually prefigures. In these dog days between event, 'All the dead voices' of tradition merely 'talk about their lives. To have lived is not enough for them. They have to talk about it. To be dead is not enough for them. It is not sufficient.' This sense of insufficiency and failure redeemed only in writing could be paralleled in innumerable Modernist texts, from 'Prufrock' and *Ulysses*, through the will-making of 'The Tower' to the Pisan Cantos. Towards the end of *Godot*, while Estragon sleeps, Vladimir has a disconcerting intuition of the perpetual discursive supersession in which we all go down to history, like the Thames-daughters and the 'neurotic woman' of *The Waste Land*:

> At me too someone is looking, of me too someone is saying, he is sleeping, he knows nothing, let him sleep on. I can't go on. What have I said?

The anxiety of history, that polysemic intertwining of discourses which is both event and narrative, leaves him emptied of meaning, knowing nothing, at this midnight of the century:

> Was I sleeping, while the others suffered? Am I sleeping now? Tomorrow, when I wake, or think I do, what shall I say of today? That with Estragon my friend, at this place, until the fall of night, I waited for Godot? That Pozzo passed, with his carrier, and that he spoke to us? Probably. But in all that, what truth will there be?

In this, the first major text of postmodernism, the secret of Modernism is out. It is all talk, waiting for an end which never comes, and speculating in the interim about the origins of action and motive which put us 'at this place, until the fall of night', 'at this place, at this moment of time . . . whether we like it or not'. In what Auden in 1949 was to call, in 'Under Sirius', 'these dull dog-days / Between event',[2]

Vladimir's questions recall another relentless patriarchal ghost who haunts the ruined century of Modernism, like that old mole in the cellarage urging Hamlet to murder and massacre. For if the title of this play wilfully recalls Clifford Odets's *Waiting for Lefty*, about a revolution that never began, the opening lines of *Waiting for Godot* call up an even more memorable intertext.

'Nothing to be done', says Estragon, exhausted, as the play begins. Not quite so desperate, Vladimir concedes:

> I'm beginning to come round to that opinion. Alı my life I've tried to put it from me, saying, Vladimir, be reasonable, you haven't yet tried every-thing. And I resumed the struggle. (*He broods, musing on the struggle. Turning to Estragon.*) So there you are again.

Estragon's final verdict offers belated answer to a question asked exactly half a century earlier, in 1902, by another Vladimir, Vladimir Ilyich Lenin: *What is to be done?*[3] As Beckett intimates, 'What is to be done?' is a question that cannot be detached from those other questions of historical exegesis and interpretation, looking before and after, 'What have I said?' and 'what shall I say?'. Estragon's judgement sets a postmodernist seal on two lean obituaries, that of Modernism, and that of the Stalinised Marxism that was its vociferous consort throughout a blathering half-century. When Vladimir 'resumes the struggle' at various points in the play, echoing the reiterated 'today the struggle' of Auden's *Spain*, he returns to that continuation of lost causes by other means which has kept an exhausted rhetoric going for a further half-century of (postmodernist) blather.

The great Modernist texts return repeatedly to remotest origins for the authority to speak, seeking in Homer, Virgil, Propertius, Li Po, Dante, etc., the authorising pre-text of their discourse. In the process, they appear to turn their backs upon Eliot's 'immense panorama of futility and anarchy which is contemporary history'. Yet everywhere in their work that repressed returns. It is not some transcendent Godot, uniting origins with ends, who walks across the stage of Beckett's play, but the master and slave Pozzo and Lucky, figuring the actual squalid history of class society which underlies all the fine lines. Lucky's repetitious monologue, when he briefly gets to wear the top hat of authority, parodies in its garbled headlong unpacking all the legitimising discourses his masters deploy to keep him down. Like Modernism itself, this monologue cannot reach any conclusion. It can only be 'abandoned unfinished'. What cuts Lucky short is not the sense of an ending, but a violent disempowering interruption, the hat of authority snatched from him, without which he falls voiceless. But hats, like Estragon's boots, are exchangeable. Power does not remain in one fixed place. Lucky himself repeatedly urges his flagging self on with words which echo but also truncate Vladimir's Marxist rhetoric. History to the defeated may say alas; but the defeated can also say, with Lucky, 'in a word I resume alas alas abandoned unfinished'.

The discourses of Modernism shadow and write large the contra-dictions of twentieth-century history, like the lengthened shadow of Sweeney straddled in the sun. For Modernism stands in dual relation to its time. On the one hand it expresses the age's will to power, to recuperating like Eliot's Tradition 'all the past', in an act of cultural conservation which identifies with the triumphal processions of the victors. On the other hand, its fractured discourses and interrupted narratives figure the reality of an historical order of exploitation founded in the inequalities of class, race, nation and gender, in exclusion, privilege and, ultimately, massacre.

In seeking to trace the origins of Modernism, this study has returned to its textual and historical sources, not from any antiquarian interest, but to understand how those sources are used to manufacture a profoundly contemporary configuration, making what Walter Benjamin called a 'constellation' of the present with innumerable pasts.[4] If the moment between 1910 and 1922 when the great Modernist texts were written is indisputably the focus of attention for any such understand-ing, this period can be comprehended only in the light of two different kinds of retrospect. The first is easy enough to understand: the Modernists themselves looked back to, and recruited, key moments of past literature and history. They are in that sense always 'after the event'. But in the two subsequent decades a new retrospective upon the moment of Modernism became possible as the late 1920s and 1930s overtly politicised the tradition it had created.

Modernism's hidden agenda came belatedly to consciousness under the cold eye of a decade that submitted all aspects of life to a political scrutiny which sought the inscriptions of power in all the ostensibly disinterested discourses of culture. T.S. Eliot's critical writing in the 1930s responds to this immanent critique, and offers clues that lead back to the material origins of Modernism's double discourse. Pound's own retrospects, in Cantos and criticism alike, undergo a similar enlightenment. Yeats's poetry from the mid-1920s onwards engages in a continuing dialogue with his own earlier productions, one of his final works, 'The Man and the Echo', almost an auto-obituary like Pound's 'Ode pour l'élection de son sépulchre', asking of his own politically complicit earlier work,

> Did that play of mine send out
> Certain men the English shot?
> Did words of mine put too much strain

> On that woman's reeling brain?
> Could my spoken words have checked
> That whereby a house lay wrecked?[5]

Another poem, published along with this in *The London Mercury* in January 1939, the month Yeats died, overtly acknowledges the truth. Called simply 'Politics', it cites for epigraph Thomas Mann's patrician judgement, 'In our time the destiny of man presents its meaning in political terms'. The poem resists the claim, unwilling to 'fix' its attention 'On Roman or on Russian / Or on Spanish politics' with 'that girl standing there', wishing instead 'But O that I were young again / And held her in my arms!'[6] But the intertwining of sexuality and politics through the figure of Maud Gonne in Yeats's earlier poetry makes this simple-minded binary of Venus and Mars no more than a banal ideological operation. Another of the *Last Poems*, 'A Bronze Head', after all, recalls of Gonne that, even at the starting-post, he had seen

> a sterner eye look through her eye
> On this foul world in its decline and fall;
> On gangling stocks grown great, great stocks run dry,
> Ancestral pearls all pitched into a sty,
> Heroic reverie mocked by clown and knave,
> And wondered what was left for massacre to save.[7]

Modernism is a retrospective artefact, a movement constituted backwards, like Beckett's series of doggy obituaries, the new dog endlessly buried for the sake of dogs to come, and postmodernism close at heel. In the 1930s, Modernism begins to inscribe its own obituaries in those texts which prefigure its dogged heir, whether in Eliot's 'Coriolan', his lectures on *The Use of Poetry* and *After Strange Gods*, Pound's Usura Cantos, or Yeats's *Full Moon in March* and *Last Poems*. Only in the retrospect afforded by the crisis years of the 1930s was it possible to discern the intimate relations between Modernism and Bolshevism, relations at once accidental and inevitable, each the promise after the other's event. In the 1930s, even Pound saw in Stalin's Soviet Union that modernisation process which had failed in the 'usurocracies' which had conceived and then abandoned the Modernist project. Beckett, a disciple of Joyce in the 1930s, writes in *Waiting for Godot* the postmodern epitaph of both those dreams turned nightmare. But, *pace* the latest postmodernists, eager as ever to write their already-dated obituaries, we stand once again not at the end but merely at the beginning of history. All that impressive rubbish cleared away, it is possible once more to say, like Vladimir at the start of a play which was always a late birth, re-hearsing itself in the wake of numberless rehearsals, 'So there you are again'.

But that is another story.

Notes

For ease of identification these notes supply full bibliographical details of all cited works on their first occurrence in each separate chapter. Where work originally appeared in journals, I have also indicated subsequent first or most available publication in book form.

Chapter One

1. Ezra Pound, 'Harold Monro', *The Criterion*, July 1932, p. 590. See also Ezra Pound, *Polite Essays*, London: Faber and Faber, 1937.
2. Laura Riding and Robert Graves, *A Survey of Modernist Poetry*, London: Heinemann, 1927, p. 258. Two of the best recent studies of the historical contexts of classical Modernism, to which I am generally indebted, are Michael H. Levenson, *A Genealogy of Modernism*, Cambridge: Cambridge University Press, 1984, pp. 71–4; and Erik Svarny, *'The Men of 1914': T.S. Eliot and Early Modernism*, Milton Keynes: Open University Press, 1989.
3. Lyndall Gordon, *Eliot's Early Years*, Oxford: Oxford University Press, 1977, p. 65 ff. For precise dates of Eliot's movements during this period, see Valerie Eliot (ed.), *The Letters of T.S. Eliot, vol.1, 1898–1922*, London: Faber and Faber, 1988, pp. xix–xxvi.
4. Ezra Pound, 'We Have Had No Battles But We Have All Joined In And Made Roads', *Polite Essays*, London: Faber and Faber, 1937, pp. 49–50.
5. Eugene Jolas *et al.*, 'Revolution of the Word: Proclamation', *transition*, vol. 16/17, 1929. The 'Proclamation' develops the argument of Jolas's article, 'The Revolution of Language and James Joyce', in *transition*, vol. 11, 1928. On all this, see Douglas McMillan, *transition: The History of a Literary Era, 1927–1938*, London: Calder and Boyars, 1975, Part 1, pp. 7–61.
6. D.D. Paige (ed.), *The Selected Letters of Ezra Pound 1907–1941*, London: Faber and Faber, 1982, p. 40.
7. Ezra Pound, 'A Retrospect', *Pavannes and Divisions*, New York: Alfred

Knopf, 1918; reprinted in Ezra Pound, *Literary Essays of Ezra Pound*, T.S. Eliot (ed.), London: Faber and Faber, 1954, pp. 3–14.

8. Ezra Pound, *The Spirit of Romance*, London: Dent, 1910; 1929. All quotations are from the third impression of the revised 1952 text, London: Peter Owen, 1970. The 1910 '*Praefatio ad Lectorem Electum*' can be found on pp. 7–9, 1970.

9. *ibid.*, p. 10.

10. Ezra Pound, 'Prufrock and Other Observations, by T.S. Eliot', *Poetry*, June 1917; reprinted as 'T.S. Eliot', in Pound, *Literary Essays*, pp. 418–22.

11. Ezra Pound, '*Prefatio Aut Cimicum Tumulus*', *Polite Essays*, London: Faber and Faber, 1937, p. 135.

12. Ezra Pound, *Spirit of Romance*, p. 8.

13. Ezra Pound, 'The Tradition', *Poetry*, vol. 3, no. 3, December 1913; reprinted in Pound, *Literary Essays*, pp. 91–3.

14. Paul Valéry, *Leonardo, Poe, Mallarmé*, trans. Malcolm Cowley and James R. Lawler, Princeton: Princeton University Press, 1972, p. 241.

15. Ezra Pound, 'A Few Don'ts', *Poetry*, vol. 1, no. 6, March 1913; first collected under the heading 'A Retrospect' in *Pavannes and Divisions* (1918), and reprinted in Pound, *Literary Essays*, p. 4 ff.

16. Ezra Pound, *Cathay*, London: Elkin Mathews, 1915; reprinted in *The Translations of Ezra Pound*, London: Faber and Faber, 1970, pp. 189–204.

17. Ezra Pound, 'Vorticism', *The Fortnightly Review*, September 1914; reprinted as chapter 11 of Ezra Pound, *Gaudier-Brzeska: A Memoir*, London: The Bodley Head, 1916.

18. Ezra Pound, *Ripostes*, London: Swift & Co, 1912.

19. Ezra Pound, *Make It New*, London: Faber and Faber, 1934.

20. Ezra Pound, *The Cantos of Ezra Pound*, London: Faber and Faber, 1975, Canto CXVI, pp. 795–7.

21. *ibid.*, Canto I, pp. 3–5.

22. J.E. Harrison, *Myths of the Odyssey in Art and Literature*, London: Rivingtons, 1882, p. 1. On the Phoenician connection, see, e.g., her account of the Sirens, p. 169. Norman Douglas expands on the Greco-Phoenician link in a way which probably influenced the *Cantos*, *Hugh Selwyn Mauberley* and *The Waste Land* in his *Siren Land*, London: Dent, 1911 (see pages 87–8).

Richard Ellmann, *James Joyce*, London: Oxford University Press, 1959, appears to think Victor Bérard, whose work Joyce knew, was the first to envisage a Semitic origin for the *Odyssey*, though he is rather vague in his attribution, speaking of 'the contention Victor Bérard first formulated about the beginning of the century, that the Odyssey had Semitic roots' (p. 421). Hugh Kenner, *Joyce's Voices*, London: Faber and Faber, 1978, p. 65, is even vaguer, speaking of a Joyce who 'took up the story, with on his bookshelf a long work by a French scholar retracing Odysseus's voyages through the Mediterranean'. Though he subsequently acknowledges (pp. 109–10) that 'there are signs that [Joyce] had read Jane Harrison's *Themis*', Kenner quotes this only in 'the useful summary of Mr Bush' (Ronald Bush,

The Genesis of Ezra Pound's Cantos, 1976), apparently unprepared to retrace Joyce's voyages through contemporary archaeo-anthropology. The debt of the Modernist writers to the Cambridge school of anthropology has not yet been properly recorded.

What he calls Bérard's 'remarkable work, *Les Phéniciens et l'Odyssée*' is discussed by Walter Leaf, *Troy: A Study in Homeric Geography*, London: Macmillan, 1912, pp. 3–4, 257–9 (see note 41 below). But Leaf is loath to associate himself with Bérard's 'obstinate refusal to see any but Phenicians in the Mediterranean' (p. 3).

23. T.S. Eliot, 'Blake', *The Sacred Wood*, London: Methuen, 1920.
24. T.S. Eliot, 'Little Gidding' (1942), ll. 50–1, *Four Quartets*, London: Faber and Faber, 1944.
25. T.S. Eliot, 'Ulysses, Order and Myth', *The Dial*, vol. 75, November 1923, pp. 480–3.
26. *The Purgatorio of Dante Alighieri*, H. Oelsner (ed.), trans. Thomas Okey, London: Dent, 1901, Canto XXVI, pp. 322–33; vol. 2 in the Temple Classics parallel text edition of the *Divina Commedia*, ed. Israel Gollancz. This is the text used by both Eliot and Pound and cited by Pound in *The Spirit of Romance*.
27. Ezra Pound, *Spirit of Romance*, p. 14.
28. Laura Riding and Robert Graves, *A Survey of Modernist Poetry*, pp. 264–8.
29. Mikhail Bakhtin, *Problems of Dostoevsky's Poetics*, as cited by Tzvetan Todorov, *Mikhail Bakhtin: The Dialogical Imagination*, Manchester: Manchester University Press, 1984, p.84. The quotations from 'East Coker' are from T.S. Eliot, *East Coker*, London: Faber and Faber 1940, *Four Quartets*, London: Faber and Faber, 1944.
30. Ezra Pound, 'A Retrospect', *Literary Essays*, pp. 3–14.
31. Ezra Pound, 'Date Line', *Make It New*, London: Faber and Faber, 1934; reprinted in Pound, *Literary Essays*, pp. 74–87.
32. Ezra Pound, *Jefferson and/or Mussolini*, London: Stanley Nott, 1935.
33. Ezra Pound, *ABC of Reading*, London: Routledge, 1934; London: Faber and Faber, 1961, p. 29.
34. Ezra Pound, 'The New Sculpture', *The Egoist*, 16 February 1914.
35. Ezra Pound, 'Watch the Beaneries', *Guide to Kulchur*, London: Peter Owen, 1952, pp. 344–5.
36. *Times Literary Supplement*, 29 January 1993.
37. Richard Ellmann, *The Consciousness of Joyce*, London: Faber and Faber, 1977, p. 4. For bibliographical details of *Hugh Selwyn Mauberley*, see chapter 5, note 1 below.
38. T.S. Eliot, 'Ulysses, Order and Myth'.
39. Frank Budgen, *James Joyce and the Making of Ulysses*, 1934, Clive Hart (ed.), London: Oxford University Press, 1972, p. 69.
40. James Joyce, *Ulysses* (1922); first unlimited edition, London: The Bodley Head, 1937, p. 21.
41. Heinrich Schliemann, *Troy and its Remains*, London: John Murray, 1875, trans. Philip Smith; *Ilios: The City and Country of the Trojans*, London:

John Murray, 1880. See also Walter Leaf, *Troy: A Study in Homeric Geography*, particularly chapter III, 'The Ruins of Troy', pp. 53–144. Leaf contributed a great deal to the climate of opinion in which Troy was restored to historicity in the popular mind. Of his *Companion to the Iliad for English Readers*, *The Saturday Review* wrote symptomatically 'It is impossible to praise too highly the excellence of [its] notes on the *Realien* of Homer . . . They help to make Homer's world live again.'

42. The 'Minoans' of Evans's reconstructed frescoes, variously exhibited in the years after excavations started in the early 1900s, caught the popular imagination with their strikingly 'up-to-date' coiffure and décolletage resembling those of fashionable *fin de siècle* Paris. Pound's references to the halls of Minos and to Minoan braids in *Mauberley* clearly reflect this fascination. In *Gaudier-Brzeska: A Memoir*, he cites approvingly a letter of Gaudier-Brzeska's in *The Egoist*, 16 March 1914, which speaks of 'The archaic work discovered at Gnossos . . . the expressions of what is termed a "barbaric people" – i.e., a people to whom reason is secondary to instinct', contrasts them with 'The pretty works of the great Hellenes' and concludes that the 'modern sculptor' is 'continuing the tradition of the barbaric peoples of the earth (for whom we have sympathy and admiration)'. A.J. Evans's *The Palace of Minos at Knossos* was published in four volumes between 1921 and 1935, but the newspapers had given extensive coverage to the Minoan style almost as soon as excavations began. See Gerald Cadogan, *Palaces of Minoan Crete*, London: Routledge, 1980.

43. Ezra Pound, 'Paris Letter', *The Dial*, vol. 72, no. 6, June 1922; reprinted as 'Ulysses' in *Literary Essays*, pp. 403–9.

44. T.S. Eliot, 'American Literature and the American Language' (1953), *To Criticize the Critic*, New York: Farrar, Straus and Giroux, 1965, p. 58.

45. 'Coole Park and Ballylee, 1931' is the poem's title in *The Collected Poems of W.B. Yeats*, London: Macmillan, 1950. In fact, the poem is at once more belated and more premature than it thinks. In its first publication, in *Words for Music Perhaps and Other Poems*, Dublin: Cuala Press, 1932, it was actually entitled 'Coole Park and Ballylee 1932'. In *The Winding Stair and Other Poems*, London: Macmillan, 1933, and three subsequent publications before *Collected Poems*, it was called 'Coole and Ballylee, 1931'. Like its speaker, then, the poem itself shifts about both in time and space, its historical and topographical dispossession reinforced, a few years later, by the builders' demolition of Lady Gregory's house at Coole Park, for 'development'.

46. W.B. Yeats, 'Meditations in Time of Civil War', *The Tower*, London: Macmillan, 1928.

47. W.B. Yeats, 'The Second Coming', *Michael Robartes and the Dancer*, Dundrum: Cuala Press, 1921.

48. I discuss this more fully at the beginning of Chapter 8.

49. W.B. Yeats, *Michael Robartes and the Dancer*.

50. W.H. Auden, *Spain*, London: Faber and Faber 1937; *Another Time*,

London: Faber and Faber, 1940. See on this Stan Smith, 'Missing Dates: From "Spain 1937" to "September 1, 1939"', *Literature and History*, Autumn 1987.

Chapter Two

1. T.S. Eliot, *Selected Essays: 1917–1932*, London: Faber and Faber, 1932; enlarged edition 1951, pp. 7–8.
2. T.S. Eliot, 'Tradition and the Individual Talent', *The Egoist*, vol. 6, September and December 1919, pp. 54–5, 72–3.
3. Valerie Eliot (ed.), *The Letters of T.S. Eliot, vol. 1, 1898–1922*, London: Faber and Faber, 1988, p. 351.
4. T.S. Eliot, *The Sacred Wood: Essays on Poetry and Criticism*, London: Methuen, 1920, reprinted with new Preface, 1928.
5. T.S. Eliot, *The Use of Poetry and the Use of Criticism*, London: Faber and Faber, 1964, pp. 9–10.
6. T.S. Eliot, 'To Criticize the Critic', *To Criticize the Critic*, New York: Farrar, Straus and Giroux, 1965, p. 10.
7. *ibid.*, p. 14.
8. T.S. Eliot, *The Use of Poetry and the Use of Criticism*, p. 13.
9. *ibid.*, p. 14.
10. T.S. Eliot, *Letters*, p. 351.
11. *ibid.*, p. 353.
12. T.S. Eliot, *The Use of Poetry and the Use of Criticism*, pp. 14–15.
13. Alan Bullock, *Hitler: A Study in Tyranny*, Harmondsworth: Pelican Books, 1962, Book 1, chapter 4 and Book 2, chapter 5, provides a vigorous and lucid narrative of this period.
14. T.S. Eliot, *After Strange Gods: A Primer of Modern Heresy*, London: Faber and Faber, 1934.
15. T.S. Eliot, 'Commentary', *The Criterion*, January 1937, p. 289.
16. T.S. Eliot, *The Use of Poetry and the Use of Criticism*, pp. 135–6.
17. *ibid.*, p. 128.
18. *ibid*, p. 38.
19. *ibid*, pp. 25–6. On this, see Eugene Jolas, 'The Revolution of Language and James Joyce', *transition*, vol. 11, 1928 and page 2 above.
20. *ibid.*, p. 27.
21. *ibid.*, p. 61.
22. *ibid.*, pp. 71–2.
23. *ibid.*, p. 74.
24. *ibid.*, pp. 75–6.
25. *ibid.*, p. 81.
26. *ibid*, pp. 84–5.
27. Peter Brooks, 'The Idea of a Psychoanalytic Literary Criticism', in Shlomith Rimmon-Kenan (ed.), *Discourse in Psychoanalysis and Literature*, London: Methuen, 1987, p. 13.

28. T.S. Eliot, 'The Function of Criticism', *Selected Essays*, p. 23 ff.

29. *ibid.*, p. 25.

30. T.S. Eliot, 'Reflections on *Vers Libre*', *The New Statesman*, 3 March 1917, reprinted in *To Criticize the Critic*, pp. 183–9; this quotation, p. 184.

31. T.S. Eliot, *The Use of Poetry and the Use of Criticism*, p. 108.

32. *ibid.*, p. 109.

33. *ibid.*, pp. 114, 116.

34. *ibid.*, p. 111. For the subsequent quotation, see T.S. Eliot, *Burnt Norton*, London: Faber and Faber, 1936, ll. 43–4.

35. *ibid.*, p. 119. For the subsequent quotation, see T.S. Eliot, *The Dry Salvages*, London: Faber and Faber, 1941, ll. 101–3.

36. 'War Paint and Feathers', *The Athenaeum*, October 1919, no. 4668, p. 1036.

37. T.S. Eliot, *The Use of Poetry and the Use of Criticism*, pp. 144–5.

38. *ibid.*, p. 69.

39. *ibid.*, p. 145.

40. T.S. Eliot, *After Strange Gods*, p. 13.

41. T.S. Eliot, *The Use of Poetry and the Use of Criticism*, p. 155.

42. *ibid.*, p. 156.

43. Bertrand Russell, *The Practice and Theory of Bolshevism*, London: Allen & Unwin, 1920, reprinted 1921.

44. *ibid.*, p. 22.

Chapter Three

1. D.D. Paige (ed.), *The Selected Letters of Ezra Pound, 1907–1941*, London: Faber and Faber, 1982, p. 40. Unless otherwise indicated, all poems quoted in this chapter are from T.S. Eliot, *Prufrock and Other Observations*, London: The Egoist Press, 1917; reprinted in T.S. Eliot, *Collected Poems 1909–1962*, London: Faber and Faber, 1963.

2. Valerie Eliot (ed.), *The Letters of T.S. Eliot, vol. 1, 1898–1922*, London: Faber and Faber 1988, pp. 44–7, 60.

3. Adelbert Albrecht, 'Professor Sigmund Freud the Eminent Vienna Psychotherapeutist Now in America: the Founder of a Most Successful School Interviewed', *The Boston Evening Transcript*, 12 September 1909. Through 1908–9 the newspaper carried a series of five reports on the Clark University Psychological Conference at which Freud had spoken. For a full account, see Alison Cassidy, *T.S. Eliot and Charles Peirce: A Study of the Influence of Peircean Philosophy on the Philosophy, Poetry and Criticism of T.S. Eliot*, unpublished doctoral dissertation, University of Dundee, 1992.

4. T.S. Eliot, 'Shakespeare and the Stoicism of Seneca' (1927), *Selected Essays*, London: Faber and Faber, 1951, pp. 130–2, 138.

5. B.C. Southam, *A Student's Guide to the Selected Poems of T.S. Eliot*, London: Faber and Faber, 1981, p. 45.

6. B.C. Southam, *A Student's Guide* notes the use of 'The Aspern Papers' in 'Burbank with a Baedeker', but does not seem to have picked up its role in mediating *Twelfth Night*'s 'dying fall' motif to 'Portrait of a Lady' and 'Prufrock'.

7. Rupert Brooke, 'The Old Vicarage, Grantchester', dated May 1912, and published in Edward Marsh's *Georgian Poetry 1911–1912*, London: The Poetry Bookshop, December 1912. Southam, *A Student's Guide* pp. 24–5 and 86, notes a possible echo of Brooke's line in *The Waste Land*, though observing that 'it is not, in the strict sense, a source'. He does not however note the almost exact and disconcerting correspondence between Brooke's line and Eliot's in 'Portrait of a Lady'. Eliot's citations of the worn-out common phrases of forgotten popular lyrics has been neglected by the source-hunters. Enquiry might reveal a great deal about the way his rhetoric of reiteration works to breathe new life into dead idioms, while placing in a 'Modern', ironic perspective the stale emotional intensities of his self-romanticising characters.

8. Percy Wyndham Lewis, *Tarr* (1918; 1928); this edition, Harmondsworth: Penguin Books, 1982, p. 188.

9. T.S. Eliot, *The Use of Poetry and the Use of Criticism*, London: Faber and Faber, 1964, p. 155.

10. Wyndham Lewis, *Tarr*, pp. 16–17.

11. T.S. Eliot, 'Tradition and the Individual Talent', *The Egoist*, vol. 6, September and December, 1919, pp. 54–5, 72–3; reprinted in T.S. Eliot, *The Sacred Wood*, London: Methuen, 1920; T.S. Eliot, *Selected Essays: 1917–1932*, London: Faber and Faber, 1932 and thereafter.

12. T.S. Eliot, letter to Herbert Read, cited in Allen Tate (ed.), *T.S. Eliot: The Man and His Work*, Harmondsworth: Penguin Books, 1971, p. 20. On the etiology and significance of this permanently self-displacing consciousness, see Stan Smith, 'T.S. Eliot: Lengthening Shadows', *Inviolable Voice: History and Twentieth-Century Poetry*, Dublin: Gill and Macmillan, 1983, pp. 73–97.

13. T.S. Eliot, *The Use of Poetry and the Use of Criticism*, p. 101. The letter to Bailey, 22 November 1817, can be found in Maurice Buxton Forman (ed.), *The Letters of John Keats*, London: Oxford University Press, 1935, p. 67. Eliot's extensive early reading in the Romantics, as in the Victorians, has been underestimated as a source for his themes and images by critics in the image of the literary revolution he forged, for whom Laforgue, Baudelaire, Dante and Donne are the reference points. For other debts to Keats, see Chapter 6, note 8.

14. T.S. Eliot, *The Egoist*, May 1918, pp. 69–70. The uncharacteristic tone here derives from the fact that Eliot is citing rather than just paraphrasing Hueffer/Ford's actual words.

15. T.S. Eliot, *Burnt Norton*, London: Faber and Faber, 1936, ll. 9–10, 146–8, 149–53, 139–40; collected in *Four Quartets*, London: Faber and Faber, 1944.

16. T.S. Eliot, *Ash Wednesday*, London: Faber and Faber, 1930.

Chapter Four

1. Ezra Pound, 'Vorticism', *The Fortnightly Review*, September 1914; reprinted as chapter 11, Ezra Pound, *Gaudier-Brzeska: A Memoir*, London: The Bodley Head, 1916.
2. Ezra Pound, *The Egoist*, 15 June 1914. Writing in February 1932 to John Drummond of 'the press-bosses' stifling of economic discussion', Pound traced the origins of the current crisis to the post-war failure of will, adding, of his new work, 'The hell cantos are specifically LONDON, the state of English mind in 1919 and 1920.' D.D. Paige (ed.), *The Selected Letters of Ezra Pound 1907–1941*, London: Faber and Faber, 1982, pp. 239–40.
3. Ezra Pound, 'Pastiche, The Regional'. According to Noel Stock, between 12 June and 20 November 1919 *The New Age* published a series of eighteen pieces by Pound under this heading, the main target of which was the provincialism of time as well as place which impoverished the modern artist. See Noel Stock, *The Life of Ezra Pound*, Harmondsworth: Penguin Books, 1985, pp. 282–3. William Cookson, in Ezra Pound, *Selected Prose 1909–1965*, London: Faber and Faber, 1975, reprints under the heading 'Provincialism the Enemy' four pieces from *The New Age* dated between 12 July and 2 August 1917 which sound remarkably similar in theme and phrasing.
4. Ezra Pound, *Selected Letters*, p. 90.
5. Mikhail Bakhtin, *Rabelais and his World*, trans. Helene Iswolsky, Cambridge, MA: MIT Press, 1968.
6. Ezra Pound, Canto CXVI, *The Cantos of Ezra Pound*, London: Faber and Faber, 1975, pp. 795–7.
7. Julia Kristeva, *Desire in Language: A Semiotic Approach to Literature and Art*, Oxford: Blackwell, 1980, pp. 72–3.
8. *Homage to Sextus Propertius*, completed in 1917, was published along with 'Langue d'Oc', 'Moeurs Contemporains' and the original versions of Cantos I–III in Ezra Pound, *Quia Pauper Amavi*, London: The Egoist Press, 1919. Four sections had previously been published in *Poetry*, March 1919. The text is available in Ezra Pound, *Collected Shorter Poems*, London: Faber and Faber, 1973, pp. 223–48.
9. Ezra Pound, *The Spirit of Romance* (1910, revised 1929, 1952). Unless otherwise indicated, all quotations are from the third impression of the 1952 text, London: Peter Owen, 1970. The 1910 '*Praefatio ad Lectorem Electum*' can be found on pp. 7–9.
10. *ibid.*, p. 39.
11. *ibid.*, pp. 84–5.
12. *ibid.*, pp. 156–7.
13. *ibid.*, p. 157.
14. *ibid.*, p. 177.
15. *ibid.*, p. 158.
16. *ibid.*, pp. 153–4.
17. *ibid.*, p. 181.
18. *ibid.*, p. 156.

19. *ibid.*, p. 220.
20. *ibid.*, p. 162.
21. *ibid.*, p. 223.
22. *ibid.*, p. 216.
23. *ibid.*, p. 204.
24. *ibid.*, p. 97.
25. H.E. Butler (ed.), *Propertius, with an English translation*, London: Heinemann, 1912 (Loeb Classical Library). This is the crib Pound used. Pound's debts to and adaptations of Propertius have been authoritatively discussed in J.P. Sullivan, *Ezra Pound and Sextus Propertius: A study in Creative Translation*, London: Faber and Faber, 1965.
26. Ezra Pound, *Selected Letters*, p. 91.
27. *ibid.*, pp. 148–50.
28. *ibid.*, pp. 178–82. Writing on 8 July 1922 from Paris, the most up-to-date time and place in the world, Pound is sure that while 'the Provençal feeling is archaic', 'the Latin is really "modern". We are just getting back to a Roman state of civilization, or in reach of it.' And he is in no doubt as to what modernity comprises: 'Eliot's *Waste Land* is I think the justification of the "movement," of our modern experiment, since 1900. It should be published this year.'
29. *ibid.*, pp. 230–1.

Chapter Five

1. Ezra Pound, 'Remy de Gourmont, A Distinction', *Instigations*, New York: Boni and Liveright, 1920; reprinted in T.S. Eliot (ed.), *Literary Essays of Ezra Pound*, London: Faber and Faber, 1954, pp. 339–40.

   Except where otherwise indicated, poems in this chapter are from Ezra Pound, *Hugh Selwyn Mauberley*, London: The Ovid Press, 1920. Ezra Pound, *Poems 1918–1921*, New York: Boni and Liveright, 1921, printed *Mauberley* as the third part of a larger sequence entitled 'Three Portraits', the first of which comprised *Propertius* and the second 'Langue d'Oc' and 'Moeurs Contemporaines'. Whether this was a wholly gratuitous yoking is still worthy of consideration. The *Mauberley* sequence is most easily available in Ezra Pound, *Collected Shorter Poems*, London: Faber and Faber, 1973, pp. 205–22. There is an admirably succinct account of the sequence's textual vagaries in Peter Brooker, *A Student's Guide to the Selected Poems of Ezra Pound*, London: Faber and Faber, 1979, pp. 183–8. The quotations passim from Cantos VII, XXXIII and CXVI are from Ezra Pound, *The Cantos*, London: Faber and Faber, 1975.
2. D.D. Paige (ed.), *The Selected Letters of Ezra Pound 1907–1941*, London: Faber and Faber, 1982, p. 239.
3. Mikhail Bakhtin, 'The Problems of Text in Linguistics, Philology, and the Other Human Sciences', quoted in Tzvetan Todorov, *Mikhail Bakhtin: The Dialogical Principle*, trans. Wlad Godzich, Manchester: Manchester University Press, 1984, p. 74.

4. Ezra Pound, *Personae*, London: Elkin Mathews, 1909.

5. Hugh Witermeyer, *The Poetry of Ezra Pound: Forms and Renewals 1908–1920*, Berkeley: University of California Press, 1969, p. 190.

6. In 'Allen Upward Serious', *The New Age*, 23 April 1914, Pound quotes at length Upward's splendid unpacking of 'glaukopis' as an epithet of Athene. See Pound, *Selected Prose 1909–1965*, ed. William Cookson, London: Faber and Faber, 1973, pp. 377–82. John J. Espey, *Ezra Pound's Mauberley: A Study in Composition*, London: Faber and Faber, 1955, p. 33, suggests that 'Yeux Glauques' derives its title from the expression 'L'oeil glauque' in Théophile Gautier's *Mademoiselle de Maupin*. 'Les Yeux glauques' is in fact the title of a well-known short story in Jean Lorrain's *Buveurs d'ames*, Paris: Charpentier et Fasquelle, 1893, though the phrase was widely fashionable in *fin-de-siècle* France. The appositeness of Lorrain's book to *Mauberley* (and indeed to *The Waste Land*) is apparent from the following summary in Jennifer Birkett, 'Masking Murder: Jean Lorrain 1855–1906', *The Sins of the Fathers: Decadence in France 1870–1914*, London: Quartet, 1986, p. 197:

> Most often, woman is the murderer. Nelly, the golden-haired Lorelei with mysterious blue-green eyes, exudes 'the philtre of Death, the fascination of Non-being' ('Les Yeux glauques'. . .). She listens, entranced, to an old legend that the woman who looks into her lover's eyes as he dies will gain his soul, and with it, the gift of eternal youth. The couple go boating together, and he drowns in a mysterious accident. In 'Ophélius', a painter lies dying of an obsession with the smile and the eyes of Botticelli's 'perversely ideal' 'Primavera', who is 'Gioconda and Ophelia combined'. Lady Viane, his English wife, has the same enigmatic smile and starry eyes. . . as had the drowned sailor he saw three months before on the beach. . . the tale concludes with a denunciation of Eve. . . 'Flaubert's Ennoïa, the eternal enemy, the dancer drinking the blood of prophets, Salome, Herodias. . .'

Likewise, in Lorrain's *Monsieur de Phocas. Astarte*, Paris: Librairie Paul Ollendorff, 1901, Phocas is obsessed with

> the '*yeux glauques*', the ambivalent blue-green gaze . . . in jewels, especially emeralds, and in women's eyes – Salome's, those of his mistress, the actress Willie Stephenson, and those of Astarte, Demon of Lust and Demon of the Sea. The contradictory image of the sea is that of Phocas' desire: for an eternal, unchanging reality with a superficially changing face (Birkett, 'Masking Murder', p. 202).

Pound would have met the same motif in Remy de Gourmont's work, in particular *Histoires magiques*, Paris: Mercure de France, 1894, an important source of *Mauberley*. See note 10 below.

7. Ezra Pound, 'Vorticism', *Fortnightly Review*, September 1914, reprinted in Ezra Pound, *Gaudier-Brzeska: A Memoir*, London: The Bodley Head, 1916. The quotation from *The Athenaeum* is dated 21 March 1908, pp.

360–3. This is of course a journal to which Pound was to become a frequent contributor.

Gaudier-Brzeska's work, and that of the Vorticists in general, was much influenced by the supposedly anti-humanist, hieratic aesthetic of Egyptian art, and references to it are scattered widely through Pound's work. The title of his series of articles in *The New Age* between 7 December 1911 and 15 February 1912, 'I Gather the Limbs of Osiris', testifies to this presence. Apart from the widespread journal and newspaper coverage occasioned by the contemporary archaeological work of Flinders Petrie, Howard Carter and others, Pound's most likely sources of information on things Egyptian would be E.A. Wallis Budge, *The Egyptian Book of the Dead*, London: British Museum, 1895; *The Gods of the Egyptians*, 2 vols, London: Methuen, 1904; *Osiris and the Egyptian Resurrection*, 2 vols, London: Medici Society, 1911; and James H. Breasted, *Ancient Records of Egypt*, 5 vols, New York: Russell & Russell, 1906; *Development of Religion and Thought in Ancient Egypt*, New York: Charles Scribner's Sons, 1912. See also W.M. Flinders Petrie, *The Royal Tombs of the First Dynasty*, London: 1901.

8. Ezra Pound, 'The Revolt of Intelligence', *The New Age*, 15 January 1920, p. 176.

9. Ezra Pound, 'Paris Letter', *The Dial*, June 1922; reprinted as 'Ulysses' in Pound, *Literary Essays*, p. 407.

10. Ezra Pound, *Selected Letters*, pp. 139–41. De Gourmont's actual phrase is 'Des femmes ... conservatrice des traditions milesiennes', Remy de Gourmont, 'Stratagemes', *Histoires magiques*, Paris: Mercure de France, 1894. See Ezra Pound, 'Remy de Gourmont, A Distinction', *Literary Essays*, p. 345, and the 'Postscript' to his translation of de Gourmont's *The Natural Philosophy of Love*, Ezra Pound: *Pavannes and Divagations*, London: Peter Owen, 1960, pp. 203–14.

11. Norman Douglas, *Siren Land*, London: Dent, 1911; reprinted with an introduction by Mark Holloway, London: Secker & Warburg, 1982. Ford's remark is quoted in the Introduction.

12. Ezra Pound, 'The New Learning', *Guide to Kulchur* (1938), London: Peter Owen, 1952, chapter 23, pp. 152–8. All page numbers in the text refer to this edition.

13. Ezra Pound and Marcella Spann (eds), *Confucius to Cummings: An Anthology of Poetry*, New York: New Directions, 1964.

14. Ezra Pound, 'Examples of Civilization', *Guide to Kulchur*, chapter 24, p. 159.

15. Ezra Pound, 'Books "About"', *Guide to Kulchur*, chapter 25, p. 163.

16. Ezra Pound, *The Egoist*, February 1917.

17. Ezra Pound, 'Affirmations: Analysis of this Decade', *The New Age*, 11 February 1915; reprinted in *Gaudier-Brzeska, A Memoir*.

18. Ezra Pound, *ABC of Reading*, London: Routledge, 1934, chapter 3.

19. Ezra Pound, 'A Few Don'ts', *Poetry*, March 1913; reprinted in Pound, *Literary Essays*, pp. 4–7.

20. Ezra Pound, *The Spirit of Romance* (1910), London: Peter Owen, 1970, p. 158.
21. Aristotle, *The Nicomachean Ethics*, edited with an English translation by Harris Rackham, Loeb Classical Library, London: Heinemann, 1926; revised edition 1934.
22. Aristotle, *The Athenian Constitution; the Eudemian Ethics, On virtues and vices*, edited with an English translation by Harris Rackham, Loeb Classical Library, London: Heinemann, 1935.
23. Umberto Eco, *Art and Beauty in the Middle Ages*, New Haven: Yale University Press, 1986, p. 20.
24. Ezra Pound, 'The Serious Artist', originally divided between three issues of *The New Freewoman*, vol. 1, nos 9–11, 1 October, 1 November, 15 November 1913; reprinted in Pound, *Literary Essays*, pp. 41–57, where it is anachronistically attributed to 'The Egoist, A.D. 1913'.
25. Ezra Pound, 'The Tradition', *Poetry*, vol. 3, no. 3, December 1913; reprinted in Pound, *Literary Essays*, pp. 91–3.
26. Ezra Pound, 'Arnold Dolmetsch', *Pavannes and Divisions*, New York: Alfred Knopf, 1918, reprinted in Pound, *Literary Essays*; see in particular pp. 433–4.
27. Aristotle, 'Eudemian Ethics', VII, iii, 10, in Harris Rackham (ed.), *The Athenian Constitution; the Eudemian Ethics, On virtues and vices*, Loeb Classical Library, London: Heinemann, 1935.
28. Ezra Pound, 'Henry James', *The Little Review*, August 1918; reprinted in Pound, *Literary Essays*; see in particular p. 300.
29. Ezra Pound, 'The Individual in his Milieu: A Study of Relations and Gesell', *The Criterion*, October 1935; reprinted in Ezra Pound, *Selected Prose 1909–1965*, ed. William Cookson, London: Faber and Faber, 1973, p. 242.
30. 'The Serious Artist', note 24.
31. Ezra Pound, interviewed by Donald Hall, *Writers at Work: The Paris Review Interviews*, second series, Harmondsworth: Penguin Books, 1977, pp. 51–2.
32. Ezra Pound, *Jefferson and/or Mussolini*, London: Stanley Nott, 1935.
33. Walter Benjamin, *Illuminations*, ed. Hannah Arendt, London: Fontana Books, 1973, p. 258.

Chapter Six

1. Valerie Eliot (ed.), *The Letters of T.S. Eliot, vol. 1, 1898–1922*, London: Faber and Faber, 1988, p. 45. The poem is included in a letter to Conrad Aiken dated 25 July 1914.

   Except where otherwise indicated, the poems discussed in this chapter are from T.S. Eliot, *Ara Vus Prec* (*sc.* 'Vos'), London: The Ovid Press, 1920, published in the United States as *Poems*, New York: Alfred Knopf, 1920. These poems are collected as 'Poems – 1920' in subsequent editions; see T.S. Eliot, *Collected Poems 1909–1962*, London: Faber and Faber, 1963.

Ara Vos Prec also contains the poems from *Prufrock and Other Obser-vations*, London: The Egoist Press, 1917. Citations passim of poems from the *Four Quartets* are taken from *Burnt Norton*, London: Faber and Faber, 1936, ll. 11–17, 154–6, 90, 99, 101–2; *East Coker*, London: Faber and Faber, 1940, ll. 76 and 95; *Little Gidding*, London: Faber and Faber, 1942, ll. 11–12, 138–9, 118–25.

2. T.S. Eliot, *Letters*, p. 368.
3. T.S. Eliot, 'Shakespeare and the Stoicism of Seneca' (originally published by the Shakespeare Association as *Shakespeare and the Senecan Tradition*), *Selected Essays*, London: Faber and Faber, 1951, pp. 138–9.
4. T.S. Eliot, 'Seneca in Elizabethan Translation', *Selected Essays*, p. 74.
5. T.S. Eliot, *The Use of Poetry and the Use of Criticism*, London: Faber and Faber, 1964, pp. 147–8.
6. T.S. Eliot, 'Hamlet and His Problems' (1919), *The Sacred Wood*, London: Methuen, 1920.
7. T.S. Eliot, *Selected Essays*, p. 91.
8. Maurice Buxton Forman (ed.), *The Letters of John Keats*, London: Oxford University Press, 1935, pp. 140–4. The letter to Reynolds, dated 3 May 1818, contains much that is scathingly reworked in *Poems – 1920*. In contrast to Gerontion's 'After such knowledge what forgiveness?' and his disgust at the chill delirium of the senses, Keats writes of how 'An extensive knowledge is needful . . . it takes away the heat and fever; and helps to ease the Burden of the Mystery'. Keats's distinction between 'high Sensations with and without knowledge', that 'in the latter case we are falling continually ten thousand fathoms deep and being blown up again . . . with all the horror of a bare shoulderd creature', joins with a later image, 'Have you not seen a Gull, an orc, a Sea Mew . . . like the Gull I may dip', to be picked up in Gerontion's 'Gull against the wind'. The 'cunning passages' of History find their precedents in Keats's remark, 'you seem . . . to have been going through . . . the same labyrinth . . . I have come to the same conclusion thus far; My Branchings out therefrom have been numerous' (contrast Gerontion's 'We have not reached conclusion'), and in the account of the 'Chamber of Maiden Thought' itself: 'Well – I compare human life to a large Mansion of Many Apartments . . . the doors of [most] being shut to me . . . this Chamber of Maiden Thought . . . becomes gradually darken'd and at the same time on all sides of it many doors are set open – but all dark – all leading to dark passages. – We see not the ballance [*sic*] of good and evil. We are in a Mist. *We* are now in that state – We feel the "burden of the Mystery".' Unlike Keats, Gerontion no longer expects any advantage from being 'explorative of those dark passages', though the author of 'Hamlet and his Problems', 'The Metaphysical Poets' and 'Whispers of Immortality' might well have endorsed the earlier remark that 'axioms in philosophy are not axioms until they are proved on our pulses . . . now I shall relish Hamlet more than I have ever done'.
9. B.C. Southam, *A Student's Guide to the Selected Poems of T.S.Eliot*, London: Faber and Faber, 1981, p. 75.

10. *ibid.*, p. 51.
11. James A.H. Murray *et al.* (eds), *The Oxford English Dictionary*, Oxford: The Clarendon Press, 1933.
12. T.S. Eliot, *Selected Essays*, p. 91.
13. T.S. Eliot, *The Waste Land: A Facsimile and Transcript of the Original Drafts Including the Annotations of Ezra Pound*, ed. Valerie Eliot, London: Faber and Faber, 1971, p. 13.
14. James Joyce, *Ulysses*, London: The Bodley Head, 1937, p. 22. On Eliot's debt to *Ulysses*, see Lyndall Gordon, 'A Note on *The Waste Land* and *Ulysses*', *Eliot's Early Years*, Oxford: Oxford University Press, 1977, pp. 147–8.
15. T.S. Eliot, 'Euripides and Professor Murray', *The Sacred Wood*, London: Methuen, 1920.
16. Gilbert Murray, *Euripides and His Age*, *Home University Library* series, London: Williams and Norgate, 1913. Page numbers subsequently cited in the text are from this edition.
17. Gilbert Murray, *Four Stages of Greek Religion*, London and New York: Clarendon and Columbia University Presses, 1912, p. 45. Page numbers subsequently cited in the text are from this edition.
18. See Chapter 1, note 22.
19. Norman Douglas, *Siren Land*, London: Dent, 1911; reprinted London: Secker & Warburg, 1982, p. 9. I have already considered this book's influence on Pound in Chapter 5, pages 87–8.
20. I.A. Richards, *The Principles of Literary Criticism*, London: Kegan, Paul, Trubner, 1924.
21. See B.C. Southam, *A Student's Guide to the Selected Poems of T.S. Eliot*, pp. 57–62, for a full exposition of the poem's sources.
22. Sergio Romano, *Giuseppe Volpi: industria e finanza tra Giolitti e Mussolini*, Milano: Bompiani, 1979, pp. 86–7. The financier Volpi's name was ubiquitous in Venice during these years, associated with plans to restore the city's former glory through a *Società Porto Industriale di Venezia*, constituted on 12 June 1917, and a scheme to connect harbour and city by a great canal. See also Christopher Hibbert, *Venice: The Biography of a City*, London: Grafton, 1988.
23. Both works are illustrated in Carolyn Keay (ed.), *Odilon Redon*, London: Academy Editions, 1977, pp. 11, 25. Redon also illustrated Flaubert's *La Tentation de Saint Antoine* and *c.* 1910 painted a Saint Sebastian (Keay, p. 21), both of which may be pertinent to Eliot's early poems. His reputation was enhanced by a description of his works in J.-K. Huysmans' novel *A Rebours*, 1884 and through Huysmans he met a wide circle of Symbolist poets around Mallarmé. By the end of the 1890s his works were being exhibited in France, Belgium, Holland, Germany and Britain, and in 1911 in the United States. See Jennifer Birkett, 'Fin-de-Siècle Painting', in Mikulas Teich, Roy Porter (eds), *Fin de Siècle and its Legacy*, Cambridge: Cambridge University Press, 1990, pp. 156–9.
24. Eugene Dubois, *On Pithecanthropus erectus; a transitional form between*

man and the apes, Dublin: Royal Dublin Society, 1896 (Scientific Transactions of Royal Dublin Society, vol.6, series 2). *Pithecanthropus erectus – a form from the ancestral stock of mankind, Smithsonian Institute Annual Report 1898*, Washington: Smithsonian Institute, 1899.

25. Lyndall Gordon, *Eliot's Early Years*, Oxford: Oxford University Press, p. 70; Christopher Ricks, *T.S. Eliot and Prejudice*, London: Faber and Faber, 1988, p. 242.

26. Andrea Verrocchio's 'Baptism of Christ', for which Leonardo is thought to have painted the angel, is illustrated in Martin Kemp, *Leonardo da Vinci: The Marvellous Works of Nature and Man*, London: Dent, 1981, p. 50. Eliot visited the galleries of northern Italy in 1914. See Peter Ackroyd, *T.S. Eliot*, London: Hamish Hamilton, 1984, p. 54.

Chapter Seven

1. The early publishing history of the poem is as nomadic as its characters: T.S. Eliot, *The Waste Land*, London: *The Criterion*, October 1922; New York: *The Dial*, November 1922; New York: Boni and Liveright, December 1922; *Collected Poems 1909–1962*, London: Faber and Faber, 1963. The manuscript variants are collected in T.S. Eliot, *The Waste Land: A Facsimile and Transcript of the Original Drafts Including the Annotations of Ezra Pound*, ed. Valerie Eliot, London: Faber and Faber, 1971.

2. Gilbert Murray, *Four Stages of Greek Religion*, London: Williams and Norgate, 1913, pp. 46–7.

3. T.S. Eliot, *The Sacred Wood*, London: Methuen, 1920, p. 75.

4. Friedrich Nietzsche, *The Birth of Tragedy or Hellenism and Pessimism* (1872), trans. Wm.A. Haussmann, Edinburgh and London: T.N. Foulis, 1910, pp. 151–6. This is volume 1 in Oscar Levy (ed.), *The Complete Works of Friedrich Nietzsche*, described on the title page as 'The First Complete and Authorised English Translation'.

5. T.S. Eliot, 'Shakespeare and the Stoicism of Seneca', *Selected Essays: 1917–1932*, London: Faber and Faber, 1932; enlarged edition 1951, pp. 128–32, 140.

6. Friedrich Nietzsche, *The Birth of Tragedy*, pp. 161–3. 'Waste and void is the sea' translates '*Oed' und leer das Meer*'.

7. *ibid.*, pp. 81–2.

8. Euripides, *The Bacchae, translated into English rhyming verse*, Gilbert Murray, London: Allen and Unwin, 1904.

9. Friedrich Nietzsche, *The Birth of Tragedy*, p. 94. Cadmus, we might note in passing, was a Phoenician sailor, described in Murray's translation of the *Bacchae*, lines 171–2, as 'Cadmus . . . who crossed the sea from Sidon and upreared this Theban hold'.

10. Friedrich Nietzsche, *The Birth of Tragedy*, pp. 174–5. In apposition to the sterile Socratic intellectual Nietzsche offers the 'cheerless solitary wanderer'

the symbol of Durer's engraving of 'the Knight, with Death and the Devil', 'the mail-clad knight, grim and stern of visage, who is able, unperturbed by his gruesome companions, and yet hopelessly, to pursue his terrible path . . . alone', whom he identifies with Schopenhauer (p. 156). This may throw some light on the antithesis of Tiresias and Fisher King/Parsifal in *The Waste Land*. The two companions add resonance to the ghostly 'third' on the road to Emmaus. Later, Nietzsche speculates that 'the German spirit still rests and dreams, undestroyed . . . like a knight sunk in slumber. . .. some day it will find itself awake . . . ' (pp. 184–5).

Nietzsche's whole account of the antagonism between the Socratic 'type of the *theoretical man*' (p. 114) and the Dionysian spirit is highly reminiscent of the language and preoccupations of *The Waste Land*: In

> the present desolation and languor of culture . . . We look in vain for one single vigorously-branching root, for a speck of fertile and healthy soil: there is dust, sand, torpidness and languishing everywhere! . . . But how suddenly this gloomily depicted wilderness of our exhausted culture changes when the Dionysian magic touches it! A hurricane seizes everything decrepit, decaying, collapsed, and stunted; wraps it whirlingly into a red cloud of dust; and carries it like a vulture into the air. . . . The time of the Socratic man is past. . . . Dare now to be tragic men, for ye are to be redeemed! Ye are to accompany the Dionysian festive procession from India to Greece. Equip yourselves for severe conflict, but believe in the wonders of your god!' (pp. 156–7).

The next section goes on to say that 'There is only one way from orgasm for a people, – the way to Indian Buddhism, which in order to be at all endured with its longing for nothingness, requires the rare ecstatic states with their elevation above space, time, and the individual' (p. 158).

11. T.S. Eliot, 'Ulysses, Order, and Myth', *The Dial*, no. 75, November 1923, pp. 480–3. For Nietzsche on myth, see in particular *The Birth of Tragedy*, pp. 173–87, which contains much of relevance both to *The Waste Land* and to Eliot's criticism. It may be here that Eliot found his precedent for valorising the pre-Socratic Heraclitus over Socrates (pp. 151–2, 184, 193–4).

12. This is the translation provided by B.C. Southam, *A Student's Guide to the Selected Poems of T.S. Eliot*, London: Faber and Faber, 1981, p. 106.

13. Sophocles, *Oedipus King of Thebes, translated into English rhyming verse*, Gilbert Murray, London: Allen and Unwin, 1911, ll. 460–2.

14. *ibid.*, Preface, p. x.

15. But see Tony Pinkney, *Women in the Poetry of T.S. Eliot: A Psychoanalytic Approach*, London: Macmillan, 1984, chapter 4. There is also an important exploratory essay on the subject by Alison Tate, 'The Master-Narrative of Modernism: Discourses of Gender and Class in *The Waste Land*', *Literature and History*, Autumn 1988, pp. 160–71. An important recent collection, Bonnie Kime Scott (ed.), *The Gender of Modernism*, Bloomington: Indiana University Press, 1990, addresses the wider role of women in the Modernist movement.

16. I have discussed this point more fully in Stan Smith, *Inviolable Voice: History and Twentieth-Century Poetry*, Dublin: Gill and Macmillan, 1981, pp. 85–6.

17. In the Conclusion to *The Use of Poetry and the Use of Criticism*, London: Faber and Faber, 1988, pp. 144–6 (see above pages 38–40), Eliot wrote that ill-health or exhaustion could produce poetry that was virtually 'automatic writing', but that no critic had yet identified the passages of his own thus produced. He had already made the first point in similar words in 'The "Pensées" of Pascal' (1931), *Selected Essays*, p. 405. According to Valerie Eliot (*The Waste Land: A Facsimile and Transcript*, p. 129), when Eliot wrote the latter he had this section of *The Waste Land* in mind. Eliot himself wrote to Ford Madox Ford in 1923 of 'about 30 *good* lines in *The Waste Land*', which he subsequently identified as 'the water-dripping song in the last part'. If this is the case, then the hallucinatory release of waters amidst a sterile landscape becomes one more instance of auto-referentiality in a poem full of self-reflection.

18. Allen Upward, *The Divine Mystery*, Letchworth: Garden City Press, 1913, quoted by Pound, *The New Freewoman*, 15 November 1913. Pound's review is reprinted in Ezra Pound, *Selected Prose 1909–1965*, ed. William Cookson, London: Faber and Faber, 1973 pp. 373–6. On the significance of Upward for Pound, and by implication for Eliot, see Noel Stock, *The Life of Ezra Pound*, Harmondsworth: Penguin, 1985, pp. 178–80; and Michael H. Levenson, *A Genealogy of Modernism*, Cambridge: Cambridge University Press, 1984, pp. 71–4.

19. Grover Smith, *The Waste Land*, London: George Allen & Unwin, 1983, p. 119.

20. T.S. Eliot, 'The Lesson of Baudelaire', *Tyro*, 1921, no. 1, p. 4. For 'Ulysses, Order and Myth', see note 11 above. Michael H. Levenson, in *A Genealogy of Modernism*, pp. 241–2, argues for a more sympathetic approach to Dadaism on Eliot's part. Certainly this would be consistent with the internally divided nature of Eliot's loyalties as described in Chapter 2 above. I share many points of agreement with Levenson's insightful reading of *The Waste Land* (chapter 9, pp. 165–212), one of the most original recent accounts of a much-considered poem.

21. Ezra Pound, *The Dial*, January 1921.

22. David Craig, 'The Defeatism of *The Waste Land*', *Critical Quarterly*, vol. 2, 1960, pp. 229–41.

23. T.S. Eliot, *The Waste Land: A Facsimile and Transcript*, p. 113.

24. Chester G. Starr, *The Influence of Sea Power on Ancient History*, London: Oxford University Press, 1989, pp. 55–6; Geoffrey Barraclough (ed.), *The Times Concise Atlas of World History*, London: Times Books, 1988, pp. 30–1.

25. Averil Cameron, *The Later Roman Empire AD 284–430*, London: Fontana Press, 1993, pp. 22, 83–4, 138–9, 188–90; M.A. Smith, *The Church Under Siege*, Leicester: Inter-Varsity Press, 1976, pp. 148–50; Barraclough, *The Times Concise Atlas of World History*, p. 32.

26. Valerie Eliot (ed.), *The Letters of T.S. Eliot, vol. 1, 1898–1922*, London: Faber and Faber, 1988, p. 351.
27. *ibid.*, p. 353.
28. *ibid.*, p. 449. On Eliot's reaction to the condition of England in 1921, see Peter Ackroyd, *T.S. Eliot*, London: Hamish Hamilton, 1984, p. 109.
29. David Stevenson, *The First World War and International Politics*, Oxford: The Clarendon Press, 1991, pp. 305–10. See also Barraclough, *The Times Concise Atlas of World History*, pp. 124–5 and 128–9. The gratuitous conjunction of rootless cosmopolitans from Smyrna and the Baltic (see next note), in a poem written in Lausanne, was ironically underwritten by history in 1923 when the Treaty of Lausanne confirmed Izmir as a Turkish city.
30. See G.L.K. Morris, 'Marie, Marie, hold on tight', *Partisan Review*, vol. 21, no. 2, 1954, pp. 231–3, for a discussion of Countess Marie Larisch, *My Past*, London: Nash, 1913, as a source of the poem. According to Valerie Eliot (*The Waste Land: A Facsimile and Transcript*, pp. 125–6) Eliot took the details verbatim from the author, whom he had met. Nevertheless, the publication of a 'shilling edition' of the book in 1915 ensured it a wide circulation, and Eliot might well have read it.
31. T.S. Eliot, reviewing Marianne Moore's poetry, *The Dial*, December 1923.
32. Richard M. Watt, *The Kings Depart: The German Revolution and the Treaty of Versailles 1918–1919*, Harmondsworth: Pelican Books, 1973, p. 416. Page numbers hereafter are given in the text.
33. T.S. Eliot, 'Religion without Humanism', in Norman Foerster (ed.), *Humanism and America*, New York: Farrar and Rinehart, 1930, p. 112.
34. T.S. Eliot, 'The Function of Criticism' (1923), *Selected Essays*, pp. 23–4.
35. T.S. Eliot, *After Strange Gods*, London: Faber and Faber, 1934. Page numbers are indicated in the text.
36. *ibid.*, pp. 61–2. The *Authorised Version of the Bible*, Ezekiel, 13: 3–4 and 14: 2–3, among other minor variations, reads 'deserts' for 'waste places'. It is unclear whether Eliot is adapting this source ('waste places' occurs elsewhere in the Old Testament) to bring the passage closer to his poem, or is using some other version.

Chapter Eight

1. Allan Wade (ed.), *The Letters of W.B. Yeats*, London: Rupert Hart-Davis, 1954, pp. 655–6.
2. W.B.Yeats, *Michael Robartes and the Dancer*, Dundrum: Cuala Press, 1921.
3. Donald T. Torchiana, *W.B. Yeats and Georgian Ireland*, London: Oxford University Press, 1966, p. 214.
4. See Jon Stallworthy, *Between the Lines: Yeats's Poetry in the Making*, London: Oxford University Press, 1965, pp. 16–25; Curtis Bradford, *Yeats at Work*, Carbondale, IL.: Southern Illinois University Press, 1965.

5. Patrick J. Keane, 'Revolutions French and Russian: Burke, Wordsworth and the Genesis of Yeats's "The Second Coming"', *Yeats's Interactions with Tradition*, Columbia: University of Missouri Press, 1987, pp. 72–105. Keane's superb account of this poem is one of many persuasive readings in a major study of Yeats's poetry to which I am generally indebted.

6. Hugh Kenner, 'The Sacred Book of the Arts', *Gnomon: Essays on Contemporary Literature*, New York: McDowell, Obolensky, 1958, pp. 24–5.

7. Richard Ellmann, *The Identity of Yeats*, London: Macmillan, 1954, p. 223.

8. Harold Bloom, *Yeats*, New York: Oxford University Press, 1970, pp. 355–6.

9. Julia Kristeva, 'Word, Dialogue, and Novel', *Desire in Language: A Semiotic Approach to Literature and Art*, Oxford: Blackwell, 1980, pp. 72–3.

10. *ibid.*, p. 66.

11. *ibid.*, p. 73.

12. See, for example, the asides in 'Mr Lionel Johnson's Poems' and 'John Eglinton and Spiritual Art', in John P. Frayne and Colton Johnson (eds), *Uncollected Prose by W.B. Yeats*, London: Macmillan, 1975, vol. 2, pp. 89 and 130–1.

13. W.B. Yeats, *Per Amica Silentia Lunae*, London: Macmillan, 1918, pp. 21–2 and 41–2. For an equivocal judgement on Wordsworth, see also p. 28.

14. Edward Engelberg, *The Vast Design: Patterns in W.B. Yeats's Aesthetics*, Toronto: University of Toronto Press, 1964, p. 3 and passim.

15. W.B. Yeats, 'A General Introduction for my Work', *Essays and Introductions*, London: Macmillan, 1961, pp. 510–11; W.B. Yeats, *Autobiographies*, London: Macmillan, 1955, pp. 135–6.

16. Thomas R. Whitaker, *Swan and Shadow: Yeats's Dialogue with History*, Chapel Hill, NC: University of North Carolina Press, 1964, pp. 197–202.

17. W.B. Yeats, *A Vision*, London: Macmillan, 1962, pp. 267–73.

18. W.B. Yeats, 'The Poems and Stories of Miss Norah Hopper', *Daily Express* (Dublin), 24 September 1898. See also 'The Irish Literary Theatre', *Daily Express*, 14 January 1899; and, for much of the imagery of *The Tower*, as well as the link of Homer to Raftery and Mary Hynes, 'The Literary Movement in Ireland', reprinted in John P. Frayne and Colton Johnson (eds), *Uncollected Prose by W.B. Yeats*, vol. 2, pp. 184–96.

19. W.B. Yeats, 'At Stratford-on-Avon', *The Speaker*, 11 May 1901; reprinted in *Essays and Explorations*, London: Macmillan, 1961, pp. 96–110.

20. W.B. Yeats, *A Vision*, p. 8.

21. Catherine Belsey, *Critical Practice*, London: Methuen, 1980, p. 68.

22. W.B. Yeats, *The Trembling of the Veil* (1922), reprinted in *Autobiographies*, London: Macmillan, 1955, p. 190. Book 1, sections 21–4, pp. 188–95, contains much that is incidental to these poems, especially in the remarks on Chaucer, on the comic/tragic cleavage, and on war and national unity.

23. *ibid.*, Notes, p. 576.

24. Julia Kristeva, 'Word, Dialogue, and Novel', pp. 64–91 passim.

25. *ibid.*, p. 77. For Derrida's discussion of 'self-presence' see Jacques Derrida, *Of Grammatology*, Baltimore and London: Johns Hopkins University Press, 1976, 'The Written Being / The Being Written', pp. 18–26.
26. *ibid.*, pp. 86–7.
27. W.B. Yeats, *Autobiographies*, pp. 192–5.
28. Julia Kristeva, 'Word, Dialogue, and Novel', pp. 78–9.
29. *ibid.*, pp. 80–3.
30. W.B. Yeats, *Autobiographies*, p. 195.
31. Julia Kristeva, 'The Bounded Text', *Desire in Language*, pp. 36–63. The sentence quoted occurs on p. 83.
32. Julia Kristeva, 'Word, Dialogue, and Novel', p. 83.
33. W.B. Yeats, *Autobiographies*, p. 191.

Chapter Nine

1. Philip L. Marcus, Warwick Gould and Michael J. Sidnell (eds), *The Secret Rose: Stories by W.B. Yeats: A Variorum Edition*, Ithaca, NY: Cornell University Press, 1981, pp. 94–5.
2. Peter Allt and Russell K. Alspach (eds), *The Variorum Edition of the Poems of W.B. Yeats*, New York: Macmillan, 1977, p. 801. This edition usefully collates the notes to Yeats's various collections of verse and, for the convenience of the reader, these notes are hereafter identified by the page numbers in Allt and Alspach.
3. *ibid.*, p. 811.
4. *ibid.*, p. 812.
5. *ibid.*, p. 813.
6. *ibid.*, p. 814.
7. *ibid.*, p. 818.
8. Lady Augusta Gregory, *Visions and Beliefs in the West of Ireland, Collected and Arranged by Lady Gregory with two essays and notes by W.B. Yeats*, foreword by Elizabeth Coxhead, Gerrards Cross: Colin Smythe, 1970, pp. 330–1.
9. W.B. Yeats, *Explorations*, London: Macmillan, 1962, pp. 3–13 passim.
10. *ibid.*, p. 25.
11. *ibid.*, p. 10.
12. Allt and Alspach (eds), *The Variorum Edition*, p. 808.
13. Marcus, Gould and Sidnell (eds), *The Secret Rose*, p. 157.
14. W.B. Yeats, 'Discoveries', *Essays and Introductions*, London: Macmillan, 1961, pp. 295–7.
15. *ibid.*, pp. 266–7.
16. Allt and Alspach (eds), *The Variorum Edition*, p. 804.
17. *ibid.*, p. 828.
18. *ibid.*, p. 829.
19. *ibid.*, pp. 828–9.

20. *ibid.*, pp. 821–2.
21. See, e.g., W.B. Yeats, *A Vision*, London: Macmillan, 1962, pp. 292–3; 'The Philosophy of Shelley's Poetry', *Essays and Introductions*, pp. 78–95; and *The Celtic Twilight, Mythologies*, London: Macmillan, 1959, p. 80: 'Did not the wise Porphyry think that all souls come to be born of water, and that "even the generation of images in the mind is from water"?'

    Yeats did not own a copy of Porphyry's *De Antro Nympharum*, but the work was available to him in the following editions: *Select Works of Porphyry; containing . . . his Treatise on the Homeric Cave of the Nymphs . . .* , trans. Thomas Taylor, London, 1823; *Theosophical Siftings*, VII, xv–xvii, pp. 3–21, London: Theosophical Publishing Society, 1895; a further reprint separately published by John M. Watkins, 21 Cecil Court, Charing Cross Road, London, 1917. The full text of Taylor's Porphyry is usefully reprinted in Robert Snukal, *High Talk*, Cambridge: Cambridge University Press, 1973, which also offers a valuable discussion of the significance of Porphyry in Yeats's work.
22. W.B. Yeats, *A Vision*, p. 268.
23. Allt and Alspach (eds), *The Variorum Edition*, p. 830.
24. *ibid.*, p. 831.
25. W.B. Yeats, note to 'The Bounty of Sweden', *Autobiographies*, pp. 579–80.
26. Allt and Alspach (eds), *The Variorum Edition*, p. 826.
27. *ibid.*, p. 821.
28. A.Norman Jeffares, *A New Commentary on the Poems of W.B. Yeats*, London: Macmillan, 1984, p. 175.
29. Warwick Gould, ' "A Lesson for the Circumspect": W.B. Yeats's Two Versions of *A Vision* and *The Arabian Nights*', Peter L. Caracciole (ed.), *The Arabian Nights and English Literature*, London: Macmillan, 1988, pp. 245–6, 254, 277.
30. Wayne K. Chapman, 'The Miltonic Crux of "The Phases of the Moon"', Warwick Gould (ed.), *Yeats Annual No. 8*, London: Macmillan, 1991, p. 65.
31. W.B. Yeats, *Essays and Introductions*, p. 337.
32. *ibid.*, pp. 339.
33. *ibid.*, pp. 339–40.
34. W.B. Yeats, *Letters on Poetry from W.B. Yeats to Dorothy Wellesley*, London: Oxford University Press, 1964.
35. W.B. Yeats, *Essays and Introductions*, p. 20.
36. W.B. Yeats, *Letters on Poetry from W.B. Yeats to Dorothy Wellesley*, pp. 86–7.
37. *ibid.*, p. 103.
38. *ibid.*, p. 153.
39. W.B.Yeats, *Essays and Introductions*, p. 28.
40. *ibid.*, pp. 51–2.
41. W.B. Yeats, *Letters on Poetry from W.B. Yeats to Dorothy Wellesley*, pp. 135–6.
42. W.B. Yeats, 'The End of the Cycle', *A Vision*, pp. 301–2.

Chapter Ten

1. Margaret Ward, *Maud Gonne: Ireland's Joan of Arc*, London: Pandora Press, 1990, provides a full biography and some measure of the extent to which Maud Gonne has become a figure of myth. On the *fin-de-siècle* stereotypes within which Gonne was configured, see Jennifer Birkett, *The Sins of the Fathers: Decadence in France 1870–1914*, London: Quartet, 1986, particularly pp. 19–34.
2. To his credit, Pound did not himself subscribe to this reading. Reviewing *Responsibilities* in 1914, he dismissed the fashion-following question 'Is Yeats in the movement?' with the riposte that 'Mr Yeats is so assuredly an immortal that there is no need for him to recast his style to suit our winds of doctrine' but added 'there is nevertheless a manifestly new note in his later work', a 'new note' which, he says, 'was apparent four years ago in his *No Second Troy*'. With the appearance of *The Green Helmet*, he continues, 'one felt that the minor note . . . had gone or was going out of his poetry' (Ezra Pound, 'The Later Yeats', *Poetry*, vol. 4, no. 2, May 1914; reprinted in *Literary Essays of Ezra Pound*, T.S. Eliot (ed.), London: Faber and Faber, 1954, pp. 378–81). For Eliot's assessment, see T.S. Eliot, *To Criticize the Critic*, New York: Farrar, Straus and Giroux, 1965, p. 58.
   The volumes discussed in the present chapter are as follows: W.B. Yeats, *The Green Helmet and Other Poems*, Dundrum: Cuala Press, 1910 (New York, 1911; London: Macmillan, 1912); *Responsibilities: Poems and a Play*, Dundrum: Cuala Press, 1914 (London: Macmillan, 1916); *The Wild Swans at Coole*, Dundrum: Cuala Press, 1917 (London: Macmillan, 1919); *The Tower*, London: Macmillan, 1928; *The Winding Stair and Other Poems*, London: Macmillan, 1933; *Last Poems and Two Plays*, Dublin: Cuala Press, 1939; *Last Poems and Plays*, London: Macmillan, 1940.
   Richard J. Finneran (ed.), W.B. Yeats, *The Poems: A New Edition*, London: Macmillan, 1984, proposes a radically different sequence for *Last Poems* from that in the standard *Collected Poems of W.B. Yeats*, London: Macmillan, 1950. The order of the latter is followed by Peter Allt and Russell K. Alspach (eds), *The Variorum Edition of the Poems of W.B. Yeats*, New York: Macmillan, 1977. On this, see Richard J. Finneran, *Editing Yeats's Poetry: A Reconsideration*, Basingstoke: Macmillan, 1990. This chapter extends some of the arguments initiated in Stan Smith, *W.B. Yeats: A Critical Introduction*, Basingstoke: Macmillan, 1990.
3. See Maud Gonne MacBride, *A Servant of the Queen*, London: Victor Gollancz, 1938; Rosemary Cullen Owens, *Smashing Times: A History of the Irish Women's Suffrage Movement 1889–1922*, Dublin: The Attic Press, 1984. For an account of the Transport Workers' Strike, see Austen Morgan, *James Connolly: A Political Biography*, Manchester: Manchester University Press, 1988, chapter 6, pp. 111–35.
4. Richard Ellmann, *The Identity of Yeats*, London: Macmillan, 1954, p. 252.
5. W.B. Yeats, *Autobiographies*, London: Macmillan, 1955, p. 219. Book 2 of *The Trembling of the Veil* (first published separately in 1922), offers a

shrewd thumbnail sketch of Hyde and of his contribution to the Irish cultural renaissance (pp. 216–19).

6. *ibid.*, pp. 439–40. This section, *Dramatis Personae*, was originally published separately in 1935.

7. C.K. Stead, *Pound, Yeats, Eliot and the Modernist Movement*, Basingstoke: Macmillan, 1986.

8. 'Twelve Southerners', *I'll Take My Stand: The South and the Agrarian Tradition*, New York: Harper, 1930. The Agrarians sought explicit precedent for their vision of the South in Yeats's fantasy of an organicist, quasi-feudal, corporatist Ireland where aristocrat, poet and peasant scorned the class-based politics of the modern world. Leading figures of the movement such as Allen Tate were clearly influenced by Yeats stylistically as well as ideologically. In the 1930s, the Agrarians seemed to offer a politics and a poetics which took a third way between capitalism and 'Bolshevism' appealing to many modern writers. At the beginning of *After Strange Gods* (1934), p. 15, Eliot, for example, speaking in Virginia, reveals that he had been 'much interested' in the Agrarians 'since the publication a few years ago' of *I'll Take My Stand*, relates this specifically to the concerns of 'Tradition and the Individual Talent', and imagines that in the South there is still 'at least some recollection of a "tradition", such as the influx of foreign populations has almost effaced in some parts of the North'. See Paul K. Conkin, *The Southern Agrarians*, Knoxville: University of Tennessee Press, 1988.

9. W.B. Yeats, *Per Amica Silentia Lunae*, London: Macmillan, 1918.

Chapter Eleven

1. Samuel Beckett, *Waiting for Godot*, London: Faber and Faber, 1965. All quotations from the play are from this edition. For a situating of these exchanges in the context of a specifically Irish history, see Stan Smith, 'Historians and Magicians: Ireland Between Fantasy and History', Peter Connolly (ed.), *Literature and the Changing Ireland*, Gerrards Cross: Colin Smythe, 1982.

2. W.H. Auden, 'Under Sirius', *Nones*, London: Faber and Faber, 1952.

3. V.I. Lenin, *What is to be Done? Burning Questions of our Movement*, London: Martin Lawrence, 1929; described as 'Written between the winter of 1901 and February 1902. First published as a separate pamphlet in March, 1902, Stuttgart, Dietz'.

4. Walter Benjamin, 'Theses on the Philosophy of History' (1941), *Illuminations*, ed. Hannah Arendt, London: Fontana Books, 1973, p. 265.

5. W.B. Yeats, 'The Man and the Echo', *The London Mercury*, January 1939; *Last Poems and Two Plays*, Dublin: Cuala Press, 1939.

6. W.B. Yeats, 'Politics', *The London Mercury*, January 1939; *Last Poems and Two Plays*, Dublin: Cuala Press, 1939.

7. W.B. Yeats, 'A Bronze Head', *The London Mercury*, March 1939; *Last Poems and Two Plays*.

Index